# LIONS *in* WINTER

## CHRYS GOYENS
## ALLAN TUROWETZ

D1166727

**McGraw-Hill Ryerson**
Toronto          Montreal

*Lions in Winter* was first published in 1986 by Prentice-Hall Canada, Inc.

1 2 3 4 5 6 7 8 9 BG 3 2 1 0 9 8 7 6 5 4

Revised edition published in 1994 by
McGraw-Hill Ryerson Ltd.
300 Water Street
Whitby, Ontario, Canada
L1N 9B6

**Canadian Cataloguing in Publication Data**

Goyens, Chrys
    Lions in winter

2nd ed.
ISBN 0-07-551712-4

1. Montreal Canadiens (Hockey team) – History.
I. Turowetz, Allan, 1948– II. Title.

GV848.M6G6 1993    796.962'64'-0971428    C93-095029-1

Cover design: Dave Hader, Studio Conceptions
Cover photograph: *The Montreal Gazette,* John Mahoney
Publisher: Donald S. Broad

Printed and bound in Canada

# CONTENTS

*For Warren, a passionate Habs fan
who helped inspire the new edition of this book*

# Introduction

Images.

Stills. Sepia-toned pictures freezing the time and place of an outdoor rink in the winter of 1931, and young men like Sylvio Mantha, Aurele Joliat, Howie Morenz and Nick Wasnie who will never grow old. In the manner of professional athletes across the generations, they stare defiantly at the camera, daring the clock to move. The fabled *bleu-blanc-rouge* is many shades of brown.

Stillness. The eerie silence that greets sportswriter Andy O'Brien on that March day in 1937 when he enters the Forum and finds it crammed full with fifteen thousand people. In a coffin at centre ice lies Howie Morenz, a scant six years removed from that day in 1931 when he and his teammates dared the second-hand to continue its sweep.

Still. Elmer Lach and Maurice Richard embracing in mid-air on an April night in 1953, their sticks high after an overtime goal, and Boston captain Milt Schmidt sitting on the ice knowing that the Stanley Cup has eluded him one more time. Or an April night the year before with the Rocket, blood streaming down his face, shaking hands with Bruins' goalie Sugar Jim Henry moments after shrugging off a concussion and the entire Boston team to score the goal that eliminated Beantown yet again.

Moving. The earliest televised black-and-white images of the fabled warriors of the 1950s—Jean Beliveau, Dickie Moore, Henri Richard, Boom Boom Geoffrion, Doug Harvey and Jacques Plante—steamrolling the opposition en route to five straight Stanley Cups.

Slow motion. Frank Mahovlich dropping a pass to Phil Roberto, and then *his* drop pass to Beliveau, who sweeps in on Minnesota goaltender Gilles Gilbert and leaves him in a confusion of green-and-gold as goal number 500 slides into the far corner.

Colour. Ken Dryden leaning on his goalie stick, watching the action 160 feet away where players such as Guy Lafleur, Bob Gainey, Steve Shutt, Larry Robinson, Serge Savard and Guy Lapointe mount a ferocious red, white and blue assault.

Splash. A young kid named Patrick Roy talking to his goalposts while the Madison Square mob hoots in derision. Three hours later "Roo-Ah" and seven rookie teammates have the last laugh. Two weeks later they complete their defiance of the odds and common sense to add *their* own silver to the biggest trophy case in North American professional sport.

Tradition.

That ugly word that hangs like a life sentence over any player who wears the *bleu-blanc-rouge* because it means that when he takes to the Forum ice, he faces not only the other team but also the bronze busts in the Forum lobby.

Tradition is images, evocations of other times and other successes that bend the time/space continuum. Tradition is commitment to those images and the people who inspired them.

Many athletes prove that they can play with pressure. Few can play with tradition.

Tradition is commitment to *la Sainte Flanelle* . . . the Holy Cloth. Whether it be the Yankee pinstripe and those monuments in deepest centre field that recall a sports stadium in the Bronx and decades of pre-eminence in baseball, or perhaps the Kelly green with white trim of the Boston Celtics and memories of players with names like Jones, Cousy, Russell . . . there is something instantly recognizable about the uniform colours of a special team in a particular sport. Few will argue that Yankee pinstripes represent baseball at its finest over the twentieth century. The same glory is attached to the Boston green and white in professional basketball.

In professional ice hockey, it is *la Sainte Flanelle* ... the red-white-and-blue and the distinctive CH of the *Club de Hockey Canadien*. As much as Harold Ballard might demur, attempting to raise the tattered standard of the Toronto Maple Leafs, that Agincourt was fought—and won— long ago.

The Montreal Canadiens and their celebrated road uniform are instantly recognized anywhere in North America—even in places where hockey is not popular. Indeed, that is probably the greatest test of a dynastic organization—the recognition factor of its colours by people with little interest in the sport.

Most of all, though, *la Sainte Flanelle* means organization. The Montreal Canadiens have become the signature team in their sport because of organization: the behind-the-scenes arranging that led to the on-ice heroics of the young men in the still and moving pictures.

But images are all foreground.

\* \* \* \* \*

This book will attempt to meld those images with the background: the organizational theory and the production of results on the ice. The authors firmly believe that the Montreal Canadiens never would have attained their full status without a strategic edge over the competition. Nor would they ever have enjoyed such an edge on the ice without a clearly articulated off-ice organizational policy.

We look at the names and try to convey what they meant then, and still mean today. Maurice Richard, the city boy, and his country cousins, Jean Beliveau and Guy Lafleur, were a lot more than mere hockey players.

They stood for something special, the pride and aspirations of a people that had enjoyed too few heroes in modern times. As a result, and no matter how hard they try, the Rocket, Gros Bill and the Flower will never be average people in the eyes and hearts of their contemporaries.

We look at the Grey Eminences who stood behind them, men with names like Dandurand, Gorman, Raymond, Selke, Pollock.

We endeavour to explain the folklore by applying sociological and organizational terms and theories to the apparatus that provided the foundation for the on-ice magic.

No one, however, can truly explain the magic. And we would be fools to try.

# An Anecdote

The year: 1983. The place: Moscow.

Serge Savard, the recently appointed Managing Director of the Montreal Canadiens, is making the almost obligatory introduction tour of the hockey hotbeds of Europe and the Soviet Union.

This is the real world of National Hockey League executives. In the best American Express tradition, no NHL General Manager should be without at least one trip to the USSR. However, NHL self-image being what it is, the club Public Relations people tell the media Savard is on a "western" scouting tour: they don't say just how far west.

Savard has been here before, with Team Canada in 1972, during that most emotional of series. That was a time of adversaries, when the Soviets would pull little tricks like constantly ringing the room telephones of Team Canada players in the middle of the night to disturb their sleep. Frank Mahovlich was a particular target.

These, however, are enlightened times. The Soviets have since won their share of games with the NHL pros, and vice versa. Hockey hegemony now is recognized to be a fleeting thing, resting on the talents of one or two superior players who define the vintage. Grudging respect is given and taken.

After the protocol is dispensed with, the vodka comes out and the hair is let down (as much as it can be under the circumstances).

Savard finds himself making small talk at a not-so-official official reception, along with a great many dignitaries.

1

Across the room, a grey-haired gentleman painfully makes his way toward the Canadian visitor. His progress is impeded equally by advanced age and infirmity and the presence of a fawning group of sycophantic functionaries.

The Red Sea of people parts in front of a curious Montrealer.

"Tell me, Mr. Savard," says the Grey Eminence, "what is happening with our Canadiens? I can hardly hold my head up in the Kremlin these days."

"We're having our ups and downs, as you may have noticed," Savard replies, equally curious and surprised.

"Yes, I know the feeling." Several minor officials, looking terribly anxious to please, press around. Eventually, the man is introduced; he is Mikhail Suslov*, member of the Politburo and the Secretariat of the CPSU Central Committee. He is known in the highest circles of international politics as the Kremlin Ideologue, the man who defined communism as it is practised in the Soviet Union.

Officials of all kinds beam benignly as the hockey man and the politician discuss matters far removed from SALT II and the Helsinki Agreement. It turns out that Mr. Suslov is a fan of Bob Gainey, Guy Lafleur and his favourite player, Larry Robinson.

His curiosity piqued, Savard wonders aloud where the elderly gentleman picked up his information.

"We in the Old Guard have been Canadiens' fans for many, many years," he smiles. "I have long been a supporter of your illustrious team and great hockey players like Maurice Richard, Jean Beliveau, Jacques Plante and others. . .

"For the longest time the Canadiens were very popular with the Old Guard in the Politburo, but now the younger men are switching. They seem to have a preference for Mr. Gretzky and the Edmonton Oilers but we have a name for them. . ."

Savard bites.

"What's that?"

"Defectors."

*Mikhail Suslov has since passed away.

# Prologue 1993

It is the perfect kind of day to be visiting this man; an early August morning partway between umbrella and string bikini, announcing a day which may eventually dissolve you in Montreal's summer heat and humidity, or drown you in an icy downpour spiced with hailstones the size of golfballs.

Meteorologists call this partly overcast, and on this morning we are alternately in bright, unfiltered sunlight, the kind that makes the back of your eyes ache and has you anxiously scanning the northern sky for the infamous hole in the ozone layer one moment, and dull leaden gloom, more reminiscent of a November day that is all grey scale, that has you casing warm dry lairs, just in case, the next.

Best call it schizophrenic. This in itself is ironic in that we are visiting the man who most probably induces more manic behaviour patterns in his fellow Montrealers than anyone else.

He is not Jean Doré, the city's diminutive mayor of the Golden Toilets, a seemingly dedicated politician with a monumental case of bad timing — a man who would promote $300,000 worth of ornate windows at City Hall at a time when it appears that the entire electorate living east of *l'hôtel de ville* is on the dole.

Neither is he Robert Bourassa, the wily politician who spent almost a quarter of a century confounding Quebec

3

voters in the province's most enduring love-hate relationship; the living manifestation of his province's erratic mood swings in all matters political.

No, this man is much more important than a mere mayor or premier because he touches more lives, and more often than either Doré or Bourassa. This man has real power, able to launch a million telephone calls a year in *la métropole*, nearly all of them to sports hotlines on French and English radio stations.

This man is Serge A. Savard, managing director of the Montreal Canadiens. Depending on his team's latest winning or losing streak, is he alternately the Stupidest Man in Creation, an utter moron totally devoid of hockey acumen, or the Wizard of Lambert-Closse, a man who has his *confrères* in the NHL eating out of his hand.

Some 225 kilometres to the northeast, in Quebec City, he is usually "that smug bastard." In *La Vieille Capitale* they have felt his sting and resented his longevity. Since his arrival in Montreal in 1983, Savard has stared down four administrations in Quebec: Maurice Filion, then Martin Madden, then Martin Madden and Maurice Filion, and now, Pierre Pagé. His record is three Stanley Cup finals, two Cups. Their record in the only city in professional hockey more desperate for a Stanley Cup than Montreal is no finals, no championship silverware.

Somehow, while the Nordiques managed to avoid the playoffs for five straight seasons, a hell that is directly related to sins committed on the ice, Savard kept his team at the top of the Adams Division. And, when the Nordiques were finally rewarded for their incompetence by a seemingly endless string of quality draft choices that had created one of the most exciting young teams in the league, the Dark Lord in Montreal rose up and smote them down with an exciting and young team of his own, built for a long conflict. Worse still for the team that dresses in an imitation of the Quebec flag, Savard's is an infinitely more francophone team as well, chock full of *accents aigu* and *accents grave*, with a few *circonflexes* and *cédilles* thrown in for good measure.

The exasperation must be felt in Boston, too, because after a generation of falling to the Montreal Canadiens, Harry Sinden managed to defeat Savard's team in four of the last five playoffs. Yet he, too, does not have a Cup of recent vintage on his trophy shelf. Neither does Gerry Meehan in Buffalo who thought he might have beaten the Habs once or twice in the past decade, and may have mortgaged his team to acquire the playoff goalie who would guarantee the end of post-season futility. And they are awfully quiet in Toronto, where they used to compete with the *bleu-blanc-rouge*. It seems that real life has blitzed by the "Hockey Night in Canada" blue-and-white puppet broadcast team that twice a year or so dusts off the tattered pennants and fragile kinescopes in the CBC archives to shill a "grand old rivalry" that has not been taken seriously by hockey fans east of Lake Ontario for a quarter of a century. If the rivalry is rekindled, it will be due to the efforts of a troika of Quebeckers — Cliff Fletcher, Pat Burns and Félix Potvin — a fact that most surely disturbs the eternal rest of one Conn Smythe.

What usually leaves local fans and critics hyperventilating is the fact that Savard is about as penetrable as a deep mountain tarn. A huge boulder — all pure violence and teeth-rattling noise — rocketing down from the highest crag and gouging a trail in the underbrush in its moment's rebellion against gravity, silently sinks in the fathomless pool that is Serge Savard, with nary a ripple. That rolling stone might be the most recent media tempest over team stars supposedly wrapping a vehicle around a telephone pole, while accompanied by young and possibly underaged young women, while AWOL from the team hotel during the playoffs. Or it might be a perceived scandal of the doctor of another Montreal woman suffering from AIDS, telling the media that she has slept with more than a hundred NHL players. Or how about two or three Canadiens getting involved in a late-night punch-up in another city, perhaps even with a pimp who was "disciplining" one of his charges, and with words like "substance abuse" bandied about.

No matter what the story, how rich the headline currency with catchphrases such as AIDS, sex, prostitution, alcohol and drug abuse, nothing seems to stick to the teflon that coats the managing director.

Better yet, the object of everyone's ire might be a hockey story pure and simple, an intransigent coach who refuses to let the pressbox dictate his decisions, a voluble veteran who does not take a benching sitting down, so to speak, or a very popular player who must leave his beloved Canadiens because there is no room for him anymore in *La Sainte Flanelle.*

Perhaps the forwards have hands of stone, and the defensemen could use twenty or thirty pounds — mon dieu, kilograms! — of stone in their hockey pants to make the weight at the blueline. Perhaps, also, the managing director is oblivious to these obvious deficiencies, even though they are as plain as the nose on his face. . . . Perhaps Mr. Savard should listen to all of us and make a trade for size on the blueline, something a wee bit more substantial, or his team can kiss off the playoffs, once again.

Or perhaps it is a normally rational sports editor who has a pathological loathing for Savard and the Canadiens, and will do all he can to take shots, in season and out. This man and his pet mathematician, whose stock in trade has been "computerized projections" on probabilities for teams winning the Stanley Cup, eliminated the home team twice during the spring, only to be buried under an avalanche of egg yellow in early June. There were smiles all over Montreal from fans knowing that there was a strong "probability" that these two had been unmasked. This editor was a very frustrated man during the summer of '93; so what might he have in store for the Habs when they inevitably crash down to earth?

"Too bad, eh?" Savard quickly and quietly savours his media antagonist's discomfort. He offers an unprintable comment or two, perhaps recognition for the editor's tenacity. That is as close as you will ever get to a public or private reaction from him.

During a mid-season talk-show appearance, Savard sits inscrutable and unassailable in a radio studio while the fans or sycophants have at him. It is great sport, and the only thing missing is sound effects, something like the death throes of a Stuka dive bomber screaming to earth, its fuselage a ball of flame, seconds away from a life-obliterating crash.

"The Denis Savard trade was the worst ever perpetrated on the Canadiens," a disgruntled fan kvetches. The talk-show host across from Savard nods sympathetically because this was his next question; *noblesse oblige* had it that his first question be gently lobbed to Savard to get things going smoothly.

Serge Savard doesn't bat an eyelash as the fan continues his tirade. He quietly explains why the trade was made then, and says he might even agree a wee bit with the caller seeing that Denis Savard is hardly playing anymore, and Chris Chelios will win his second Norris Trophy. However, he is careful to careful insist that, "In my office, I don't have the benefit of 20/20 hindsight when I'm on the telephone with another general manager."

Or a nationalist might try to stir up controversy: "You traded away francophone superstars like Stéphane Richer and Claude Lemieux. . . . How could you?" Conveniently omitted are the facts that Richer's leaving brought the team's future captain, Kirk Muller, to Montreal, and that Lemieux was traded because Pat Burns was going to punch him in the head any day now, and it might even have happened at the team bench during a game on live TV because that's how bad the enmity got before Savard threw the switch on the safety valve.

"We traded Claude heads up for another French-speaking player, Sylvain Turgeon, even though he didn't work out, either," he responds gently.

"But, I had to take a gamble on Turgeon because he was the best I could get under the circumstances," he says, revealing something that many journalists did not know. "Despite his talent and scoring ability, Claude Lemieux's reputation preceded him and nobody wanted him out there, 30 goals a year or no 30 goals a year."

The caller is a pit bull, equal parts ferocity and inability to overcome the  vehemence of a single, poor idea. "You can say that, but still you traded away francophone stars. '*Les gars d'icitté*,' two good homeboys who have been banished to an exile worse than death in the wilds of New Jersey. "

Savard is a veteran of talk-show situations, even though a meticulously protective Canadiens' public relations phalanx does its level best to keep his live exposure to a minimum during the year. He quietly awaits the end of the rant, and while the caller is either taking a breath of air, or wondering why the operator in the control booth has smoothly tuned him out, Savard returns to the fray, all measured tones and reasonableness.

"Yes, but I improved my team, and in case you haven't noticed it, we have players with names like Daigneault, Desjardins, Brisebois, Roy, Damphousse, Dionne and Brunet in the line-up." He could go on and add Racicot, Sevigny, Lebeau, Roberge. Or the names of French-Canadian players who had their names enscribed on the precious Cup before it was time to move on: Savard, Bélanger, Dufresne.

The talk shows are a necessary evil, and an arena in which he performs to the highest NHL standards, but Savard prefers the anonymity of his office and a work world connected by conference call.

Once a player with the talent to gain admission to the National Hockey Hall of Fame, "The Senator," as some still call him, has many things on his mind this morning. Actually, he has only one thing on his mind, what to pay the best player at his position in the league, the player who made life eminently more livable in a metropolis that has grown ragged about the edges by winning the Stanley Cup two months previous.

Generations of Montrealers have lived with three constants, come peace or war. They are, in order: cold, damp winters; hundreds of municipal workers swarming over the thousands of miles of city streets in April filling in the potholes that represent asphalt's loss in the tug-of-war between winter freeze and spring thaw; and the Stanley Cup parade along the same, now smooth and even, city streets sometime in May or June.

In recent years, *Montréalais* have had subsisted on a starvation diet of the cold, damp winters. No Stanley Cup, lots of year-round potholes. This does not amuse them, and it is Mr. Savard's task to bring the local batting average to .667 by icing a hockey team that provides the parade. (He refuses, however, to interfere with the Public Works Department at City Hall.)

Savard is acutely aware of this responsibility, even though this Atlas-like burden does not generate even the slightest flicker of doubt or concern in his placid features.

When he played in the National Hockey League — 17 seasons, seven Stanley Cups, one Conn Smythe Trophy as playoff MVP in 1968-69 — the rangy 6-foot-2, 210-pound defenceman was reputed to be the steadiest player at his position, in a career that shared playing time with legends like Harry Howell, Bobby Orr, Tim Horton, Gary Bergman, Bill White, Pat Stapleton, Jacques Laperrière, Jean-Claude Tremblay, Larry Robinson, Denis Potvin and Brad Park. While others garnered the headlines and the First Team All-Star designations, Savard collected the big prize and played a quiet game.

Which is not to say he went unnoticed. He served with distinction on the 1972 Team Canada that outlasted the Soviet Union in the eight games of the Hockey Summit. Many observers say that only two broken legs in three seasons prevented him with competing regularly with Bobby Orr for the Norris Trophy during the Boston blueliner's heyday in the late 1960s and early 1970s.

Savard's game on the Second Floor is exactly the same as it was on the ice: distinguished, effective, recognized by his peers, and occasionally spectacular. And, of course, the results are there.

It is because that Savard is on top of his game and forever honing his skills that he is worried on this August morning.

"The game has changed . . . the money is going through the roof and the players think they'll be able to line up and automatically receive huge salaries," he says. This summer's main task is to sign Patrick Roy, the goalie who delivered the Stanley Cup to the building at Atwater and St. Catherine neatly giftwrapped. Savard already has had one "good meeting" with Pierre Lacroix, a good match as one of the few agents as inscrutable as he, but the subject of filthy lucre was not broached. It will be soon, and already hints have been received to affix a string of six zeroes after the numeral five or six, and to add the two-word phrase, "per year" somewhere in the same sentence.

"What can I do?" Savard muses aloud. "Mario Lemieux got $43 million for six years. Players in the NBA, NFL and Major League Baseball are getting huge deals, even if their teams are going broke and even with the networks cutting back on the broadcasting deals. And no matter how much we talk about fiscal restraint, good management and building for the future, the players' association accuses us of holding out on the players."

Savard's counterpart in St. Louis and predecessor in Montreal, Ronald Caron, has raised eyebrows by offering Los Angeles free-agent defenseman Marty McSorley a five-year deal worth almost $10 million. (Or, in terms of illegal stick measurement in the heat of the NHL final, about $4 million an inch.) We discuss the issue, and while not wanting to cast aspersions on the management practises of other managers, agree that perhaps the wily Caron has found an ingenious way to force Bruce McNall, Rogatien Vachon and Nick Beverly to divest themselves of some of the Walt Disney money received for renouncing their territorial rights to Anaheim.

"Marty is in his thirties and is a good defenseman," Savard says, "but this kind of package will be more trouble than good for management. There are many defensemen out there who might be rated higher and aren't getting anywhere near that money." Does that mean that the Disney or Blockbuster Video money will venture forth, trying to buy talent like the Florida Marlins of baseball's National League?

"I'm not sure about that," Savard replies. "These people made their money be being smart businessmen, and they've hired good people in Bobby Clarke and Bill Torrey in Florida, and Jack Ferreira and Pierre Gauthier in Anaheim. I don't think they are going to try shortcuts." He turns out to be right; the St. Louis offer is matched by the Kings, who then turn around and trade McSorley to Pittsburgh, the newcomers in the new "Adams-Division-plus-one" grouping which will now be called the Northeast Division.

"Will signings of players like McSorley to such contracts hurt the Canadiens in their attempts to sign Patrick Roy?"

"Not at all. Patrick Roy is the best goaltender in hockey and he will be paid accordingly. If you're going to make comparisons for Patrick, you have to talk about Mario Lemieux, Wayne Gretzky, Eric Lindros, Steve Yzerman and players like that."

"What about Félix Potvin's salary demands in Toronto? This kid may already be the second or third best in the league."

"No comment. Neither Mr. Potvin nor Cliff Fletcher need my advice in this area." The teflon is working overtime.

Will McSorley's signing upset the salary applecart at other levels?

"Yes." You can almost hear the clicking of the abacus beads in Savard's mind. He says this knowing that five players, Benoît Brunet, Eric Desjardins, Mike Keane, John LeClair and André Racicot are moving into option years of their contracts, and that he has an outstanding obligation to renegotiate Kirk Muller's $925,000-a-year pact which has two years remaining (one and an option year).

"What are you, and pro hockey going to do about it? Are you going to take it to the wall, just like baseball appears likely to do?"

The Gallic shrug is permanently anchored.

"I can't say, but we'll have to head it off long before we find ourselves in an ultimatum situation just like baseball."

Many veteran hockey observers think it might already be too late. Several teams, San Jose prominent among them, have tried novel ways of circumventing the league's nebulous free-agency system, with offers to Craig Simpson and Kelly Miller that pop out of a file called Imaginative Financing 101. The Sharks offered the Edmonton winger a relatively small salary but a huge reporting bonus in an attempt to sidestep the league's compensation legislation, obviously anxious to upgrade the third-year team with quality players, and not lose quality players or draft choices in return, à la Brendan Shanahan-Scott Stevens. The ploy by Chuck Grillo, San Jose's director of player personnel, was so imaginative that the NHL almost went into stasis. (At press time, commissioner Gary Bettman had vetoed the deal, pending his own investigation, and the NHL Players' Association had taken the issue to the courts, disputing Bettman's jurisdiction.)

As well, the NHLPA's collective bargaining agreement with the league expired September 15 with no deal in sight, but, unlike baseball, no hint yet of walkout. Savard shares all of these concerns with his fellow team executives across the league.

The longest season in Montreal Canadiens' history ended June 9, and that, too, is part of what professional hockey is quibbling about. In mid-April, Montreal radio stations began broadcasting among the many little daily briefs that "on this day, the Canadiens won their fourth Cup" or "on this date, the Canadiens won their twelfth Stanley Cup." And that was before the playoffs had even begun.

In another era, the players reported in mid-to-late September, worked themselves into shape, and began the new season in mid-October. In mid-to-late March, the regular season ended, playoffs began, and then ended with the coronation of the new champion in late April or early May. Seven or eight months at the outside, and another season was done.

For the Montreal Canadiens, the season began in late August, 1993 with an early training camp appearance and a quick trip to London, England for a two-game "friendly" with the Chicago Blackhawks. Actually, it had started even earlier as many players gathered in early August to begin their own private scrimmaging at a suburban rink. It is expressly prohibited by the NHLPA collective bargaining agreement for a team to call for informal practise sessions or early camp appearances. However, today's professional hockey player knows he must report in playing shape, ready to push the performance curve near the high end within a week or two of arrival at camp. Playing oneself into shape at leisure is very much a thing of the past in the NHL.

Ironically, the only thing that might interfere with this regimen is success; a team that wins the Cup suddenly finds its summer calendar overloaded with appearances and outside events, and some of the marquee players may not have the time to maintain a rigorous off-season program.

All of these facts, especially the gentle tug-of-war between marketing and hockey concerns, are loaded into the Savard database and weighed. Another Gallic shrug. And maybe even a nervous glance at the Molson hockey calendar. The next season officially gets under way scant days away with rookie camp on September 8.

In the rapidly shrinking three-month interval between playing seasons, Savard has been retooling. Gone are five players whose names appear on the team's twenty-fourth Stanley Cup — Denis Savard and Donald Dufresne to Tampa Bay, Jesse Bélanger to Miami, Sean Hill and Todd Ewen to Anaheim. The experiment with the two Patriks from Sweden, Carnback and Kjellberg, is already over with Carnback joining Ewen and Hill as a Mighty Duck and Kjellberg opting to remain in Sweden. And a once highly touted Quebec junior, Steve Larouche, is yet another former Habs farmhand who couldn't portage past the logjam of youth and talent in Montreal and will try to capture Lightning in a bottle in Tampa Bay.

Arriving soon is another of those good crops of players, patiently nurtured in junior, college, international or minor pro hockey: Brian Savage, a big, mobile All-American centre from Bowling Green who reminds many observers of John LeClair; Turner Stevenson, 220 pounds of all-purpose winger; Pierre Sévigny, a heads-up forward blessed with outstanding vision in traffic; and two trees on defense, Sweden's Peter Popovic and Brent Bilodeau of the WHL, bookends who top out at 6-foot-5.

And then there are a pair of diminutive Russians, Oleg Petrov, who honed his North American hockey skills in Fredericton for much of the previous season, and Pavel Buré's kid brother, Valeri, who finished second in scoring in the Western Hockey League in 1992-93 with 68 goals and 79 assists for 147 points in 66 games. Valeri was a "home draft," picked at the Forum on June 18, 1991, and the cheers from 14,000-plus Canadiens fans when his selection was announced, still ring in "The Senator's" ears.

"Valeri tells me he is going to make this team," Savard grins.

The prospect delights him, in all senses of the phrase.

It has been a wonderful summer. However, the pragmatist also knows that it has been the Summer of Their Discontent just up the highway in the provincial capital and that an aroused Quebec Nordiques team will be quietly planning to explode from the blocks in early October.

The Nordiques, too, will probably find room for their top junior, René Corbet of Drummondville Voyageurs, scoring champion of the Quebec Major Junior Hockey League last season with 79 goals and 69 assists for 148 points in 63 games. And the Whalers will be improved . . . the Penguins will play in this division . . . the Sabres have something to prove . . . and only a fool would ever discount the Bruins before the season starts.

Savard also knows that he goes into the new season with a Stanley Cup coach in place, all real and perceived dressing-room rifts healed, a young, healthy, talented and improving team that is anxious to silence its detractors. Last, but not least, a local sports media that will have to bide their time through the honeymoon period.

A banner will be lifted into the rafters on Wednesday, October 6, as the Canadiens launch their new season against the Hartford Whalers.

And then it will be business as usual.

# 1

## Setting the Stage

*"Time is but a stream I go fishing in."*
Henry David Thoreau

The Forum, ice hockey's Holy Place, is quite unlike most shrines or churches in Montreal. One who is not familiar with the city but who has grown up on the legend of the Canadiens and has seen the inside of the Forum hundreds of times through the eyes of television will no doubt be disappointed. The Forum should be more like the Montreal churches that Mark Twain wrote about: overpowering, imposing, opulent, classic. The Forum should be as representative of hockey history as were those churches of Quebec's once pervasive Roman Catholicism.

Yet unlike the teams that have made the Forum great, the building itself is squat and functional. The only concessions to architectural élan are the escalators on the St. Catherine Street side of the building. The sides of the escalators feature fluorescent panels. Viewed from outside, at night, the image is of crossed hockey sticks.

Inside, the Forum is just another hockey rink at first glance. If you've visited any arena of size in the National Hockey League, the impression here will be one of overwhelming sameness. The team colours prevail—red, white and blue in ascending order of seats ringing the ice

15

surface. But for those colours, you reason, it could be the Forum in Inglewood, California, or the Capital Center in the middle of nowhere between Baltimore and Washington. Second glance will uncover a series of visual clues that indicate the familiar and the fabled.

The stylized CH at centre ice will be the first reminder of what this building has meant to the sport. But that isn't the key to the Forum either. There must be something else that reveals the true Forum, home of the Flying Frenchmen, birthplace of firewagon hockey, one of the most famous sports gathering places anywhere in the world, known from Kitimat, B.C. to Antigonish, N.S.; from Atlanta, Georgia, U.S.A., to Tiflis, Georgia, U.S.S.R.

Where is the real Forum? Look up. Straight above your head, in the rafters. There you'll find the real Forum. There, high above the ice, they hang silently. To call them just pieces of cloth is like describing an Arras tapestry as just another wallhanging. They reveal what the Forum has meant to ice hockey, and the reason why this rink can be like no other. Only this Forum holds twenty-four separate white panels on which these words are written in blue with red trim: "Montreal Canadiens, Stanley Cup Champions".

No other rink can present players, referees, journalists and spectators with such an imposing view. Even the Russians look up and take notice when they visit. And they are psyched, because this has to be the most intimidating view in the game.

Ice hockey's dynasty of dynasties hangs high. Unequivocably *the* club team of the sport, the Canadiens are also the team that has come to epitomize the sport, the Soviet national team included. A paean to enlightened management techniques and specialized know-how; a certain way of doing things since time immemorial. A red, white and blue strategy. Hockey history cut from whole cloth. But, as the Bard wrote: "There's the rub."

Looking up at those banners you become instantly conscious of how history can lie, how the trappings of a dynasty present a picture that is larger than life ever was or ever could be, and how myths are perpetuated.

Look up at the banners hanging silently in their glory and you can see the incomparable Howie Morenz stick-handling fluidly at centre ice. Look at those that end 1956-57 or 1958-59 and picture Rocket Richard steaming in on Glenn Hall or Terry Sawchuk, his eyes blazing like the single light on an overnight freight. Look up at the Forum and see Jean Beliveau, a *seigneur* of the twentieth century, a true aristocrat on ice. See Doug Harvey single-handedly controlling the entire game for minutes on end, or Guy Lafleur, blond hair streaming behind him, sweeping down the right wing and firing a laser blast into the far corner, ankle high to the goalie's right. Remember Ken Dryden, all 75 inches of him, leaning forward on his goalstick in his characteristically pensive pose while his teammates swarm all over the opposition 180 feet away.

Look at the banners and fall into history's trap. Communications consultants have spent their careers building this folklore of the Montreal Canadiens.

Today's researchers and analytical hockey insiders, who are far more familiar with the infrastructures of the modern corporations that most professional ice hockey teams have become, would work up a quite different kind of perspective on the club's glory than that of the common fan. They would identify acute insight, long-term strategic planning, an integrated and systematic recruitment program and an intense commitment to the hockey organization as a family as the elements which have contributed to an important and highly visible tradition.

George Kendall, Leo Dandurand, Joe Cattarinich, Louis Letourneau, Tom Gorman and even to some extent Frank Selke could not explicitly envision the *Club de Hockey Canadien* as a multi-level corporation, yet they managed it along corporate lines. The introduction of solid business principles and an all-encompassing work ethic helped to shape the organization's direction and guaranteed its growth and continuity.

The average hockey fan had trouble separating the hockey club from the business organization for a lot of reasons, most of which would keep a phalanx of sociologists publishing until the end of this century and well into the next: the common man (read working stiff) identifying with a winning tradition that helped ease the drudgery of his everyday life; the French Canadian's association with a winning collectivity, especially at a time when he might have felt insecure in a province dominated by an English-speaking economic elite, and many others.

How does a sports organization come to be perceived as a viable business arrangement? More significantly, how does a sports organization sustain its standards of excellence over time, while others remain unsuccessful or mired in mediocrity?

The answer to the first question is that the organization develops constancy—a consistent presence and image. Secondly, it faithfully maintains that constancy with its fans. In other words, the organization enters into a social contract with its followers.

It would be futile to delve into the mystique, history and impact of the Montreal Canadiens without pausing to look at the team from a fan's viewpoint. Over the years, there have been many celebrated team followers, among them Jockey Fleming, Dutchy, and Kid Mercury.

In our minds, the most irrepressible was Harry Brown. He is our Common Fan and he has a way of putting history in its place. To look at Harry and his world is to put the impact of the Canadiens into context.

If you had ever met Harry Brown, or happened to be discussing him with friends today, the first remarks might be something like: "It's a good thing Harry isn't alive to see this." "This" being the sportsworld of the 1980s—the world of agents, hockey players who have shopping centres written into their contracts, hair dryers in the dressing room—the sports world of the Information Age.

Harry was a product of another Information Age, a time of cigar-chomping journalists who imparted their bon mots from Olympian press boxes to sports fans who related to life in black and white. He became known as the Great Prognosticator because he started work as a messenger "pushin' a bike" up and down Montreal's celebrated city core—"where downtown is *really* downtown" —delivering for the telegraph people. He later moved inside where he would see all the copy the journalists and newspapers would send to each other. Like many wire operators, he became good at picking horses by accident. Because he punched out the pre-race programs and post-race results so often, some names were subconsciously filed away—only to re-emerge when Harry discovered the tracks. Hence the Great Prognosticator.

Today, years after his passing, there are those who will swear that he was Leo Gorcey, that he had lifted the accent of the Bowery Boys and carried it home to Montreal. Others, amateur philologists perhaps, would have recognized Montrealese—a curious patois spoken in this city's blue collar English community. It is a hybrid of cross-cultural communications with the other side—English kids who grew up scrapping and playing with French-speaking neighbours in Point St. Charles, Notre-Dame-de-Grace and Rosemont all speak it.

Harry was street people, a celebrated mooch, and downtown Montreal was his turf.

If you were a writer and connected with sports in even the most remote way, or fancied yourself a part of the *centreville* tableau, you would occasionally find yourself talking with, and trying to escape from, the Great Prognosticator.

He was the city's most indefatigable purveyor of the facts—pronounced "facks". In his early eighties, he also was without a doubt the most bowlegged man to ever live: "You jam a leather bicycle seat up your ass every day for twenty years and see where it gets ya, sonny," he would tell all and sundry from his perennial perch at the Montreal Press Club. Harry sidled along at about a mile a year like a fiddler crab, but even the fleetest of foot could not escape his inexorable approach.

Harry ran the Press Club. Oh, the regular journalists with pretensions of professional association would actually go through the trouble of holding nominations and electing one of their own every second year or so, but Harry ran the Press Club.

And there he would be at four in the morning, starting a fight in the poker game ("ya sunnuvabitchin' sandbagging tomatacan, ya held out on me!") and there would be a horrific crash as Harry tossed his cane at the sliding doors of the poker room. Seconds later, his walking stick recovered, Harry would sidle out of the room, throw some travelling profanity over his shoulder, and head for the men's room.

About thirty minutes later, one of the more daring souls in the club, noting the protracted absence, would timorously venture into the WC and invariably discover Harry asleep on his feet like an egret against a urinal, his cane wedged against a partition for balance.

He was in his element in early May. The Run for the Roses was on the horizon in Louisville and the Canadiens were involved in their annual Run for the Silverware.

The Montreal Men's (changed after a major league feminist furor in 1971) Press Club at the Mount Royal Hotel was the unofficial Stanley Cup headquarters. Harry was the unofficial NHL host. The wee hours usually found him and NHL veterans like Red Sullivan and Milt Schmidt at the club's dilapidated piano singing Broadway show tunes from the forties. If any member of the NHL chorus forgot a lyric, or challenged Harry on one, the Great Prognosticator would silence them with an embarrassing tidbit from the transgressor's career like, "How'd ya ever get into the Hall of Fame, Schmidt? Go out into the front hall. There's a picture of tha Rocket scoring a Stanley Cup winner and you sittin' on ya ass like a baby." You sang the songs Harry's way.

Before he passed away in the early 1970s, he loved expounding on Montreal's sports teams. What he called the Alouettes is a sound that cannot be repeated in any manner, including phonetically. What he thought of the Expos, then a struggling expansion team, was not much. He would start talking about the denizens of Jarry Park, would make a connection with this name or that name and you'd find yourself back in the glory days of the 1940s, talking about the Royals, Jackie Robinson, the

Duke and Delormier Downs. But mention the Canadiens and the philosopher-cum-historian would be in his element.

"The facks is," he would begin, gently hooking you by the elbow with his cane, (after all, he was going to hit you for a drink as payment when the consultation was over), "tha Habs are tha best team in the history of tha game. They *are* tha history of tha game and I don't care if Conn Smythe croaks when I say it. All you gotta do is go down ta tha Forum and look up. Tha facks are there for all to see."

The Great Prognosticator was a notorious bottom line man—"tha horse comes in, or it don't. It makes all the difference in the world, tomatacan"—and "facks" were his stock in trade. To Harry, history was finite and absolute, and measured in terms of win, place and show.

To most hockey fans, history is finite and absolute. But, while hindsight may afford one an unimpeded view of things, its perspective is very poor when you're a betting man. Harry bought the pennants hanging in the Forum rafters because they were common currency— just like winning tickets in your hands on your way to the pay window at the track. His long years had taught him that the past is the only thing you can take to the bank. No matter how good you were at handicapping the horse, the deposit you made wasn't always the one you thought you did.

Although Harry Brown was old enough to have been there when the Canadiens began and to follow the team through more than fifty years of history, even his eyewitness history could blur with the passing decades.

Harry's history was a little off; but his buying into the Canadiens' mystique was not. At the outset, the Montreal Canadiens were neither a dynasty nor a major force in hockey. They eventually emerged as both because Tommy Gorman instilled a business ethic and then Frank Selke provided the meticulous planning and direction that would make them a business first, a hockey team second.

Perhaps the most accurate gauge of Selke's political and social astuteness was that although he built a business dominated by English-speaking managers, he purposely played down the business aspects of the organization and played up its most acceptable side: the hockey team. It was no accident that management kept a low profile in those days.

Sports franchises become successful when the members of the sports audience in a given area become committed supporters of that organization and buy into its future (by accepting its past and supporting its present). Selke knew this instinctively and worked at obscuring the roles of the people who wore suits to work and kept the organization running smoothly.

Everything depended on a carefully cultivated image. Public relations and marketing directors are very aware of how to trade on such a commodity, no matter how superficial it may appear. In the Canadiens' early days, the social and cultural attachments seemed more visceral as an entire class took the club's daily doings to heart. These attachments long pre-dated the relatively young sciences of public relations and marketing.

In a detailed and systematic fashion, the hockey club became a part of the community's everyday activity. Defeats were taken personally while successes were honoured and recognized regularly.

The hockey club managed to build an Ivory Tower, complete with imaginary drawbridge, which was occasionally lowered to allow the fans to visit—quite unlike other barriers in certain areas of Montreal which remained forever raised, cutting off a large part of the population from the city's riches and beauties.

The team crest or logo became a symbol for Montreal and Quebec fans. The players who bore the crest bravely on their chests were charged with a meaningful set of responsibilities, for they were perceived as advocates of the community, rather than just simple representatives of a hockey team. In a sense then, the *Club de Hockey Canadien* was undergoing an institutionalization process, one which was external to the individual and beyond his control.

One does not have to study institutional power for a long time to understand its significance. Not only do institutions exist, they are perceived as having the moral right to exist. The Canadiens' mystique and credibility were nurtured within the context of these institutional arrangements. A sense of honour came to be associated with the opportunity to perform within the club's ranks. A special feeling of overwhelming servitude and enthusiasm engulfed the novice.

This deep-rooted commitment embraced the neophyte, the hockey rookie, so that the need to motivate him was diminished. For generations young hockey players have said, "Playing for the Montreal Canadiens is more than enough motivation," and they believed it. That feeling would become very evident during the 1986 Stanley Cup playoffs. In the sports world, this kind of hyper-commitment is a luxury afforded few teams.

It was achieved primarily by Selke and embellished by Sam Pollock. Selke orchestrated the situation in such a way that the novice actually believed the club was doing him a favour by permitting his participation in the team. How many millions of dollars have corporations spent in trying to exhort new recruits to believe in an enterprise's potential and to share in the long-term commitment to its success? For the Canadiens, external motivation came from the community, which had adopted the presumed success potential of the team. Internal motivation derived from the players' shared-belief system, which was gently introduced throughout the organization.

If a youthful hockey player comes to believe in the expected success of a franchise, he is more likely than not to set his sights on playing for that franchise. That was certainly the case in Montreal and Quebec before the National Hockey League introduced the universal draft; family, friends and acquaintances would find a way of letting the Canadiens know when and how well a young prospect was developing. Thus, the organization's recruitment process was facilitated wherever hockey was played. The young player believed that he would acquire all of the necessary knowledge and skills as a consequence of his involvement with those seasoned veterans who had been injected with the ten cc.'s of commitment and ten more of both expertise and personal discipline.

The process of transmitting the knowledge and skills was further enhanced by the rich oral history which emphasized the importance of winning ... and how it came to be expected.

Simply put, these are the sociological reasons why the people embraced the myths. People bought the tradition and the rich cultural tapestry which was being woven because in doing so they became part of it all.

History dwells on the rise of the Roman Empire, but it comes close to ignoring the fall. Lots of famous people, some historians, some not, have said that about the historical process. The consensus is that your history is only as good as the club public relations man who will write it many years later. And the people who were there and will go along with it. There is no problem finding folks to fit into this latter category. We all want to say we were there, and that includes the 415,000 people who saw Bobby Thompson hit his "shot heard around the world" in person at the Polo Grounds back in 1951.

"History is something that never happened, written by a man who wasn't there," is one of the most famous quotes about the subject. History teachers generally start new semesters with it. A lovely pithy statement, it is snickered at politely.

History, Montreal Canadiens' version, certainly happened. It just didn't happen quite the way you've been led to believe. The "facks"—those twenty-three ghostly shrouds hanging above the Forum ice—attest to the consistently best professional hockey team the world has known. And, with twenty-three Stanley Cup championships, and a remarkable twenty-seven final series appearances, they pay tribute to a sports organization whose exploits are the sport of ice hockey.

However, permit us a historical asterisk. The facts can, and do, lie.

There can be no doubt that with the advent of the new millenium, when the historians and anybody else with the ability to put a few words down begin chronicling the superlatives of the hundred years past, Montreal Canadiens will be known as the ice hockey team of the twentieth century. Even if the Habs don't win another Stanley Cup in the next fourteen years. Even if another team goes on a prolonged winning streak. That much is in the bank.

Yet the real glory they will reap is recent glory. Yes, Montreal Canadiens, eighty-three years old in 1993, have defined professional hockey in North America. Yes, they have provided much of the sport's romance, especially south of the border in the Flying Frenchmen era.

It wasn't always that way. In the team's first forty years, 1909-10 to 1949-50, they won six Stanley Cups. Since then, however, the team has won seventeen NHL championships in convincing fashion. Many fans easily recall the "five straight" team of the late 1950s and the "four straight" team of the 1970s. In fact, many forget that only a Toronto upset in 1967, the last year of the six-team NHL, prevented another "five straight" team from 1965 to 1969.

With that kind of recent glory, especially in the television age, it is no wonder that the red, white and blue is compared with the New York Yankees.

There was a time, however, in the 1920s and 1930s, when the Canadiens not only failed to capture the imagination of the hockey world, they couldn't even win over the fans in Montreal. Things got so bad during the Depression era that there was even talk one year of transferring the franchise to (horror of horrors) Cleveland. In these days of revisionist and instant history, the myth obscures the reality.

The *Club de Hockey Canadien* was born at a time when Montreal was one of several hockey hotbeds. The pre-First World War era was busy for Canada. The country was literally pulling itself up by the bootstraps and fortunes were to be made in "that there wilderness". Canada was definitely a hewer of wood and drawer of water, as well as a miner of silver, gold and most of the valuable minerals upon which old-time fortunes were made.

Teams with names like the Kenora Thistles, the Renfrew Millionaires, and the Dawson City Klondikers all would challenge for the Stanley Cup and, in the case of Kenora, actually win it, in 1906-07. Towns like Cobalt and Haileybury challenged Renfrew in northern Ontario for highest concentration of silver millionaires and best "store-bought" hockey teams. As Trent Frayne writes in *The Mad Men of Hockey*:

> In the spring of 1909 the silver magnates brought the Ottawa Senators and the Montreal Wanderers to the north country for an exhibition series. When the teams returned home, half the players stayed behind to cash in on the bonanza. The whole area was hockey crazy.
>
> Tens of thousands of dollars were bet on each game; often thousands changed hands on a single goal. Miners in the crowds fought in the rinks during games and up and down the streets after them, and during that wild period the best hockey players in the world were performing in this backwoods league formed to take advantage of the silver discovery.

Up to and during this era, the enduring hockey power was a team from Montreal called the Wanderers. It won the Stanley Cup four times between 1905-06 and 1909-10, after breaking the Ottawa Silver Seven's string of three straight Cups. The Wanderers were the pride of the Eastern Canadian Hockey Association and brought glory to their league in years when champions of various leagues challenged for the Cup. At one point in 1910, there were twenty-five professional ice hockey teams in Canada alone, including the fledgling *Club de Hockey Canadien* of the new National Hockey Association. Montreal was home to five such teams: the Canadiens, Shamrocks, Nationals, Wanderers and Victorias. The Canadiens' beginnings were singularly inauspicious as they finished the first NHA season with two wins in twelve games. Year two was quite different, mainly because a different team wore the Canadiens' name. In 1909-10, the NHA team called the Canadiens was owned by J. Ambrose O'Brien and T.C. Hare of Cobalt.

The league, well aware that ethnicity was box office gold, granted the two men a franchise to ice an "all French Canadian team," which they did, hiring the celebrated Jack Laviolette as coach and manager.

In 1910-11, a challenge to the team name and right of franchise was forwarded by George Kendall, owner of the *Club Athlétique Canadien*, a very popular French-speaking sports club in the city. He told the National Hockey Association board of directors that he owned the rights to the *Club Canadien* name and would undertake very expensive and time-consuming litigation if a franchise was not forthcoming. League management quickly saw his argument, and also understood that the popularity of the *Club Athlétique Canadien* would almost ensure a successful fan base for the team, and Kendall (also known as Kennedy) received his franchise. With Georges "the Chicoutimi Cucumber" Vezina in goal and stars like Didier Pitre and Jack Laviolette, Kennedy-Kendall's Canadiens won their first Stanley Cup in 1916.

For the team's first three seasons, it was Montreal's French team, by NHA rules and constitution. In 1912-13, the league relented and allowed the Canadiens to dress two English-speaking players while the other teams could sign as many as two French-speaking players each. The Kennedy-Kendall era ended five years later, when the popular Montreal sportsman died in the influenza pandemic (1918 to 1920) that killed more people around the world than the First World War.

Thus began the first modern era of the Montreal Canadiens. The team was purchased for $11,000 by three Montreal businessmen-sportsmen, Leo Dandurand, Joseph Cattarinich and Louis Letourneau. It became part of the brand new National Hockey League, intending to make a big impact south of the border.

In 1924, a Boston franchise was added, and teams from New York and Pittsburgh followed a year later. Chicago

Black Hawks and Detroit Cougars were next, in 1926, and the early foundations of the NHL were set.

Teams would come and go in the 1920s and '30s— among them the Ottawa Senators, Pittsburgh Pirates, Philadelphia Quakers, New York Americans and Montreal Maroons—but the Original Six (as they would become known) were in place: the Canadiens, Toronto St. Pats (later Maple Leafs), Cougars (later Red Wings), Bruins, Rangers and Black Hawks. The Canadiens, still very much the Flying Frenchmen of the old NHA days, became popular gate attractions around the league and especially tough rivals of the Quebec Bulldogs, Maroons and Senators. The team, which featured a collection of stars with names like Newsy Lalonde, Aurele Joliat, Howie Morenz, Joe Malone, Sylvio Mantha and the infamous Cleghorn brothers, Sprague and Odie, won three Cups between 1923 and 1931.

It also set about developing its historical character. Yet the *Club de Hockey Canadien* did not immediately stand the NHL or the sports world on its ears. The fabulous Flying Frenchmen were just one of many teams, no more, no less. But they were an organization that would eventually develop what sociologists call an "occupational culture" which was to foster a winning tradition by stressing the importance of success.

One would assume that most work organizations naturally generate such strong beliefs and commitments among their employees. The truth is that these qualities take years to cultivate.

In the case of the Canadiens, those athletes and administrators not willing to commit themselves to the degree considered necessary for success were selectively eliminated from within the organization.

Can you imagine how successful most corporations would be if their potential recruits were straining at the leash to work for them?

In the corporate world, IBM (Big Blue to Montreal's Red, White and Blue) fostered a parallel belief system. Preaching loyalty, dedication, hard work and integrity as core variables, Thomas Watson Jr. combined history with culture to create a sense of belonging to a winning tradition within his organization. Like Frank Selke with the Canadiens, Watson was a grand master in the area of strategic long-term planning and systematic recruiting. He was acutely aware of the importance of human resource development and was highly selective when choosing a plan for growth and development of what we now call corporate synergy.

Just as Selke would expose new recruits to legendary tales of the great superstars and their accomplishments, by the simple expedient of turning their everyday dressing room into a museum, so did Watson dwell on IBM's early days when his highly motivated workforce, supported by brilliant Research and Development people, began to make inroads in the marketplace.

Sociologist Orrin Klapp calls this an identity voyage, a fantasy ride that allows new recruits to identify with the legends and folk heroes of their particular organization. One reason why Detroit Red Wings have been so feeble in recent years is that only the city's hockey fans identify with Gordie Howe, Ted Lindsay, Sid Abel and Alex Delvecchio; the players cannot and do not.

Imagine the uproar in Montreal if Maurice Richard were allied with another hockey team, as is Gordie Howe (with Hartford). The close identification of present players with the team's legends helps to build camaraderie and generates cohesion from within.

Ken Reardon, Sam Pollock and Toe Blake were experts at the task of transmitting the central components of the occupational culture. When Irvin, charged with the same responsibility, failed to keep his superstar Maurice Richard sufficiently motivated to rank individual urges below the importance of team activity (the 1955 outbreak which led to his suspension and the notorious Richard Riots), he was quickly replaced by Selke, a close friend. The lessons of commitment are followed by all, at all levels of the organization.

In April, 1986, forty-nine years after Howie Morenz died, the Montreal Canadiens are skating through a strenuous workout and preparing to meet the Hartford Whalers in the Adams Division final. Head coach Jean Perron and his assistant, Jacques Laperierre, put their charges through their paces for ninety minutes.

High in the east-end reds, the decades meet. Toe Blake, who as a junior was scouted by Morenz and who played with Joliat, sits quietly watching the colourful swirl on the ice. He chats with Ronald Corey, Jean Beliveau, Serge Savard, Doug Harvey, André Boudrias, Jacques Lemaire and Carol Vadnais. Except for team president Corey, all have played for Montreal at one time or another and sport Stanley Cup rings.

Down on the ice, the players occasionally glance up and notice the cabal. They know what those people represent and they possess the drive to achieve some of that glory.

Five weeks later, rookie Brian Skrudland wipes champagne from his eyes in a Calgary dressing room, hugs the Stanley Cup and says:

"This is what Larry Robinson, Bob Gainey and Toe Blake meant."

History, whether purely factual or that wonderful synthetic thread woven into a folkloric tapestry, is an integral part of this hockey team.

# 2

## Assembling the Cast

*"We will now discuss in a little more detail the struggle*
*for existence."*
Charles Darwin

One thing that has distinguished the Montreal Canadiens throughout the team's history has been the almost unbroken succession of superstars who have epitomized the team.

While most have been true Flying Frenchmen, handing the torch down from generation to generation (Richard to Beliveau to Cournoyer to Lafleur), the first was a Swiss-Canadian from small-town Ontario.

Howie Morenz, the Stratford Streak, was the catalyst and the superstar whose name first defined the Montreal Canadiens in their true beginnings, the 1920s and 1930s. Teamed up with colourful characters like Aurele Joliat, Billy Boucher, Armand Mondou, and Sylvio Mantha, Morenz was arguably the best player to don skates in his era.

That is quite a claim, when it is considered that athletes bearing surnames like Patrick, Boucher, Conacher and Shore played in the same period. Perhaps the best way to make the case for Morenz is to step outside the sport for a moment.

The 1920s, as most observers will tell you, was the beginning of the golden age of sport. That is largely

because most avid sports fans would rarely, if ever, actually see their sports heroes in action. It was the era of the
re-created sports event—when radio announcers, impro-
vising sound effects, would take play-by-play off the
wires and re-create sports contests such as baseball
games, championship boxing matches, or great track-
and-field matches.

It was a time when "spectators" were found at home,
straining to hear the descriptions of fevered action
emanating from a Motorola or Philco crystal set and
letting their imaginations envision the scene.

On the playing fields were herculean characters like
Babe Ruth in baseball, Red Grange in football, Bill Tilden
in tennis, Bobby Jones in golf. In the ring were incompa-
rable champions like Jack Dempsey and Gene Tunney.
Olympic swimmers like Johnny Weismuller and Buster
Crabbe went right from the Olympic Pool to Hollywood.
Women's sports were also well represented, with names
like Helen Wills and Gertrude Ederle in tennis and golfer
Babe Didrikson.

Even the supporting casts were full of people larger
than life—baseball managers like McGraw, McCarthy,
Huggins and Ott; coaches like Rockne; promoters like
Tex Rickard and writers like Grantland Rice, Ring
Lardner and Damon Runyon.

What the fans never really saw, and never really heard,
was re-created and reproduced for them by these titans.
A Grantland Rice story would instantly elevate the pe-
destrian to Olympian heights. It was vicarious hero worship three times removed.

Into this world slipped the fledgling National Hockey
League. Not only did the league, its teams and its players
have to compete with other sports for the sports dollar,
always the case in any era, it had to find someone who
would make the American sportswriters sit up and take
notice.

And it had to be someone who could join Ruth,
Dempsey, Jones *et al* in the pantheon of the golden greats.
Someone whose very presence would actually coax an
adjective or two from a kingmaking scribe and who
would be written up as an honest-to-goodness legend.

That person was Howarth W. Morenz, and the man who found him was Canadiens' owner Leo Dandurand, a man who loved the horses and was fully light years ahead of his peers in his understanding of the value of public relations and promotions in an era built on them.

Mere mention of Morenz to his contemporaries still gets results a half-century later. Eyes glaze over and memories play on a private video recorder of the mind. The superlatives flow easily.

"Howie Morenz was in a class by himself, the greatest player I ever saw." Heady praise. The source was the late Frank Clancy, a man who spent seventy years in and around the National Hockey League as a player with the Ottawa Senators and Toronto Maple Leafs, referee, coach and executive. He was right-hand man to the late Toronto owner, Harold Ballard, in the 1970s and early '80s.

"He was the best in his day, the best I played against and the best I've ever seen. He could get to top speed in one stride, he was a threat to go from end to end through an entire team at any time and he shot the puck as hard as any man who ever played."

Clancy the executive takes over from Clancy the player, coach or referee. He begins to discuss the real value of Morenz in the 1920s. The Roaring Twenties. The Golden Age of Sport.

"He sold one hell of a lot of tickets at a time when hockey really needed somebody who could pull in the fans.

"If you went to a baseball game and saw Babe Ruth powder one over the fence, you didn't need to know first base from the ass of your pants to realize that you had seen something special. It was the same thing with Morenz. You didn't need to know the difference between a hockey puck and your belly-button to know that when you had watched Morenz play the game, you had seen something special."

Of the Three Musketeers who owned the Canadiens at the time, Dandurand was the man with the street smarts, the man who knew that the product was the thing that mattered, and that it was competing against other products that were well established. When he plucked the flashy Morenz out of the wilds of Ontario, he knew that the introverted player would have to become the super-hero of the sport, if it was going to stand a chance of survival.

In Morenz's first professional season—1923-24—the league was struggling to survive with three solid clubs: the Ottawa Senators, Toronto St. Pats and the Montreal Canadiens, plus an anemic Hamilton Tigers franchise. On Canada's West Coast, the Pacific Coast Hockey Association was flirting with financial ruin, reduced to three teams which were losing large amounts of money.

Three years later, in 1926-27, the NHL was a ten-team league, with six of those franchises in the United States, where the money was. The arrival of the Boston Bruins in 1924, Pittsburgh Pirates and New York Americans in 1925, and the New York Rangers, Chicago Black Hawks and Detroit Cougars in 1926 moved the game to the United States in a big way. Dandurand flogged Howie Morenz and the Flying Frenchmen like Colonel Ruppert sold the Sultan of Swat and Murderers' Row. The league went along for the ride.

"When the Canadiens and Howie Morenz came to town, the American teams beat the drums hard about the games," Dandurand said. "That attracted the casual fan who went to see hockey out of curiosity. But they only had to watch Morenz play the way he did and the Canadiens' approach to the game and they were hooked.

"There was only one Morenz and there has been none like him since," Dandurand wrote in *The Hockey Book* (edited by Wilfrid Victor "Bill" Roche) in 1953.

"Full speed going both ways—giving his brilliant all— all of the time. The game has changed considerably since his days and I doubt there will ever be another like him."

Hyperbole certainly, because people like Eddie Shore, Bun and Bill Cook, the Patricks and the Bouchers more than did their jobs for their respective franchises. Yet the Canadiens had that something extra which made them special. They were the Flying Frenchmen, romantic foreigners from the Far North who spoke of a romantic North American tradition—Radisson, Marquette, the *coureurs de bois*, colourful fur traders.

Dandurand understood the promotional punch of golden boys and foreign myths. He merged the two successfully in Morenz and the Canadiens. Thousands of American hockey fans grew up believing that Morenz was a famous French Canadian name in Quebec. *Mais oui* —sell, sell, sell! Even when Morenz would do a very rare radio interview south of the border, the fans would strain to hear his peculiar French accent. Howie Morenz could have been exactly the same superstar with the Toronto St. Pats, later the Maple Leafs. But the impact would never have been the same in the United States. He needed the Canadiens and their mythic potential as much as the team needed him and his prolific on-ice exploits. One wonders if Morenz and the NHL could have survived his playing for another team. That almost happened.

Morenz shone at hockey at an early age, starring for four years with the Stratford Midgets, a perennial junior hockey power in southwestern Ontario in the post-First World War era. Morenz played on a line with Roter Roth and Frank Carson, the latter a future star with the Montreal Maroons of the NHL. Stratford also had a senior team playing in the Ontario Hockey Association and this team would often call up Carson and Morenz to bolster their lineup.

Although the teams in the fledgling National Hockey League sent scouts to beat the bushes for talent, quality young players did not automatically gravitate towards the upper echelons of the sport once they had finished their junior years. Such was the case with Morenz, who took a job as an apprentice machinist in the Stratford railway shops.

Larger companies in those days sponsored sports organizations for their employees, and a few judiciously selected ringers. The railways were famous for this. After all, who could better assure transportation for tournament-bound players? It was at such a tournament in Montreal that Morenz was spotted. Morenz scored nine goals for the Stratford CNR team against Montreal's Point St. Charles machine shop team at the old Mount Royal Arena (where the Montreal Canadiens first played) on a warm Saturday afternoon in the spring of 1922.

The referee for that contest was Ernest Sauvé, a former player with Cecil Hart's All-Stars, a collection of hockey players that was one of the best amateur teams in Canada in 1913. After the game, he got on the telephone to his former coach, and Dandurand dispatched Hart to Stratford to sign him.

It was a long summer, however, and local pressure was applied to force Morenz to remain in Ontario, if not with the local Stratford seniors, then with Toronto in the NHL. Just before training camp, Montreal received a wire from the young centreman stating that he had changed his mind about playing for the Canadiens and could Mr. Dandurand please tear up the contract?

No dice, said Dandurand. Morenz was to play professional hockey. Despite Morenz's doubts, this was an entirely good idea, since the young man was as terrible with his personal finances as he was good with his stickhandling on the ice and had run up a few debts back home to the tune of $800. (In those days that sum could buy one a new car and still leave enough left over to pay a couple of months' rent.)

The telegram didn't work, so Morenz sent Dandurand a letter:

> "Dear Sir;
>
> I am enclosing a cheque and contract to play hockey with your club.
>
> Owing to several reasons, of which family and work are the most to consider, I find it impossible to leave Stratford.
>
> I am sorry if I caused you expense and inconvenience, and trust you will accept the returned contract in a sportsman-like way.
>
> Yours truly,
> Howarth Morenz"

"Monsieur Leo" hadn't acquired his impressive reputation by falling for every line handed to him, no matter how genuine it seemed. He described the incident in *The Hockey Book.*

> The letter was written on August 10, but the postmark on the envelope shows that it did not reach Montreal until August 23. Howie had evidently carried it around and thought about it before he finally put it in the mail. I promptly phoned Morenz at Stratford, told him there would be a railway ticket for him at the stationmaster's office in Stratford, and asked him to get on an evening train and come to Montreal for a personal conference with me. Howie agreed to meet me at my office the next day.
>
> He arrived on time, too. But he was adamant in his refusal to turn pro, declaring that he would never report to the Canadiens or any other NHL club. During our conversation, Morenz insisted that with his job in the Stratford car shops and with what he was 'getting on the side' to play OHA intermediate hockey, he would be better off to finish his shop apprenticeship and stay out of professional hockey.
>
> Then I told him as kindly as possible that business was business, and he would have to comply with the terms of the contract he had signed.
>
> Morenz broke down and wept. With tears running down his cheeks, he declared: 'I don't believe I'm good enough to make a place on your team, and you will be everlastingly sorry you forced me into pro hockey. You'll have to take the responsibility of depriving me of my livelihood and my amateur standing.'

At that, Dandurand was sorely tempted to call the deal off, but he remained steadfast.

Within a week of training camp, and a tough week it was, because rookies were severely tested by veteran incumbents, Georges Vezina and Sprague Cleghorn were convinced that the introverted young hockey player would be a great one. They were absolutely right.

Morenz on the ice, Dandurand upstairs. It was the first in a series of famous upstairs, downstairs Canadiens' couples that would make this a hockey franchise like no other.

Aurele Joliat remembered both well.

Joliat came to the Canadiens in 1922, in a controversial trade for Newsy Lalonde, the Habs' most popular player at the time, but well past his prime. The trade made Dandurand so unpopular in Montreal that he had to have his phone disconnected. Lalonde, the spirit of the Canadiens in their first decade, did not complain. Dandurand had negotiated a new contract for him worth more than double what he was getting in Montreal.

Joliat, an Ottawa native, had a French name, but he was the son of a Swiss Protestant and he was the first to tell you his French was lousy.

"Still, it was easier for Dandurand to trade Lalonde for me than for a Dick Smith."

At trade time, he was playing for the Saskatoon Sheiks and barely weighed 135 pounds soaking wet. Still, he was a fast-skating, smart left winger and scored twice in his first Montreal game, finishing his rookie season with a very respectable 13 goals.

"Dandurand stuck his neck out for me and I had to deliver."

Montreal would finish in second place that year and would be edged out in playoff action by a tough Ottawa team. The next summer would see Dandurand at his best, and two rookies named Mantha and Morenz join the team.

Joliat has his own private little joke for those who must ask the obvious question: "What was it like playing with Morenz?"

"I never played with Morenz," is a response guaranteed to send the questioner right into the archives.

"Wait a minute. It says right here that you guys were on the same team, hell, the same forward line, for more than a decade."

Joliat pauses, letting the full impact of his little joke build up.

"I'll tell you . . . I played with him, but not exactly with him, if you get what I mean. I was always in front of him or behind him. I could never stay even with him, that's

for sure. Jesus Christ, could he go! End to end rushes ...
none of this back and forth passing to get there. ..."
Joliat doesn't notice it, but he is speaking much faster
now, in short, clipped phrases, his words bunched together, and with that faraway look in his eyes ... "He
went straight from end to end."

Morenz on the ice, Dandurand and his people like Cecil
Hart upstairs: it was a combination that produced
legends.

Leo Dandurand was something of a celebrity in Montreal in the 1920s. Without a man like him, the Canadiens
might never have made it. He was the ideal man to take
over after the death of Kendall-Kennedy and keep the
dream of the *Club Athlétique Canadien* alive.

> Hockey always has been a game of weight and power, and a
> small man needed a great deal of skill to make it as a pro. I
> believe that speed and skill are the best ingredients of the
> game. I view the Canadiens as playing a very fast, slick game
> but not being bullied by anyone. I don't want hoodlums, but
> I do want he-man hockey talent to meet all and any situa-
> tions, to be able to win by whatever means are needed.

That was Leo Dandurand's hockey philosophy all
wrapped up in a neat quotation uttered the day he
masterminded the purchase of the Canadiens. From his
remarks it would seem that the team he was buying into
was a collectivity of listless, less-than-spectacular journeymen who simply weren't effective when the going
got rough. With names like Laviolette, Vezina, Pitre and
Lalonde on the honour role, that obviously was not the
case.

Still, Dandurand was the consummate showman and
he wanted to start selling an image right away. The
image would be "Firewagon Hockey"—something that
the Flying Frenchmen could market very well south of
the border. Dandurand, who knew "south of the border"
very well—it was his backyard—got on the job right
away.

Dandurand, Joseph Cattarinich and Louis Letourneau
were Montrealers who had been around. They were

popularly referred to locally as the "Three Musketeers". Dandurand, who traded on his name as a native-born French-Canadian, actually was born in Bourbonnais, Illinois and moved to Canada at the age of sixteen, in 1905.

He was thoroughly outgoing, known for his flamboyant lifestyle and pluck. His fame in Montreal was sufficiently widespread that he was referred to simply as "Monsieur Leo". Dandurand had a broad interest and involvement in sports and was a promoter *par excellence*, whose executive ability matched his imagination and congeniality.

He carefully nurtured the myth that he was the "man with the Midas Touch" and maintained a reputation of always backing winning ventures. Of course, his successes depended on wisdom, shrewdness, promotional ability and good research—but he wasn't the man to give a successful formula away.

His interest in sports was not always in the wings. He began as a founding father of the Canadian Amateur Hockey Association and even refereed in the old National Hockey Association, where he had several celebrated run-ins with Kennedy, the man he would succeed at the helm of the Canadiens.

Joe Cattarinich also started out on the ice—as goalie for the Canadiens in the club's inaugural 1909-10 season. Cattarinich was such a team man that he suggested the club woo Georges Vezina, the man who was to replace him between the pipes. When the time came to purchase the Canadiens, he was a successful Montreal businessman who had done well in other ventures on both sides of the border with Dandurand.

Of the three, Louis Letourneau was the most carefree, a well-to-do amateur sportsman and partner with the other two in various undertakings, including ownership of a thoroughbred race track in Cleveland. When word came down that the Canadiens would be sold at auction, all three men were busy with the summer meeting in the Ohio city. Dandurand sent word to an acquaintance, Cecil Hart, to function as his agent at the auction and go as high as necessary to buy the team. Two other groups were interested—Tom Duggan, representing the Mount Royal Arena Company; and NHL president Frank Calder, speaking for Ottawa interests. Bidding opened at $8,000 and Hart immediately bumped it to $8,500. Calder then stepped in and asked for time to consult his backers.

The auction resumed a week later and this time Duggan dramatically laid ten $1,000 bills on the table.

The theatrics were wasted, however—Dandurand had picked his man well. Hart calmly got on the phone to Cleveland, described what had happened, and was told to do whatever was required. He offered $11,000, the other two potential buyers backed off, and the Three Musketeers had a hockey team.

Dandurand later offered his memorable quote about the kind of hockey player he envisaged wearing the *bleu, blanc, rouge*. He immediately set about living up to it. His first acquisition bespoke a man who had spent years in horse racing. He went for bloodlines when he acquired Billy Boucher, a slick Ottawa native and member of the family that would eventually provide four NHL players, including older brother Frank, a future Hall of Fame member. Despite Dandurand's claim that he would never brook the presence of hoodlums on his team, he next sought the services of hockey's premier enforcer—a Montrealer with the colourful name of Sprague Cleghorn.

You might go up to Sprague Cleghorn or his brother Odie and jokingly mention that his name sounds like a root fungus. You would do it exactly once, and you would never do it again. Along with Cleghorn, in a trade with Hamilton, came Billy Couture (often known as Coutu) a former Canadien with a penchant for ash surgery, who as a Boston Bruin in 1927 would be banned for life from hockey for attacking a referee.

With Coutu and the Cleghorns on the team, the fleeter skaters and playmakers could operate with relative impunity—in those days that meant the opposition wouldn't attempt to rearrange your facial features more than once or twice a game.

After a celebrated rift with Lalonde in the new management's rookie season, Dandurand gave Sprague Cleghorn the job of team leader, the equivalent of team captain. He never regretted it. Cleghorn's tenure gave all appearances of being a short one, however.

In a game at Ottawa, February 1, 1922, Cleghorn decided to get even with his former team for trading him. His single-game savagery would probably net him a life sentence in today's much more civilized game. The best description of the on-ice mayhem is to say he simply excised the opposition's top three players from the game.

He began with star defenceman Eddie Gerard, who was dispatched with a five-stitch gash just above an eye. Scoring ace Frank Nighbor followed, smashed to the ice with a vicious check that injured an elbow. A butt end to Cy Denneny's face opened up cuts on the nose and over the eye and had the first aid people scrambling for medical supplies.

The punishment for all this? A match penalty and the recommendation by referee Lou Marsh that he be banned from the sport. Ottawa strongly protested Cleghorn's behaviour and asked for a life sentence, but Toronto and Hamilton refused to go along with the suggestion. Since unanimous approval was necessary, Cleghorn dodged a bullet.

The tough Montrealer, quite a dandy off the ice (players on his team often joked that he and Odie spent as much time in front of mirrors checking out the latest additions to their wardrobe as they did playing—but never to their faces) was never repentant. In later years he would admit to purposely injuring the three Senators and claim proud participation in "more than fifty stretcher-case fights" during his career.

If King Clancy can rhapsodize about the ephemeral hockey talents of Morenz, his description of Sprague Cleghorn is in more down-to-earth language.

"Sprague was just tough and mean, the best at using the butt-end of his stick that I ever saw," Clancy recalls. Rather than the faraway look elicited by his recollections of Morenz, you get the feeling he's looking over his shoulder as he recounts this tale.

"He also wouldn't hesitate to give you a hook in the face or cross-check you in the back of the head."

In Trent Frayne's excellent book, *The Mad Men of Hockey*, Clancy describes the following incident.

> He was just a terrible man to have to play against, a terrific stick-handler, a master with the butt-end, and tough, holy Jesus he was tough. One night he broke loose with the puck and sped towards our goal. There was just one man between him and it. I came rushing back and as Sprague neared the last man I tapped my stick on the ice a couple of times like you do when you want the puck, and I yelled: 'Over here, Sprague.' Well, he naturally thought it was a teammate and he slid me the puck without looking, and I sped the other way with it. So when the period was over I was feeling pretty good as I walked to our dressing room and the fans were applauding me and just as I was going in the room, I heard this friendly voice, 'King', and I turned around to see who it was. Well, I want to tell you, my friend, did I ever get a sweet whallop in the kisser. It was Sprague all right, just quietly turning off my lights. Jesus, did he hit me a beauty.

Cleghorn was not all muscle, though. He scored 17 goals, high for league defencemen in that era, and "only" had 63 minutes in penalties. The Canadiens finished the Three Musketeers' first season with a 13-11 record and Dandurand pledged to continue improving his club.

That summer, he met George Boucher, Billy's brother, at the racetrack (where else?) and the Ottawa star mentioned a player in Saskatchewan who might be a star. Not long afterward, Aurele Joliat was on his way to Montreal.

A year later, of course, Morenz would join him. The subtle blend of superstar forward (Morenz), skilled muscle (Cleghorn) and front office know-how (Dandurand) was coming together for the first time in Canadiens' history. It would be repeated over and over again in the next sixty years.

Yet, although the Canadiens were assembling their on-ice team, little was being done about developing the front office team. To be sure, Dandurand was nobody's fool and as good a sports entrepreneur as there was at the time. And for all of his braggadocio, his "Midas Touch" and the "Monsieur Leo" all over Montreal, Dandurand showed a lot of common sense when he hired the quiet Cecil Hart to run his team.

Nevertheless, there were few efforts to build a front office organization that would ensure the on-ice product would never be diluted. A major reason was that, although the Canadiens constituted a high-profile sports and business venture, they were not Dandurand's main business interest. In those days, ice hockey was at best a four- or five-month endeavour while horse racing—harness and thoroughbreds—was a year-round preoccupation, especially with Dandurand's interests south of the border.

There was very little work done to develop a minor-league or feeder system of teams, or a network of scouts who would eventually beat some of Canada's most isolated bushes in search of young men who could play the game.

Marketing and promotion were practically unheard of. Management would trade on the names of their star players, as is done today, but would go little further. Endorsement contracts and third-party promotions were rare. Selling the team usually involved only the simple act of publishing schedules.

As for a comparison of the Montreal Canadiens' nuclear family of the modern era with the teams of the 1920s, there is none to be made. The players then were as close as today's because success was directly linked to on-ice cohesion. But that was as far as it went. As Mrs. Georges Mantha reminisces:

"While there was a certain status in having a family member on the team, the city was not yet the Montreal Canadiens hotbed it would become later. There was little in the way of facilities for wives and relatives; if you wanted your wife to be there, you bought a ticket. As for physical facilities, forget it! The wives of the players had an unofficial lounge, a restroom on the second floor. There were some pretty good fights in there, let me tell you!" It seems that Mesdames Morenz and Joliat, who enjoyed their status as the *grandes dames* of the Montreal Canadiens, would brook no challenges to their authority.

Conversely, today's Canadiens family is an extended one and includes spouses, girlfriends, parents and children of the players. Everything is done to make these people feel comfortable at a game—whether they are related to a ten-year veteran or a youngster just called up from Sherbrooke (AHL) or a junior team. If you are going to demand loyalty from your employees, Frank Selke reasoned, you must show them respect and fair treatment.

Today's front office follows that dictum to the letter.

The Three Musketeers, Dandurand, Cattarinich and Letourneau, were in the hockey business to make money, or at the very least to gain a little public respect that might help overcome the taint of their involvement in horse racing. Wasting a lot of time or energy coddling the friends and families of their players was not on their agenda.

They were businessmen of their time, operating on handshakes and personal relationships that would be anachronistic in this day and age. One example of that closeness took place in 1926, when the New York Rangers were being assembled by Conn Smythe, and later the Patrick family. Leo Dandurand helped the Patricks negotiate their way through a variety of player deals after they sold the Pacific Coast and Western Canada leagues and moved east to join the NHL.

The names involved in the deals read like a list from the Hockey Hall of Fame: Eddie Shore, Ching Johnson, Taffy Abel, the Cooks, Frank Boucher and Red Dutton. After the wheeling and dealing had ended, Dandurand invited the Patricks over for dinner at his home.

"How about Herb Gardiner?" he asked. The fine defenceman had not yet been included in any transaction.

"He's yours if you want him," Lester Patrick replied.

"How much?"

"One dollar."

"Done."

Gardiner was a mainstay of the defence that played in front of George Hainsworth in 1928-29, when the little goalie allowed only 43 goals in 44 games and compiled 22 shutouts.

Business was up close and personal in that era and a tad less scientific than in today's corporate world.

All of that notwithstanding, Dandurand and his fellow Musketeers put together a team that won the Stanley Cup in Howie Morenz's first year, 1923-24, and two more in 1930 and 1931.

"We almost lost the Cup after the first one," Dandurand wrote.

The team was invited to the Université de Montreal after they downed Ottawa, Vancouver and Calgary in the playoffs. (It was only after 1927 that the Cup would become an exclusive NHL trophy.) The Stanley Cup was presented to the Canadiens during a special ceremony and all of the players headed to Dandurand's home in the high-rent district. In Montreal, they don't exaggerate when they say high-rent district. Dandurand's home was high atop Mount Royal in Westmount.

After the game, several players, including Sprague Cleghorn, Sylvio Mantha and Vezina, piled into the boss's Model T for the trip. Things were going fine until the car encountered Côte St. Antoine Road, a sight that would gladden the heart of many an Alpine downhiller. Cleghorn had been carrying the Cup on his lap when all three players piled out to give Monsieur Leo and his Tin Lizzy a push up the hill.

The rough defenceman gently set the Cup down on the curb, and the car was pushed to the crest of the slope. About two hours later, Mrs. Dandurand was ladling out refills of her famous punch when she chanced to remark: "By the way, where *is* this famous Cup you've all been talking about?"

Cleghorn, never at a loss for words, replied: "Uh-oh!"

Dandurand and Cleghorn sped back down Côte St. Antoine to the spot where the Model T had originally stalled. The Cup was still sitting there.

Several years before he passed away, Dandurand was asked about the business side of hockey in his day.

"Let's just say it was a less complicated time," he replied.

In 1932, the Montreal Canadiens were barely a framework for the modern-day business organization. Frank Selke was fourteen years away. And a good part of those fourteen years would represent the worst period in the club's history.

# 3

## The Darkness Descends

Nowhere can the myth of the invincibility of the Montreal Canadiens be shattered more easily than in the Depression Era.

Those who might today purposely or unconsciously manipulate history to say that the Canadiens were always the best, always at the top of the heap, forever the Flying Frenchmen, might be very surprised to discover how bad the team was in the 1930s and '40s. And those who believe that the team never trades its top superstars, such as Richard, Beliveau and Lafleur, may be stunned to learn that Howie Morenz was dealt away to Chicago in 1934.

If you can look beyond popular mythology to the facts, you will find them very revealing. The Dandurand-Morenz Era peaked in 1929-30 and 1930-31 with consecutive Stanley Cups. The next time the Montreal Canadiens would win Lord Stanley's prized hardware would be in 1943-44. That thirteen year drought was the longest in the club's history. During that period, Detroit won three times (1935-36, '36-37, '42-43), and Toronto (1931-32, '41-42), the New York Rangers (1932-33, '39-40), the Chicago Black Hawks (1933-34, '37-38) and the Boston Bruins (1938-39, '40-41) all won twice. The city of Montreal's drought was not as long as the Canadiens' because their arch-rivals, the Maroons, managed a Cup of their own in 1934-35. Not only were the Canadiens not winning, it seemed that everybody else was. Some dynasty.

The troubles did not descend on the team all at once. As the saying goes, they were long in coming, and even longer in staying. They began shortly after the 1930-31 Stanley Cup win, off the ice. The nucleus of the Stanley Cup winners, George Hainsworth, Sylvio and Georges Mantha, Marty Burke, Aurele Joliat, Morenz, Pit Lepine and Johnny Gagnon, remained intact for the next two years. The changes took place in the front office. Dandurand, Cattarinich and Letourneau had done the team proud since its purchase in 1921. They had hired qualified management, which in turn put together competitive and exciting teams on the ice. They stayed on top of all developments in hockey in the city, including wresting the Forum away from the Maroons.

A frequent topic of conversation in Montreal in the early 1930s was: "Which team will move?" The Canadiens and Maroons, arch-rivals on the ice, were even more competitive off the ice, as everyone involved realized that only one team could survive in the long run. Talk of merger was heard occasionally, with fans openly fantasizing about the powerhouse that would result from such a benevolent matrimony. Merger discussions were often heard in higher financial circles, and discreet feelers would go out from one camp to the other at almost regular intervals.

The partnership continued for two more years but it was doomed to failure; the principals had too many other interests making demands on their time and effort. Insiders say that Dandurand, always on the lookout for excitement, had gotten bored. Enter "Tay Pay" (from the French pronunciation of T.P.) Gorman.

To better understand what was happening, it is necessary to take a sidetrip via Ottawa and Chicago. Ottawa was the hometown of sports entrepreneur Thomas Patrick Gorman. For all of those modern-day sportswriters who firmly believe they know better than the sports managers they cover, Tommy Gorman is an inspiration. He not only said so as sports editor of *The Ottawa Citizen* in the pre-War era, but when he was given the opportunity he went out and proved it with the three Cups his Ottawa Senators captured in 1920, 1921 and 1923.

"The Great Gorman" was the title of the March 1, 1946 article in *Maclean's*. Sportswriter Jim Coleman wrote:

> Mr. Gorman combines some of the characteristics of P.T. Barnum, Shirley Temple and a very shrewd banker. His hockey antagonists frequently regard him with chagrin, but Mr. Gorman can afford to chuckle at this discomfiture—he is the only surviving member of the four men who originally formed the National Hockey League.
>
> Also, even if he has no other claim to fame, he would go down in history as the only former police reporter who had a chance to make a million dollars from a thoroughbred horse. However, he was the victim of a fate which can befall only an Irishman or a newspaperman—the horse thoughtlessly took ill and died!

Tommy Gorman's first job was as a page boy in the House of Commons and his energy was such that he attracted the attention of Charlie Bishop, a reporter with *The Ottawa Citizen*. Bishop got Gorman a job at the newspaper and his boundless energy served the young Irishman well; he advanced through the ranks from copyboy to police reporter to sports editor in jig time.

"Tommy soon realized that you couldn't do what he liked to do best—make money—working for a newspaper, so he left in 1917 to become publicity man for L.N. Bate, the owner of the Ottawa hockey club," Coleman reminisces.

Within a year, Gorman and Ted Day, owner of the Ottawa Arena, purchased the Ottawa club for $2,500 and Gorman was sitting at the table in Montreal's Windsor Hotel forming the four-team National Hockey League with Frank Calder, Mike Quinn of Quebec and George Kendall of Montreal. Within five years, the Ottawa Senators had won three Stanley Cups.

You couldn't keep Gorman in one place for any length of time. In 1925, he sold his share of the Ottawa Senators to Frank Ahearn for $35,000 and all of the latter's stock in Connaught Race Park outside Ottawa. Two days later, he joined Tex Rickard with the New York Americans. The Gorman family owns the Connaught track to this day.

Tex Rickard and friends were big money boys; they liked to make it and spend it, and even to spend it while making it. Gorman was in his element and it took him only a few days to convince Rickard to buy the Hamilton Tigers, lock, stock and hockey sticks, for $75,000.

It was a fast crowd in New York, sometimes too fast, and Gorman was a veteran of the police desk. He realized that some of his bosses might be using their speed to stay a step ahead of the law. Gorman's intuition never failed him. The club's owner shortly thereafter found himself in the Atlanta federal penitentiary in a one-way dispute with the U.S. Internal Revenue Service, *à la* Al Capone.

In 1928, Gorman left hockey and joined his friend Jim Crofton, a.k.a. Sunny Jim Coffroth, at the new Agua Caliente racetrack just outside Tijuana, Mexico. The track was an immediate success, the finest facility in the southern California area at a time when the sport of kings was banned in that state. Messrs. Crofton and Gorman were in the chips and a wonderful business opportunity galloped into view in 1932.

A large gelding from Down Under with the improbable name of Phar Lap was setting the racing world on its ear, winning races with ridiculous ease. The horse's ownership and entourage consisted entirely of "horse people" who had lucked into a moneymaker but whose lack of business acumen was severely reducing their earning potential. Phar Lap won the Agua Caliente Handicap without difficulty, and Gorman convinced the Australians to let him arrange a series of races across North America, culminating "back East", where all the money was.

Disaster struck quickly. Phar Lap died under mysterious circumstances and his handlers were convinced that he had been poisoned. Then legislators in Sacramento decided that horse racing in California was not a bad thing at all, and Hollywood's finest no longer had to travel to Agua Caliente to bet on the thoroughbreds.

Hockey beckoned anew.

You'll draw a smile from his son, Joe Gorman, when

the stories turn to his dad, a handsome Irishman whose eye for the ladies was well-known. Tommy had a gift of the blarney, but he also was a workaholic, who never feared putting in an eighteen-hour day.

"Dad was involved in hockey, horses and baseball in Ottawa and Montreal and was a good friend and business acquaintance of Dandurand and Cattarinich. Dad was on his way back to California in 1932 when they pulled him off the train. They had $50,000 invested in the Chicago Black Hawks who were owned by Major McLaughlin and they wanted him to keep an eye on their investment. So they made a deal with McLaughlin that Dad take over coaching the team."

In the language of that era, Major Frederic McLaughlin was a "beaut." Reports indicate that Major Hoople might have been closer to the truth. The rich son of a man who had made his fortune in coffee importation, he was a tall, movie star type who affected a clipped moustache and bow ties. He played polo and was a prime mover in the social whirl of the City With Big Shoulders. The Black Hawks were named after the famous 85th Black Hawk Division of the U.S. Army, to which the Major had belonged during the First World War. The Major must have felt he had never left the trenches and his machine-gun battalion behind, because he ran his team accordingly.

Four years before he created the Chicago franchise, the Major married movie star Irene Castle, of the famous Castle and Castle dancing team, and he really began putting on the ritz.

Tommy Gorman appeared on the scene in 1932, when the fortunes of the Black Hawks had definitely begun to wane. Up until that time, Chicago had finished third, last, last, second, second and second in the NHL's American Division. Every time the Hawks threatened to bust out into a good team, McLaughlin dumped another coach.

In six-plus seasons, Pete Muldoon, Barney Stanley, Hugh Lehman, Herb Gardiner, Tom Shaughnessy, Bill Tobin, Dick Irvin, Godfrey Matheson and Emil Iverson had stood behind the Chicago bench. Consistent with the Major's idiosyncratic behaviour was his hiring of Matheson. They met aboard a train in the U.S. Midwest and struck up a conversation. Matheson mentioned that he was a Winnipegger and the Major's eyes lit up. If this man was from Canada, the Major reasoned, he must know quite a bit about hockey. When the train arrived in Chicago, Matheson was the new coach of the Black Hawks.

That kind of sublime silliness put the team into financial hot water. Chicagoans loved the sport, but they were not going to stand still for a second-rate team. Their attitude and a bad frost in Brazil had the Major scrambling for working capital. Enter Dandurand and Cattarinich.

"Dad had orders to improve the team so that Dandurand and Cattarinich could get their money back, and that's what he did," says Joe Gorman.

Gorman picked up the coaching reins in the 1932-33 season and the Hawks finished dead last. The following year, Gorman made a few judicious player moves and the Hawks finished second in their division and third overall in the league. A veteran crew which included Taffy Abel, Lou Trudel, Lionel Conacher, Paul Thompson, Leroy Goldsworthy, Johnny Gottselig, Mush March and Chuck Gardiner wreaked havoc in the playoffs, sweeping Detroit in a four-game final to win the Stanley Cup.

In Major McLaughlin territory, that could be both good and bad news for the coach. McLaughlin had been feuding with the Norris family, who owned the cavernous Chicago Stadium, ever since 1928, when he refused approval for a second NHL franchise in Chicago.

In response, the Norrises founded the Chicago Shamrocks of the American Association in 1928, and they played before larger crowds in the Stadium. When that league went belly-up in 1931, McLaughlin signed a three-year contract with the Stadium and was happy for a while, until the Stadium began to lose money and was bailed out by the Norris family.

"The Norris and the Wirtz families owned Detroit and New York and they wanted Chicago and the Stadium. Wirtz and my father discussed the Chicago-Detroit series, and at that point, my father knew he was finished. He knew he was going to get the squeeze and he did not want to finish there on an unsatisfactory note. Whatever his impression of what Wirtz was trying to say to him about the series, my father told me that he wanted no part of any discussion about games, and that was that. They won against Detroit (1-0) that night and my father, who was living at the Sherman Hotel, packed up all of his belongings and left them in his car, which he parked about five blocks from the Stadium. When the game was over and the celebrations quieted down, he went out to the car and started to drive home to Canada."

Gorman had been away for a while and discovered to his dismay that Stanley Cups won in Chicago did not endear him to all Canadians. Crossing the border at Windsor, he was stopped for expired licence plates and tossed into the hoosegow for an overnight stay. Canadians awoke to pictures in their morning dailies of the Stanley Cup-winning GM en route to jail.

That didn't faze him and he continued on to Montreal for a meeting with Dandurand.

"At the time, the Canadian Arena Company owned the Maroons and they were having all sorts of problems with them at the Forum. The building was mortgaged to the skies and there was serious talk of turning the Forum into a streetcar barn to serve the west end of the city. Joe and Leo got their money back but they were still in trouble financially."

Dandurand and Cattarinich recommended to Senator Donat Raymond, co-owner and chairman of the Canadian Arena Company, that a job be found for Gorman, a top-notch hockey manager and businessman. He was appointed manager of the Maroons.

"My father brought in Lionel Conacher as coach, and players like Alex Connell and Allan Shields to go along with guys like Toe Blake, Cy Wentworth, Jimmy Ward,

Hooley Smith, Bob Gracie and Herbie Cain and the Maroons finished second in their division and won the Stanley Cup."

No book on the Canadiens of this era would be complete without a look at the Maroons, Montreal's other team. In fact, many oldtimers will tell you that it was the Canadiens who were the other team. The Maroons-Canadiens rivalry was one of the few things that could get cash-strapped Depression era hockey fans into a rink in the '30s, especially since the English-French animosity was built in right from the start.

In 1924, Dandurand, the consummate showman, sold one-half of his territorial rights to Jimmy Strachan, a Montreal businessman and owner of the Canadian Arena Company. Sold might be too strong a word; he almost gave them away for $15,000.

A seasoned horse player, Dandurand was taking a calculated risk. The thing that has made Montreal hum for centuries, any politician or sociologist could tell you, has been the finely calibrated cultural tension between the English and French communities.

If anyone was tuned into this cultural phenomenon it was Dandurand—a French Canadian who had spent the first sixteen years of his life in the United States. His impeccable English and French allowed him to circulate freely in the two communities. His inherent sense of showmanship told him these were the things of which great rivalries, and profits, were made.

In *The Hockey Book*, edited by Wilfrid Victor (Bill) Roche, Dandurand explained his reasoning.

Allowing the Maroons to get into the Montreal hockey picture was no big-hearted gesture on my part. I saw in them an important and lucrative local rivalry, as well as a fine addition to the league and to hockey in general.

I let Maroons in for only $15,000, which was considered, even by the Maroons directors, to be very reasonable. It was understood among the other three member clubs of the NHL that year—Toronto St. Pats, Ottawa Senators and

Hamilton Tigers—that the $15,000 was to go to the Canadiens.

That price, incidentally, established a precedent for the submission fee of franchises of Boston (1924), Pittsburgh and New York Americans (1925) and New York Rangers (1926). However, the $15,000 caused an NHL rumpus. Toronto, Ottawa and Hamilton began to think they ought to share equally with the Canadiens in the money which Maroons paid to enter the league. That didn't suit me because it had been privately agreed that the cash would go to Canadiens. The rub was that there was no written record of any such agreement, nothing in the minutes of the league.

The Canadiens finally did get all of the money, and from then on a stenographer was present to take the minutes of every NHL meeting. Dandurand insisted on it.

Dandurand's estimates of the rivalry were proved right the very first time the teams faced off in their Forum. When the *bleu-blanc-rouge* took to the ice against the maroon-and-tan, anything could happen on the ice and in the stands. Both teams were epitomized by one player or a specific line. For the Canadiens it was Morenz, Joliat, Black Cat Gagnon and their go-go speed. For the Maroons, it was slower-paced, hardnosed hockey as personified by the Three "S" Line of Nels Stewart, Babe Siebert and Hooley Smith.

"Hooley was just about the meanest guy you ever saw," is the standard quotation from any Maroons or Canadiens fan from that era. Legendary tough guys like the Cleghorn brothers had long retired but the Canadiens had the likes of the Mantha brothers, Georges and Sylvio, Albert "Battleship" Leduc, Pit Lepine and Joliat.

How bitter was the Canadiens-Maroons rivalry? The answer best comes from Maroons defenceman Red Dutton, a western cowboy who would also star with the New York Americans, and serve six years as NHL president. Getting antsy before a game while the referee hunted for three ounces of black, vulcanized rubber, Dutton offered the famous line: "Never mind the goddamned puck, let's start the game!"

Even Dandurand had no immunity from the rivalry: in one game he got involved in a fight between Smith and Newsy Lalonde!

"They were bigger than us and they played that way," Joliat reminisces. "But we couldn't back down. We had nowhere to hide, we were playing all of our games against them in our own city and everybody knew that each game we played meant a lot more than others. Especially in the mid-'30s when nobody knew which team was going to survive in the city. By the time we got there, it was like we were playing to be the team that deserved to stay. Man, I'd say they were tough . . . I can't remember anybody who was tougher than Hooley Smith. There were guys like Eddie Shore who would never back down from anybody, but Hooley took care of him. Battleship had a couple good scraps with those guys, too. I have to laugh when today's hockey fans cry about the Big Bad Bruins or the Philadelphia Flyers because they have a fight or two during a game. In those days, these guys were surgeons with their sticks. When a fight started on the ice, it might end up in the seats or under the stands, and everybody was in it."

The Maroons entered the league in 1924. They won their first Stanley Cup two years later. In 1927 and 1928, the Maroons-Canadiens rivalry was set in stone, with the Habs nipping their crosstown foes in a best-of-three series the first year, and the Maroons returning the favour the next.

In 1928, the Maroons extended the New York Rangers to five games, losing the deciding game on home ice in a game that could be charitably described as poorly re-fereed. The fans weren't in such a charitable mood; they tried to penalize the unfortunate official, who needed a police escort out of the building.

The Maroons were nothing if unpredictable, dropping into fifth place in the Canadian Division in 1929, then storming back the very next year to win the division and lose to the Bruins in the playoffs. And while the Canadiens may have been unhappy at losing the regular-season championship to their hometown foes, they took solace in the Stanley Cup championship, their first of two.

After the consecutive championships, it was the Maroons who captured the hockey headlines in the city. They took the much favoured Toronto Maple Leafs into overtime before succumbing in the 1932 playoffs and were eliminated by the Detroit Red Wings and Chicago Black Hawks respectively the next two years. In 1935, however, their time came as they squared off again with the vaunted offensive machine of the Maple Leafs' "Kid Line"—Charlie Conacher, Joe Primeau and Busher Jackson. Playing tough in the corners, gang defence and relying on the red-hot Alex Connell in goal, the Maroons won the Stanley Cup—the last that would be awarded a Montreal representative until 1944.

Almost as soon as it had started, it was all over for the Maroons. Both teams had financial problems in the Depression Era, but it was the Canadiens who were in the direst straits. A bad, almost directionless team, the Canadiens were getting used to playing before crowds of 2,000 and less and were losing a lot of money. The nadir for Montreal hockey fans came in 1937, the year that Howie Morenz returned to the Canadiens and died; a year when almost every description of the teams started with "financially strapped."

On September 17, 1935, it appeared that the merger rumours would be borne out, when the team was sold to Ernest Savard, Louis Gelinas and Colonel Maurice Forget. The three had formed a syndicate and were linked indirectly with the Canadian Arena Company. The latter had two main properties, the Forum and the Montreal Maroons.

"Montreal had to become a one-team arrangement and that was part of the deal that was kept quiet. The team was purchased and the plan was to move the franchise to St. Louis, but Conn Smythe, that man of wonderful vision, scotched that," said Gorman.

"At that time my father was out of it, because the Senator turned the hockey operations over to Ernie Savard, a drinking buddy. He might have done that because, once again, Dad was too successful and won the Cup that first season. It isn't easy to fold a Stanley Cup winner to keep a seventh-place team (the Canadiens). That kind of move would have been dynamite, French majority or no French majority."

The 1935 Cup champions maintained their momentum by winning the Canadian Division in 1936, but lost in the first round of the playoffs. The next year, they finished second in the regular season and went into the playoff semi-finals. In 1937-38, the once haughty Maroons expired with nary a whimper, failing to make the playoffs with 12 wins, 30 losses and 6 ties in the 48-game regular-season schedule. On August 25, before the next season would start, the Maroons ceased operations. It had been decided in the boardroom that if any team would survive in Montreal it would be the Canadiens; after all, the population base for the city was seventy percent French-speaking and the Canadiens were their team.

Nobody gloated. The Maroons had won the respect of their adversaries in their brief lifetime; winning two regular season championships and two Stanley Cups in a scant fourteen years. And the fans who had packed the Forum for Habs-Maroons games knew that they would miss the special "family feud" that those two teams represented. There were a lot of distraught Maroons fans, too, who felt that they could never support a team they had loathed so long and with so much passion. In time, however, most came round to support the Canadiens.

"The saddest thing is, that once the Maroons were folded, Savard messed up completely. Instead of moving the Maroons to St. Louis and rebuilding the Canadiens, they amalgamated the two teams. But they gave away most of the good players, like Gracie, Cain and Dave Kerr and kept Wentworth and Stu Evans, who were both on their last legs."

Gorman was still very much a part of the Canadian Arena Company and his job as business manager was to fill the big building on as many nights as possible.

"My father quietly began building up the Quebec Senior Hockey League. They had several teams from the Montreal area and also from Valleyfield, Shawinigan, Ottawa and Sherbrooke, and they used to play Sunday doubleheaders at the Forum. The QSHL was a winner and it happened at the Forum. How do you keep a building going?"

The answer would do Hulk Hogan, Nikolai Volkoff and Andre the Giant proud. Gorman "discovered" professional wrestling, which was becoming popular all over the United States.

Eddie Quinn was the big Montreal promoter and a yet-unknown French Canadian named Yvon Robert was about to become a bigger draw than the Canadiens.

"Dad was into everything in those days, and the Forum was starting to look a whole lot better, profit-wise. Wrestling took up a lot of summer and fall dates, and ice shows helped fill the quiet nights in the winter and spring."

The Canadiens were still alive, although not kicking very much. In 1938-39, they finished sixth in a seven-team league and in 1939-40 they dropped to dead last with 25 points on 10 wins, 33 losses and 5 ties in 48 games. Something had to be done, and Senator Raymond stepped in.

William Northey now was running the show and a deal was made with Lester Patrick in New York to have some of the Rangers move to the Canadiens and to bring in Frank Patrick to manage the club. This was not a particularly bad idea. The Rangers had finished second twice in a row during the regular season, and sparked by the goaltending of Dave Kerr (remember him?) and the play of Phil Watson, the Colvilles, the Patricks (Lynn and Muzz), Babe Pratt and Bryan Hextall, had skated away with the Stanley Cup in 1939-40.

The Patricks had a superb hockey reputation and it was hoped that Frank would help pump new life into the Canadiens. He started by suggesting former New York great Bun Cook as coach.

Northey went to Toronto to consummate the deal and

interview his new coach. There was a knock at his hotel room door. When Northey opened it, Bun Cook literally fell through, dead drunk. The interview ended on the threshhold, so to speak.

Tommy Gorman then was dispatched to the Big Apple to discover what was going on. After all, the 1940-41 season was rapidly approaching.

"Lester Patrick hemmed and hawed and my Dad said: 'Listen, I don't have a lot of time to fool around. Training camp opens in a couple weeks. Lay it on the line.'

"Lester cleared his throat and said: 'The directors won't go for the deal.' Dad got back on the train to Montreal. What else could he do? Now he had to report back that the Canadiens essentially didn't have much of a team."

Gorman was not completely helpless. He knew where he could find a top-notch coach in a hurry because Toronto sportswriter Andy Little had tipped him off to the fact that Dick Irvin was through in Toronto and would soon be replaced by Hap Day.

Joe Gorman, who by now was his father's "gofer", accompanying him everywhere, was sent to the Mount Royal Hotel to meet Irvin and drive him to Ste. Adèle, about forty-five miles north of Montreal, in the Laurentians.

"Dad gave Dick the lowdown, he wanted him to know exactly what he was getting himself in for. We did not have a hockey team and we were going to have to start from scratch to put one together."

That kind of assessment made no friends with the hierarchy, especially Senator Raymond, who resented Gorman's implied criticism of his friend Ernest Savard. Senator Raymond also knew that the indomitable Irishman thought little of his bona fides, too.

If French-speaking Quebec thought Senator Raymond was a top society man and politico, the treasurer to the Quebec Liberal Party and power behind the scenes, what with his genteel cattle and horse breeding farm in Vaudreuil and his connections in the Quebec legislature and

House of Commons, Tommy Gorman and his buddy Maurice Duplessis, the Union Nationale leader who would be Quebec Premier for more than twenty years, contemptuously dismissed Senator Raymond as little more than a Liberal party bagman.

Their hostility remained unspoken because both men recognized that they needed each other. Gorman's business acumen had begun to show dividends for the Forum. He was actually making a profit, something totally alien to the Old-Boys-Club style of management that had existed before.

"When Dad returned to Montreal, he found out that these idiots had signed away everything . . . the concessions, advertising, the game program . . . to all of their friends. He put a stop to that in a hurry and made recovering these things his first priority."

Gorman made his point to Raymond and other disbelievers about the collective worth of the Canadiens in the most graphic way possible. He put the entire team on waivers, with the exception of Toe Blake. There were no takers. Dick Irvin heard the real story during that meeting in Ste. Adèle.

"Dick got something like $4,500 or $5,000, which was pretty good money in those days. The whole dressing room had to be cleaned out and he had to do it."

Frank Patrick was still in the picture, the remaining evidence of Senator Raymond's pique, but not for long.

"Frank was a nice man, from a good hockey family, but there had to be a reason Lester let him come to Montreal. He was totally off the wall. He kept talking about taking the team to train in Sun Valley, Idaho, and making a movie about it. My father kept asking what team he was talking about. What they had in Montreal was a complete disaster."

Gorman and Irvin eventually began to build a team and slowly put together the elements of a winner. Toe Blake was the one-man nucleus, but he was joined that year by a raw defenceman from Winnipeg named Ken Reardon. He picked up former Canadiens defenceman

Jack Portland from Chicago, and Elmer Lach, a rookie centre from Saskatchewan, also joined the team that year.

Another member of that team would achieve notoriety in a completely different fashion. Antonio "Tony" Demers was a smooth-skating right winger with a devastating wrist shot who scored 13 goals and assisted on 10 others in 46 games in 1940-41. Nine years later, the season after he was voted the most gentlemanly player in the Quebec Senior Hockey League, he became the first and only former Montreal Canadien ever to be accused of murder. He was later convicted of manslaughter in the beating death of his girlfriend, and sentenced to fifteen years in prison. He served half of that sentence at St. Vincent de Paul penitentiary before being paroled.

The patchwork quilt Canadiens finished sixth in 1941 and 1942 but were showing signs of developing into a team, especially after such promising young newcomers as Buddy O'Connor (1941), goalie Paul-Emile Bibeault (1941), Butch Bouchard (1941), Maurice Richard (1942), Glen Harmon (1942), Mike McMahon (1943) and Bill Durnan (1943) came aboard. The 1942-43 team moved up two places in the standings, ending a four-year play-off drought for the Canadiens.

A year later, everything came together at once. The Canadiens, led by the Punch Line of Blake, Lach and Richard, the rock-ribbed defence of Reardon, McMahon, Frank Eddolls and Bouchard and the goaltending of Durnan, set a regular season points record—83—on an unbelievable 38 wins, 5 losses and 7 ties in a 50-game season. Detroit finished second with 58 points. It was the first of four straight Prince of Wales championships for the Canadiens.

The Habs topped off their greatest season with a 4-0 icing of the Chicago Black Hawks in the final round. Dick Irvin and Tommy Gorman had done the job.

More importantly, Quebec senior hockey, which Gorman had actively cultivated, was beginning to pay dividends. Montreal was acquiring a number of quality players, many of them French Canadians, who graduated from junior ranks and preferred to play senior closer to home rather than moving to the United States or Western Canada for seasoning in the minor pros.

The Canadiens did not win the Stanley Cup in 1944-45, but came back with a vengeance the following year to cop another. Everything was going well, on the surface. However, beneath the surface, the Gorman-Raymond feud was raging.

"In 1946, my father had about all he could take from Raymond. He had done his job and the Forum was in great shape. They were debt free and showing some profit because of ice shows and wrestling. The Canadiens were packing them in and the Senior Hockey was still drawing big crowds too. The company had about $600,000 in the bank."

Tommy Gorman had a network that fanned across the province. One fine summer day, defenceman Mike McMahon came into his office and told the general manager that he had found the Canadiens' next goalie. About two weeks later, McMahon walked into Gorman's office with a fifteen year-old from Quebec City, named Gerry McNeil. McNeil, at the ripe old age of sixteen, wound up with the Montreal Royals seniors.

"That was the whole point to the network that was feeding my father at the Forum," Joe adds. "McNeil cost the Canadiens nothing; neither did the entire line of Blake, Lach and Richard. Blake came when the Maroons folded, Richard came up through Quebec hockey and Lach came to Montreal after a tryout with the Rangers. They cut him and he passed through Montreal on his way back out west, staying at the Queen's Hotel. Gordie Cannon drove him out to our training camp in St. Hyacinthe for a look-see and that was that."

A Toronto referee named Bert Hedge tipped off Gorman on a young player named Ted (Teeder) Kennedy, and the general manager added him to the Canadiens negotiations list. Kennedy was traded to Toronto two years later, for Frank Eddolls and Joe Benoit, two players who would be important cogs in the Canadiens team of the 1940s.

Gorman received a lot of criticism for that trade, because Teeder Kennedy became one of the very best players in the NHL and the inspiration for a Toronto team that won four Stanley Cups in five years between 1947 and 1952.

"What most of these people didn't know was that when Teeder was eighteen, he and his father came to Montreal and met with my dad. Mr. Kennedy explained that his son was Toronto born and bred and that he had only one desire in life: to play with the Maple Leafs. My dad could have insisted that he play in Montreal but he respected what the young man and his father were saying. So he traded him to Toronto."

It worked out for both teams. Gorman's connections reached even further than the boondocks of Quebec or Saskatchewan. He was an Ottawa boy, and in that civil service town, that meant he grew up with more than a simple nodding acquaintance of some government VIPs.

When the Second World War got under way, the question was whether or not the National Hockey League and other professional sports organizations would be able to maintain operations. A long debate in Congress finally decided that major league baseball and other sports could continue in the United States, and Canadian sports entrepreneurs lobbied for a similar decision north of the border.

Here, however, they ran into a stone wall in the person of James Layton Ralston, a staunch Maritimer and Minister of Defence in the Liberal cabinet of Prime Minister Mackenzie King. Senator Raymond, for all of his connections, had no say with the Minister because the men were on opposite sides of the Conscription issue. French Canada voted almost ninety percent against a draft that would send their young men to fight in what was considered a British war; English Canada voted the opposite way in almost the same proportion.

King walked a political tightrope when he compromised: young Canadians could be conscripted for service in the armed forces but they could not be sent overseas. Ralston was outspokenly against that decision; he favoured overseas conscription. He also was dead set against business as usual for professional sports and said so.

Other well-connected NHL representatives, like Conn Smythe and league president Red Dutton, tried to dissuade Ralston but to no avail. Without conferring with Cabinet, he unilaterally decreed that all sports were over and that Canadians had to engage in the war effort as a total activity.

"My Dad had grown up with the three Lynch girls, as they were known in Ottawa. One married into the Labatt family, and another married D.C. Coleman of Toronto, a member of the Canadiens' board of directors and father of sportswriter Jim Coleman. More importantly though, when she was a young woman, she was pursued by two men, Mr. Coleman and Mackenzie King, and it turned out that she had been the love of the Prime Minister's life and he still had a soft spot for her.

"She telephoned the Prime Minister and arranged an appointment with Mackenzie King for my father, Mr. Dutton and one of the Norrises, in King's office. When they got there, the Prime Minister took them down the hall, ushered them into Mr. Ralston's office and said something like, 'Take care of these gentlemen.' The message was clear: Mr. King wanted professional sports to continue and Mr. Ralston should pay serious attention to that fact."

Ralston's objections were also tempered by the fact that Dutton, a decorated war hero in the First World War, was petitioning that hockey continue even though he had recently had two sons killed in action, a week apart.

That incident was a coup which raised Gorman's worth around the league. Nonetheless, by the war's end, the Gorman-Raymond acrimony meant that the partnership was destined to end. And when Tommy Gorman was in the Senator's bad books, he couldn't win for losing.

"I remember an incident where Senator Raymond's wife wanted to go up to the country house in the

Laurentians. The Senator was out of town and besides, he had put up his car for the winter. My father suggested that Gordie Cannon drive Mrs. Raymond and their four children up there, which he did. When Raymond found out, he raised holy hell."

The last straw was Atwater Park, a long-time baseball field across Atwater Street from the Forum where Babe Ruth had once played a game, many years before, on a barnstorming tour. Gorman, ever alert to potential revenue, suggested that the Canadian Arena Company purchase the park and use it for parking in the short term, while keeping a sharp eye on the long-term real estate development possibilities.

"Dad knew they could get it for $125,000 and the parking revenues in one season would take care of the purchase price. As well, the team was planning to raise ticket prices and Dad figured that the parking facility would allow the club to cancel the ticket increase. By this time, however, Senator Raymond was against everything my dad suggested. What the Senator did was take all the profit out of the company. My dad was a businessman with an eye to the long term and he wanted to plough all the profits back into the company. He couldn't stay under those circumstances."

There are always two sides to a story, of course. The other side in this case was a gentle hint from the Forum that Tommy Gorman was actually let go for reasons relating to alleged irregularities involving ticket sales. It seemed that some famous Montreal scalpers, Jockey Fleming among them, were getting choice seats to sell "off market", and suspicion fell on the general manager. None of this was ever proven, and Joe Gorman vehemently denies the allegations.

This chapter essentially has been Tommy Gorman's chapter, and with good reason. His contribution was virtually expunged from the Canadiens' historical record over the years as the Selke-Pollock story grew. Whether Frank Selke did it on purpose or not, the impression is that Selke came to Montreal to a franchise that was in utter disarray.

Nothing could be further from the truth.

Frank Selke walked into an operation that for the most part was thriving. The Canadiens had won the Stanley Cup April 9, 1946, with a 6-3 win over Boston at the Forum. The team line-up had names like Lach, Blake, Richard, Mosdell, O'Connor, Bouchard, Reardon, Eddolls and Durnan. It was coached by the redoubtable Dick Irvin.

The time had come for the Senator and "Tay Pay" to part company. The clincher was a replay of Chicago, 1934.

The Gorman family still talks about a telephone call Irvin received before the fourth game of the final series in Boston, with the Canadiens leading the series 3-0. It came from someone high up in the Canadiens organization and it contained instructions to bench Toe Blake. If Boston won that night, the teams would return to Montreal for the fifth game. The story goes that Irvin was fit to be tied when he came away from the telephone.

"What do I do?" he asked aloud.

For Gorman, it was a case of *déjà vu*.

"My dad confronted Dick and said he didn't much care what happened but Blake was going to play, even if he and Irvin would be out of a job the next day. The Canadiens lost that game legitimately that night, and won the Cup back home in Montreal."

A short time later, Tommy Gorman was gone, for all intents and purposes, a non-person in the Canadiens' history.

He returned to Ottawa and the Ottawa Auditorium, which he owned in addition to the Ottawa Senators senior hockey team. He enjoyed a healthy, happy career with his baseball, hockey and horse racing interests until he died in 1961.

Phar Lap may not have delivered the goods for him but a lovely young girl named Barbara Ann Scott did. After she won the 1948 world figure skating championship, the rising young star was frozen out of the lucrative U.S. ice show market by some short-sighted and chauvinistic American promoters. T.P. stepped in and personally set up a tour of Canadian cities and rinks that made both skater and promoter a respectable profit.

Perhaps the reason for his faint appearance in the archives of the *Club de Hockey Canadien* can be traced to one very revealing comment Frank Selke made to us many, many years later.

Senator Raymond was the director of a Toronto bank and attended that institution's Annual Meeting in May, 1946. While in Toronto, he called Selke, who had already left Smythe and the Maple Leafs.

"I told him I couldn't work for Mr. Gorman. Mr. Raymond told me they were going to retire him at the end of their business year, the first of July. So I came down."

Why couldn't Selke work for Gorman?

"He was an odd person. Tommy was the kind of guy— I don't mean this wrong—if the truth served better, he would still tell you a lie. Tommy was a wonderful guy in many ways. Did a lot of things. But he was a peculiar person. And he had gotten himself in wrong and they had gotten rid of him."

To paraphrase the proverb, the truth will always belong to the last historian.

# 4

# Maurice Richard
# The Lion Rampant

The New York Yankees had Babe Ruth. He was the star of the dynasty that gave birth to Yankee tradition. That is why Yankee Stadium in the Bronx is called The House that Ruth Built. The legitimization of baseball, especially after the Black Sox scandal of 1919, rests on Ruth's shoulders. He gave the sport character, notoriety and definition. Before Ruth, baseball had been perceived, like most other professional sports, as something tawdry, a jock *demi-monde* inhabited by barely literate farm boys, greasy hucksters and colourful characters; in the 1920s, it became respectable and joined the mainstream of North American life.

"He launched baseball . . . he had the largest following in the history of the game—no doubt about it," said Branch Rickey in *The Old Game.*

"In the 1920s, baseball needed a revival of faith and Babe Ruth was exactly that. He was a necessary focal point for public adulation." Ruth's astonishing 59 home runs in 1921, and his 60 homers in 1927, captured the imagination of a post-War generation like few other sports feats. Everything about the Babe was genuinely heroic.

Which is not to say that the Sultan of Swat was Caspar Milquetoast. On the contrary, he was true to his origins

—a saloon and orphanage in Baltimore. He, and others including Ty Cobb, Walter Johnson, Pie Traynor, Lou Gehrig and Connie Mack, gave America what it wanted: believable heroes, a Pantheon of Homeric figures untainted by scandal. Boxing, horse racing and hockey strove valiantly to join baseball on this Doric pedestal, but with little success for many years to come.

Boxing and the horses made great movies because they contained the stuff of life, all the elements of the human condition wrapped up in a sports contest. They pitted shining Good Guys against villainous Bad Guys and characters of all the shades of grey in between. The trouble was, too often those sports were featured outside the sports pages, as this week's petty gambler, or last week's mob figure confronted a Grand Jury to explain the mechanics of the Big Fix.

Apart from the Black Sox scandal, baseball was remarkably free of such taint. Football, having taken the college route of academic respectability, would eventually join baseball in the ranks of mass popularity sports that were above suspicion, but that wouldn't happen until the 1950s. Basketball also did not achieve universal popularity until later. Hockey, especially in Canada, would also receive its benediction in the 1950s.

Any cursory examination of sports history will be misleading because it cannot accurately paint the whole picture. To clearly understand the mood and feelings of an era, one has to emerge from the sports pages and do a time line study of the period. Scouring the microfilm library of a newspaper, or viewing the fragile kinescopes and film of the 1930s and '40s, paints a distorted canvas. The sports reporters and recorders of the time were consummate professionals and the honoured ancestors of today's media professionals. Like today's counterparts, they sold sports with magnificent reporting of events and stars. But a simple search of the sports section of the day could not tell us what was inside the heads of the people who sat in the seats.

Were sports heroes then comparable in stature to the media superstars of today? Was Jack Dempsey as big as

Muhammad Ali? Could the Manassa Mauler almost single-handedly stop a generation of young people from
going to war as Ali did ("I ain't got no quarrel with the
Viet Cong") with the youth of the 1960s? Did athletes
get involved in politics? Were they big in advertising and
commercials? When they spoke, did anyone listen? What
did the fan in the stands feel about his sports heroes?
What did he feel about his social condition? What kind of
a day did he have prior to attending the sports contest?
How did he respond to the media coverage of sports?

All of those questions, and especially their answers,
would be essential to anyone attempting to gauge the
true impact of a sport or an athlete within his social
context.

No picture of the era would be complete without a
basic comprehension of where the athletes stood with
the public when they were away from the playing fields
and locker rooms. The verdict was far from unanimous
but the majority opinion was that most professional athletes were "rubes", dumb hayseeds scant weeks removed
from isolated farms, barely literate and unable to function in civilized society. Those men who rose to lofty
heights on the playing field, whose exploits were legend
in the sports pages, were forgotten souls when the contest was over.

To say that a majority inhabited a special jock *demi-
monde* is no exaggeration. They were not the solid suburban citizens today's athletes have become, commonly
perusing the stock market tables and addressing the
monthly luncheon of the Advertising and Sales Club,
when they aren't calling up their agent to complain that
they have been benched because the manager doesn't
understand them, not because of their .244 batting average.

In the 1920s, Ring Lardner's comic strip "You Know
Me, Al" was quality satire, a sensitive and knowledgeable
send-up of Jack Keefe, a fictional hayseed Chicago White
Sox pitcher, writing home about his exploits to boyhood
buddy Al Blanchard in Bedford, Indiana. The White Sox,
of course, were a terrible team, decimated three years

earlier by the Black Sox scandal when eight starters were banished for life for throwing the World Series to the Cincinnati Reds. The best teams of the time were the New York Giants and Yankees. One thing all the clubs had in common, whether good or bad, was that the ballplayers were depicted as boorish oafs, with few redeeming qualities beyond those necessary for making a living at the game. "You Know Me, Al" was popular satire because it was thinly veiled truth, or accepted as such, anyway.

A sample of Jack Keefe's letters home:

> Dallas, Tex., March 31 Well friends I never would have loose this game to the giants only for Schalk and when Young come up in the 8 innings I wanted to give him a curve ball but Schalk insisted on a fast one and Young hits it out of the ball pk. and if that is getting any help out of your catcher I am nuty and the next time you can bet that I wont pay no tension to a catcher just because they got a reputation.

While the good burghers of the middle class paid as willingly for their athletic thrills as they did for other kinds of entertainment, the people employed in these industries did not enjoy the upscale images of today's athletes. A professional athlete in most sports during that era was just above bank robber and con artist on the social scale. Yes, he was a colourful character; but usually because he was so uncouth that every third word was profane. He spent his entire salary on cheap booze and women and was headed for the junkpile the moment his athletic skills deserted him. The young son in a middle class household might announce to his parents that he wanted to be a pro athlete when he grew up, and receive the same amused response as if he had decided to be a cowboy, but as he matured he would receive a subtle message: this is no kind of life for an honest citizen. And if you think that attitude was ridiculous or self-right-eous, think about this question: How many of today's enlightened parents in the middle class would react favourably to a son's announcement that he would like to become a professional boxer?

If it seems that we are belabouring the issue, there is a reason. It establishes the true context for what Ruth and a few others accomplished. It also illustrates just how tough it was to attain respectability for professional ice hockey.

If other sports and their athletes were considered beneath the pale, that was especially true for hockey. The men who played the game most often were under-educated farm boys, or city kids who had dropped out of school to pursue it, a situation which continued well into the 1970s until the arrival of the U.S. college players and the Europeans. The players of hockey's first decades were mercenaries, pure and simple, and let loose the dogs of war on each ice rink where they played. They were mostly hard-drinking (those train rides could be wild) gambling womanizers who reacted with scorn to the alarms of the bourgeoisie.

On the ice, they routinely knocked each other's teeth out, carved intricate designs on each other's faces and generally comported themselves in a manner that would get them thrown in the slammer should any of their mayhem stray off ice. Quite often it did—a hockey crowd was no place for the faint-hearted in the 1930s and '40s.

While people like Morenz, Taylor, Shore, Joliat, Lalonde, the Cooks and the Patricks laid the game's foundations, the sport simply did not enjoy the respectability of baseball. For that, a Babe Ruth was needed, someone whose skills were sublime, someone whose name would fill the rinks with all ranks of society. A superstar. Someone who could, as Branch Rickey said, "launch" the sport.

They found him. His name was Joseph Henri Maurice Richard.

Born August 4, 1921, Maurice was the eldest son of Onesime and Alice Richard, who were part of the post-War exodus to the cities by young francophones all over Quebec. Onesime and Alice left their native Gaspé and settled in Montreal, where he went to work as a carpenter for Canadian Pacific Limited. After a short time spent in the Plateau Mont-Royal area, they moved to the isolated Nouveau Bordeaux district, north of the city and across the Rivières des Prairies from Laval. It was on that river, and in the schoolyards of the Bois-de-Boulogne and Laval that Maurice Richard developed his formidable talents.

Like a great many young hockey players of talent, Maurice Richard would play six or seven days a week during the season, as a member of a school team, a parks or recreation league team and perhaps a third sports association team. He began to attract the attention of hockey people all over the city, but there was no specific meeting with a hockey scout who would pronounce the fateful words: "Maurice, how would you like to play for the Canadiens?"

"It never happened that way," Richard says. "It might have a couple years later, but then the Canadiens did not have the kind of organization Mr. Selke built. They owned four or five junior teams and controlled senior hockey too, but it was run like a bad orchard. They waited until the wind would blow the apples out of the trees.

"If you were any good, you would eventually work your way up and they would notice you. It was nothing like today's Junior Leagues and articles in the newspapers for ten year olds."

In his teens, Richard came under the tutelage of Paul Stuart, who despite his name, was a French-speaking Montrealer who did his best to ensure that young francophones would get a fair shake in the pros. He was in charge of the almost forty hockey teams that played in the midtown Parc Lafontaine area, and mentor to hundreds of boys. Richard was introduced to him at the juvenile level and Stuart immediately saw in him something special. He also knew that a rising young French-speaking star in the NHL would have to learn to take care of himself, and enrolled the thin, fragile youth in boxing lessons with Harry Hurst, a Montreal prize-fighter. Not just content with attaining a level of pugilistic proficiency that would stand him in good stead in any hockey rink, Richard entered the Golden Gloves competition and acquitted himself well.

"But I was a hockey player, first and foremost," he says. "I really enjoyed boxing as a one-on-one competition, but hockey was my game. I will say that my ability to take care of myself with my fists around the NHL allowed me to play hockey a lot more. In those days, nobody gave you anything in hockey—if an opponent sensed a weakness, he would be on you every game."

The establishment, and some observers of the time, would argue that the absence of a process of natural selection in Montreal could easily have cost the Canadiens the services of Maurice Richard. The only factor militating in the club's favour was that the other teams in the league were even shorter in organizational talent. Montreal was a hotbed of hockey and a prominent nursery of talent, but most of the other teams stayed away, giving the Canadiens free rein.

The clubs did have territorial agreements, and the Montreal Canadiens generally had *carte blanche* to proceed as they saw fit with hockey talent in Quebec. The other teams were by no means barred from searching for talent in the city and environs. Most of the time, they just did not bother.

Stuart and Paul-Emile Paquette, who ran his own juvenile team, saw the raw talent of Maurice Richard and tried to tell the Canadiens. Yet in those days, Flying Frenchmen or not, the club was not about to chase after every talented young French Canadian who came along. With the demise of the Maroons, and the transfer of former Maroons like Toe Blake, Herb Cain, Jimmy Ward, Bill MacKenzie, Cy Wentworth, Stew Evans and Babe Siebert, the club had a decided "anglo" tint. That carried on into management, where Tom Gorman, who had managed the 1933-34 Chicago Black Hawks and the 1934-35 Maroons to Stanley Cup victories, now was general manager of the *bleu, blanc, rouge*. Cecil Hart, Pit Lepine and Dick Irvin were his coaches, Lepine only as a fill-in in 1939-40 after the death of Siebert.

Irvin was fresh from Toronto, where he had coached the Maple Leafs for a decade. Hart, who coached the Canadiens for ten seasons, seven in the late 1920s, and three more in the 1930s after a five-year hiatus, was a

well-respected hockey man as well. But neither had connections in the French-speaking community.

"So don't be so surprised that these people didn't come
after me when I was younger," Richard cautions. "The
amateur leagues received some media coverage in those
days. But it was nothing like the attention Bobby Orr,
Guy Lafleur and Wayne Gretzky received when they
were young. Those guys were ten, twelve or fourteen
years old and they were in the newspapers and on television a lot. Not in our days."

Stuart was a very talented hockey man and was offered an opportunity to coach the Canadiens' top feeder
team—the Canadiens Seniors. He accepted on one condition—the club would favour the development of French
Canadian talent. The Forum demurred and Stuart stayed
in Parc Lafontaine. Both Paquette and Stuart realized
that someone would have to pay attention to their protégé so they went to see Arthur Therrien, coach of the
Verdun Juniors, one of the Canadiens' five junior teams
in the metropolitan area. The message was simple:
"Come and see this kid, you will not waste the trip."
Therrien could not help but be impressed. Richard, then
a left-winger, was averaging six goals a game and typi-
cally would score a couple at the end of rink-long rushes.
Along with 125 other hockey players, he was invited to
Verdun's training camp, but no promises were made.

"Quite a few of the other players there were the stars
of their juvenile or midget teams from all over the province too," he recalls. "Just being invited to camp at that
level meant something special in those days." Richard
impressed during his first scrimmage with two goals that
involved through-the-opposition manoeuvering. He
made the team, but not as a regular.

"I spent some time on the bench early in the season
and I would play on the third or fourth line a lot. But as
the schedule went on, and I got more confidence, I
started playing better and better and pretty soon was
playing on the first or second line. That was when I knew
that I would one day get a chance to try out profession-
ally. The top juniors always got a tryout and that year I
led the league in scoring during the playoffs."

The next step up came very quickly, when Richard was invited to the Canadiens Seniors training camp the following September. He played well, made the team and had already scored two goals when the teams went into the third period of the Canadiens Seniors first regular-season game. Richard picked up the puck just outside his own blueline and steamed up-ice. Just inside the opposition zone, he was knocked off balance and slammed into the corner boards. His skate caught in a rut at the base of the boards, his body's momentum swung him back towards the ice, and his ankle snapped. Season over.

In 1941, he returned to the Canadiens Seniors where he was converted to a right winger and played well for the first twenty games of the year ... until a broken wrist in the twenty-first game sidelined him for the rest of the regular season. He came back to score six goals in four playoff games and was considered a shoo-in for a post on the parent club's 1942-43 edition. That summer, Maurice Richard worked hard as a machinist and married his childhood sweetheart, Lucille Norchet. He also tried to enlist in the Canadian army but was turned away because of his ankle injury in 1940. (Richard would try again in 1943, with the same result).

Training camp came and went and Richard's participation could be wrapped up in one sentence uttered by coach Irvin: "The kid is a natural."

The kid might have been a natural but Irvin wasn't going to tell him that personally. That wasn't his or the Canadiens' way. Jacques Plante, who would join the Canadiens ten years after Maurice Richard, tells of the Rocket's earliest beginnings and an apocryphal story which would be used to prove a point to all Habs rookies down through the years.

"When Rocket first came up in 1942, to show you what kind of guy he was, he was a rookie at the same time as Bobby Fillion of Thetford Mines. Dick Irvin was coach and he played them off against each other. Both players would skate in the pre-game warm-up but they didn't know until after the warm-up which one would be playing. After it was over Irvin would tell them who was playing and who would have to get undressed. One day

Rocket was told to go to the room and he just kicked the door right through, he put his foot right through the door, and then went in to shower. He was twenty-one years old, a rookie, and to do that to Dick Irvin showed that he had a lot of character. This was the type of guy Irvin was looking for. Irvin would love a good fight on the ice during practice. He would instigate things, people would blow off steam, and then laugh about it afterwards."

Dick Irvin's blasting cap to Rocket Richard's dynamite stick was an ideal combination as the Canadiens began to rebuild. However, thirteen years later, the combination would have devastating side effects.

General manager Gorman agreed with Irvin's assessment of the rookie after that initial training camp, and Richard graduated to the big club, signing his first professional contract (two years) two days before Hallowe'en. Less than a month later, he would begin amassing Ruthian headlines such as "The New York Rangers beat Maurice Richard 5-3." Things went well for the first six weeks of the season as Richard began proving his worth in every rink in the league. Two days after Christmas, in a game against the Bruins, he took a hard check in the third period, fell awkwardly, and fractured his right ankle this time. Later that evening, Irvin wondered aloud to the press: "Richard may just be too brittle to play in the National Hockey League."

"Three major injuries in three years—I wondered too," Richard says. "I knew I was a lot stronger than they gave me credit for and that I could play against anybody in that league but I was going to have to prove it. It is hard to fight against the other teams and your own coaches, management and team-mates. Getting a reputation that you are injury-prone is something very hard to get rid of. I also knew that if I hurt myself again in the next season or two, the Canadiens might ship me just about anywhere."

It was indicative of the management practices of the age that no one would discuss these issues with Richard himself. It was also the beginning of his disenchantment with the people in the front office, a bitterness that lingers even today.

"What bothered me the most was that nobody would come up to you and talk about such things, man-to-man, face-to-face," he says. "That is not pride or egotism . . . it is honesty and respect to treat someone this way. I was a very young man starting out in hockey and, so far, very unlucky. Instead of recognizing that, the club worried publicly about whether I would be able to last in this league. Tommy Gorman never said this to me but he did talk about it to the papers. I did not appreciate that but I was young and he was the boss . . . I could say nothing."

Compounding the troubles with Richard were the ongoing problems that the club experienced in the era: the Canadiens had been down for so long that few fans remained to support the team.

"When I was playing senior hockey, quite often we would fill the Forum while the Canadiens played to a half-full Forum," Richard recalls. "Most of that was because they had been such a bad hockey team for so long. But a large part was because they had few recognizable French Canadian stars. Maybe that is why they were so nervous about me making the team. If I could be successful, and a few others like Butch Bouchard and Fernand Majeau, we could get the people back."

The Canadiens and Maurice Richard would be most successful, far beyond their wildest dreams, in 1943-44. They would post one of the best records in the history of the NHL, 38 wins, 5 losses and 7 ties in 50 games; Richard would score 32 goals, 23 of them in the last 22 games of the season—after missing a large part of the early season with yet another injury, this time a dislocated shoulder. The season started with Richard receiving permission to switch uniform numbers to 9 from 15. He was a happy man and proved it with two goals in each of his first two games as he played alongside two new linemates—Toe Blake and Elmer Lach. His bad shoulder put the brakes to his scoring but the New Year came in with a bang. Richard, fully recovered from the injury, scored his first hat trick Dec. 30, 1943 (against Jimmy

Franks of Detroit), and went on a tear. By season's end he was only the fourth member of the Canadiens (Joe Malone with the league record of 44 in 22 games, Newsy Lalonde and Howie Morenz) to score 30 or more goals in a season.

Richard's value to the team was without question as the playoffs beckoned.... The Canadiens, with essentially the same lineup, had finished in fourth place the year before. With the additions of goaltender Bill Durnan and Richard, they catapulted into first, and awaited the post-season tournament with optimism and some newfound cockiness. That was quickly drummed out of them in a 3-1 loss to Toronto. Bob Davidson, the Bob Gainey of the era, threw a checking blanket over Richard and the Forum crowd went home muttering to itself.

"I remember going up to their goalie Paul Bibeault near the end of the third period and telling him things would be different in the next game," Richard says. "I didn't know how right I would be ..."

Like most great athletes, Richard can recall his greatest moments in the most minute detail, recounting events as if they were happening in the present. Also like most great athletes, he is at a loss to explain why those moments came about. He cannot analyze them now and never could.

In this case, most National Hockey League veterans agree, the superstar was born. The date: March 23, 1944. The place: the Forum.

"We went through the first period scoreless," recalls Ray Getliffe, the Montreal centre who had nicknamed Richard "Rocket" earlier in the season, "and it looked like they were going to shut Maurice down forever. But he had other plans."

The breakthrough came in the second period, when Richard finally shook off Davidson and scored three times.

"He was on another planet, in another world," said Getliffe. "He had that look in his eyes; like the other players against him weren't even there ... like he was all by himself on the ice. I played with him, and sometimes when I was on the ice with him, and I saw him coming in my direction with that look on his face, I wanted to jump right over the boards out of his way. Can you imagine what the opposition felt?"

On that March day, it would not be hard to imagine how the Leafs felt: Richard added two more goals in the third period, and the final score read: Richard 5, Toronto 1. No other hockey player had ever scored five goals in a playoff game. The Richard legend was born.

Ten days later it was Richard 3, Chicago 1. The Canadiens swept the Black Hawks in four games and Richard scored 12 goals in 9 playoff games. After thirteen very long years, the Stanley Cup returned home with the Canadiens. The drought was over and a new age beckoned.

In 1927, as the Bambino pursued his sixtieth home run, the event was of such significance that the press coverage moved from the sports pages to the front page. In 1944-45, Maurice Richard muscled aside the Second World War and earned his way to page one. Germany was collapsing on all fronts in February and March, 1945, and the same could be said of opposition defences and netminders in the National Hockey League. Richard was on the trail of the elusive scoring record of 44 goals held by Joe Malone.

His pursuit of the record was about as easy as the Allied mop-up operations in Europe; everywhere Richard turned he found an adversary poised to use any tactic necessary to stop him. One such hired thug was Bob "Killer" Dill, a player who had been banned from the American League and the nephew of two famous prizefighters, Mike and Tommy Gibbons, from whom he had acquired a certain pugilistic prowess. Richard was scoring at an unbelievable rate of a goal a game and the challenges were mounting. Before he would go into an enemy rink two questions were bandied about liberally in the papers. How many goals would he score that night? And who was the designated hitman for the opposition?

The Canadiens were scheduled for a Madison Square Garden contest against the Rangers a week before

Christmas and every hockey writer from miles around was speculating on the "inevitable" Richard-Dill confrontation. In those days, the sportswriters were not under pressure from crunchy granola publishers to clean up the game and downplay hockey violence. They knew the fans loved it, as they do today, and played it up. Some pre-game stories were "Tale of the Tape" boxing-style pieces. The rather unique Garden fans were fairly slavering over the prospects of their man stopping the Rocket in more ways than one. The puck was dropped to start the game and Dill immediately made his presence known, ramming Lach into the boards. Throughout the first period, the Rangers player did everything he could to goad Richard into a fight, but with no success.

In the second, he got his wish. Dill and Chuck Scherza began a scrap behind the Rangers net with Lach and Blake, two men who could take care of themselves. It appeared that the referee had sorted things out and players were milling about when Dill manoeuvered near Richard and said something to the effect of: "Is the frog scared?"

Richard scored a one-punch knockout, a right hook that lifted Dill off his feet and left him in a crumpled heap on the ice. The belligerents repaired to the penalty box area where a somewhat revived and chagrined Dill began vociferously planning his revenge. Before entering the penalty box, the players came together a second time.

The headline in the New York *Daily Mirror* summed it up best: "Dill Pickled." Richard caught the Ranger with a series of punches, the most devastating being a right to Dill's left eye, which opened a large cut. After serving his double majors, Richard scored the game-tying goal, his 19th in 19 games. After the game, Rangers' coach Frank Boucher ranted: "If he doesn't learn to control his temper, that crazy Richard will kill somebody one of these days."

As for Dill, he met Richard after the game on 49th Street, smiled broadly as he told the Montreal star it was the hardest anyone had ever hit him, and accepted Richard's dinner invitation! And so it went in Richard's ascension to superstardom.

Three days after Christmas, Richard showed up in the Canadiens' dressing room at the Forum and headed straight for the trainer's table. Sprawling on it, and looking exhausted, he announced that he had been moving house all day with his brother and could hardly move. "You'll have to do it without me tonight," he concluded.

Three hours later, Richard was in the same dressing room, trying to explain to reporters how he had scored five goals and added three assists in a 9-1 dismantling of Detroit. He couldn't, but that bothered no one. Most of the reporters admitted they just wanted to get close to greatness, even if the quotes were starvation rations.

Seven weeks later, he scored twice against the same Red Wings in a 5-2 victory; his 42nd and 43rd goals of the season, tying Cooney Weiland for second-highest goal total in NHL history. What was so astounding was that the Rocket scored the 43 goals in 38 games. In Toronto the next week, he tied the Malone record of 44 and received a standing ovation from the normally reserved Maple Leaf Gardens crowd, even when the P.A. announcer refused to acknowledge the record-tying feat.

A week later, the same teams were at the Forum and the Leafs were determined that Richard would not set the record against them. Everywhere Richard went that night, two, three and four white-and-blue shirts faced him. Nick Metz and Davidson, top defensive wingers, shadowed him mercilessly and the tension grew as the first two periods went by. The tension on the ice was palpable—at the slightest provocation, Canadiens and Leafs players would drop the gloves and go at it. With such attention paid Richard, his team-mates found themselves with open ice and led Toronto 4-2 midway through the third.

Almost 14,000 fans jumped out of their seats when Richard picked up a loose puck, shook off two checkers and bore down on Toronto's Frank McCool. McCool held his ground and made the save and 14,000 disappointed fans sighed, and sat down as one. There were about four minutes remaining in the contest when Blake hit Richard with a little flip pass in the Toronto zone. The Montreal winger never hesitated, even though he was at a bad

angle out near the faceoff circle. The puck hit his stick
and he let it go simultaneously ... into the net past a
startled McCool.

There was a sudden hush. And then the Forum exploded. The Canadiens streamed out onto the ice, Blake
made straight for the net to retrieve the puck, which
later would be presented to Richard by Malone. The
game would not resume for another fifteen minutes.

And so it went. The magic 44 eclipsed, people began
speculating whether Richard could score 50 goals in 50
games, an unheard-of feat, easily the match of Ruth's 60
circuit blasts. With eight games remaining, could Richard
score five more goals?

When would Richard score his fiftieth? Where would
he score it? The tension mounted as the season wore
down to its conclusion. The Canadiens played against
Chicago Black Hawks in their home ice finale and
Richard was a man possessed that night. He had 49 goals
to his credit and appeared ready to sell his soul to the
devil to score number 50 at home. Late in the third
period (like the preceding Toronto game) a magnificent
opportunity presented itself with Richard all alone in
front of the Chicago goalie. A sprawling defenceman
tripped him at the last minute and a penalty shot was
awarded. It was not to be. Richard missed and scored his
fiftieth in Boston.

50 goals in 50 games. In a six-team league. In an era
where just about every hockey player thought it was his
sacred trust to separate an opponent's head from his
shoulders if the latter had the audacity to attempt to
score against the former. It was a momentous feat and
set the Richard legend in stone. Hockey was well on its
way to respectability and acceptance ... on the streaming
shirt-tails of Maurice "Rocket" Richard.

After 1944-45, Maurice Richard's stardom was as-
sured, even with the ascension of Gordie Howe of Detroit. If anything, Howe was Gehrig to Richard's Ruth; a
quiet farm boy with prodigious hockey skills, who would
eventually rewrite the record books in a career whose
longevity still baffles experts. (Howe would play against
both Richard and Gretzky, which is a little like playing

baseball against both Ruth and Aaron). You can still start a fist fight in certain drinking establishments in the old six cities by simply stating that Richard was vastly superior to Howe, or vice versa.

It would be easy to continue the recitation of Richardian anecdotes and facts. The pages would quickly melt away and a thick tome would emerge. However, this work concerns itself with the Montreal Canadiens, the birth of their legend, and the organization that learned to make that special status work for the team. Without giving Maurice Richard's career short shrift, suffice it to say that he was the superstar who truly launched the on-ice dynasty. His was the most special Canadiens legend, eclipsing even that of the fabled Howie Morenz, who once had lain in state at centre ice of the Forum.

If there was any doubt what Richard meant to hockey, especially in French Canada, that doubt was erased on St. Patrick's Day in 1955. The Canadiens were defending Stanley Cup champions that March and were winding down another season in fine style. Unlike the teams of the late 1940s, of which French Canadians formed a definite minority, the '54-55 Canadiens overflowed with French Canadian players of all-star quality: among them Bernard "Boom Boom" Geoffrion and the regal Jean Beliveau. Coming down to the last four games, Richard, Beliveau and Geoffrion were 1-2-3 in the NHL scoring race and Richard was fighting for his first-ever Art Ross Trophy and the $1,000 in prize money that accompanied it.

On March 13th, against Boston, Richard and Hal Laycoe hooked up in a brutal stick-swinging incident that saw the Canadiens forward go berserk after Laycoe (a former team-mate) cut him for stitches on top of the head. Richard attacked Laycoe and decked him; then picked up his stick and hit the Bruins player with it three times, all the while fighting off linesman Cliff Thompson, who was trying to separate the two.

"At this point, it was almost like he discovered the existence of the linesman," said coach Dick Irvin the next day. "I still don't know whether or not Maurice recognized who he was."

That will remain a moot point. Even Richard can't or won't say for sure, almost thirty years later. His personal Official Secrets Act has not yet reached its statute of limitations.

What happened next was that Richard turned on Thompson and hit him twice in the face. He was immediately assessed a match misconduct and NHL president Clarence Campbell was called in to investigate the incident. Earlier in the season, after a fight with Toronto's Bob Bailey, Richard had taken a swipe at linesman George Hayes and was given a match penalty for his efforts.

To this day, many people believe there was a movement to "get" Richard, and that its main proponents were at the highest levels of the league . . . the owners of the other five franchises.

"Even today, I have not shaken the feeling that certain people felt it was time to punish Richard for the way he acted on the ice," said Frank Selke in 1983. "Although I hoped for the best, I expected the worst when Campbell announced his decision."

Richard, Kenny Reardon and coach Irvin were summoned to Campbell's office in Montreal's Sun Life building. The verdict was harsh—Richard was suspended for the rest of the season and the Stanley Cup playoffs as well.

Clarence Campbell, a pillar of White Anglo-Saxon Protestant rectitude, had spoken. Until his last day, he maintained that he took the correct action. Until that very same day, a lot of people in the know swore that he sold out to the other owners and that his action was a calculated slap at the Canadiens, Richard, and French Canadians in particular. He would receive evidence of the popularity of such sentiments very soon.

Richard insisted, also until Campbell's last day, that the suspension had been a mistake. Pressed by a journalist for his thoughts on the former NHL president at Campbell's Montreal funeral in 1984, Richard stated simply: "He was wrong."

The day after handing down his decision, Campbell and his fiancée took their seats at the Forum for a game between the Richard-less Canadiens and Detroit, Campbell proving once again that he was totally out of touch with the French-speaking majority of the city in which he lived. He simply did not realize that the hardheaded attitude he had demonstrated was nothing short of an incitation to riot. Earlier that day, the Montreal police and City Hall both had contacted the NHL president and asked him to stay away from the Forum. They had received all sorts of threats of violence against him, as did his own office. Several callers were emphatic: if Campbell walked into the Forum, he would be carried out.

Campbell entered the Forum that night in spite of the warnings, and, inevitably, the fans' anger erupted.

Shortly before the game got under way, a large crowd formed outside the Forum, at St. Catherine and Atwater. Many had tickets and would enter the building shortly before the 8 p.m. start. Many others, however, had no tickets, but were there to express their displeasure in the Richard sentence. Many carried placards and signs depicting Campbell in the rudest fashion. Inside the building, a "he'll show, he won't show" guessing game was going on in the stands. The game started and Campbell's two reserved seats remained empty. Scattered throughout the building were as many as 150 special policemen hired for the occasion.

About halfway through the period, Campbell and his fiancée took their seats. What seemed to compound matters was the fact that the Canadiens did not appear to have their minds on the game. After the league president's arrival, Detroit scored three quick goals and led 4-1. The crowd began yelling, *"On veut Richard—à bas Campbell"* (We want Richard—down with Campbell) and the NHL executive sat stoically through the verbal onslaught. By the end of the period, the hostilities were no longer merely verbal; fans began throwing everything in reach ... fruit, hot dogs, rubbers, and programs ... at Campbell, as people in his vicinity scrambled for cover. He maintained his stiff upper lip until a young man attacked him physically and was pulled away by Forum security at the last moment. Then it really hit the fan. A tear gas canister went off just a few feet from Campbell, and the fans who had toughed it out thus far abandoned ship, tears streaming down their faces. The Forum was ordered evacuated by Montreal fire marshals and the game was forfeited to the Red Wings. Nobody knows to this day whether the canister was thrown by a policeman or a disgruntled fan—a later investigation proved that it was the kind sold to the Montreal police by the manufacturer.

The people inside the Forum stormed outside and were joined by hundreds of angry fans who had been unable to attend the game. The rioting began.

From the surge of spectators exiting the Forum, many of them with tears streaming down their faces because of the tear gas, those waiting outside received their signal. Anything that could be thrown was hurled in the direction of the Forum and the sound of breaking glass filled the air. The barrage was so concentrated that police supervising the evacuation inside had to turn several thousand spectators around and escort them out via the side exits. Cars, taxis and buses on St. Catherine and Atwater became moving targets and drivers and passengers alike had to hit the floor to avoid a shower of glass as windshields and side windows exploded. The wail of sirens joined the street music and was followed by the sound of running feet as rioters scattered in all directions, trashing storefronts all along St. Catherine. Newspaper kiosks were overturned and set ablaze as police arrived in force. But they, too, had to advance carefully, as they came under bombardment from the agitated crowd. Several police cars were heavily damaged and more than once a policeman who had arrested wrongdoers and was preparing to take them away had to surrender his prisoners when surrounded by crowds of rioters.

Dozens were arrested, and St. Catherine Street was a river of glass all the way to University (about two miles east of Atwater) before the outburst was tempered around midnight. The newspapers had a field day on March 18, with French and English dailies taking opposite sides. The Canadian Press wire agency described the uprising as the "worst seen in Montreal since the anti-conscription riots which marked the last War."

Thirty years later, historians and sportswriters alike look at the Richard Riots as a watershed in the development of Quebec society. Rejean Tremblay of *La Presse*, a sports columnist who started out as a Latin and Greek teacher, says:

"If, at the time, many anglophones were unwilling to acknowledge that the Campbell-Richard confrontation had political consequences, I don't think that is the case today. Too many people say Quebec's Quiet Revolution did not begin in 1960 with the arrival of Jean Lesage and the Liberals, but with the Richard Riots. That told us that this backhanded attitude of the English establishment would no longer be tolerated." Maurice Richard was not just a hockey player; he was the French Canadian incarnate.

Sociologist Orrin Klapp has written that hero worship is a yearning relationship in which the individual escapes his own frustrations or inadequacies by wishing or imagining himself to be like someone whom he admires. The profound impact of Maurice Richard can best be explored through analysis of the ways in which local fans made deep commitments to him.

Ever since humanity's earliest societies, heroes have been used by the masses for what sociologists now call individual dream realizations—to supply a type of psychic mobility for those who cannot make it on their own initiative. This generally is most prevalent in an adolescent population, for it is here that idealization is freshest and most impetuous—part of the process of parental control giving way to the influences of peer group pressures and the need to embrace a fairly precise and all-encompassing belief system.

For the French Canadian of the 1950s (and they were still called French Canadians then), the identification with the Montreal Canadiens and the success of the team's French Canadian stars was particularly overpowering. In fact, it was so pervasive that Frank Selke worked extremely hard to downplay the huge contribution of the primarily all-English front office. At a time when thousands of francophone Montrealers chafed under an anglophone bit in the workplace, Selke felt, quite rightly, that the players should and would get all the attention.

And no one wore the *Sainte Flanelle* with more pride and character than Maurice Richard. Three decades later, Richard himself is very aware of the symbolism of St. Patrick's Day, 1955.

"Yes, I realize I was important to a lot of people as a symbol, but I could not look at the politics of it," he says. "Even discussing it along these lines makes me feel a little funny. How would you feel to be discussed by historians like this? I was a hockey player; I have always been a hockey player ... it was my *métier*. When you talk about the politics, you talk about people manipulating things that happened, a long time after they happened."

Yet there could be no doubts about the influence of Richard. That was recognized the night of the riot, when Selke called him and asked him to come back to the Forum and personally ask the crowd to disperse.

"I told him that would only make the situation worse," Richard says. "They would have probably carried me down St. Catherine on their shoulders and started something worse."

Montreal was in turmoil the next day, a Friday. Mayor Jean Drapeau, who had experienced uprisings during the anti-conscription riots as a member of the Bloc Populaire, laid the blame squarely on the shoulders of Campbell. The mayor said that Campbell's attendance at the Forum was overt provocation, and that nothing untoward had happened during the first ten minutes of the game prior to his arrival. A war of words began between the two, with Campbell expressing his concern that the first magistrate of the city of Montreal would take him to task because he refused to acknowledge the threats and warnings of "several hoodlums" to stay away from the game.

Campbell himself spent the day answering telephone

calls from journalists all over the world and had to deny a rumour that he was about to resign as league president. "Me resign?" he scoffed. "The league governors have all called me and congratulated me for attending last night's game," he replied, once again proving in the minds of the suspicious that something more than a simple hockey fight was behind the Richard suspension.

Richard was receiving telephone calls too, many from influential friends who were worried about a replay of the previous evening's festivities.

Later that evening, a sombre Richard, impeccably dressed in a grey suit, sat in the Canadiens dressing room at a small table. On it was a veritable forest of microphones, bearing the flashes of Montreal's radio stations and the French and English networks of the Canadian Broadcasting Corporation. At 7:15, the hockey player began to speak, in French and in English. Richard began by admitting his disappointment over the severity of the sentence, and how he would miss not being with his team-mates in the playoffs. He spoke quietly, in a very subdued manner, but his words carried immense weight. There was to be no more talk of riots and revenge. Maurice had spoken.

And on this, the most traumatic evening of his career, Maurice Richard was confirmed as the quintessential superstar of the game ... the Babe Ruth of professional hockey. His influence transcended the mere 200 feet by 85 feet enclosure on which he plied his trade.

Yet oddly enough, it also was the beginning of his eclipse as team leader as well. Maurice Richard would return to the Canadiens and captain his team-mates to an unprecedented and unmatched five straight Stanley Cups. He would end his career with 544 regular-season goals, another 82 in the playoffs. He would have seasons of 38 and 33 goals the next two years, but would tail off to 15, 17 and 19 goals in 111 injury-plagued games between 1957 and his retirement in 1960.

That does not mean he did not contribute. Far from it. Ralph Backstrom, a soft-spoken native of Kirkland Lake,

Ontario, and the best third-string centre in hockey at the time, became a regular in the 1957-60 period when Rocket's star was on the wane.

"I was in awe of Rocket. I did not know what to say to him so I sat in the dressing room in a catatonic stupor during the first few weeks I saw him as a team-mate. The man hated to lose. If the team suffered a defeat, he would stalk around the dressing room glaring at people. He wasn't chastising any particular individual but was generally aggressive and visibly upset. It was important for me to watch him that way. He was communicating some significant values and I realized at that point that if he wasn't satisfied with the performance on the ice, I could never be content either. But the hockey tradition, the one that Mr. Selke fashioned, was really carried on by the Pocket Rocket, Maurice's brother Henri. He was my role model throughout my playing career."

The Rocket, the Lion Rampant, could only snarl his frustration at his own shortcomings in his latter years. He could inspire, but he was not the leader his brother Henri would be, nor that Jean Beliveau was, for that matter.

Still, he was pure competitor. Jacques Plante played with Rocket throughout his professional career, but his most vivid images of the Rocket are from Richard's early retirement years.

"In his playing days, Rocket was not the greatest skater or the most efficient playmaker, but he had the biggest heart in the league. They can tell all the stories they want about Gordie Howe but the Rocket played with fire in his eyes. He would do anything to win the game. The most fascinating thing about him was that he was no different in practice. The closer he came to the net, the faster he moved. Then all that you could see were those big black eyes staring you down. It was like being mesmerized by a cobra; he had a hypnotic ability about him.

"The irony, of course, is that he did not change his style even after his career came to an end. We used to

practice every Saturday afternoon from one to three at
St. Vincent de Paul arena—we called ourselves the Saturday Gang— and since I was the better of two goalies, I
always played against Maurice. The guy still had contempt for his opponent and if I stopped him during a
rush, he would become incensed at me and come at me
again—it was almost as if we were competing in an
important match. That's where you could see Rocket's
true character. Even then, he was constantly looking for
the edge and that is exactly what Frank Selke was looking for when he recruited him."

Although he was still ferocious in his declining years,
the Lion could always find time for novices. Rod Gilbert,
a handsome French Canadian winger who, along with
Jean Ratelle, escaped the Canadiens' recruiting dragnet
and went on to star with the New York Rangers, has a
more pleasant memory of the Rocket in his last season.

"I was a rookie just up with the Rangers from junior
and I spotted him in a coffee shop at a hotel near Madison
Square Garden one day late in the season. I was really
nervous about approaching him, but I did and I asked him
if he had any tips to give someone who was just coming
up. He really surprised me when he told me he knew
who I was and had read good things about me. He said
something like, 'Sure kid,' and agreed to meet me at
Madison Square after both teams had practised. He told
me to bring my skates and stick."

Gilbert, a little timidly, showed up at the appointed
time and Richard skated out onto the ice carrying his
stick in one hand, a bucket of pucks in the other.

"He dumped the pucks all over the ice in one end and
spread them out all over the ice surface," Gilbert recollects. "And then he just started wheeling and shooting
them into the goal from every angle—backhand, fore-
hand, wrist shots, slapshots—and just about every one of
them went in.

"I must have stood there with my jaw hanging down
when he skated up to me and said: 'If you want to play in
this league, kid, you have to know where the net is.' He

then just skated off the ice."

No one knew better than the Rocket where the net was.

The Campbell suspension robbed him of his only chance to ever win the league scoring championship. He would never get another; even on the Canadiens he was to be eclipsed by players with names like Beliveau, Moore, Geoffrion and his brother, Henri Richard.

To this day, there are Montreal fans who curse Campbell in his grave.

# 5

# Father Frank's Masterplan

The Canadiens' dynasty began August 1, 1946, when a short, bespectacled man in a crew cut, a dead ringer for comedian George Gobel, strolled into the Forum.

The first two words of French that Frank Selke had learned were *carte blanche*. That was what he had been given days before by Senator Donat Raymond.

"Mr. Selke, do what you must do to make the Montreal Canadiens the most impressive team and organization in professional hockey," Senator Raymond told the native of Berlin (Kitchener), Ontario. "You are in complete charge of the team. What you say, goes."

Frank Selke smiled, remembering the celebrated feud with Conn Smythe that had driven him to Montreal, and went to work. Using the third word of the French language that he had learned, he issued his first order, the prime dictum that was to launch one of the proudest teams in club sports.

"Clean the toilets: this place stinks like a *pissoir!*" It was a beginning that lacked the romance and impact of a jeroboam of champagne swinging in a high arc to splinter against the bow of a new ocean liner. Yet from this mundane christening, a championship team was born.

The little man in a baggy business suit who took over the fortunes of the Canadiens that sweltering August day looked like a shy, retiring bookkeeper. As with many famous leaders, however, Selke's small stature (5 feet 2 inches and 150 pounds) hid a giant intellect and mastery of details. At fifty-three, he had already been involved in ice hockey management for thirty-nine years, starting at the precocious age of fourteen in his hometown of Berlin, which would change its name to Kitchener during the First World War.

The son of a Polish immigrant farmer, Selke turned to organizing and coaching in his early teens and put together his first good team—a juvenile aggregation with the improbable name of Berlin Union Jacks—when he was nineteen. Although they formed a younger and smaller team than most in Ontario, the rough and tumble Polish and German kids from a working-class neighbourhood stunned observers by not losing a single game en route to the 1913-14 provincial championship.

"We were the kids from across the tracks and everybody looked down on us," Selke reminisced. "It seemed we always had to fight just to stick together and play, so we turned into a team of real scrappers. We owned the corners and we were proud of it."

The following year, the Union Jacks were accepted into the Ontario Hockey Association junior league and were handed the raw end of the scheduling stick by the resident teams. They need not have bothered: Father Frank's boys won the league title anyway, only to lose in the championship playoffs to the pedigreed Toronto Varsity Juniors, captained by a man named Conn Smythe.

The First World War barely interfered with Frank Selke's budding hockey career. He joined the Canadian army for a three-year stint and, while awaiting his posting overseas, was asked to organize recreation for the troops. Selke put together a quality team that played at the intermediate level and, to raise money to support it, he even organized a variety show that sold out the auditorium of St. Jerome's College in Kitchener.

Well before the war, Selke had left school at a young age and, in 1911, began an apprenticeship as an electrician. He resumed that trade in 1917 when he received a medical discharge from the army and also took up where he had left off as an organizer of hockey teams.

It was in the latter capacity that he stopped off in New Hamburg, Ontario one winter to scout a young goaltender named Schmidt, one of three brothers who played between the pipes. He found his goalie, and also the goalie's sister, Mary. Frank married Mary shortly after receiving his army discharge.

After the war, there was an exodus of Canadians from the countryside to the big cities. The Selkes headed for Toronto, where Frank went to work for the University of Toronto as an electrician and coached the University of Toronto Schools team to the Ontario junior hockey title in 1918.

He left UTS after that season and coached several other teams in the Toronto area before taking the reins of the Toronto Marlboros in 1924. The Marlboros' junior and senior teams were to become the prime feeder clubs for the soon-to-be organized Toronto Maple Leafs and Selke was only a few short years away from a career in professional hockey, leaving the life of an electrician behind forever.

The Selkes' attention to the family aspect of hockey stood Frank in good stead with the higher amateur leagues and, eventually, the pros, because family friends would turn out to be stars when they grew up. Mrs. Selke had seven of her own children, but she was also den mother to countless others. As she told a Montreal newspaper in 1964:

> I'd have to say that Toronto's Kid Line of Harvey (Busher) Jackson, Joe Primeau and Charlie Conacher were my earliest pets. I'd been the family chauffeur for years. Many a winter I packed six or seven boys like Harvey and Charlie into our old Reo and took them to games around Ontario.
>
> One boy I remember as well as any ... was Red Horner. He was our grocery boy. He loved to pause in our kitchen for a glass of milk and homemade biscuits.

The Selke family knew well the value of minor league clubs to supply the big team. Frank put together a powerhouse Marlboro team with those very same boys: the three members of the Kid Line, Horner and Alex Levinsky on defence and another forward named Bob Gracie.

At this time, a familiar name surfaced in Selke circles, that of Conn Smythe, the old Toronto Varsity captain whose team had beat out the Union Jacks for the OHA junior crown in 1913-14.

While Selke was building his hockey career, Smythe was also making a name for himself as a hockey manager in Toronto with the Varsity Blues and, later, the Varsity Grads.

So good were Smythe's teams (Varsity won the Canadian intercollegiate championship at a time when Canadian college hockey really meant something and then went to the final of the Allan Cup) that his fame spread southward. In 1924, the National Hockey League opted to expand to the United States and, after the auspicious beginning of the New York Americans, management at Madison Square Garden decided that a second team in the Big Apple would also draw well. In March, 1926, the New York Rangers were born and Colonel John Hammond was placed in charge. The timing was right, merging with Smythe's Varsity successes, and when Conn's name was suggested, Colonel Hammond sent for him.

Smythe was signed to a three-year contract and charged with putting together, and then managing, the Rangers. One of the first players Smythe signed was a tall and taciturn goalie named Lorne Chabot, the very man whose acrobatics had carried his Port Huron team past the Varsity in the Allan Cup final. The old Western League was folding and Smythe went hunting for talent. He picked up Winnipeg's Ching Johnson and Taffy Abel, both talented defencemen. Then he heard that two Saskatoon players, Bill and Bun Cook, were being courted by James Strachan of the Montreal Maroons and were on their way east to sign with that team. The ever-resourceful Smythe waylaid the brothers in Winnipeg and $5,000 in bonuses turned them into Rangers. Bill Cook recommended a centre who had played for Vancouver and Frank Boucher was signed as well.

When Smythe was done, the New York Rangers had spent $32,000 and the Big Apple had its second professional hockey team. The irascible Smythe had done it his way and the results would be visible to all when the team took to the ice. However, before the Rangers could skate out for their first game, Connie was gone.

Smythe did not intend to move to New York, a major mistake for anyone hired by a New York sports organization, and began setting up the Rangers' training camp in Toronto. His premature departure centred on the non-signing of former NHL great Babe Dye, who had been offered to the Rangers. Smythe refused to sign Dye, even after several telephone calls from Colonel Hammond, whose ears were being bent by local experts in the Big Apple. Hammond went to Toronto to bring his team home and brought a replacement manager, Lester Patrick, with him. Smythe met them at the railway station and was told about the managerial change. He was so upset that he allowed Hammond to buy him out for $7,500.

That year, the expansion Rangers finished first in their division and third overall in the National Hockey League. A year later they were the Stanley Cup champions. On the Stanley Cup it says Lester Patrick, manager. A few people, Madison Square Garden president Tex Rickard among them, knew that this was Smythe's team, although everyone acknowledged that Patrick was a first-rate coach.

Among those who recognized Smythe's contribution was Jack Bickell, one of the top men with the hapless Toronto St. Pats franchise. The club was so bad that halfway through the 1926-27 season, half of the team's owners wanted out. An offer to buy and transfer the team to Philadelphia was being seriously entertained when Bickell contacted Smythe.

Would he take over the team? Not if it moves to Philadelphia, replied the staunch Torontonian. If Smythe could match the Philadelphia offer of $200,000, Bickell replied, the team could stay in Toronto. Smythe threw in $10,000 of his own money and began pounding on every door in sight. He convinced Bickell to keep his $40,000 interest in the club and found investors with another $75,000. With that money in his pocket, and a promise to pay the remaining $75,000 within thirty days, Smythe killed the St. Pats. On Feb. 15, 1927, they were reborn as the Toronto Maple Leafs.

Smythe, ever ungracious in victory, would spend the rest of his days taking credit for the Maple Leafs. A single-minded, tough-talking, straight-shooting (most of the time) egocentric who flirted with megalomania, Smythe was the very antithesis to Selke. Yet this was the man for whom Selke soon would go to work.

The ensuing feud became an NHL legend. Smythe described some of its high points in *Conn Smythe, If You Can't Beat Them in the Alley*, written with Scott Young:

> My loss of faith in W.A. Hewitt didn't take long, but I really didn't get onto Frank Selke for many years, probably because he was a good hockey man and a hard worker, even if some of his hard work turned out to be against me. When I first hired him before the Gardens was built, I paid him out of what I was getting. I thought that was fair; he was doing some of my work, so there was no reason for the Gardens to pay me for that work, and pay him too. A sportswriter at the *Globe*, Ralph Allen, later nicknamed him Little Rollo. I'm not sure exactly what that means, but Selke tended to be sanctimonious in his dealings with other people. Years later in an interview in the *New Yorker*, Selke described me as a brilliant but sometimes impossibly egotistical man, which might be true, but to my mind it's better than being the way he was. I like things to be out in the open, seen, and understood. He worked another way. As this is written, it is more than fifty years since I first hired Selke. I think he did well from being my assistant, but when the crunch came it was plain that he had no loyalty to me. Because of his hockey knowledge, hard work, and sobriety he was a good man up to a point, but then he was a minor leaguer, as far as I was concerned.

A psychiatrist reading those lines might draw some very interesting conclusions about Conn Smythe. The truth of the matter was that Smythe did resurrect the Toronto NHL franchise, but it was Selke who delivered the players that allowed the Maple Leafs to win their first Stanley Cup. Before Selke was hired, Smythe was struggling with a bad team that invariably failed to make the playoffs. One day he called in Selke and Bill Christie, coach of the senior Toronto Marlboros, to ask, "How in the world are the Maple Leafs ever going to take the Stanley Cup away from the Montreal Maroons?"

Selke, the man whom Smythe would call duplicitous, underhanded and disloyal, answered in character: "I'll tell you how. Just fire the old men you have playing with your team now. Replace them with these young bucks I have with me on the Marlboros."

Always gracious with the free advice of others, Smythe retorted: "There are times when I think there's something wrong with your head," and a wonderful working relationship was born. Two years later, when the Leafs moved into the brand new Maple Leaf Gardens, and celebrated with the club's first Stanley Cup, the players who delivered the silverware were Frank's boys—Charlie Conacher, Joe Primeau, Busher Jackson, Alex Levinsky, Red Horner and Bob Gracie.

They had been moulded into a fine hockey club by a new coach found by Smythe, a hockey innovator from Saskatchewan named Dick Irvin.

Even before the team won the Stanley Cup, there was the matter of building the Maple Leaf Gardens, a project that became a monument to Smythe's persistence and drive. Smythe was everywhere in the Queen City while the Gardens were being built: one moment on the construction site, another hustling Garden shares, and the next sweet-talking worried bankers and investors. He put everything he had into the project, but even here Selke quietly helped him out. While Frank was assistant manager of the Leafs—a job description that included such esoteric tasks as publicity man, advertising salesman, game program editor and hockey scout—he managed to put his old electrician's background to good use, having retained his union card as an honorary business manager of the International Brotherhood of Electrical Workers.

As hard as Smythe had driven himself, it appeared that the sale of stock in the Gardens would fall short of the amount necessary to start construction. Selke went to his union connections and asked the electricians if they could convince the other workers in the building trades to take twenty percent of their pay in Gardens stock. They agreed and Smythe was able to coax a similar agreement out of the banks. Smythe, of course, took credit for the entire plan.

Smythe and Selke set about building a strong franchise in Toronto and the Leafs won two more Stanley Cups by 1946. In 1939, with the Second World War under way, a middle-aged Smythe was one of the first Canadians to volunteer for active service. He was called up in 1942 and the team essentially passed into Selke's control.

Smythe formed a battery which became part of the Seventh Toronto Regiment, Royal Canadian Artillery. He put all of his prodigious energy into the task and was given the rank of active Major and named Commanding Officer of the Thirtieth Battery. While Smythe dedicated most of his time to preparations for war, Selke was at home taking care of the store. After the 1940 season, Smythe did take the time to engineer a move to Montreal for Dick Irvin because, "I didn't think he was tough enough, without me backing him up, to do what needed to be done." He hired Hap Day to coach the Leafs, then went into the army and spent the year at Camp Petawawa, training to go overseas.

In September, 1942, Smythe moved to England. Two years later he was wounded in action. Smythe returned to Canada, where he promptly became embroiled in a major army scandal. He came home on a hospital ship, and with characteristic honesty told the *Globe and Mail* that Canadian soldiers were not being adequately reinforced in the European theatre of operations. The real scandal was that the Mackenzie King government was going to have Smythe court-martialed until the federal Minister visited the ETO and confirmed everything that Smythe had said.

Even though Conn Smythe returned home from Europe in September, 1944, and soon would be discharged from the army, he was in no condition to return to the Leafs. He would not see his first hockey game in three years until February 1, 1945, and it was a Chicago-Montreal contest at the Forum which Smythe attended because he was in Montreal for a meeting of the NHL Board of Governors.

Nevertheless, a little more than a year later—May, 1946—Smythe had returned to Maple Leaf Gardens with a vengeance and forced Frank Selke to resign. Nearly all of the main players have since passed away, including the two principals, and chances are that we will never know the real reasons why Selke was fired.

Years later, both men were still taking their shots.

"I think he respected my worth as a hockey manager but he could never admit that my ability for identifying hockey talent and moulding a team were far ahead of his," Selke said.

"That rankled. It really bothered Conn to have to overhear other NHL governors and managers dropping the little lines like: 'Yeah, but he's got that Selke doing all of that for him.' It drove him crazy. I remember some incredible messages he would send me from his overseas office. How in God's name can you run a team from France? Besides, winning the Stanley Cup in his absence did not mean a thing: he still had me down as the publicity man and Conn took all of the credit."

One version of the story relates that the situation came to a head over a trade engineered by Selke in 1943. A young defenceman, Frankie Eddolls, was moved to Montreal in return for a centreman named Ted Kennedy. The substance of the trade did not upset Smythe; the fact that it was consummated without his stamp of approval did.

"That bothered Conn and he let me know it in no uncertain terms in a note from Europe," Selke recollected. "Time has surely proved we were right in our estimation of Kennedy. Kennedy had no equals in taking face-offs, or in coming up with the winning plays in the clutch games."

Of course, the Selke and Smythe versions diverge.

"Frank Selke always said for public consumption that he and I parted company because of a trade he made without my permission, while I was overseas. This is not true but probably sounds better, which is why Selke would say it. Certainly I was furious about not even being consulted. Eddolls had joined the Air Force soon after signing with us and I thought trading him was a stinking trick to play on a man who was going overseas. But if that was to be the end of Selke with the Leafs, why did I wait three years before telling him to walk the plank? And why didn't I fire Hap Day, too? Hap had a bigger voice than Selke in deciding on the trade."

Smythe explained that Selke was out because he sided with the wrong people (Ed Bickle and Bill MacBrien) in a Maple Leaf Gardens power struggle which was eventually won by himself. Both versions probably contained more than a kernel of truth. In the end, the two lifelong antagonists parted company.

Why so much information on the inner workings of the fledgling Toronto Maple Leafs in a book about the Montreal Canadiens?

With Selke en route to Montreal, Smythe finally could boast that he had an undisputed hand in building an NHL dynasty. The catch was that the dynasty would turn out to be the Montreal Canadiens, not the Toronto Maple Leafs. Had Smythe and Selke been able to work together, the odds are great that the Toronto Maple Leafs would be acknowledged as professional hockey's dynasty. But the true dynasty did not start until that humid August day in 1946, when Frank Selke followed his nose into the lobby of the Montreal Forum.

Some thirty-seven years later, on Canada Day in 1983, Father Frank welcomed us to his Rigaud farm and spoke about the big moment. "I'll never forget that first afternoon at the Montreal Forum. The place was filthy and the stench of poorly managed urinals knocked you down when you opened the front door. I had come from the working class and I would not stand for sloppiness at any level."

Hockey always had been a family oriented activity for the Selkes and Frank's first responsibility was to the fan who bought tickets to the games. "The local fan deserved to sit in comfort and enjoy a high quality of entertainment, so my first task was to invest more than $100,000 in a new plumbing system and undertake major renovations in the building." His hockey family's *raison d'être* was to welcome other families into its home, the Forum, and so this home had to be maintained with pride.

A hockey rink was a respectable place, with no room for rowdyism from fans or poor manners from staff. If you could remember those simple rules you would always be in Father Frank's good books.

Yet his order to renovate was more than a mere device to clear the air at the Forum. It was also Frank Selke's first totally independent decision in professional hockey; he now had the autonomy to build the kind of hockey organization he always had wanted.

"I'll never forget that day, August first," says Camil DesRoches, who had begun working part-time for the Canadiens in 1938. "Mr. Selke walked into the Forum and very quietly let everyone know that he was the boss and would be the boss for a very long time to come. He did something that impressed me very much; he went around the whole building and introduced himself to everyone, ushers, carpenters, plumbers, ticket people. And from that day on, he always would have a hello and nice words for his people, no matter where they worked in the Forum." To DesRoches, who became the club's publicity director in 1947 and is still with the Canadiens, Selke was a second father: "I called him Daddy and he treated me like one of his sons."

Everywhere in DesRoches' office on the second floor of the Forum are reminders of the Canadiens' storied past: over here a colour picture of the three Flying Frenchmen—Richard, Beliveau and Lafleur—over there a black and white shot of Camil at centre ice with Toe Blake and Frank Selke; beside his desk a signed picture of Prime Minister Brian Mulroney and Mrs. Mulroney. The most important picture is directly across from DesRoches' desk—it is the picture of the 1959-60 Montreal Canadiens, the team that was to win its record-setting fifth straight Stanley Cup later that season.

"That was Frank Selke's team all the way," says Des-Roches. "He built it from the bottom up."

To appreciate properly what Father Frank had wrought, one must return to 1946 and Selke's arrival at the Forum. It would be wrong to suggest that the Montreal Canadiens were a poor team prior to Selke's arrival. After all, the 1943-44 Canadiens had lost only five games —an all-time league record—en route to the Stanley Cup, and would repeat that success with a Cup victory in 1946. But they were far from the Flying Frenchmen of sports lore: both teams had only five French Canadians— Maurice Richard, Butch Bouchard, Fernand Majeau, Robert Fillion and Leo Lamoureux in 1943-44 and the same group, with Gerry Plamondon replacing Majeau, in 1945-46.

"One thing we had instilled in Toronto was a certain way of doing things, right throughout the organization," Selke recalled, "and I felt that the only way to guarantee long-term success for the Canadiens would be to do the same. But we had to do two things; build an organization which on one hand could recruit the very best talent available right across Canada, and at the same time develop the pool of players in our backyard, Quebec."

A young man from Montreal's West End named Sam Pollock, and defenceman Kenny Reardon, who retired from the Canadiens after the 1949-50 season, were given the task of running the sprawling minor league system with Selke. The Selke tentacles reached everywhere, with Montreal-sponsored teams in British Columbia, Saskatchewan, Manitoba, Ontario and Quebec feeding young players into the various levels of the professional leagues, in which many more Montreal teams were set up.

Selke, who in later years would become a recognized breeder of thoroughbred horses and prize chickens, likened the burgeoning system to farming. "I've always been a gentleman or *ad lib* farmer, always doing something around the house like landscaping or fixing things that needed it. I operated those clubs like a farmer, nurturing good potential players like plants and helping them come up and ripen in the system until they were good enough to join the big club."

The Selke farm system was vast. "We helped teams everywhere in hockey. We had ten teams in the Winnipeg area and we paid for the whole amateur system in Regina. And at one point, we were paying $300,000 a year in amateur development in Edmonton." Those kinds of expenses deterred other NHL managers, but not Selke. He ran his system as a farm and each year harvested a crop.

"We never interfered with the teams at the local levels. All we were interested in was developing good players and that we did. It paid for itself because we were able to sell about a quarter million dollars worth of quality players every season." They were sold to the other five clubs, of course, sales which would benefit the Canadiens in the years ahead.

"It was very convenient for some of the other organizations to save their seed money and they came to depend on us to beat the bushes for quality players for them," Selke smiled. "That meant, of course, that they bought players who were a level below our best, and that we knew everything there was to know about those players. This would eventually work out to our advantage."

When Selke rolled up his sleeves and went to work in 1946 he was dismayed to learn that he had come up against a formidable foe—himself—when the season got under way. The Canadiens lost the Stanley Cup final that year to the Maple Leafs, the team that Frank had built. Teeder Kennedy would lead Toronto to three straight Cups, lose one to Detroit, and win a fourth in 1950-51 on Bill Barilko's overtime goal against Montreal.

No matter that Selke could not win a Stanley Cup during his first six years at the Forum; he was building a system that would deliver championships like clockwork once the apparatus was wound. In 1947-48, a raw rookie from west-end Montreal named Doug Harvey took over Frankie Eddolls' Number 2; a year later a young Winnipegger named Tommy Johnson joined the club during the playoffs. In 1949-50, kids with proud French-Canadian names like Bernard Geoffrion, Dollard St. Laurent and Jean Beliveau had tryouts with the team, and in 1951-52 · Dickie Moore and Don Marshall surfaced.

The Quebec junior system, with teams like the Canadiens Juniors, Royals, Nationals, the Verdun Maple Leafs and Quebec Citadelles, delivered an astonishing number of top-quality players. Selke's investment was paying off.

Yet it was not merely the simple expediency of buying an extensive farm system or paying for a Quebec Junior league that would make the Canadiens something special. Any other team with a similar idea could duplicate those feats. Selke also instituted a particular Canadiens' way of doing things at all levels of the organization.

The feeder hockey systems were full of bright-eyed, talented young hockey players with a dream. They all flashed their stuff and, if their talent was sufficient, they moved up a level approximately every other season. To the outsider, this was a glamorous lifestyle, holding the promise of much greater riches at the top. Many young boys became very conscious that they were the objects of constant observation and assessment, and they learned that the whole dream could end abruptly, cruelly. Most teams preyed on the positive side of the promise, and lost many young talents along the way because they failed to realize that the occupational or job culture they had created also contained a negative side. Selke, who had been telling hockey players that they just weren't good enough since he was fourteen, recognized both sides of the coin and saw to it that his players did too.

He knew that hockey's occupational culture locked the individual into a situation which left him with less than a magnificent set of alternatives. In Selke's eyes, young hockey players were vulnerable and easily influenced. They could be directed, but it had to be a gradual process. The *Club de Hockey Canadien* adopted a particular set of strategies which underscored the significance of the minor leagues as a training ground for the all-stars who were preparing to enter the higher professional ranks.

As the young players progressed through the various levels of expertise, they underwent a socialization process during which the cultural values of winning were stressed more and more. Other factors which came into play were the influence of the media, the selection of current Canadiens' stars as role models and the formal and generalized system of coaching throughout the system.

The Montreal Junior Canadiens, Quebec Citadelles or the Regina Pats player shifted in focus from play to work, a shift that was characterized by a changing lifestyle which further integrated the life of the potential professional into the occupational culture. As a result, the Canadiens' juniors tended to be a little more serious, a little more mature than their counterparts in other organizations. While this could never be a substitute for pure hockey talent, when it came down to two players of equal on-ice skills, the Canadien usually would show more character. As a result, many young players who laboured long in the Canadiens' system only to fall short at the very last stage, still found employment as valued NHL players on the other five teams.

Selke had identified four stages in a young player's recognition of the professionalization process. They were: 1) the awakening of interest in a pro career; 2) the crystalization (resolve) of this interest; 3) the consolidation and commitment to that career, and 4) a review of that commitment. Most young hockey players who advanced to the junior ranks usually found themselves forced to move to a small town and were systematically cut off from family and friends. A large portion of a young player's life and energy would then revolve about practice, games, equipment preparation, meetings with management, and travel. Educational pursuits had been left behind, usually at a very young age, and the players were forced into a regimented way of life governed by the schedule and team curfew. The team scouts were always around, watching games and trying to assess the intangibles. As cruel as it sounds, the survivors were generally hockey players of character.

Floyd Curry, who came up to Montreal for the first time in 1947-48, and to stay two seasons later, described the process. "Junior hockey was more helter-skelter; [some good] players didn't play their positions quite as well [as they could have] while others looked much better than they really were. As we progressed, the speed increased, the guys became a good deal tougher and the demands of the hockey club became more acute. It really wasn't all that different because we were still playing hockey, but the sweater and the pride associated with this organization made matters much more complex."

Some twenty years later, when Ken Dryden moved into the NHL, the Selke message had spread to players at all levels of hockey. "I saw few differences in the transition from university to the professional club, since I always thought of myself as a professional. The necessary preparations for winning the contest were paramount in my mind and that commitment never left me. There were few differences in drills, practices or approach to the game; curfews were observed judiciously and the camaraderie flourished as always within the ranks of the team. I suspect that the most significant difference rested in the fact that you were playing against guys who were generally better than you."

Selke looked for three essentials in his players: a strong hockey background; a deep commitment to winning or an equally strong aversion to losing; and the sense of self-confidence, self-direction and self-motivation necessary in a player who would be asked to accept the team's regimentation. He wanted his players to adopt a shared perspective, rather than just an individual one. Personal expectations, attitudes and motives had to become team expectations, team attitudes and team motives.

Those players who made it received all the support in the world; they became part of the Canadiens family team and were protected and organized to ensure maxi-

mum performance. Frank Selke treated the Forum carpenters, telephone receptionists, publicists and ice makers as part of his family, and the men who wore the club
uniform were expected to respond in the same way.
Supportive communication and interaction were encouraged at all levels among team members.

As Jean Beliveau recalls: "It was much easier to be
involved in a family experience in those early days because we travelled by train. During the trip, most of the
guys, especially the veterans, would review the evening's
contest and you learned a great deal just by listening to
them. With air travel, these kinds of discussions do not
take place, so that if the coach doesn't offer a strategy for
success, the guys never get to talk about their mistakes."

Another centre, Ralph Backstrom, echoes Beliveau's
sentiments. "We were very close to one another, but I
think that winning was the most important thing that
we had going for us. When things were not going well,
we were frank with one another. Doug Harvey would
call a team meeting and we would all show up early at
some local bar to have it out. Sometimes we deliberated
for hours during the long train rides between cities, but
in the final analysis, we policed ourselves. Our coaches
gave 110 percent but it was really the players whose
pride and deep feelings of commitment sustained the
family entity."

In one way Beliveau was wrong: the demise of train
travel did not diminish the Canadiens' habit of socializing
as a team, especially on the road. If that custom was a
strong point of the powerhouse team of the 1950s, its
1970s counterpart also socialized in much the same manner, even though the train travel, a natural mixer, was no
longer available. The major difference of the 1970s was
that the players had to work a little harder at maintaining the sense of togetherness.

"We were always able to go out as a group, to a bar or
someplace when we were on the road, and talk things out
when we were not doing well," says Steve Shutt. "Players may have had best buddies and all that, but when the

team went out, the *team* went out and if there were any problems to hash out, we did it then and there." This system worked, even though it may have caused difficulties for the coach who was used to taking the leadership role in problem-solving. Scotty Bowman experienced occasional problems with team unity and the club's committee of veterans for the very good reason that the process of developing team unity depended on the players coaching themselves to some degree.

"This was pointed out in funny ways, sometimes," laughs Shutt. "I remember that we were out in Oakland one night and had one of our meetings and the boys all crawled back to the hotel very, very late, way past Scotty's curfew. Was he ever steamed, and he even felt worse when the Seals took a 2-0 lead on us in the first period! Now when Scotty got really pissed at us, he could scream and rant with the best of them. This time was different, he was almost subdued and some of us were going 'uh-oh' when he came into the room between periods. 'All right, that's it, you guys. If you don't want to play, I'll be damned if I'm going to coach you,' he said in the softest voice, and then he stomped out of the room. He wasn't kidding. He didn't say a damned thing for the next two periods so we coached ourselves, took care of all the line changes and played the game. We won, 6-2." Frank Selke had been gone for eight years when Shutt was drafted by the Canadiens from the Toronto Marlboros, but his legacy remained. The players in the '70s could occasionally get along without their coach, or father figure, because they were a tight familial unit.

There were never unclear lines of authority with Selke. Clear, concise coaching and leadership were important to Selke, and for many years he was happy with Dick Irvin, who had preceded him to Montreal by six years and won two Stanley Cups in the interim. Whether Selke's coach had a smooth disposition or was as abrasive as a brick wall did not matter. The coach had to be able to spell out the rules, set standards of performance, and call the plays. He was required to be a disciplinarian and stern taskmaster, and he had to believe in the product and remain highly committed to the task at hand. As a clever decision maker, Selke fervently hoped that his coaches would have enough personal strength to forego popularity.

Dick Irvin qualified for that job description, even though Selke admitted that Irvin gave him fits during key games.

"I remember the playoff series with Toronto in 1947. Richard had been suspended for two games and we had fallen behind. I was convinced that we would not come back, but in the sixth game we had them on the run. With thirty seconds left in that game, they pulled their goalkeeper for a sixth attacker and won the right to face off in our end. What does Irvin do? He pulls Curry, Mosdell and Mackay off the ice in favour of Rocket and Lach. I was so upset that I jumped up out of my chair to get Irvin's attention. Why would he choose to put the goal scorers on the ice when we were in desperate need of defence? Senator Raymond told me to relax and sat in his chair smugly, convinced that we had the game in the bag."

Selke's voice, thirty-six years later, still contains the exasperation he felt that night. "Kennedy won the draw and passed the puck to Smith. Before I could turn my head, the light went on. I rebuffed Senator Raymond for interfering with my plan. But that was Dick's record all along. He could never win the big one. He wasn't Toe in the clutch."

That might not be a fair observation; after all, Irvin had won the Cup with the fledgling Leafs, and then twice with Montreal before Selke arrived there and would win it once more in 1952-53 with the Habs. If Selke had his doubts about Irvin, he took his time in expressing them because Irvin remained coach of the team until the aftermath of the Richard Riots in 1954-55, taking his team to seven games in the final against the Red Wings that year despite the suspension of Maurice Richard. But Selke was firmly convinced that Irvin had exacerbated the

Richard situation and that the times called for a coach who could cool down the tempestuous superstar when the situation called for it.

Another problem was Selke's close friendship with Irvin. Both men were fanciers of fine specially bred chickens and pigeons. As Selke wrote in his autobiography, *Behind the Cheering*, in 1962:

> I am sure that some of the best days of my life were those spent with Dick and the fancy chickens and pigeons we used to keep out at Gordon Green's farm near Ste. Thérèse. Since 1956, I have had a lovely farm of my own near Rigaud; and as I putter about the assortment of good birds I keep there, I cannot help but think of how wonderful it would be if Dick could just come down the lane some day, with a carload of the birds he loved so well, and dump them in the barnyard. Our disagreements about the finer points of hockey were sometimes bitter; but we always enjoyed the arguments we had about fine feathers.

Selke told Irvin that he could no longer coach the Canadiens, but that there would be a position for him elsewhere in the Canadiens' organization if he wanted it. The Canadiens' general manager also knew that Irvin had an out, that he had been talking quietly with Chicago during the season about a return there. Given the alternative, Irvin chose Chicago.

"What none of us knew at the time was that, all that year, Dick had been suffering from a form of bone cancer. It was to culminate in his untimely death two years later. So he had reason enough to be restless and miserable. But, to this day, I miss this lovable, truculent Irishman who never learned the meaning of the word 'quit' in a hockey game."

If Irvin, the innovator of hockey coaches in the 1930s and 1940s, was going to Chicago, where could Selke find a quality replacement?

What better man than quiet Hector "Toe" Blake, the classy left winger who for years had been Richard's partner (along with centre Elmer Lach) on the celebrated Punch line? But hiring Toe Blake was not as easy as it seemed and at one point during that summer, Selke began to regret having forced Dick Irvin to move to Chicago.

"The board of directors and the French Canadian players wanted a French coach, while I supported Blake. I could sympathize with these people; French Canada was supplying so many wonderful hockey players and yet no one was giving jobs to French Canadian coaches, who were as good as anybody around.

"If Montreal Canadiens didn't hire French Canadian coaches, who would? I found that to be pretty sound reasoning, but I was personally committed to Blake. I thought he was the ideal man to keep Maurice in line and take our young veterans to the Stanley Cup. I thought a good deal about our former captain, Butch Bouchard, but I didn't think he had the knack or patience to become the team coach." Selke stuck to his guns, subtly reminding Senator Raymond of the *carte blanche* he had received nine years before, and Blake became the new coach of the Montreal Canadiens. It proved to be the right decision in the long run, but Selke made sure that it was cleared by Richard, during a long meeting arranged to receive the Rocket's blessing.

There is, however, another version to the Blake hiring which differs considerably from the Selke story. After Toe retired, he spent some time coaching in the Quebec Senior League with Valleyfield, and then moved on to the Canadiens' AHL club in Buffalo. Blake then left the club in mid-season, and Selke reputedly had said he would never again coach in the Montreal organization.

"I got the story from several sources," said Joe Gorman, "that Frank Selke was all set to hire Billy Reay as the coach when Maurice Richard came to my father and said he would quit. The press conference announcing it was to be held the very next day."

According to Gorman, his father suggested that Richard call writer Marcel Desjardins and give him the scoop that the players all wanted Blake to coach them.

Doug Harvey, who had worked for Joe Gorman at

Connaught Raceway, across the Ottawa River from the Canadian capital, said he had confirmation of the Gorman version from another source.

Whatever the circumstances of his hiring, and the Gorman-Selke feud that reaches beyond the grave, Blake proved to be one of the best-ever professional coaches, in any sport. Said Jacques Plante: "The guy knew how to prime you for a game; he knew what button to push to get the most out of guys because he always wanted to maintain the edge. Even if it was a so-called nothing game near the end of the season, he would always be saying things like, 'We might see this team in the playoffs so don't let up. If they give you a good run tonight, we'll have them believing that they can beat us and then we're in real trouble.' Toe kept us alert and always prepared."

Blake's reputation is sterling from all angles, on-ice and off. Hockey referee Red Storey: "Toe was the strongest guy behind the bench that I've ever seen. For me a good coach is the guy who can get the most out of his players, push them to the limit, discipline them when necessary but consistently retain their respect and admiration. That was Blake. He was loyal to both the team and the organization.

"I remember that he would close the dressing room door after a bad game and raise the roof in there. But when that door opened to the media, you never heard a bad word from him about any of his players. That kind of class will keep you in white shirts for a long time."

Blake took the Canadiens, now definitely the team that Father Frank built, to five straight Stanley Cups, from 1956 to 1960. After a three-year domination by Toronto Maple Leafs in the early 1960s, Blake coached Montreal to three more championships before stepping down after the 1968 season, having accumulated eight cups in thirteen years of coaching.

Once Frank Selke's machine was assembled, it hummed smoothly over the next few years, and even the sale of the Montreal Canadiens in 1957 did little to affect it. Senator Raymond, by then seventy-five years of age, wanted to slow down, but he would not sell his Canadiens to just anybody. He settled on a fellow Senator, Hartland de M. Molson, scion of a prominent Quebec brewing family with long roots in the province. Senator Molson and his brother Tom took over the *Club de Hockey Canadien* and the Canadian Arena Company in late September.

Little changed. Frank Selke continued as managing director and talented younger men like Pollock and Bowman moved from square to square on the organizational chart in places like Peterborough, Hull-Ottawa and Houston, Texas. In 1963, Father Frank celebrated his seventieth birthday and some gentle pressure was exerted to persuade him to retire and enjoy his later years, secure in the knowledge that he had been the architect of the best hockey team ever, a feat which he knew would stick in the craw of his perpetual antagonist, Connie Smythe.

Yet like many very active people, Frank Selke was the last man who wanted to retire. He just couldn't see the sense of turning away a sharp, experienced mind, only to replace it with someone new whose experience was still to come.

"Senator Molson asked me to retire. He said Molson's had a mandatory retirement policy at age seventy and my time had come. I told him to put me up against any man near my age and he'd see. He agreed with me but kept pressing and this distressed me. My skills had not diminished, like those of a hockey player physically past his prime. I knew full well that I could continue to run the team for many years to come."

It was not to be. Waiting in the wings was Sam Pollock, a man who had learned the ABCs of hockey management at Selke's knee and who would prove every bit as astute and influential as his mentor. "I can only guess that there was a very real fear at the board of directors level that if a place wasn't made soon for Sam Pollock, he would leave the organization and go to another team, or into the business world," Camil DesRoches recollects.

"As far as I can recall, Sam never even hinted at such a thing, but these people were pretty smart businessmen and they didn't want to take any chances. And when you think of what Mr. Pollock would accomplish for the Canadiens over the next fourteen years, you can understand why the board was nervous."

Senator Molson negotiated a compromise; Pollock would become the new Managing Director in 1964 and Frank Selke would, in that most famous corporate euphemism, "move upstairs" as a special adviser.

"So they set me up in a beautiful office, and nobody bothered to come and see me," Selke complained. "I was a vice-president and member of the board but it meant nothing. I was never invited to attend board meetings." Selke stayed active in parts of the hockey world, remaining as chairman of the selection committee for the Hockey Hall of Fame, an organization he had practically invented a year after joining the Canadiens.

He dedicated himself to his family and the full-time pursuit of activities that had previously been hobbies. Selke purchased a 220-acre farm near Rigaud, Quebec, about forty miles west of Montreal, where he raised prize chickens and thoroughbreds, as well as Galloway cattle. Only the latter turned a profit for Rolling Range Farm, but that did not matter.

Father Frank had a place for his family, as the spread contained three homes (two married daughters and their families lived there) and a guest house. He lived there for more than twenty years before he passed away at age ninety-two on July 3, 1985. Throughout the last two decades of his life, he was a Forum regular in Box 2, Seat 10, where he watched his team, now Sam's boys, roar into the television age and expansion. Occasionally the television cameras would flick over to that spot, as if silently imploring Father Frank to give his blessing to the events taking place before him. Whether he knew the cameras were on him or not, he appeared to sit there with a small smile at the edge of his mouth as the *bleu, blanc, rouge* swirled all over the ice, usually against inferior opposition. It was a smile of proprietorship, the same look his wife Mary must have seen when he stood behind the bench of the Berlin Union Jacks in 30-below temperatures at the outdoor rinks of southern Ontario some sixty years before. Sometimes, with the camera still on him, Frank Selke appeared to be looking across the rink, where his old adversary Conn Smythe might have been standing and glaring at him. Well over a century of hockey antagonism had passed between these two old war horses.

"The funny thing is," Camil DesRoches recalls, "that the Smythe-Selke feud seemed to be more for public and media consumption than anything else. I always wondered if both men were afraid of admitting to the other the kind of respect they felt for each other. All I know is that I worked with Frank Selke for many, many years in Montreal and many times when I had to go to Toronto on team or Forum business, he would give me a note and say, 'When you get there, go see Connie and tell him you're there for me, he'll fix you up.' Both of them were involved in thoroughbred horses, Selke breeding them and Smythe racing them, and [they] would occasionally get together in the hockey off-season. Smythe, "the enemy", died in November, 1980.

On July 4, 1985, Father Frank paid his last visit to the lobby of the Montreal Forum. There he lay in state, arrangements of funeral flowers tastefully arrayed about him. The place smelled a lot fresher and a whole lot more successful than it had on that faraway August afternoon in 1946. And you did not have to approach the casket to know that Frank Selke had that quiet little smile on his face.

# 6

# Jean Beliveau
# The Lion Regal

It is a surprisingly brisk August day in 1976, a reminder that the warm afterglow of the recently extinguished Olympic Flame too soon will be replaced by the glacial Arctic winds that sweep down from the north and across the St. Lawrence lowlands every winter. Jean Beliveau is well-protected against the gusts in a three-piece pin-striped wool suit. The navy suit is moulded to his large frame and sets off his silver hair. He stands six feet, three inches tall and carries 215 pounds on a very large frame, "about five to ten pounds over my playing weight," but he looks even larger than he is. When he first rose to prominence in hockey he was a skinny 170 pounds and disarmingly handsome.

Forty years later, his face would be described as inter-esting, from his aquiline nose to the high cheekbones and eyes sheltered by a prominent, chiselled forehead. He has the aristocratic features you might find in a portrait of some long-lamented *sieur* hanging among those of several generations lining a hallway in a French chateau, or with that nose, in profile on a Roman coin. He has a presence that makes heads turn, even in places where they have never heard of ice hockey.

The chill wind is refreshing for the vice-president of corporate communications of the *Club de Hockey Canadien.*

It was a long trip from Frobisher Bay the night before. He was asked by an administrator of an orphanage in that Arctic settlement if he could deliver a short speech. Forewarned by meteorological forecasts that the weather would be uncertain at best, Beliveau went anyway. "I made a commitment," he sighed gently, remembering the turbulence on the return flight.

Beliveau got home late but was at the office early. He had an appointment with a journalist, and his general rule applies to all situations. After the interview, we leave the Texan Restaurant, across Closse from the Forum, and head east down St. Catherine Street, the main downtown thoroughfare. A voracious reader, Beliveau is on his way to a nearby bookshop to pick up another text. Unlike many young hockey players who came out of junior ranks in his day, Gros Bill had finished his high school studies. He refused to leave it there, however, and sometimes during his playing days more energetic teammates anxious to go out and take the edge off would chide him for having his nose buried in yet another book. "I looked forward to having much more time to read when I retired. . ." He lets the statement trail off with a smile of resignation. Today, with his Canadiens job, his Foundation and several corporate directorships, he has even less time for his beloved books. Yet it seems that every day he still finds himself in a downtown bookstore somewhere, poring over the titles in French and English, oblivious to the stares and pointing fingers of other bibliophiles.

At Fort and St. Catherine Streets, still several blocks west of Beliveau's destination, an obviously inebriated citizen of the streets cuts across our path. Standing directly in front of us, with that curious list to one side that identifies winos everywhere, he sports a tattered suit and long, multi-coloured beard.

"*Ah, le Gros Bill,*" he says, his eyes alive with recognition. "I will never forget the goal against Boston in '71". Jean smiles gently, and you could see the mental wheels turning quietly as he asks himself, "Which one?"

The drunk demonstrates prodigious recall. "The second game when they had you down 5-2 after two periods. Early in the third period, you and Ferguson took the wind out of their sails with early goals. Do you remember?"

"*Ah, oui*," Beliveau replies, his voice surprisingly soft. And two hockey fans spend ten full minutes happily discussing The Seven Games That Broke Boston's Heart. Dozens of pedestrians step gingerly around them, their faces a curious mix of contempt for the wino and starstruck awe for Number 4.

Time is fleeting, there are several appointments on the afternoon agenda. "I must go now," Beliveau announces quietly.

"Thank you, Jean," says the wino, perhaps wondering if this encounter has really happened. "You're welcome," Beliveau smiles quietly, and shakes the hockey fan's hand.

In 1125 regular-season games over 18 full seasons (plus two amateur tryouts) and another 162 playoff games, not one negative word has been uttered about the man who wore Number 4 for the Montreal Canadiens. Harry Sinden, a ferocious competitor and innovative hockey mind, said it for everyone: "It would be like desecrating a monument."

If Maurice Richard, despite the competition from the great Gordie Howe, trailblazed for the modern era of professional hockey, Jean Beliveau consolidated the sport's acceptance into the entertainment mainstream of North America. Richard was Ruth to Howe's Gehrig, and Beliveau was hockey's Joe DiMaggio. As to relative importance with the Canadiens, it might be best to say that Richard epitomized the back of the sweater, the celebrated Number 9, while Gros Bill perhaps best described the front of the sweater, the legendary CH. No one ever has or ever will wear the *bleu-blanc-rouge* with more distinction than Jean Beliveau. The scope of that statement can only be truly understood when one takes a moment to pause and recall the greats who wore it with pride over the decades and now reside in the Hall of Fame.

As well, no one has ever worn a "C" on his hockey sweater with more impact, on any NHL team. Jean Beliveau was leadership personified.

In many ways, his childhood bordered on a small-town Depression-era Quebec cliché. He was born August 31, 1931 in Trois-Rivières, the eldest of seven children, five boys and two girls (a third girl died in infancy). His birthplace is significant, located as it is about halfway between Quebec City and Montreal. It is, perhaps, an omen of the celebrated tug-of-war that would come two decades hence.

The Beliveau family did not remain in Jean's birthplace long. Arthur Beliveau, a lineman with Shawinigan Power, moved his brood to Plessisville and then on to Victoriaville when Jean was three. Here he grew up and first came to the attention of the hockey world.

"I grew up right next door to a church, and as was the case with many young French Canadian boys of that time, I became an altar boy. You would have a lot of early Masses in those days and when the other boys couldn't make it on time because of weather conditions, there would be a knock at our door. As it turned out, I was on the altar nearly every morning."

After Sunday Mass at Les Saints-Martyrs Canadiens church, Jean would exchange his censer for a well-taped hockey stick and join the couple of dozen boys playing hockey on the rink Arthur Beliveau constructed every winter in the family's spacious backyard.

"The deal was almost a Quebec tradition," Jean smiles. "My dad would put up the rink and flood it; we had to shovel it clean before our games. If you get six or seven boys with shovels and the rest with their hockey sticks, the rink gets cleaned pretty fast. We would play all morn-ing until it was time for Sunday dinner. Most of the Quebec-born players I played with on the Canadiens remembered starting out this way ... if it wasn't on a homemade backyard rink, it was on a frozen lake or river."

There was one rule in the Beliveau Backyard League: every man for himself.

"That's where the really good NHL stickhandlers started out. There were few rules and the teams changed every five minutes, this kid switching to that team, those two coming over to this one. It was a scrimmage and you tried to hold on to the puck as long as you could. The bigger boys would stickhandle and keep the puck away from the little guys, who would start out by learning to check. As the little guys grew up, they became the boys who manipulated the puck. We didn't have organized leagues or teams with sweaters and all that; we really didn't even have rinks but we all learned to play and play well. The first real rink I would play on would be that of the Sacred Heart Brothers."

Jean played for teams at his first two schools, the Académie de Saint-Louis de Gonzague and the Collège Sacré-Coeur. He began to show his talents at an early age. It was while he was a student at the College studying technical education (electricity, in case he decided to follow his father to Shawinigan Power) that local hockey people began noticing him.

Maurice Richard was making waves in the NHL when the Victoriaville stringbean began to show his stuff in ice hockey. The Second World War was over and Jean was sixteen when he began to play intermediate hockey, perhaps the best-named league of them all. In the mid-40s, Quebec hockey revolved about the powerful Senior semi-pro league and a handful of smaller, less important junior leagues. (All of this would change within months as Frank Selke and the Canadiens began reforming the junior hockey picture).

Both the Senior and Junior leagues were for players with a future or, in the case of the Seniors, for old pros who still enjoyed the game and might seek to pick up a few dollars close to home.

Intermediate, or in-between hockey, was comprised of teams stocked with players of all ages who might not be quite good enough to play Senior or, in Jean's case, did not have a junior franchise nearby. These teams would be a mix of young talents like Beliveau and players in their twenties and even thirties who might be a step too slow or a mite short in overall ability to play Senior. Suffice it to say that junior-age hotshots were considered fair game and that this was probably the toughest league in which Jean Beliveau ever was to play.

"I played for the Victoriaville Panthers and we were owned and run by two local businessmen, Mr. Robitaille, who owned an auto parts store and Mr. Buteau, who acted as our coach. The coaching then was not very scientific and we spent most of our practices in full scrimmages. These were tough enough but the games were something else." Beliveau was so good that he often played the whole game, skating at centre until he tired and then dropping back to defence for a rest. By the midway point in the season, he had scored 47 goals and was attracting a lot of interest around the province.

In 1948-49, Victoriaville was awarded a franchise in the Quebec Junior Hockey League, which Frank Selke was trying to buttress with more funds, expanding what had been a four-team league to eleven teams. The new team's management came looking for the tall young centreman who had shown his ability in intermediate hockey.

"We would like to sign Jean to play for us," they told Arthur Beliveau.

"There is one condition," Beliveau replied. "Jean retains his own rights." Knowing full well that Beliveau and another local boy, Paul Alain, were their best players, the owners agreed.

"My Dad was looking out for my interests. He knew that I could go far in hockey and that if I committed to one team, one management, that it might not do me any good. He was right, of course, the Victoriaville team lasted one year in the league and then folded."

That one season with the Victoriaville Tigers launched Beliveau. The Tigers' gold-and-black uniforms with a tiger's head superimposed on a large black "V" impressed the people of Victoriaville but few others. Playing with strictly homebrew talent, they were easy prey for powerful teams from the Quebec City and Montreal areas. Still, Beliveau, then already six-feet, three-inches tall and weighing 170 pounds, scored 48 goals and added another 27 assists in a 48-game season for a club that finished out of the playoffs.

"The most important thing about that season was the coaching. Roland Hebert was the man who coached me and he believed in giving me as much ice time as I needed to develop. He felt it was the only way I would learn and I believed him. Hockey is a game where ice time is very important; the more you play, the better you will get. Practice time is nice and so are drills but game action is what creates the best players."

Professional scouts now were sitting in the stands, scrutinizing the tall skinny kid who was playing for his hometown team. There was a lot to see; Beliveau was on the ice forty minutes a game, and although the Tigers were not a winning team, he showed enough talent during that year to impress everyone. The Quebec Citadelles formed one of the league's powerhouse teams that season, and when they met the Tigers at home, they were confident that they would easily extend their 16-game undefeated streak. The late Jacques Plante tells the story.

"In those days, if teams were tied after regulation, you played overtime and not sudden death either. Jean was playing his usually great game and kept his team in against us—I think he scored the goal that tied the game in the third period—and then assisted when Victoriaville scored to take the lead. That did not bother us all that much because we had pulled out of several games like that already so we pressed to the attack. Our guys were in their zone when our defenceman took a shot that hit the post. One of their defencemen just swung at it, it hit the boards and I look up and there is Jean skating for all he is worth trying to catch up with it over our blueline. I had no choice. I rushed out at the puck because it was closer to me and I was just about to hit it away when he reached out with those tentacles of his and poked it past me. So there I was lying on my stomach halfway out to the blueline and Jean had an empty net and the puck. He didn't miss and we lost."

Performances like that excited the scouts. After a single season at home the Victoriaville franchise folded, and Jean became the most sought-after player in the junior league.

"They had a trophy they gave to what they called the best professional prospect and I won it. After the Victoriaville team folded, I was a free agent and able to sign with anyone I wanted. Montreal and Quebec both wanted me and I could choose, which was my father's idea all along. It was a tough decision to make because both teams were exceptionally strong and had excellent players. There were people like Bernard Geoffrion, Dickie Moore and Dollard St. Laurent playing for some of the Montreal-area teams and others like Jacques Plante in Quebec."

The Montreal-based teams played out of the Forum or the Verdun and Palestre Nationale rinks. They were powerhouses: the Junior Canadiens, the Montreal Royals, the Verdun Maple Leafs and the Nationals. They all wanted Beliveau.

"A representative of the Forum came to Victoriaville offering me all kinds of contracts to play with Junior Canadiens, and Quebec was after me, too."

Roland Mercier, who later would serve as president of the Canadian Amateur Hockey Association, and also would be instrumental in securing Guy Lafleur for another Quebec City junior team, was general manager of the Citadelles. The owner was Frank Byrne, an important figure in the pulp and paper industry. They were relentless.

In the end, geography and urban sprawl were the deciding factors. Victoriaville was closer to Quebec City than Montreal. As well, the smaller, more comfortable Quebec City would provide less culture shock to a former altar boy from Les Saint-Martyrs Canadiens.

The Montreal-Quebec bidding war and his performance with Victoriaville during the previous season led to bigger and better headlines during the off-season. A third factor also was involved. The old Colisée had burned down during the spring and construction was proceeding apace during that summer to ensure that the new building would be ready for the hockey season. That explained Mercier's and Byrne's anxiety as far as the tall centre was concerned. Both men were convinced that Beliveau was the attraction who would fill the new rink, and help pay off the mortgage. They were proven right on all counts.

There was someone in Montreal who was not terribly upset by the Quebec City decision. Frank Selke already had his mitts on the junior and the way he discovered him showed just how small the world of ice hockey really is.

"Rollie Hebert, his coach at Victoriaville, attended the wedding of my daughter to Paul Bibeault, the goalie. He came up to me at the wedding and said: 'Mr. Selke, I have a player who plays for me in Victoriaville that you should sign. He is a big, strong fellow and he will be an excellent professional one day.' So I went down to Victoriaville and talked to him and his father. I had an interpreter for his father and me. I signed him to what we called a Form B, which gave us an option on his services if he decided to turn professional, provided we could satisfy him financially. There was no way of forcing him to take a bad salary then. The terms had to be entirely satisfactory to him."

Arthur Beliveau's shrewdness had paid off yet again, as Frank Selke was to realize two years later. Unlike most other hockey players signed to the universal "C Form", which made them chattels of the team in question, Beliveau had independence of movement. If he was still good enough after his junior hockey days, the Canadiens would have to come after him with something a little more substantial than a "for show" signing bonus and the NHL minimum salary.

At that moment, however, it was up to Beliveau to prove that his performance in Victoriaville meant more than just the easy goals of a talented local boy scoring big without any pressure on him. From now on Beliveau would be playing on a team in the thick of a championship race and the opposition would be gunning for him.

The tall centreman, who seemed to add about ten pounds a year to his large frame, lit up the junior league. He came up against some superb hockey players, among them his nemesis, Dickie Moore, with the Sam Pollock-coached Juniors, and Skippy Burchell and Geoffrion with the Nationals. Joining Beliveau on the Citadelles was Camille Henry, a diminutive winger who would star with the New York Rangers for many seasons during the 1950s and early '60s.

The new Coliseum was unfinished as the season began, so the Citadelles played the early part of their 1949-50 home schedule in Victoriaville, a nice treat for their star centre.

"We held our training camp in Victoriaville because the Colisée was not ready and then ended up playing our home games there until December. In reality, I didn't leave home for the first time until the Colisée was ready, just before Christmas 1949. And ready is not quite the word; we had to dress in the older rink about 300 yards away, and carry our skates to the new Colisée in December, January and February."

Those who wondered if the Citadelles' new centre would fill the rink had their questions answered early. Tradesmen were still hard at work finishing the building when the first crowd of 10,000 showed up and the Citadelles were on their way. For the rest of the season and the next, 10,000-plus crowds were the rule in the Colisée.

"We set records in the Colisée that they couldn't break today because of the way the rink was renovated six years ago. Back then we had a playoff crowd of 16,800 or so against Barrie Flyers but now the stadium capacity is only 15,400. There is no standing room there now and that's what made the difference with the big crowds."

The big crowds also came out in Montreal to fantasize about the "Class of '31"—Beliveau, Moore and Geoffrion —who one day might graduate to the big team and help the Canadiens become *une équipe extraordinaire.* Beliveau and Geoffrion battled for the league scoring lead all season long with Moore a half-length behind. Better still, the fans' fantasies were stoked by the fact that the three players complemented each other, with Beliveau playing centre, Moore at left and Geoffrion at right wing!

Three years before Jean Beliveau became a Canadien, Montreal sportswriters were regularly indulging themselves in "What If?" pieces. The entire province sighed in anticipation of the blessed event, with the only vote of dissension registered by the solid citizens of *La Vieille Capitale*, who would do anything to keep Jean "home" in Quebec City. Everywhere else in the National Hockey League, scouts who had covered Quebec, and noted the coming of Beliveau *et al* were drawing a gloomy picture for their medium- and long-term team fortunes.

Everywhere else, perhaps, but Toronto, where that noted talent man Conn Smythe held sway. Tommy Gorman, no longer with the Canadiens but still very much involved with the Quebec hockey and horse racing scenes, was passing through Toronto with his son Joe when he decided to pay a courtesy call on Smythe. They were joined by Toronto coach Hap Day and spent parts of an agreeable spring afternoon swapping tall tales.

"At one point," said Joe, "Connie asked my Dad if he had any good hockey players for him in Quebec."

"Sure thing. There's a kid who can't miss called Beliveau from Victoriaville playing with Quebec City."

"Conn and Hap started laughing like they were going to split a gut."

"Beliveau? He will never amount to anything!" roared Smythe. "We saw him play against Barrie Flyers in the Memorial Cup and they put him in their back pocket."

The senior Gorman looked at the Toronto Twosome with stupefaction. "You're going to lay all of this off on one game?"

"We saw what we had to," was the gruff reply. "And in any case, we have this kid called Eric Nesterenko who is going to make everybody forget about this Beliveau."

The Gormans later discovered why Beliveau and his team-mates were blown out 8-3 in the Barrie game. Flying was still an adventure in the early '50s and the

Citadelles had spent twelve hours sitting around airports during the day of the game, finally flying into Toronto just before game time.

Joe Gorman confides, "Dad really respected Smythe's hockey know-how after that."

Jean played two superb years in junior hockey, despite the fact that he was the rope in a protracted tug-of-war between Frank Byrne and Frank Selke during that entire time. The top junior players who had signed B or C forms were invited to the Montreal Canadiens' September training camp every year and Beliveau was no exception. Gros Bill, Geoffrion, Moore, Dollard St. Laurent and Don Marshall were among the young players who showed up and impressed management.

Beliveau was the jewel, however, and his value increased every October when he would politely, but firmly, turn down Frank Selke's offers and return to Quebec City. The pressure was really turned on after both Moore and Geoffrion signed right out of junior. These two talented kids cried out for a centre! The whole team cried out for a centre! Elmer Lach was on his last legs.

But Beliveau felt he had commitments in Quebec City and could not make the move until all of these were met. In his last year of junior hockey, the team and Quebec fans bought him a 1951 Nash and it bore the special licence plate "9 B" for his number 9. Jean had signed an endorsement agreement with a dairy and the senior Aces were talking of offering him anything the Canadiens might, just to keep him in that city.

"I was paid very well in Quebec City; Frank Selke could not give me more money because then I would be getting more than people like Maurice Richard and he could not have that on his team. For three years I came to the Canadiens' training camp and they were kind of scared. In those days they put players who signed the B Form on a special negotiating list and they could only keep two or three players on it. When they signed or released a player, then they could protect someone else."

Like many of the teams in the senior league, the Quebec Aces were a company team, owned lock, stock and barrel by Anglo-Canadian Pulp and Paper. Money was no object, especially since Beliveau would be responsible for three or four thousand extra patrons during every home game.

How popular was Jean Beliveau back then?

In October, 1952, the Dean of (English) Canadian hockey writers of the day, Andy O'Brien, was despatched to Quebec City by *Weekend Magazine* to discover what the fuss was all about. Jean Beliveau was to be the subject of a full-colour cover story headlined: "He's Hockey's Most-Wanted."

He writes:

> We drove from the auditorium in a swank, cream-coloured convertible, the second car presented to the twenty-one-year-old whiz by his admiring fans (the first had been presented at age nineteen). It bore a special Quebec licence plate with the number '2 B'; the then Quebec Premier, Maurice Duplessis, has '1 B'.
>
> Jean parked his convertible directly in front of the main entrance of the famed Château Frontenac Hotel and we went up to my room. He poured himself a beer and was in the act of lighting up a cigar when there came a knock on the door. I opened it and in walked a Quebec City policeman. Taking off his fur cap, the cop said in French:
>
> 'If you let me have your key, Jean, I'll park your car.'
>
> Without interrupting his discussion, Jean threw the cop his keys. The cop backed out of the room apologetically. Frankly, I was awed—but I shouldn't have been.

Jean Beliveau, the Anointed. Guy Lafleur would tell of a similar incident twenty years later when he and his family drove into Montreal to attend the NHL draft that would make him a Canadien. They were lost downtown and desperately searching for the Queen Elizabeth Hotel. When they found it, there was still a problem: the Lafleur family car was on the wrong side of the six-lane Dorchester Boulevard heading west and there wasn't a left turn in sight to bring them back to the hotel. At a red light, a local cop recognized Guy and helped him make an illegal U-turn across five lanes of traffic so that he could have his meeting with destiny. Clearly, rules were for mere mortals.

In 1950-51, while still a junior, Jean Beliveau served up *un petit apéritif* to Montreal hockey fans when he scored a goal and an assist against Chicago in the second game of a two-game trial. At the end of that junior season, it appeared that he would head to Montreal. He could sign with the Canadiens or find a job and play Senior hockey.

After long deliberation, and yet another Canadiens' fall training camp session that left Montreal's management drooling, Beliveau returned to Quebec, this time to play for Punch Imlach and the Aces. He now was a strapping 190-pounder and ready to play with the big boys. But how could he accept money to play with the Aces when the Canadiens owned his professional rights, acquired when he signed the B Form? Quite simply, the Quebec Senior Hockey League was classified semi-professional, even though all players in it were paid. A few, like Beliveau, were paid salaries that matched those received by pros, but that was just quibbling.

The Aces were as strong as many very good American Hockey League teams and included such players as Dick Gamble, who would later play for Toronto and Montreal; Marcel Bonin, fresh out of junior and a future Red Wing and Canadien; Ludger Tremblay, the older brother of Gilles Tremblay, and former Leaf Gaye Stewart. After a slow start, Beliveau caught fire and won the league scoring championship with 45 goals and 83 points. He was Rookie of the Year, centre on the First All-Star team, and best pro prospect in the league and the Aces' team MVP.

He was, as Punch Imlach invariably replies when asked the inevitable question, "The best player I have ever coached."

He was also a rapidly maturing hockey player coveted not just for his prodigious on-ice talents but also for his leadership qualities.

"I think one thing that has always struck people, apart from his tremendous talent, is Jean's leadership," says Imlach. "At the beginning, he would lead by example through what he did on the ice—making passes, checking, scoring goals. Later, especially in his second year, he would take over the leadership of the team. It seemed a natural thing to happen. He did not go looking for it; it went looking for him."

The 1952-53 season in the Quebec Senior Hockey League was combination ice hockey and soap opera. Beliveau filled the rinks all over the circuit, often drawing crowds of 15,000 to the Forum and the Colisée. But was it really Beliveau by himself? Absolutely. If Gros Bill was injured, the arena was half-full; if he played, it was standing room only.

The soap opera could have been called "An Act of Faith". Most QSHL fans went to see Beliveau play fully convinced that each game would be his last, that the Canadiens could not afford to leave him in semi-pro hockey as they fought their way to the Stanley Cup. It was well known that Gros Bill had made a commitment to Frank Byrne and Roland Mercier. It was equally well known that Frank Selke wanted him and Selke usually got what he wanted.

Punch Imlach threw out the challenge to the rest of the hockey world: "The NHL certainly must know by now that my boy rates only with Gordie Howe and Rocket Richard in their league," he told the newspapers.

The challenge was picked up ... by Beliveau. He was called up for a three-game trial, the maximum allowable under NHL rules, and wearing Dickie Moore's Number 12, scored five goals, three against the New York Rangers. This time it was no junior who faced the NHL defencemen.

Beliveau was fully grown at six-feet, three-inches and 205 pounds, a monster to opposing defencemen who were, on the average, five inches shorter and twenty pounds lighter. He was a deceptively smooth skater and possessed a very heavy half-windup slapshot that could tear a goalie's catching glove from his hand. The most dangerous part of his game was his formidable wingspan, a long reach that got him to pucks even when he arrived simultaneously with opposition players. Beliveau bearing down on a defenceman was a frightening sight: "Will he shoot? Will he take my best check and bounce off? Will he fool me with his speed? Or will he just simply make me look sick with a couple of moves and go around me like I'm not even there?" Some coaches and general managers in the league scoffed at Imlach's brave proclamation. All of the best players in the world were in the NHL, they boasted.

"Not yet," retorted those players who went up against the Quebec Aces star, "not yet!"

It was a very tough time for Beliveau, and it was not helped by the legend he was forging in the senior league.

"Just like Guy Lafleur many years later, I found myself caught in a vise, with the media pushing me to break all records the first night I hit the ice. Of course, that was impossible and it made life very, very difficult for me." Beliveau bore this with characteristic stoicism, preferring to dwell on its positive side.

"Of course, when it came to negotiating my first contract, I had an ace in the hole."

After the three-day trial, driven by an almost hysterical media onslaught, Selke went to the Victoriaville native with a new offer. The total package would be $53,000, broken down into a $20,000 signing bonus, and a three-year contract at $10,000, $11,000 and $12,000 a year. The only player close to making that money in Montreal was a little-known winger named Richard.

Beliveau turned it down.

Word came down from the President's office: "Mr. Selke, I know you have been given *carte blanche* to run the hockey operations any way you wish and I am not to interfere, but we must have Mr. Beliveau," was the message delivered by Senator Raymond. The reply was quick and uncharacteristically submissive from a Managing Director who was generally ruthless in repelling all attacks, real and imagined, on his hockey hegemony: "You're right!"

That summer, the toast of Quebec City married *une belle de la vieille capitale* and hundreds of well-wishers waved them off on their honeymoon.

Three months later, another longstanding courtship was sealed with an unusual dowry. Frank Selke, tired of being spurned by a man some called the best hockey player in Quebec, Rocket Richard or no Rocket Richard, found the solution to all of his problems.

If Jean Beliveau's B Form stipulated that his professional rights were owned by Montreal Canadiens, and everyone knew Beliveau was being paid as much as Richard by the Aces, it was time to establish that the Quebec Senior Hockey League really was a professional league. That could be done in one of two ways. The Canadiens could take the entire league to court and argue that it was professional and, therefore, Beliveau belonged to them. That would be costly and could take a long time.

The second solution might be just as expensive but a real timesaver: buy the league. Selke chose the second solution, and the Quebec Senior Hockey League became the Quebec Senior Professional Hockey League.

In October, 1953, with the television and film cameras rolling, and flashbulbs popping, Jean Beliveau signed a $110,000 contract which contained a sizable bonus, a five-year guarantee and a raft of bonus clauses. As Beliveau signed, Dick Irvin, who was standing behind him, put up a V for Victory sign and Frank Selke cracked a rare smile. Moments later, in one of his first TV interviews, Selke was asked how the Canadiens finally convinced the Aces star to sign.

"It was really simple," he replied, in his best why-didn't-we-think-of-this-earlier tone. "All I did was open the Forum vault and say, 'Help yourself, Jean.'" There was an air of levity, but Selke was not joking.

In the 1980s, it is much easier to remember the hoopla that surrounded the arrival of Guy Lafleur to the Canadiens, and the subsequent letdown as the rookie appeared to struggle in his first several seasons. Lafleur's start, in all ways, mirrored that of his idol.

Both players joined a Stanley Cup winner: Beliveau after second-place Montreal defeated Chicago and Boston to win the Cup in 1952-53; Lafleur after the Canadiens downed Boston, Minnesota and Chicago to win in 1970-71. In both cases, Montreal fans foresaw an uninterrupted string of championships and immediate individual glory for the former Quebec City heroes. In both cases they were wrong.

Beliveau disappointed those fans who felt he would win the scoring title in his first year. Plagued by injuries, he played only 44 of 70 regular-season games in 1953-54 and finished 26th in scoring with 13 goals and 21 assists for 34 points. He showed his mettle in 10 playoff games, however, with two goals and eight assists, and veteran hockey observers were often quoted as saying that the eruption was imminent.

In the second year, Beliveau moved well up in the standings, scoring 37 goals and 36 assists for 73 points in 70 full games and added 13 more points in 12 playoff games. The 73 points were sufficient for third place in the scoring championship, two points behind Geoffrion and one after the Rocket, who lost his bid to win his first-ever title in the famous suspension that followed after he slugged a linesman in Boston.

"The most disappointing thing for me was that we didn't win the Stanley Cup those first two years. Both times we could have, losing to Detroit in seven games twice and with Rocket suspended in 1955. When we came to training camp in 1955, we all knew we were going to do something."

United with all of his adversaries from junior days— Moore, Talbot, Plante, Geoffrion, St. Laurent and Marshall—and a young kid named Henri Richard who had joined his older brother with the *bleu-blanc-rouge*, Beliveau was the star of the Canadiens' youth movement that would pay dividends for the decade to come.

It was during the 1955-56 season that Beliveau bloomed and proved to the entire hockey world that he was a player of star quality. Doug Harvey describes it as "the year Jean got tough."

"In his first two years, Beliveau showed everyone he could play the game but he took an awful lot of punishment. They went after him every chance they got and

Jean rarely retaliated. I got on him all the time, and so did Dickie Moore and the Rocket. That third year in training camp I told him that if anything started, go for the guy and we'd all be right there."

In his first two seasons, Beliveau had 22 and 58 penalty minutes respectively. In 1955-56, he was nearly leading the league with 143. The following two years he had 105 and 93 minutes and after that he was left alone. The newly aggressive Canadien crunched all comers until there were no more challengers. Whenever the rough-housing threatened to spill over, well-respected fighters like Moore, Olmstead, Richard and friends covered the flanks.

When the season ended, Beliveau had won the league scoring title with 47 goals and 88 total points, nine better than Gordie Howe. Along with the title came the Art Ross Trophy, the Hart Trophy for league MVP and selection to the First All-Star team.

The best prize was yet to come. Beliveau's 12 goals and 7 assists for 19 points in 10 playoff games were highest in the league and led the Canadiens to the Stanley Cup, the first of five straight. In the 80 games he played that year, Beliveau scored 59 goals and 48 assists for 107 points, a post-expansion era scoring performance in the days of the Original Six. The hockey player had arrived, and the great leader was in full development.

How did Jean Beliveau come to assume the latter role? Why was it not assumed by someone else, a teammate like Bernard Geoffrion, Doug Harvey or Dickie Moore?

Veteran referee Red Storey traces the turnaround to the pivotal third season.

"Jean Beliveau was a man with great class and ability. I remember when he came to the league; he was very talented but also very timid. He was a gentleman, he played like a gentleman, he never retaliated. As such, everybody used to take a shot at him and somewhere during that first summer, between seasons, I think the proper people contacted him and told him how to handle himself with respect to the stick, the elbow and the body. A year later he had the respect of the players on the other team and he didn't have to play that way any more."

The recipient of special dispensation from the game of the trenches, Beliveau towered head and shoulders above the rest, playing a hurly-burly sport with an almost aristocratic sense of tradition and dignity that rendered simple statistics next to meaningless.

"You could see his effect on this team, this team that featured such great veterans as Rocket Richard and Harvey. You could see that the Rocket, who never was a great oral communicator with his teammates, was almost glad that someone like Beliveau was there to handle that. Jean spoke to all that surrounded him, he educated and coached his peers, he trained the young kids and worked diligently for the Canadiens from the day he first arrived to the present day.

"As far as I'm concerned, Beliveau represents what hockey is all about or should be about. Guys his age, like Moore and Geoffrion, did not seem to resent his leadership ability. They listened just as hard as the other guys."

Floyd Curry was one of several veterans who greeted the arrival of this very mature rookie without the slightest rancour. This was not the kind of rookie you could haze or shave bald in first-season high jinks. Jean escaped the rites of passage inflicted on his peers.

"It goes beyond class when you speak about Beliveau. I know him now as a businessman and his efforts transcend the hockey world with respect to the kinds of things that he does and how he does them. Jean is loved by everybody, even people who don't know him. All that you have to do is take one look and you feel this enormous presence."

Beliveau's leadership role became more pronounced as the years went by, but it was not until the 1961 season, after Doug Harvey was traded to New York, that he was named team captain. Curry felt that Beliveau's role was more inspirational than confrontational.

"There never was one guy on the team or in the dressing room who was singled out as the leader beyond all question. The team always had six or seven leaders and the rest of us were followers. That tradition of the 'committee of veterans' is still in force today, thirty years later."

Gump Worsley, who came to Montreal in the 1963 trade that sent Jacques Plante to New York, saw the practical side of leadership.

"The coach is the team psychiatrist, who has to be able to make twenty egos work for the team good. The captain keeps everybody together. It is his job to keep the room calm, to keep bickering down between players or their wives. That can be a big problem. When two wives pair off and get into an argument, soon enough the two players aren't talking anymore and that can lead to all sorts of dissension on the team."

The off-ice inspiration could not work without on-ice performance, especially at times when the chips were down. Despite a career that had obvious peaks and valleys, 18 goals in 1961-62 and 1962-63, a mere 12 in 1966-67, Beliveau always seemed to rise to the occasion. His toughness and grace under fire became the Canadiens' toughness and grace under fire. When he was injured and not present on the team bench, the resultant void was a chasm.

His kind of leadership helped Montreal deprive two great teams, the Chicago Black Hawks of the 1960s and the Boston Bruins of the late '60s and early '70s, of their proper due. The Black Hawks, with such stars as Bobby and Dennis Hull, Glenn Hall, Stan Mikita and Pierre Pilote, should have won more Stanley Cups in the 1960s than they did. After breaking the Canadiens' string of five in the 1960–61 semi-finals, the Hawks beat New York to capture their first Stanley Cup since the Tommy Gorman days. It turned out to be their last.

First it was Punch Imlach's defensive Maple Leafs that stopped the Hawks in a six-game final in 1961-62 to launch a string of three straight Cups for Toronto. Three years later, the Toronto streak over, Montreal and Chicago went to a seventh game at the Forum to decide the title.

In most sports, the home advantage disappears when the championship hinges on one game. Montreal fans were well aware of this, and they knew that Glenn Hall was the type of goaltender who could turn back the Johnstown Flood for sixty minutes, even if he had the disconcerting habit of throwing up before every big game.

They need not have worried. Gros Bill put the puck into the net at the 14-second mark of the game, the earliest Cup-winning goal ever in Stanley Cup history. The Habs added another three tallies before the first period was over and smothered the Hawks under a suffocating checking blanket for the rest of the evening. It was delicious irony that Jean Beliveau was awarded the first-ever trophy given to the best playoff performer—the Conn Smythe award. During the presentation, Smythe was not laughing as he had that day twenty years before when Tommy Gorman came to visit Maple Leaf Gardens.

Six years later, the Big Bad Bruins of the Esposito-Orr era were well on their way to eliminating the Canadiens, having finished 24 points ahead of the Habs during the regular season. Boston won the first game of their best-of-seven quarterfinal 3-1 and was coasting 5-1 midway through the second period of the second game. Beantown's Leatherlung Brigade sat back happily enjoying the slaughter ... the game, and the series, were in the bag. No matter what Montreal did at the Forum, they would not be able to overcome the methodical Big Bad Bruins and their scoring machine.

So there were little more than a few murmurs in Boston Garden at 15:33 of the middle frame when Henri Richard stole the puck from Bobby Orr and beat Eddie Johnston to put the game within reach. A moribund Montreal offence began to shake off the cobwebs during the remaining four minutes of the middle frame but Johnston, stung by the Richard goal, was vigilant, stopping everything that came his way for the rest of the period.

Few Bostonians or Montrealers will ever forget what happened after intermission.

Beliveau had assisted on the game's opening goal by right winger Yvan Cournoyer in the first period before Boston roared back with five straight. At 2:17 of the third, referee Art Skov sent off Phil Esposito for cross-checking and the Beliveau-Cournoyer-John Ferguson line (finesse, speed and pure menace) went to work. With Cournoyer flitting all over the Boston zone like a water bug and Ferguson cruising the slot like a Panzer, the puck was worked around the points and in front of the net. Ferguson shot, the rebound came to Beliveau at the side and it was 5-3 Boston.

Still two goals behind, the Canadiens seemed to be surging while the Bruins sagged noticeably. On his line's very next shift, Beliveau struck again, converting passes from Cournoyer and Ferguson at 4:22 and the Boston Garden was deathly quiet. From high up in the galleries came a plaintive wail: "Come onnnnnnn, Brooooons!" The smell of impending doom, a tangible electrical scent, invaded the Garden.

At 8:34, Frank Mahovlich and Wayne Cashman traded high sticks and with the teams playing five aside, Jacques Lemaire pounced on an errant puck at the Boston blue-line and blistered a vicious drive just under the crossbar one second shy of the halfway mark.

Impending doom was replaced by a pall of inevitability. When the Beliveau-Cournoyer-Ferguson line skated onto the ice with five minutes remaining in regulation time, there was a buzz in the crowd. At the other end, a lanky rookie named Dryden had just stoned Esposito on a shot in the slot and a rebound. Espo sat on his bench looking haggard.

Jean Beliveau, four months shy of his fortieth birthday, should have been gasping for breath on his bench while the Young Turks fought it out in the trenches. Instead it was the younger players on the Bruins who had their heads down. With five minutes left he skated out for yet another shift. The teams lined up for the face-off, Beliveau looking intent, Cournoyer impatient and Ferguson homicidal. At 15:23, Number 4 slipped the puck to Number 22 for the game winner. Three minutes later, Frank Mahovlich added an insurance goal. Montreal 7, Boston 5. Series tied.

At 19:14, almost as an afterthought, Boston's "Young Turk", Derek Sanderson, slashed Beliveau and Gros Bill repaid the compliment. There was a tiny smile on his face when he skated to the penalty box for a well-earned rest with his thoroughly defeated, twenty-three year old tormentor. Jean finished the game with two goals and two assists and would add but three assists over the next five games as Montreal upset the Bruins in seven games, with two wins in Boston.

Frank Mahovlich won the playoff scoring title with 27 points that spring as the Canadiens went on to defeat Minnesota and Chicago to win the Cup. Beliveau's 22 points on 6 goals and 16 assists, and his inspirational leadership, were major contributions in his last playoff series.

That inspirational leadership was spotted early by Frank Selke and it was channelled toward off-ice efforts by both Selke and Sam Pollock. The master altar boy, with his early maturity, fierce dedication to the work ethic and almost saintly demeanour, was to be developed into a goodwill ambassador *extraordinaire* for the Canadiens, and by extension, for the National Hockey League.

As Beliveau was winding down his career, the world of hockey was changing its face. New needs had emerged with respect to marketing, organizational planning and public relations. No longer could an ex-All Star, who had put in fifteen or so years of stellar on-ice performance, assume a high-profile post in the front office or behind the bench without the appropriate human resource training, for himself and his employers.

Great stars like Gordie Howe and Bobby Orr suffered when they "moved up", not because they were not prepared for it, but because the organization was not prepared for their arrival. Where to place them? What to do with them? Often the team administration was at sea, and as Howe said of his short-lived stint in the Detroit front office, before he returned as a player: "They were content to keep me in the closet growing mushrooms, opening the door to throw in fertilizer once in a while."

It was the Maurice Richard syndrome all over again; take the aging star out of uniform and have him show up at every sports banquet in sight to sign autographs and hand out beer coasters. It was an insult to the intelligence of astute people like Richard, Howe and Orr and all three rebelled.

In Beliveau's case, there never was any thought of hiring an autograph machine to represent the Canadiens; his demeanour and his statesmanship precluded any thoughts of taking the low road. He had established early his awareness and understanding of organizational needs and had a highly developed sense of fair play, which made him capable of perceiving the core of most issues.

Jean Beliveau's major attraction for the Forum front office was that even while he wore the hockey uniform, he thought like a member of the corporate entity on the second floor. He acted purposefully and confidently in both uncertain and structured situations. He was a most effective communicator, expressing himself unequivocably and directly in all situations, yet presenting himself as a most responsive listener, open at all times to the attitudes, needs and ideas of others.

Many of his teammates have said often that Beliveau left very little doubt in their minds what he thought or how he felt about important issues. If you asked Jean Beliveau for a favour, if you wanted him to integrate information from diverse sources in order to provide a coherent picture, or if you asked him to try and analyze or anticipate long-range consequences and to evaluate existing talent, you received a comprehensive response that combined insight and simplicity.

These qualities made Beliveau not only a great captain of a storied hockey team, but also a valued corporate executive. The movement from young newcomer to valued veteran to team leader took about eight years.

"I was especially fortunate in that I joined the team at a time when train travel was still the big thing. We spent a lot of time together on trains, in hotel lobbies and in restaurants and this helped promote team unity. There was always something to talk about and something to share."

In Beliveau's case, these conversations were conducted quietly, out of the limelight. More often than not, they were short affairs. Sometimes, however, Jean might spend an hour or two trying to convince a rookie to do certain things that would raise his contribution to the team.

"I remember an evening during my seventh or eighth year. Butch Bouchard was gone, so was Elmer Lach, and the team was really changing. Henri Richard arrived in 1955 and new young players seemed to be joining us at a rate of one a year. It suddenly came to me that I had a new set of responsibilities. I was one of the veterans being counted upon to head the team. A year later I was elected captain and I was surprised a bit, because I had not even been an alternate. Now I had a bigger commitment to the team." Yet another of Beliveau's special talents was an ability to read his teammates.

"Everybody is tense before a game . . . hockey players are up-and-down people. I believe that even the most confident of us feel nervous inside. People used to say that Doug Harvey wouldn't get excited if lightning struck right beside him, but I'm not sure about that. Some players liked to give you an impression of composure while they were churning inside."

Craig Ramsay, a coach with Buffalo Sabres and a premier defensive forward in the NHL for fourteen years, agreed with Beliveau's sentiments.

"I wish that as a hockey player I could have experienced something other than the constant highs and lows, bouncing back and forth from pillar to post. Whatever happened to plain old mediocrity?"

In the cases of Beliveau and the Canadiens, mediocrity was anathema; the pressure was always intense and expectations were always overwhelming. The latter were shared, not only by management, coach and players, but also by the fans in Montreal who bought the tickets to watch Jean Beliveau perform. The opposition, of course, did everything they could to ensure that the performance was less than brilliant.

"I played against Dave Keon for years, so he must have been a good match for my particular style. But we all did that, didn't we? While someone was trying to impede my performance, I was doing the same to them. I played against Frank Mahovlich for years, especially when he was with Toronto, and I had my own book on him. The trick was to check him in his own end, whenever possible, because once he really got moving, he could build a real head of steam." His ability to understand the true nature of competition, to elevate it to a higher plane than simple war-on-ice, made Beliveau a better player and a classic leader.

In the end, Jean managed his non-playing career just as he had his playing years. In 1969, a year before he was to retire, he incorporated himself to take advantage of the many non-hockey opportunities which had come his way. At the end of the 1969-70 season, Beliveau visited with Sam Pollock. He had scored 19 goals and added 30 assists for 49 points, his worst season in years. The captain in him noted the lesser contribution, analyzed it, and sought to implement a solution.

"It's time to retire. I'd like to call it quits now and move on with my career."

The Canadiens were in transition. A solid nucleus of veterans, among them Ferguson, Terry Harper, Jacques Laperriere and Yvan Cournoyer were paired with a plethora of raw rookies and the team chemistry left a lot to be desired. As well, Sam Pollock had assembled a formidable collection of young professionals who would become the Montreal Voyageurs that fall. Pollock asked a favour.

"Please stay another year. We have a number of good young players on the team and we're in transition. I want you around for the kids—we need somebody in the older crowd who is able to relate to them and whom they will trust. I'm not worried about your point production, you'll get your share." Pollock was prophetic—Beliveau turned in 25 goals and 51 assists for 76 points in his last regular season and led the generation gap Canadiens to yet another championship. Then came the playoff success and Beliveau's tenth Stanley Cup.

The extra year paved the way for a milestone, Beliveau's 500th career goal. As usual, the great event was accomplished with that special Beliveau touch.

Going into the February 11 game with Minnesota North Stars, Beliveau had 15 goals for the season, and 497 for his regular-season career. At 5:55 of the first period, scant seconds after John Ferguson had returned from serving a minor penalty, Gros Bill teamed up with the "Twin Beanpoles," Terry Harper and Jacques Laperriere, to give Montreal a 1-0 lead. It was opportunism at its best, Beliveau racing onto the ice as the extra attacker during a delayed penalty.

Two shifts later, at 8:39, Beliveau beat Minnesota's Gilles Gilbert on deke, stealing the puck at the faceoff circle and walking in unmolested. The crowd went wild. With 51 minutes left in the game, Beliveau had a tremendous opportunity to score goal 500 and a hat trick at the same time! The crowd smelled an opportunity to witness history, as Beliveau would be joining exalted company in the NHL 500 Club; the Rocket, Gordie Howe and Bobby Hull.

Beliveau skated through four more shifts that period with few opportunities in the opposition zone. The second period was six and a half minutes old when Frank Mahovlich picked up the puck near his own blueline and glided over the Minnesota line. There he dropped a pass to the hard-charging Phil Roberto (replacing an injured Yvan Cournoyer) who veered off toward the right wing and left the puck at the top of the faceoff circle, taking a defenceman with him. Coming up behind Roberto, Beliveau had a clear path to the goal. He skated in on Gilbert and tucked the puck behind the goalie on a backhand. Mahovlich was on the lip of the crease and the puck came tantalizingly close to his stick. Would it go wide? Could he afford not to tip it in in a 2-1 hockey game?

Big M had assisted on Gordie Howe's 700th goal in Detroit and recognized history when it stared him in the face. He pulled his stick away from the path of the puck, it nicked the inside of the goalpost and lodged inside the cage. Number 500 for Number 4! The 16,158 fans did not stop cheering for five minutes.

Six weeks later, Rollie Hebert, Punch Imlach and Toe Blake stood at centre ice and joined in a special tribute to *le Capitaine*, who was joined by his parents, Mrs. Beliveau and fourteen year old daughter Hélène in gracefully accepting the accolades.

The club held the tribute night for their superstar, but only after they met his conditions.

"Jean refused to allow us to give him anything like a car or a cheque," said Sam Pollock. "So the Jean Beliveau Foundation was established and he was able to donate $155,000 to the start-up fund on that night." The Canadiens' sense of occasion paid off yet again in a 5-3 win over Philadelphia the same night. The only low point came when Beliveau returned home to find that burglars had stolen some jewellery and other valuables.

Thus Beliveau's extra season also allowed the Canadiens to close off his career the same way it had begun, with class. The year gave them time to prepare for his departure and their transition, just as both had prepared eighteen years ago for his playing career.

His personal preparations for re-entry into the off-ice working world were totally unnecessary. While Jean Beliveau played hockey for the Canadiens, he had also worked full-time for Molson's brewery, even during the season.

"We used to practice at ten o'clock and it would be over by noon. Whenever we were in Montreal, I would go to the brewery, have lunch with the employees in the cafeteria, and go to work. I had a small office there and one winter I would specialize, working and reading all the material they had on marketing. The next winter I might study production and another winter, transportation. By the end of my hockey career, I also had eighteen years at Molson."

Maurice Richard suffered when the time came for transition. For Jean Beliveau there was no transition.

"I think the only transition there would be was that I would not be going downstairs to put on the sweater. I just started to add new things to the job, mainly because there were no more ten o'clock practices and road trips in the way."

When it came time to retire, Jean left gracefully, with the applause of his peers ringing in his ears. On June 9, 1971, the day before the Canadiens drafted Guy Lafleur, Jean Beliveau delivered an emotional retirement speech to a standing-room-only crowd of hockey people and reporters in the Grand Ballroom of the Queen Elizabeth Hotel.

The Stanley Cup was home and it was time to quit, said the thirty-nine year old veteran, flanked by Sam Pollock and Canadiens' president J. David Molson. The club president then took the podium.

"It gives me a great deal of pleasure to announce that Jean Beliveau has accepted an executive position with the club. Effective immediately, he will be the new vice-president and director of corporate relations. In addition to being an executive officer of the club, he will be responsible for the development of corporate relations with particular emphasis directed towards the press, radio and television media. In effect, he will become the official spokesman of the *Club de Hockey Canadien*."

Molson's announcement was about ten years late. Beliveau had been the club's official spokesman in all but name for a decade already.

Two summers later, someone in Quebec City had a better idea. The World Hockey Association's Nordiques were desperate for recognition. They played in a hugely inferior league in a small city far from the beaten paths of North America's media outlets. Jean Beliveau would give them instant respectability, if only he could return to the ice. The offer was in the neighbourhood of one million dollars. Quebec and the Colisée wanted Gros Bill back and they were willing to pay.

Jean deliberated for well over a week, knowing full well in his heart that he loved his front office job, and that his sixteen year old daughter now enjoyed the presence, albeit belated, of a full-time father.

"I knew I was happy, but a million dollars is not something that goes out of your mind very easily. They wanted me to play because they needed me on the ice to sell tickets. I kept saying no to myself and the dollar signs kept popping up. Finally, I said no for sure and told them that."

On an early August afternoon in 1985, Jean Beliveau sits in his comfortable office and reminisces about his career. He is making plans for a long trip; he has been selected as Honorary Captain of the Canadian team at the Maccabiah Games in Israel and leaves two days hence. A week ago, he eulogized Frank Selke at the latter's funeral.

It turns out that some 6,000 miles away from the Forum, the Beliveau magic still dazzles. Almost fifteen years retired, Gros Bill is the biggest attraction in the camp of the Canadian contingent and the willing target of a large number of autograph hounds in Tel Aviv. He is surrounded not only by young members of the Canadian delegation, many too young to remember how he played, but also by many Israelis who were born and raised in Montreal a generation ago and who go home for a few, brief moments with Gros Bill.

# 7

## The Fabulous Fifties

Camil DesRoches, who has been with the Montreal Canadiens in both official and semi-official capacities since 1938, becomes animated when the subject turns to the Fabulous Fifties and the real Flying Frenchmen.

"We have had many great teams in Montreal but I think none of them comes close to the 1959-60 team," he declares with the conviction of one who has wrestled long and hard with the question.

A diminutive man with a ready smile, DesRoches is very protective of his boys. You don't get word one from him without a detailed explanation of what, exactly, this book will be about. If others in the Canadiens' hierarchy might be lambasted for their shortsightedness, not so DesRoches. He has been around the organization for forty-eight years and has seen all sorts of bosses come and go. Moreover, the young men staring ahead confidently in the hockey photos that span generations are not just legends of the sport; they are his friends. Once convinced of your *bona fides*, however, he becomes a veritable fount of knowledge.

Camil's office may be a lot smaller than most on the Rue Lambert Closse side of the Forum but it makes up for that in the memorabilia it contains. All four walls are covered with meticulously cared-for pictures of the greats and near-greats. The conversation gets around to the Big Question: which edition was the best?

Camil gets up from his chair and walks around his desk to the wall facing it. There, just to the left of his office door, the last thing he sees every night when he turns off his office light is a vivid red, white and blue photograph of the Canadiens. Every office on the second floor at the Forum has such a picture, so one doesn't bother to look closely anymore. Camil makes you look and then you realize that the picture coming into focus isn't the standard photo of the current edition team—in fact, many members of the current team were not even born when this picture was taken.

"You want to know what made the five Stanley Cups so special?" He jabs a finger at the players on the 1959-60 team as he moves up and down the rows.

"Junior Langlois, Marcel Bonin, Phil Goyette, Henri, Jean Beliveau, Dickie Moore, Donnie Marshall, André Pronovost, Claude Provost, Jean-Guy Talbot, Boom Boom, Doug Harvey, the Rocket, Jacques Plante, Charlie Hodge . . . they were all Montreal boys."

Well not exactly, one interjects, Plante was born in Mont Carmel and grew up in Shawinigan, Pronovost in Shawinigan Falls, Langlois in Magog . . .

"Makes no difference. Once a Quebec boy found himself in Montreal, he was a Montrealer. These guys all made their homes here. There was no question of going home for the summer when the season was over. They were proud to live here. They were proud of what they meant to the community and they got involved. When it came time to play hockey, they had more at stake than players on a lot of the other teams."

The team of the '50s was Frank Selke's through and through and showed how well his minor league sponsorships were progressing. Practically shut out of Ontario, the Canadiens went to the talent-rich Prairies. The Montreal boys smiling at the photographer in Camil DesRoches' picture had teammates like Ab McDonald and Tom Johnson from Winnipeg; Scepter, Saskatchewan's favourite son, Bert Olmstead, and Bill Hicke and Bob Turner of Regina. The only Ontarian, Ralph Backstrom of Kirkland Lake, was swept away from the clutches of the Toronto Maple Leafs and the Boston Bruins when he was sixteen, and played four years of junior hockey in Montreal.

The combination of what the sportswriters of the day called "Gallic flair" and "Prairie hardnose" was impossible to beat, as the other five teams discovered during that era. The best part was that the Prairie boys had some of the flair and the native-bred Montrealers loved the hard-nose part of the game too.

However, by no stretch of the imagination were Montreal Canadiens alone atop the league in the 1950s.

The team that Tommy Gorman put together won the Stanley Cup in 1943-44 and 1945-46 but would not skate off with Sir Stanley's silverware for another seven years. They were in a perennial dogfight with Toronto and Detroit. The statistic that backs up this claim is startling: after the Boston Bruins won the Cup in 1940-41, it became the exclusive preserve of the Canadiens, Maple Leafs and Red Wings until 1960-61, when Chicago would triumph. And Montreal and Toronto would share it for the next eight years after that!

The team that Tommy Gorman had built was a sound one and, with a minimum of tinkering by Frank Selke in the late 1940s to replace such stalwarts as Toe Blake and Kenny Reardon, battled hard at the top of the league with the Detroit Red Wings and the Toronto Maple Leafs. Detroit won an unprecedented and unequalled seven straight Prince of Wales Trophies for the regular season championship between 1948-49 and 1954-55, a tribute to the superb craftsmanship of Jolly Jack Adams and the talents of Howe, Abel, Lindsay, Kelly, Reibel and Sawchuk. Detroit's winning margin was substantial in six of those years; the closest runner-up lagged six points behind (Toronto 101-95) in 1950-51.

However, in that same seven-year period, the Red Wings would win only (!) four Cups, losing two to Toronto and one to Montreal. Chances are they would not have won a fourth had it not been for Clarence Campbell's largesse in suspending Maurice Richard for the playoffs. As it stands, the 1954-55 Stanley Cup should have been renamed the Clarence Campbell Bowl and should forever contain an asterisk in the record books—"donated to Detroit". Campbell's draconian decision against Richard—or to place it in another context, his overly generous award to the rest of the league—had three main repercussions: Detroit was able to catch and pass the Rocketless Canadiens on the last weekend of the season for the Prince of Wales championship and home-ice advantage in the playoffs; the Rocket lost his only chance at ever winning the league scoring championship; and Detroit was taken to a seventh game (in Detroit, of course, thanks to number one) by the Rocketless Canadiens before the Red Wings triumphed.

Has an off-ice decision by a league president or commissioner ever affected so many outcomes in any major sport, before or since? Is it some kind of ironic justice that Detroit has never won another Cup?

The sad part is that the Red Wings were innocent of any wrongdoing, apart from some normal lobbying by Jack Adams at the league executive level in the wake of the Richard-Laycoe incident in Boston. Yet if any team suffers in the historical context it is Detroit because, to this day, even the Red Wings players will never know if they could have won that year had the Rocket faced off against them.

Detroit won seven straight league championships between 1948-49 and 1954-55 but during the same period Montreal appeared in five consecutive Stanley Cup finals (they would go on to make it ten straight, a record which will never be broken in a four-division set-up). After losing the 1950-51 Stanley Cup final to Toronto on Bill Barilko's overtime goal in the fifth game, Montreal deservedly fell, in four games, to a great 1951-52 Wings team which had finished 22 points ahead of them during the regular season. A year later, however, Sid Abel was in Chicago and third-place Boston bumped off the Red Wings in six tough games before succumbing to the Canadiens in five games. Detroit would save some face with Cups in the subsequent two seasons, both times in seven games. Then Montreal would take over.

The 1952-53 team was a transitional squad, half Gorman, half Selke. Gerry McNeil was the regular goalie and his understudy was Jacques Plante. Today's hockey fan might marvel at the imagined feats of such a stellar netminding duo, comparing them with today's netminders, who tend to share the load 50-50, or at worst, 70-30. That was not how it worked back then, Plante reminded us.

"Gerry was the goalie, I was in Buffalo. Each team played seventy games back then and the starting goalie was expected to go all seventy if he could. Few teams carried two goalies. The other guy would come up only if there was a major injury and the starter could not go on."

Plante played three games that season, allowing four goals for a 1.33 goals-against average. Still, he wasn't going to dislodge McNeil, the Quebec City native, who allowed 140 goals in the other 66 games, posting 10 shutouts and a 2.12 average. The Second Team All-Star added another two whitewashes in eight playoff games before he was injured, and Plante registered one shutout himself in the other four games.

Plante's statistics belied his emotional state of mind during the semi-final series against a very determined Chicago team. He was pure rookie.

"I was playing in Buffalo when they called me up during the season to replace Gerry McNeil who had been hurt. Gerry got hurt again in the playoffs. The team was behind 3-2 in games and we were playing in Chicago, of all places, with the loudest crowd in the league. We were at the LaSalle Hotel and the team was just about to leave for the rink when I came downstairs. Dick Irvin called me over and says: 'Jacques, you're playing tonight. You're going to get a shutout.' I started to shake so hard that I could hardly walk to the rink. I wasn't prepared for this kind of pressure."

As Plante dressed for the game, he ran into an unexpected snag: he was literally shaking so hard that he couldn't tie his skate laces. The sight must have been a touch disconcerting to his teammates, who were getting ready in a dressing room that was quieter than a Roman Catholic church during Good Friday services. Rocket Richard walked over to the goalie and sat down quietly beside him. Jacques had no idea what to expect, but he had been around the team long enough to know that Maurice didn't believe in long speeches.

"Don't worry about it," Rocket said softly. "There isn't a guy in this room who isn't shaking inside just like you. You'll feel better once we're on the ice."

Three minutes into the game, Pete Babando skated in alone and put the rookie goalie on his bum with a nifty deke. Plante stunned the Chicago forward and the crowd with a desperate lunge, got his skate on the puck and made the save. Some nineteen years later, another rookie goaltender named Dryden would turn a series around with a similar larceny off a winger named Pappin in the same building.

"After that save, the pressure was gone. We won 3-0 and went home to Montreal, where we won the series final 6-1. I finished the series against Chicago and played the first two games against Boston. We won the first and lost the second and Gerry McNeil returned and won the last three games for us."

Jake the Shake would become Jake the Snake, a Hall of Fame netminder. Yet Plante, the epitome of the *bleu, blanc, rouge* goalie, almost ended up playing for the hated Red Wings.

"I grew up in Shawinigan with Marcel Pronovost. We were close friends and played a lot of hockey together. I almost ended up going to Detroit with him. What happened was, a Detroit scout from Quebec City came to Shawinigan to look at four players, Marcel, the Wilson brothers, Johnny and Larry, and me. I wasn't there that night so he signed up the other three and went back home. It was lucky for me that I didn't sign with them. Their regular goalie was Harry Lumley and they had young guys like Terry Sawchuk and Glenn Hall in the system at the time and I might never have gotten a chance to play. I would have disappeared somewhere, especially in Ontario where they had their farm clubs and I didn't speak a word of English. I would have been lost. Going to Montreal, I think, was the best thing that could have happened to me."

Plante would replace McNeil over a three-season period, taking over for good in 1954-55. Other players were also moving in the transition from the team of the '40s to that of the '50s.

The 1952-53 Cup team's defence was anchored by veterans like team captain Emile "Butch" Bouchard, and Doug Harvey. They were ably seconded by young rear guards Tom Johnson and Dollard St. Laurent, who became regulars in 1950-51 and 1951-52 respectively.

Up front were oldtimers such as Elmer Lach, the Rocket, Billy Reay, Kenny Mosdell and Floyd Curry and some of the kids, Bernie Geoffrion, Dickie Moore and Bert Olmstead.

Centre was a position that desperately needed reinforcement. Reay retired after the Stanley Cup win and Lach played one more injury-plagued season, in 1953-54. They were adequately replaced, however, when Jean Beliveau finally ended the suspense and signed for the new season, and Henri Richard joined the team, in 1955-56. By then, the Selke Machine was in high gear and the steady stream of young talent from Quebec, especially, and the West, became a flood.

A quick chart paints the clearest picture of the Selke airlift. Depicted below are the years the players indicated first came up to Montreal. Many of them would have several trips to the minors before they stuck with the big team.

These were the first crops of a farm meticulously seeded and cultivated by Selke, Reardon and Pollock.

| Year | Player | Position |
|---|---|---|
| 1950-51 | Bernard Geoffrion | Right wing |
| | Tom Johnson | Defence |
| | Dollard St. Laurent | Defence |
| | Bert Olmstead | Left wing** |
| | Paul Masnick | Centre |
| | Paul Meger | Left wing |
| | Jim McPherson | Defence |

| | | |
|---|---|---|
| 1951-52 | Dick Gamble | Left wing |
| | Dickie Moore | Left wing |
| | John McCormack | Centre |
| 1952-53 | Jacques Plante | Goalie |
| 1953-54 | Jean Beliveau | Centre |
| 1954-55 | Charlie Hodge | Goalie |
| | Don Marshall | Left wing |
| | Jackie LeClair | Centre |
| 1955-56 | Henri Richard | Centre |
| | Jean-Guy Talbot | Defence |
| | Claude Provost | Right wing |
| | Bob Turner | Defence |
| 1956-57 | André Pronovost | Left wing |
| | Phil Goyette | Centre |
| 1957-58 | Marcel Bonin | Left wing** |
| | Albert Langlois | Defence |
| 1958-59 | Ab McDonald | Left wing |
| | Ralph Backstrom | Centre |
| 1959-60 | Bill Hicke | Right wing |
| | Jean-Claude Tremblay | Defence |

These players were the nucleus of the Canadiens' reconstruction. The asterisks beside Bert Olmstead and Marcel Bonin indicate that these two valuable wingers were obtained in transactions: Olmstead was traded to Montreal from Chicago; Bonin, who started his NHL career with Detroit, was drafted from Boston.

The others came up through the Selke system of Quebec flash and Prairie brawn.

The majority of the superstars, Johnson, Harvey, Beliveau, Geoffrion, Moore and Henri Richard, were part of successive Quebec junior league bumper crops that were harvested in the first half of the decade.

After the two Detroit disappointments of 1953-54 and 1954-55, the team that came together for the 1955-56 training camp knew that something was going to shake loose.

"We were just too good to hold down for too long," says Doug Harvey. "Toronto and Detroit had made changes but they weren't enough. We had lost a lot of good veterans and Butch Bouchard had let us know it was going to be his last year. But we had all of these super young players and we were very hungry. On top of that, the Rocket was like a bomb ready to go off. He was jobbed out of the scoring title the year before and he was damned if he ever was going to lose anything again."

The catalyst was Richard, but not the one everybody was talking about. He proved to be a small centre, all of five feet seven inches tall and 160 pounds, named Joseph Henri Richard, fifteen years younger than Joseph Henri Maurice Richard, his big brother.

"He was up for almost a courtesy look-see," Selke recalled. "He had played very well with the Junior Canadiens the year before and was only nineteen. He was invited up with our young kids and we fully planned to ship him out for another year of junior."

One fine September day, Father Frank was busy with the paperwork when a Forum employee burst into his office.

"Mr. Selke, come quick! Richard has been knocked out!"

"Which one?"

"Both of them."

Maurice and Henri were on opposite sides in a full scrimmage when Rocket zigged and Pocket zagged. Splat.

Rocket came to in the trainer's room, to find Henri, who had grown up idolizing his older brother, anxiously peering down at him. Henri had been revived first and needed only a few stitches; his lesser height meant that he had come in under Maurice and caught him a beaut when their heads clashed.

"I think Maurice had about fifteen stitches from that one," says Henri.

Maurice shook his head three or four times to clear out the cobwebs and looked sternly at young Pocket, who still was holding smelling salts under his nose.

"Henri, you gotta watch out. You could get hurt out there."

Two weeks later, training camp was winding down and the kid who had come up for a courtesy call was still in camp. Toe Blake had no choice but to keep him up, since Henri wouldn't let anyone else have the puck. It came down to the last few cuts and Selke and Blake were at loggerheads.

"There's nothing wrong with sending him back for one more year of junior," said Selke, who liked things neat and tidy, with no surprises.

"The kid is ready now," Blake countered. The matter was left unresolved.

Montreal played their last exhibition game that year against Chicago and Henri dressed. He scored twice and assisted on three other goals. A few days later he was in Frank Selke's office with the Rocket acting as interpreter, because Henri understood very little English.

Maurice opened the discussion with a simple statement: "Henri wants to play with the Canadiens."

Selke had been through this discussion with Blake several times and he countered with his one-more-year-of-junior argument, but more for form's sake, since he had been swayed by the facts. Maurice translated and Selke watched the Pocket shake his head. No dice, in any language.

"How much money does he want?"

The Rocket translated. If an injury ended his hockey career, a job at the United Nations beckoned . . .

"The money doesn't matter, Mr. Selke. He just wants to play with the Canadiens." Maurice and Henri conferred some more before Rocket offered: "How about a $2,000 signing bonus and the rookie rate, $100 a game ($7,000)?"

Selke pulled out a contract and Henri signed it.

"We were going out the door when Mr. Selke told us to hold on a minute," Henri recalls. "He took the contract back, tore it up and increased my signing bonus to $5,000. Maurice said Mr. Selke told him that he didn't want me to think later that he took advantage of my young age. He didn't know that I was almost ready to pay him for playing with the Canadiens."

Two years later, Henri was the first team, all-star centre in the league. He would retire with 11 Stanley Cups, the most ever.

In a book which attempts to focus on the personality of the so-called Big Three French Superstars (the capitals are lifted directly from the newspaper headlines that routinely described them that way), we could not have done justice to the Canadiens if we had ignored the supporting cast.

Maurice Richard, Jean Beliveau and Guy Lafleur were not surrounded by mere "quality players". They, too, had superstars for teammates. Doug Harvey won the Norris Trophy as Best Defenceman in the league seven times between 1955 and 1962, his consecutive streak interrupted only by Tom Johnson in 1959.

Jean Beliveau, Dickie Moore and Boom Boom Geoffrion won five scoring championships among them, two each for Geoffrion and Moore. Moore's 96 points in 1958-59 was challenged in 1960-61 by Geoffrion, mostly on the strength of Boomer's 50 goals, and stood until Bobby Hull edged it out with 97 points in 1965-66.

Jacques Plante won five straight Vezina trophies as top netminder between 1956 and 1960, and won again in 1962. There were a lot of smiles on the faces of hockey veterans in 1969 when Plante, then aged forty, and Glenn Hall, also forty, of St. Louis Blues teamed up to win yet another.

From 1950 to 1960, there were 120 all-star berths available to the entire league. Montreal claimed one-third of them and these selections were divided among thirteen different Canadiens.

Montreal won six Cups, and came whisker close to three more in the 1952-61 period because players like Donnie Marshall, Phil Goyette, Ralph Backstrom, Bob Turner, André Pronovost, Dollard St. Laurent, Jean-Guy Talbot and Charlie Hodge backed up the superstars. And because the superstars had character.

"Henri Richard might have been the toughest competitor I played with," said Dickie Moore.

"Dickie Moore might have been the best of the lot," said Harry Sinden. "The guy won two scoring championships on one leg. His knees were so bashed up and yet he played a one hundred percent physical game."

"Doug Harvey was the best defenceman I ever saw because he could control a game like nobody I have ever seen," said Red Storey. "Bobby Orr could break open a game at any time and was an incredible player. But Harvey could take it over. If Montreal got a goal up on you and Harvey decided you weren't going to score, that was it. Go take your shower, the game is over."

It is common to hear similar testimonials for Plante, Beliveau, Geoffrion, the Rocket and Tom Johnson.

Camil DesRoches sits in his office. We are looking at the colour picture of the 1959-60 Canadiens. The authors are from a younger generation and favour the 1975-76 Canadiens with the Lafleur, Shutt, Mahovlich, Gainey and Lemaire front line, the Big Three on defence and Dryden in goal. But the fans agree with DesRoches.

A fan vote in 1984 picked for the all-time Montreal Canadiens team five members of the 1959-60 version: Plante, Harvey, the Rocket, Moore and Beliveau. The other player to crack the line-up was Larry Robinson. No second team was named, but imagine the battle that might have raged for the two spots on defence among Johnson, Butch Bouchard, Savard and Lapointe. Or how about the goalie vote among Dryden, McNeil and Durnan?

Would Steve Shutt, Guy Lafleur, Jacques Lemaire and Pete Mahovlich have been able to outscore Henri Richard, Boom Boom Geoffrion, Toe Blake and Elmer Lach as forwards on Team Two? Where would stars such as Yvan Cournoyer, Jacques Laperriere, Gump Worsley, Ralph Backstrom and Mats Naslund fit?

1950s *versus* 1970s. Which team was better?

No less an authority than Sam Pollock puts in a bid for a third contender, the 1960s edition, which but for an upset at the hands of a red-hot Terry Sawchuk and the Maple Leafs in 1967, would have won another five straight Cups between 1965 and 1969.

"Of all of the teams we have had, this is the one that everybody seems to forget," says Sam, a characteristic grimace of pain etched on his face.

"Beliveau, the Pocket, Backstrom, Ted Harris, Terry Harper, J.C. Tremblay, Gilles Tremblay, John Ferguson, Savard, Claude Larose, Dick Duff, Cournoyer, Gump Worsley and Rogie Vachon — that team was as strong as they came."

The longtime observers are split. Dick Irvin Jr., son of the former Canadiens' coach and the dean of current National Hockey League broadcasters, opts for the 1950s, because he says it doesn't take much stretching of the imagination to see how close the Canadiens came to an incredible eight Stanley Cups in a row in that era.

"They won in 1952-53 and the next year they went seven games against Detroit, only to lose it 2-1 on a Tony Leswick goal in overtime. And the year after, they went to seven games without the Rocket. You see how little would have had to change to make it eight in a row? And at the other end, they went to seven games against Chicago, had two overtime goals disallowed, and lost in the second overtime to end their streak in the 1960-61 semi-finals."

Montreal took the end of the streak with characteristic grace. Toe Blake hammered referee Dalton MacArthur.

The Black Hawks went on to win the Stanley Cup in 1960-61 and with good reason; five of the team members were Dollard St. Laurent, Ab McDonald, Eddie Litzenburger, Murray Balfour and Reg Fleming—all former Canadiens.

Hindsight is selective, the skeptic might argue. If Canadiens fans could change history with a deflection here, a judicious referee's ruling there, could not the same imaginary happenstance have befallen them with unfortunate results during their fabled five-year run?

Not quite. In those five years, Montreal was taken to a sixth game final only once (1957-58), winning three of the finals in five games and the other in four. That left little room for the fortuitous circumstance of a deflected puck or disallowed goal.

Last but not least, what might have happened if Jean Beliveau had joined the club a year or two before he did?

It is during this kind of delicious argument *en famille* that it dawns on you. This is what they mean by dynasty.

# 8

# Good Trader Sam

In 1978, the Queen Elizabeth Hotel hit upon a novel way of celebrating its twenty years in Montreal. The hotel began a "Great Montrealers" promotion, aimed at celebrating excellence in many fields of endeavour during those two decades. The promotion was an unequivocal success—the Great Montrealer dinner held each year since then has become a popular celebration of the city's best.

In the sports category, the first selection committee had a pantheon of local greats to pick from: Sam Etcheverry, Hal Patterson, George Dixon, Peter Dalla Riva and Terry Evanshen from the Canadian Football League and the Montreal Alouettes; Maurice and Henri Richard, Jean Beliveau, Guy Lafleur, Serge Savard, Larry Robinson, Guy Lapointe, Yvan Cournoyer and Jacques Lemaire from the Canadiens; Claude Raymond, Ron Piche and Bill Stoneman from the Expos and major league baseball, and a host of athletes in other professional and amateur sports. Everybody had a favourite candidate and it became obvious early on that the final choice would please few and upset many, many more.

Therefore, it was almost ironic that the man they selected was the physical antithesis of the jock: short and portly and resembling an armchair athlete more closely than a sports hero. He never played a minute at the Forum, Delormier Downs, Molson Stadium, Jarry Park, the Autostade or Olympic Stadium. But he was the best choice by far, and not one voice was raised in complaint.

The first Great Montrealer in sports was Sam Pollock, vice-president and general manager of the *Club de Hockey Canadien Inc.* Some call him the most enlightened sports franchise administrator of his time in North America. Trader Sam, the man who took over the reins of the organization from Frank Selke and improved on everything. The man who brought the Montreal Canadiens nine Stanley Cups in his fourteen-year tenure. Only one other manager in professional sports, the Boston Celtics' guru Red Auerbach, could boast of such an accomplishment, especially considering that Pollock's team won their tenth championship in fifteen years, the season after Trader Sam retired. Sam was gone but the 1978-79 Stanley Cup champions were very much Sam's boys.

"The man was quite simply the best there was," said Lou Nanne, Minnesota North Stars GM when Pollock announced he was stepping down in 1978 to pursue other business interests.

"I think that not only Montreal, but the league, has lost a tremendous person. He was the biggest leader in the game today. I know that when I was in the Players Association we were always talking about parity. I said at the time the easiest way to do it would be to loan Pollock to each team for a year. He was never wishy-washy. He was a great innovator and a leader. His ideas and examples are something we are going to emulate. He was so successful because he was just a few steps ahead of everyone else at all times."

Heady praise, and unanimous too. While many of Pollock's associates felt on occasion that he had taken them to the cleaners in a deal, the transaction still was a learning experience. Sam Pollock would always deliver value today for future considerations and you could not fault the man because his foresight was 20/20. It was a lesson that most of hockey's executives were slow to learn. But it was a lesson that, once absorbed, improved the talent in the front offices throughout the league. For among his other bequests, Sam Pollock left the National Hockey

League with a legacy of superb business sense. Gone
were the recycled old war horses in ill-fitting, three-piece
suits. Sitting in their seats at draft meetings and other
NHL sessions were professional hockey businessmen.
Those who learned the lesson best would profit soonest,
among them Bill Torrey of the New York Islanders, Cliff
Fletcher of the Calgary Flames and Lou Nanne.

"When I started, front office management might have
been 50 percent hockey acumen and 50 percent business
skills," Pollock says.

"By the 1970s, it was 25 percent and 75 percent. Now,
I think it is 15 percent hockey sense and 85 percent
business skills. If you want to be successful in this business, you have to follow sound business principles. That
means keeping expenses low and profits high. If you
follow good business principles, you will do your financial homework.

"That usually means you'll do your hockey homework
too and you'll have a competitive team. Winning is what
this is all about and the best way to ensure you'll win is to
do your homework, all the time. Because just like on the
ice, there is a competitor out there doing his homework
and waiting for you to make a mistake.

"If the guy running your organization has trouble
reading a balance sheet, the organization will be in trouble. Today's sports administrators have to be first class
businessmen and alert to all opportunities."

Pollock demonstrated his alertness and management
skills at a very young age, joining the Canadiens when he
was twenty-one. Under the tutelage of Frank Selke, he
would learn his hockey and management skills from the
ground up.

Sam was a product of the de-militarized zone between
Snowdon and Notre-Dame-de-Grace, west-end city dis-
tricts, but it was in the latter that he made his reputation.
Despite its French name, Notre-Dame-de-Grace was
mostly English. "En, Dee, Gee," as it is popularly known,
was a veritable cradle of athletic abilities, producing some
of the best talent in hockey, football and baseball anywhere in Quebec. As a young man, Sam Pollock was a

capable athlete, competing with distinction in the three major sports and playing the others in the shoulder seasons.

Nevertheless, he was much better at managing other players than at playing himself. Almost every street or park in NDG those days had a team in the three sports. If the players weren't competing in house leagues or school competitions, they would get together for semi-organized contests that were the closest thing to NDG all-star matches.

Sam Pollock, the son of a storekeeper who had parlayed shrewd business abilities into an impressive portfolio of real estate holdings, seemed to have a knack of bringing together the best talent. At seventeen, he was icing some of the best hockey teams and fielding some great baseball teams as well. He also managed to put together fastball exhibitions in which the star attractions were members of the Canadiens like Toe Blake and Bill Durnan. As a result, people in the upper echelons of sports management in Montreal began to take notice of "that kid in NDG."

After leaving high school, Pollock joined many of his peers in the work force in a popular job in Montreal at the time: junior clerk for a railway. In 1946, he was convenor for the Canadiens' minor league teams in the Montreal area. Essentially, Pollock's job was to keep track of the players in the Canadiens' system and to be alert for boundary infractions committed by his counterparts representing the other five NHL teams. He also signed on as manager of the Junior Canadiens.

He handled both positions with his characteristic panache and thoroughness and proved to be a good talent scout as well. Those qualities were the reasons why, at the ripe old age of twenty-one, Trader Sam became the youngest-ever coach of the Junior Canadiens.

"Sam Pollock got the job because he worked the hardest and was very shrewd," says Frank Selke.

"Financially, he was one of the smartest guys I ever knew. He asked for a chance to coach the Junior Canadiens and I let him. If anybody ever deserved it at that

age, Pollock did. And we built up a pretty good organization and won the Memorial Cup (junior), Allan Cup
(senior) and Stanley Cup."

When Selke received the blessing of Senator Raymond
to build a Montreal organization as he saw fit, he set
about the task immediately, and a young kid by the name
of Pollock got the opportunity of a lifetime to be in on the
action.

"We began to work hard at bringing all the pieces
together in the late 1940s," says Sam. "A lot of people
might not believe it today, knowing the history of the
club in the last three decades, but Montreal Canadiens
just were not organized until Frank Selke came over
from Toronto and began putting the system together. I
was supremely fortunate to be there at the time. I was
coaching the Junior Canadiens and handling the business
end, too.

"In those days, you just didn't have the front office
support staff you have today. A coach trained the players
like today's coach; but he also scouted them, negotiated
contracts with them, paid all the bills and made all the
arrangements when the team went on the road. The
coach represented the organization as far as the players
were concerned. It was the best possible education in
sports management you could ever get."

Pollock took full advantage of this opportunity, meld-
ing his strong business instincts with his talent for handling athletes and forming cohesive teams. Within three
years, the Junior Canadiens had won the first of two
Memorial Cups with Sam Pollock as coach. Dickie
Moore, a tough kid from Montreal's Park Extension, was
a member of that first Memorial Cup team in 1949-50
and later on would share in six Stanley Cups with the
parent Canadiens.

"What kind of man was Sam? I think in many ways he
was a very good copy of Frank Selke. But he had his own
ideas, I would think. Sam was very, very astute, very
intelligent."

However, Moore, an athlete whose play was fuelled on
emotion, refuses to buy the popular belief that Pollock

was a cool-headed, cold-hearted business robot who was fixated on balance sheets and bottom line considerations.

"I think that was part of Sam's act; he learned very early on that you don't get too close to a hockey player whom you might have to trade tomorrow," says Moore.

"So he often would stay in the background, away from the limelight, but I think that was because he was basically shy and a very private person. But he cared about his players and his teams and if he could help you out when you needed it, he would. I once saw Sam on a TV show saying that running a hockey team was like running a chicken farm. He said it was all business, forget emotion, it was all business. I just think that a lot of this was a front put on by a very astute man who saw the necessity of keeping his distance."

This is not to say that Sam could not get emotional. One of the images that remains with Guy Lafleur is that of a distraught Pollock agonizing in the dressing room during or after a bad game by the Canadiens.

"You always knew things were happening when Sam would get to nervously wringing his handkerchief in his hands," Lafleur laughs. "The veterans who knew better would be checking out his coat pockets to see if an airline ticket to someplace like Oakland was sticking out."

"Absolutely right," chimes in Steve Shutt. "Our joke was 'How do you spell Relief? A-I-R-C-A-N-A-D-A.' Over and out. It wasn't hard to stay motivated with Sam running the show, emotion or no emotion."

In 1951, Frank Selke had completed phase one of his rebuilding project. The Canadiens now had a network of amateur teams all over Quebec and across Canada and were building a solid professional farm system on both sides of the border. They also had the parent team, which had moved into the league's upper echelons and was constantly fighting Detroit Red Wings and Toronto Maple Leafs for the Stanley Cup. The second phase of the plan commenced.

That year, Selke began devoting most of his attention to the NHL team, and divided the Canadiens' elaborate

farm system between Pollock and Ken Reardon, the former Canadiens' all-star defenceman who was also son-
in-law of Senator Raymond. Pollock and Reardon got
right down to work, solidifying weak franchises, stocking
them with talent discovered by an increased scouting
staff. If there was a talented player anywhere in Canada,
he was either playing in the Canadiens organization or
being thoroughly analyzed by Canadiens talent scouts.
Rare was the new player who graduated to an NHL foe
without an updated file sitting in Forum headquarters.

"People have asked me many times how someone goes
about building the kind of tradition the Canadiens have
enjoyed for so long," Pollock says. "It is really quite
simple. You build a top-notch organization manned by
the best people at all levels. You get each man doing his
job on the ice and off the ice and all of a sudden, you're a
winner."

Believe it or not, that's the easy part. Where most
sports organizations go wrong is in letting up once they
have reached, or are near, the top of their sport.

"Once you're a winner, you keep improving on perfec-
tion. You keep making the trades and changes that will
strengthen the team, even if they aren't popular at the
time. You go about your business. That is where we
might have been different from other franchises. Once
we started winning, we worked even harder to continue
winning. Too many organizations relax at this point."

Frank Selke and Sam Pollock managed to instill traditional values into the organization. Many are preached
with near-evangelical zeal even today.

Did they set out to build tradition?

"You can never set out to build tradition," replies Pollock. "You start out to build a winner. If you can perpetu-
ate that winner, you might end up with tradition. But
tradition is a by-product. It can only be measured after
the fact. But the obvious fact, too, is that success breeds
tradition. In the case of the Canadiens, the oldest team in
professional hockey, they have been blessed through the
years with one or two superstars; they've always had the
Hall of Fame players. That and the fact that tradition will

build up when you're winning because when you are talking about a championship team, there is a lot more stability than you will have in a losing club. Winning clubs don't change players, coaches or management as often as losing clubs. That's where tradition is built up."

No matter how far a proud franchise might stray from its days of heady success, it will always have something to return to quickly if it begins to win again, Pollock believes.

We discuss the New York Yankees, and especially the teams of the Yankee Stadium drought from 1965-1974. For a decade, that team stumbled and lurched through dismal seasons and yet, when the Thurman Munsons, Lou Piniellas and Reggie Jacksons ignited the pyrotechnics of the late 1970s, it was as if the Yankees had never been away. A decade of bad memories had been wiped from the slate.

In the dismal season of 1983-84, the Canadiens mirrored the Yankee situation. After turning in the club's first sub-.500 season in forty-three years, the Canadiens lit up during the playoffs and it was as if the regular season had never happened.

"I can't say exactly why but I think I know why that is," says Pollock. "People will always recall the good memories and today's good times will reinforce that. Once you have had something, accomplished something or shared something, you can go back to it. It's an intangible but you can use it. Everybody who has ever been in the organization shares in it. That is why the Yankees, Celtics and Canadiens are so intimidating. They have history on their side."

After coaching the Junior Canadiens, and while he was managing one-half of the farm system, Pollock took charge of the Hull-Ottawa Canadiens, and built a strong team in the shadow of Canada's Parliament Buildings, winning two championships in the Eastern Professional Hockey League. He moved on to the Central Hockey League, and two more titles at Omaha, and sent a steady stream of quality players to Montreal.

He held that position at the end of the 1963-64 season when Frank Selke was asked to retire by Molson's, the owners of the Canadiens who had bought out Senator Raymond and his partners in 1957. Their policy was mandatory retirement at age seventy. Selke was seventy-two when he stepped down.

Suddenly, a very shy organization man who was one of the best-kept secrets of the hockey world found himself sitting at the biggest desk in the Forum, running the most celebrated franchise in professional ice hockey. Gone was The Old Man, who in seventeen years had moulded the Canadiens into a powerhouse while quietly cutting a major slice of the glory. The Canadiens were very definitely Selke's team.

In his place was a still quieter businessman who would spend his fourteen years at the helm shunning the limelight with even more vigour. Sam Pollock had arrived. The National Hockey League would never be the same again. (Just reading those two sentences would make Sam blush a deep Canadiens red and start to fidget.)

After the long years of Selke rule, the Canadiens were left with one of the top sports franchises in the world, although the team had been eliminated in the first round of playoffs four years straight. It would have been very easy for Selke's successor to coast, to bask in the reflected glory and play it safe. Pollock took a different route, turning up the throttle, and adding his own work ethic and prodigious skills to the task at hand. If the Canadiens had grown good under Selke, they were to become great under Pollock.

"Sammy Pollock took over an empire and I'd say he did a hell of a job when he took over," says Red Storey, former NHL referee and member of the Hockey Hall of Fame.

"Sam Pollock had a tremendous secret that put him far ahead of his opposition. He was very, very dedicated and worked eighteen and twenty hours a day while the other managers were working eight or ten. He not only worked harder, he was smarter, and a guy who can put those two together is going to be more successful, don't you think?"

More importantly for Storey, who had seen the best and worst of managers come and go in his decades in the game, Pollock's character was his strongest advantage. "I liked him a lot because he was down-to-earth, he had no delusions of grandeur. I think his biggest reward was being successful at what he was doing. He did not need anything else."

When this observation is repeated to the subject himself, the reaction is vintage Pollock. He squirms in his chair, his feet out straight from his body. He crosses them this way, then that. And then, naturally, he tries to deflect the question.

"Well, I never thought personality entered into it," he says, reddening visibly. "If I could accomplish the job, it wouldn't really matter if I chose to stay in the background or spent a lot of time in front of the media, would it? All that would matter would be that someone was taking care of business and that we were winning."

But someone who spent a lot of time grandstanding for the media or entertaining them and playing up to fragile egos in the press would be mismanaging valuable time better spent doing the club's work, right Sam? The response is a "you-got-me" wounded look.

"There could only be one boss, one person in charge of where the team and the organization were going to go," he declares. "Responding to the media, or playing to the media, or listening to the fans is the quickest way to start losing. The fans are great, but the thing they respect the most is a winner.

"The thing they know the least is managing a sports franchise. They have their favourites and strong emotional attachments with them. A sports administrator who wants to be successful can never think that way."

That kind of rationale and business pragmatism helped Pollock outwait Ken Dryden when the rangy goaltender-lawyer insisted on a renegotiated deal in mid-contract; and trade away popular favourites like Ralph Backstrom, Peter Mahovlich and Ted Harris when he felt he could make deals that would strengthen the franchise in the longer term.

Pollock served the Canadiens best in the decade of 1966-1975. Two major upheavals struck the microcosm of the National Hockey League during that period: the 1967 Expansion and the formation of the World Hockey Association five years later.

In the latter case, Pollock was one of the few NHL bosses who held firm against the onslaught of the WHA in the mid-1970s. While other teams panicked and began signing all-star and journeyman alike to guaranteed long-term deals, Pollock let people like Frank Mahovlich, Jean-Claude Tremblay, Marc Tardif and Rejean Houle go to the new league. No player, no matter what his past contribution, was better than the team itself in the organizational scheme of things. A player may be more valuable to his team than a teammate, but he could never be more valuable than the team. One policy covered every man who donned the red, white and blue, be he superstar or plumber.

Ken Dryden learned that lesson when he spent 1973-74 articling for a Toronto law firm at $135 a week. The other burgeoning superstars on the team—Guy Lafleur, Larry Robinson, Guy Lapointe, Serge Savard, Jacques Lemaire, Peter Mahovlich and Steve Shutt—went to school on Dryden. If Pollock was able to stand firm against the goalie, winner of the Calder (rookie) and Vezina (best goalie) trophies in his first full season, he could certainly stand firm against an individual forward or defenceman.

The policy was simple. The players would earn their superstardom. Then they would be paid accordingly.

"I felt that a player would have to prove his worth as an individual and team member before he could be considered a superstar," Pollock explains.

"Some were quite upset to hear my definition of superstar. I felt that a superstar was a player who had produced well-above-average performance for a period of time. This definition was given a severe test during the WHA war. Teams in that league were giving journeymen $100,000-plus a year, teams in our league were following suit, and I was trying to convince our players that their paydays would come if they produced for the best hockey team in the world."

Pollock's strategy worked. All of the great young players stayed with the team, with the notable exceptions of Tardif and Houle (although Houle would return later). In addition, Pollock saved a lot of money by refusing to enter the bidding wars. So respected was he by his players for the courage of his convictions that Dryden had to sound out a few intermediaries before he could approach Pollock about a possible return. "Will he talk to me?" Dryden asked.

Hurt by Dryden's defection, Pollock nonetheless was still the consummate businessman. Dryden was welcomed with open arms and, after a spotty performance in his first few months, would backstop Montreal to another four Stanley Cups.

Even today, many years after the fact, the Dryden episode rankles. The year that the goalie sat out was the first of two in which the Canadiens found themselves out of the Stanley Cup final. Two good young goalies, Wayne Thomas and Michel "Bunny" Laroque played well; but neither was a Dryden.

What also hurt at the time was that two former Canadiens, Tony Esposito and Rogatien Vachon, were dazzling the league with their acrobatics between the pipes.

And if there was a player on the team who would best understand where Sam Pollock was coming from, it had to be Dryden, the articulate and intelligent Cornell grad who was combining law studies at McGill University with his job as Montreal Canadiens' top goaltender.

"We had an honest difference of opinion," Pollock says wistfully.

"That's what it was," agrees Dryden, an individualist who guards his privacy as fiercely as Pollock. Both refuse to discuss the matter any further.

The Canadiens' GM was not upset with the reinforced bargaining position now held by the best players.

"The worst thing at the time wasn't what the WHA was paying top players," he says, "it was how the whole scale was thrown off. All of a sudden, career minor leaguers and unproven rookies were getting all sorts of money they didn't deserve. You can't pay a prospect

$50,000 a year when he's only worth $25,000. A lot of people in the league argued that $25,000 at a time when we were controlling million-dollar budgets wasn't all that much difference. I said, multiply it by ten and you're talking a quarter of a million dollars." Pollock's parsimony not only saved money, of course, it made money. It also made him the envy of his peers in both leagues, if peer means counterpart, and not equal.

Nevertheless, one must quickly dispel any impression that Pollock was a fiscal Simon Legree, keeping his slaves in line with starvation rations. He had to find the middle way between the no-responsibility, no-incentive fat contracts that turned some hockey players into non-producers, and those that represented modern-day indenture, not recognizing the realities of the current-day market. A stolid insistence on value paid for value received would have hurt the team eventually, no matter how efficient the Canadiens' farm system.

The answer was simple: bilateral contracts that would provide both security and incentive to hockey players. Guy Lafleur signed such a contract in 1975, a ten-year deal with a veritable staircase of raises that would maintain him as one of the best-paid athletes in the game, especially if he performed as one of the best. If, at any time, either party was dissatisfied with the arrangement, they could sit down and discuss the matter rationally and with the most amicable relations.

"I learned at this time that long-term contracts were useless unless they had a reasonable form of renegotiation built in," Pollock says. "You had to build in flexibility because you could predict that somewhere down the road, one side or the other was bound to be unhappy over something." This pragmatism was respected by his athletes and freed them to concentrate on their performances. Pollock established the rules early in the game and then lived by them.

If Pollock was not overly generous with his players' salaries, neither did he underpay them. When Lafleur was drafted in 1971, he immediately became the highest-paid rookie ever to play with Montreal. He received a

$55,000 signing bonus and $25,000 a year for the 1971-72 and 1972-73 seasons, for a total of $105,000. Built into the contract were bonus clauses worth between $1,000 and $5,000.

Did this special treatment upset team veterans?

"Not at all," Pollock replies. "They, better than anyone, knew the value system on the team and the emphasis placed on performance. Lafleur had been recompensed for his performance in the junior ranks and the fact that he was the first draft choice overall. His salary was not out of line with the club's salary structure and his play as a team member would be rewarded by bonuses." Instead of opening the bank vault and inviting his players in, Pollock hit on the novel strategy of opening the door and giving them a quick glimpse, nothing more, before closing it on their noses.

This rational approach to financial motivation seemed to escape most of his counterparts in the other NHL front offices who blithely signed twenty-two year olds to large long-term contracts with few incentives but to show up and put on the uniform and skates.

Silent Sam preferred that his charges make their money the old-fashioned way: by earning it. The bonus system was the great equalizer in Montreal, and many of the bonuses were team-oriented.

"The bonus system was in effect for about twenty years by the time we signed Lafleur and we had had a great deal of experience with it. However, I must point out that if you are discussing basic salary, that's another story. No young player, no matter what he has accomplished in junior hockey, commands a higher salary than that given to an established veteran and Guy Lafleur was no exception. He could not possibly expect to receive more basic salary than an established star."

This even-handed approach was respected by players and agents alike.

Nevertheless, even Pollock was able to come up with an imaginative stretching of his principles when Lafleur was tempted by the WHA. Nothing could be more natural than for the new Quebec franchise in the WHA to be interested in Lafleur, the young man who had starred in that city for almost six years before he moved on to the NHL.

When the Montreal Canadiens retreated to their Stanley Cup playoff hideaway in the Laurentians in April, 1973, the upstart Nordiques chose that moment to offer Lafleur a three-year contract at $90,000 a year and a $50,000 signing bonus. As heady as those numbers sounded, however, Lafleur was not impressed, because other WHA franchises had opened the vaults for people like Derek Sanderson, Bobby Hull and Gerry Cheevers. Lafleur and his agent asked for $200,000 a year, or about what Cheevers was getting from the Cleveland Crusaders.

The major stumbling block was whether or not the contract could be guaranteed, given the shaky financial status of several WHA franchises. After Lafleur's agent, Gerry Patterson, expressed his misgivings on this score, the Nordiques returned with their final offer; a $465,000 three-year package which included a $60,000 signing bonus and salary of $125,000, $135,000 and $145,000 over three years.

Now the ball was in Pollock's court and only some nifty footwork could get him into position to play it cleanly. Pollock knew that one player he could not afford to lose was Lafleur, not with superstardom beckoning to him. More importantly, he could not have Lafleur return to Quebec, where he might help the Nordiques to seriously challenge the Montreal Canadiens for the loyalty of hockey fans across the province. Last but not least, he did not need team harmony disrupted as the Habs entered the playoffs. It was a managerial mine field.

The pressure to have Lafleur return to Quebec was formidable. Guy had constantly filled the Colisée during his days with the Remparts and was mobbed by autograph seekers wherever he went in that city, especially after the tumultuous 1971 Memorial Cup series. *La métropole* had stolen Jean Beliveau in the 1950s and had repeated the dastardly deed two decades later with Beliveau's heir apparent. But now the WHA had given

Quebec the opportunity to repatriate Lafleur. The fans circulated petitions and the radio talk shows stoked the fires. Even some of Quebec City's financial movers and shakers like Marius Fortier and Roger Barre involved themselves in the plans.

That is what Pollock faced when he went to the Canadiens' Board of Directors.

"This is the one young man we cannot afford to lose," he told his bosses. "He will lead us to the Stanley Cup in a couple of years, and probably more than once. If he goes to the other league, he will help them establish credibility in Quebec, something they have in only a few places, with people like Bobby Hull. We'll lose in several ways."

The board of directors expressed their faith in Trader Sam's judgment and he returned to Gerry Patterson, Lafleur's agent. The deal was a ten-year, million dollar contract, plus signing and performance bonuses. Lafleur was free to renegotiate after three and six years, in case the NHL salary scale raced ahead of his contract. Last but not least, the Montreal Canadiens took out a one million dollar life insurance policy on Lafleur.

Patterson and Lafleur both agreed; it was a tremendous deal and would make Lafleur the Canadiens' first-ever millionaire. A week later, Sam Pollock and Irving Grundman were the proud hosts at a tasteful press conference and reception at the Forum press lounge where the new contract was announced.

How important a feat did Pollock accomplish in retaining Lafleur? A month later, the Canadiens won the Stanley Cup final in six games on a goal by the other right winger, Yvan Cournoyer, against Tony Esposito in a final game 6-4 victory. A month after that, Lafleur married the daughter of Roger Barre, one of the Quebec City negotiators.

A lovely reception was held afterward for family and a few close friends at Barre's home in suburban Ste. Foy and after the toasts had died down, Barre cornered Patterson.

"You know, Gerry, time alone will tell if you have made the right decision for Guy," he said in the wounded tone of a rejected suitor. Patterson couldn't resist. "Roger, Guy makes up his own mind. I had nothing to do with his decision to marry your daughter."

By the time the NHL was involved in total war with the WHA, the Canadiens' patriarch was well established and considered the major mover in the league's upper echelons.

Pollock had arrived on the scene in 1964, just as the National Hockey League was seeking to expand its horizons. Ever mindful of the fact that television was becoming the major medium for professional sport, and that the league would never have a chance of shaking the U.S. money tree without better geographical distribution of its teams, the league studied expansion. Some teams favoured measured expansion, two teams at a time every two years over the period of a decade or so.

Pollock led the group that recommended the league immediately double in size. He and his allies were up against league conservatives who felt that the shock of such a large-scale expansion would devastate the NHL and its calibre of play for a generation. They were blind to new possibilities, among them the fact that the United States and Europe would soon be providing quality hockey players to the NHL in record number, thereby swelling the talent pool. Of course, these would be the same people who would later complain about the "foreign" incursion into the sport.

"Their approach would not have worked," reflects Pollock. "We had to immediately guarantee geographical balance. We could never hope that the U.S. networks would even consider us if we had no teams out west, for example. We had to get into some of the top markets as soon as possible."

Pollock, and a few other visionaries, pushed hard for major expansion, recommending it as a good business decision. Others, many of them purists dedicated to the quality of the game, worried about diluting the talent base.

"Diluting the talent base, or watering down the product, as quite a few people were arguing, was not the priority expansion was," Pollock recalls. "We had to get into some important markets in the west and midwest. Chicago could use the competition from Minnesota and St. Louis. New York could use the competition from Pittsburgh and Philadelphia. And we needed teams in California so we could cover the United States from coast-to-coast. Those were important considerations if ever we were to penetrate the American TV market."

Also, many hockey players who had been labouring long in the American and Pacific Coast hockey leagues were quality players, and could easily step in and play for the new NHL franchises.

The league voted for a six-team expansion and the winning applicants were Philadelphia, St. Louis, Minneapolis-St. Paul, Pittsburgh, Los Angeles and Oakland-San Francisco.

The next step was to decide on parity. How could these teams be stocked with players and become competitive in the space of one summer? Very few of the Original Six wanted to lose their top players. Many of the team GMs were also leery of losing their protected players in the organization, those young kids who were a season away from maturing.

Most important was the fact that they really didn't want to give up protected territories, such as the Canadiens' protected area (Montreal) which provided so many quality players each year.

"But a lot of these things had to be done away with," says Pollock, "or this thing would have never worked. One solution was to bring in the universal draft of amateur players, where all twelve teams would have a shot at the best juniors and college players graduating each spring and the last team in the previous NHL season would draft first."

In recognition of the original teams' junior development system, which was soon to be dismantled to provide players for the six new franchises in the new draft system, Montreal was given the right to select two French Canadian players in lieu of their first two draft choices for a five-year period in the mid-sixties. However, because of the phasing-in period, 1969 was the only year in which this special provision helped. At that time, the Canadiens selected Rejean Houle and Marc Tardif. If this system had lasted one more year, they would have been able to draft Gilbert Perreault the following year.

"I don't know how many times sportswriters have written that we maintained our strength for years because of this so-called unfair advantage," Pollock said. "It just never happened that way."

Pollock also recommended that there be a moratorium of two to five years on trading draft choices, so that the clubs could mature with these players and, although they might suffer for two or three years, would find themselves with a solid nucleus five years down the road.

The other clubs turned that suggestion down. That bout of myopia would cost them dearly, as Pollock turned out to be the best manipulator of draft choices and veteran talent ever seen in the league. Going into the expanded NHL, Pollock was sitting atop the best organized and richest franchise. Top young and veteran talent sat in places like Houston, Cleveland, Springfield and other cities. New franchises, hoping to become competitive earlier than the opposition, turned to Pollock for help. He helped them, but they paid a price.

In 1969, Montreal drafted Rejean Houle and Marc Tardif 1-2 and selected another speedster, Bobby Sheehan of St. Catharines Black Hawks, number 32. A year later, Pollock went into high gear. Goalie Ray Martiniuk of Flin Flon Bombers was picked number 5 and forward Chuck Lefley of the Canadian National team was number 6. Lower down in the order came Rick Wilson of the University of North Dakota, a player who would toil on the Montreal defence for one season and then be despatched for more draft choices.

A year later, jackpot! Guy Lafleur was selected first overall but he was not alone. Number 7 was Chuck Arnason from Flin Flon and number 11 was a tall, classic skater from the Ottawa 67s named Murray Wilson. If that wasn't enough, Pollock took a flyer on a skinny defenceman with Kitchener Rangers in the number 20 spot and Larry Robinson became a Hab. Further down in the order came players like Greg Hubick, Mike Busniuk and Peter Sullivan, all of whom would toil in the organization for several years before moving on to other organizations for more draft picks.

The Lafleur pick, of course, was the most famous product of Pollock's wheeling and dealing, exchanging value today for future considerations. In 1970, Pollock sent forward Ernie Hicke and a draft choice to Oakland in exchange for their first-round pick in the 1971 draft.

Such was Pollock's reputation by then that everybody began reading ulterior motives into virtually every transaction he made. Late in the 1970 season, the story goes, Pollock awoke to the fact that he had been too generous to the Seals, when they threatened to overtake Los Angeles Kings. Sam needed a last-place finish by the Seals, so that the inverse order of the draft would give him first selection. He quickly despatched veteran centre Ralph Backstrom to the Kings and Backstrom did his job, helping that team improve and stay ahead of Oakland.

That story has been in print for fifteen years, and one version even claims that the Canadiens secured the re-transmission rights for the first Muhammad Ali-Joe Frazier fight for the Forum from Kings' owner Jack Kent Cooke.

Pollock has a one-word response: "Bunk!"

In 1972, Montreal used its accumulated picks to select Steve Shutt, Michel Larocque and Dave Gardner in the 4, 6 and 8 spots respectively. Defencemen John Van Boxmeer and Bill Nyrop were numbers 14 and 66.

And so it went. Whether or not the top choice panned out, and that wasn't always the case (for example, Cam Connor in 1974), Montreal usually found itself with an abundance of high choices and, even after the other teams started to refuse draft choice swaps, managed to find more good players in the lower echelons of the draft. In 1974, Montreal drafted Connor, Doug Risebrough, Rich Chartraw, Mario Tremblay, Gilles Lupien, Marty Howe, Jamie Hislop and Dave Lumley (number 199)—all players who would play in the NHL for a variety of teams. Three years later, it was Mark Napier, Normand Dupont, Rod Langway, Alain Côté, Gordie Roberts,

Robert Holland, Richard Sevigny, Mark Holden and Craig Laughlin.

Montreal could pick high; they could pick low. Two celebrated grinders, Canadien Chris Nilan and Boston's Louis Sleigher, were Montreal draft choices in 1978 and numbers 231 and 233 overall. Two star players, Mats Naslund and Guy Carbonneau, were selected numbers 37 and 44 in 1979, and St. Louis Blues goaltender Rick Wamsley was number 58 the same year. In 1980, the Doug Wickenheiser draft year, Montreal found Craig Ludwig at 61, Mike McPhee at 124 and Steve Penney at 166.

Trader Sam traded for draft position, and he delivered quality to the expansion teams. While experts of the day took Minnesota GM Wren Blair to task for draft choices he sent to Montreal, they will conveniently forget, of course, that players like Ted Harris, Gump Worsley, Danny Grant, Jude Drouin, Dave Balon, Andre Boudrias and Claude Larose were the backbone of the North Stars for many years, and, in fact, came close to upsetting Montreal in the 1971 Stanley Cup semi-final.

The St. Louis Blues received a raft of Canadiens farmhands and found themselves in the NHL final for three straight years between 1968 and 1970. Players like Noel Picard, Jimmy Roberts, Red Berenson, Ernie Wakely, Bill McCreary, Christian Bordeleau and Fran Huck became household names in Missouri.

"Restocking the team was important to us and we quickly realized that the draft was going to be the major area of importance," Pollock says.

"That meant we had to increase our scouting staff, to ensure that we saw all of the best players available and were able to assess them. That also meant that we would draft for specific players with specific talents."

A prime example was Bob Gainey, famed Canadiens captain and now coach of the Dallas Stars. He is acknowledged by many as the best defensive forward ever to play the game. As strange as it might sound, Montreal acquired Gainey by dropping down five positions in the draft.

"The Gainey draft developed out of a very large set of

circumstances," says Pollock. "I always tended to look at the overall or big picture, such as how many players we had, and how many players we were going to have to protect in a given year. Very seldom was my philosophy to win a championship first, especially at the expense of developing a good team, because if you worried about winning the championship in one particular year, you could make some very bad mistakes.

"Two things distinguished the 1973 draft year. First, it was probably the most competitive year between the NHL and the WHA. Second, there were more high-calibre players available that year, even though the first choice, Denis Potvin, was head and shoulders above everyone else. And there was absolutely no chance of trading up a spot for Potvin; Bill Torrey let everyone know that Potvin was a franchise player and would be an Islander for life."

Montreal traded the second pick to the Atlanta Flames for two first round picks, the number 5 pick that year and another first round pick another year. The Flames drafted Tom Lysiak, a flashy centreman whom *they* felt would be a franchise player. Not long afterward, the St. Louis Blues came calling and said they were desperate to draft a tall goaltender with Calgary Centennials named John Davidson. The Blues feared that the Boston Bruins, drafting sixth, would take Davidson, whom *they* felt was a franchise player. If Montreal would switch their number 5 choice for St. Louis's number 7, the Blues would kick in an extra first round choice at a later date.

It was a good gamble for Pollock. The Canadiens' scouting staff had the first five selections down pat and the club was gambling two new first-round picks that the Boston Bruins and Pittsburgh Penguins would not take Gainey. It worked. Boston opted for a former team-mate of Guy Lafleur, a flashy Quebec Remparts centre named André Savard, and Pittsburgh selected high-scoring winger Blaine Stoughton.

"So we got Gainey, a player who had a reputation of being a great defensive player and who had learned defence under the best, Roger Neilsen in Peterborough."

You could hear a pin drop at the Mount Royal Hotel

when the Canadiens announced their draft choice. "Bob *qui?* How many goals has he scored lately?" You had the feeling that Harry Brown would already be squawking downstairs in the Press Club.

When it came to draft futures, Montreal's so-called knowledgeable hockey fans went for the glitz, just like everyone else. Defensive forwards were anathema to them, despite the fact that people like Kenny Mosdell, Jim Roberts and Claude Provost had been protecting the rears of more gifted scorers for decades at the corner of Atwater and St. Catherine.

Pollock acknowledged the criticism, but made a strong point, one which was quietly enforced over the years. Whether the Canadiens fans were knowledgeable or not, and every cab driver in town knows he can run the Canadiens better than the current GM, Pollock ran the team.

"The fans represented the bottom line and our success would be measured in the numbers who came to the Forum and paid to see our hockey players," he said.

Nevertheless, Sam Pollock could not have the fans running the hockey team. Decisions would have to be taken with the best information at hand, and accepted. The same rule applied to the media mavens who were a step removed from their *confrères* in the cars with dome lights.

Other GMs had rabbit ears, and were a little too quick to acknowledge the howls and downturned thumbs. Sam would thoroughly plan his move, assess it and go ahead, fully expecting to be judged by history somewhere down the road. More than a dozen years later, the Gainey move clearly proved right.

"Just like in any other sport, your first-round picks are usually not defensive linemen and even if there isn't a terrific quarterback available, they usually tend to be great offensive players," says Pollock. "We were looking for a great defensive player." Ever the diplomat, Pollock returns their self-respect to Montreal cabbies and sports-writers. "Don't get me wrong, we were very conscious of our fans. But we ran the team."

After years of learning from Frank Selke, and helping

build up an organization whose tentacles reached into every corner of hockey-playing North America, Sam Pollock was the first hockey man to know when the time had come to get rid of expensive and cumbersome operations.

"We were as much a victim of the television age as was baseball and all of its minor leagues," he says.

"By the mid-60s it became apparent that most minor league franchises could not pay for themselves and the simple reason behind that was the fact that people in those cities could watch the National Hockey League for free on the TV sets instead of paying to see the American Hockey League or another league."

Free agency, television and the 1967 Expansion were the first steps, and the WHA was the last. Pollock quickly moved to cut away the excess in the organization. The pride of Frank Selke, the extensive system of professional feeder clubs, was outdated and no longer profitable. Sam the businessman had spoken.

It was a move that Frank Selke probably would have made himself. If there was a major difference between Selke and Pollock it was that Selke was a front-line producer, a farmer-businessman, while Pollock was the quintessential entrepreneur or middleman. Frank thought in terms of seeding, weeding and feeding (no rhyme intended) and taking the produce to market. Sam thought in terms of the deals that could be swung in the marketplace.

Each man was a visionary in his own era. Such leadership is at the heart of the Canadiens' tradition of success.

# 9

## The Surprising Sixties

*Blessed are those that nought expect,*
*For they shall not be disappointed.*

This quotation from John Walcot, Lord Mayor of London in the fifteenth century, may best summarize the credit and the curse of the Montreal Canadiens' Team of the Sixties.

"I really don't understand why everybody is so anxious to compare the Montreal Canadiens of the 1950s with the team of the late '70s. There was a team in the middle that might have been as good."

That is the opinion of Sam Pollock, general manager of the Montreal Canadiens from 1964 to 1978, the architect of two of the three Canadiens' powerhouses.

With respect to Lord Mayor Walcot, the credit to which we refer is for winning five Stanley Cups. Here we add our own asterisk: the Stanley Cups won by the 1960s team came in 1965, '66, '68, '69 and 1971. The championship won at Toronto, April 14, 1960 was won in the 1960s if you use the calendar as your only rule; the same qualification applies to the cup won in Chicago, May 18, 1971. Had it not been for unbelievable goaltending by Johnny Bower and the late Terry Sawchuk in the 1967 playoffs, the 1960s Canadiens would have duplicated the feat of five straight.

The 1960 Cup, the fifth in a row, most obviously belonged to the 1950s edition of the Canadiens. The 1971 championship was a glorious close to a chapter of the club's history that is unjustifiably ignored. As for the 1973 Cup, the best that can be said is that it was won by a team in full transition, two years after the team of the 1960s retired gracefully and two years before the team of the '70s began toying with any and all comers.

To help you understand our point of view, and explain why this chapter begins with a quotation from a Mayor of London who lived five-and-a-half centuries before the 1960s Canadiens skated at the Forum, it is necessary to return to the 1950s.

There was no real reason to believe that the Montreal Canadiens that won five straight Stanley Cups would stop there, as the Age of Camelot on the Potomac dawned. Up front, Jean Beliveau, Bernie Geoffrion and Dickie Moore were twenty-nine years old and other stalwarts like Henri Richard, Ralph Backstrom, Billy Hicke, Phil Goyette and Don Marshall were even younger.

On the blueline, Doug Harvey, Tom Johnson, Jean-Guy Talbot and Bob Turner anchored a stingy defence. They were, respectively, thirty-six, thirty-two, twenty-eight and twenty-six. Goalies Jacques Plante and Charlie Hodge were thirty-one and twenty-seven. As well, very capable rookies like the Tremblays, Gilles and Jean-Claude, and Bobby Rousseau, were being worked into the line-up slowly. The Canadiens also had legions of good young players scattered throughout North America, awaiting the call to the Forum.

Maurice Richard hung up his skates one day during September training camp (after scoring four goals in a morning scrimmage) but the team that had ravaged the league during the previous decade was basically intact. The Canadiens proved it by finishing first in the regular season with 92 points, the same total as the year before, and would better that mark with 98 the following season. In all respects, the team of the Fifties was still alive and thriving.

The derailment, as would be the case in the early 1980s, came in the playoffs.

"We still had a very competitive team," Frank Selke recalled, "and we made few changes in those two years because we had few to make. You do not go about disassembling a first-place team because of a playoff setback. The team was sound in 1960-61 and we had every right to expect a good result in the playoffs."

How sound were the Canadiens? Jean Beliveau and Bernie Geoffrion finished first and second in the scoring race, with Boom Boom scoring 50 goals, only the second time ever that feat had been accomplished. Dickie Moore and Henri Richard joined their two teammates in the top ten in scoring. Beliveau, Geoffrion and Harvey were on the first all-star team, Moore and the Pocket on the second.

In the playoffs they ran into a Chicago Black Hawks team that had been under construction for almost a decade. Jim Norris and Arthur Wirtz had spent a lot of money in the late 1950s to give Chicago a winner and they had received some significant help. The National Hockey League was well aware that a franchise in Chicago was a necessity, and they knew that the Black Hawks were being held back because they lacked the most important thing of all: the ability to play as a team.

After some success in the 1930s, the Black Hawks headed for the league's nether regions and took up permanent residence there. Between Stanley Cups (1938 and 1961) the Black Hawks finished last ten times and never higher than third. Emile Francis, a goalie with the 1950-51 team, remembers that quality players did not seem to last a long time in Chicago.

"We had a rookie left winger named Bert Olmstead with us that year and the word got out that the Canadiens wanted him. Before you knew it, Montreal, Detroit and the Black Hawks made a three-way deal and he was on his way to the Forum. It wasn't easy playing for Chicago back then; it was the place where teams unloaded excess baggage."

Bringing back the Black Hawks to respectability became an NHL reclamation project, not unlike the Marshall Plan that resurrected Europe in the post-War years. Players like Eddie Litzenberger, Ab McDonald, Dollard St. Laurent, Reggie Fleming, Murray Balfour and Bob Turner came over from Montreal and joined Toronto castoffs like Tod Sloan, Eric Nesterenko and Jim Thomson, former Red Wings Al Arbour and Ted Lindsay and longtime New York Rangers defensive stalwart Jack Evans. The latter four and Montreal's St. Laurent were despatched to Chicago by their respective teams as punishment for their abortive efforts to establish a players' association in 1957. When the 1960-61 season rolled around, however, they were no longer complaining.

There they joined the first crop of "original" Black Hawks, raised in the Chicago farm system, most of them in St. Catharines, Ontario: Bobby Hull, Pierre Pilote, Stan Mikita, Kenny Wharram and Chico Maki. Goalie Glenn Hall was acquired in a trade with Detroit and centreman Red Hay came out of college ranks.

That was the team that bumped off the Montreal Canadiens in successive semi-finals in 1961 and '62, winning the Stanley Cup the first year in a six-game series with Detroit then losing it to Toronto in the same number of games the following season.

The Canadiens were still a strong club, finishing in first with 98 points in 1962, 13 better than second-place Toronto who were 10 points in front of third-place Chicago.

"We handled Toronto all year but a combination of injuries and a very physical Chicago club did us in both years," Frank Selke recalled.

The first moves at disbanding the team of the 1950s came in the 1961 off-season when Doug Harvey was dealt to the New York Rangers, even though he had won a spot on the first all-star team and the Norris Trophy as the league's best defenceman. He felt it was his punishment for union activity of the same kind that had resulted in so many one-way tickets being issued to Chicago four years earlier.

"Of course it was that. If I hadn't won the Norris Trophy from '57 through '60 and if we hadn't been winning all of those championships, I would have been long gone. But Selke wasn't stupid; he knew if he traded me in 1957, they would have lynched him at the corner of Atwater and St. Catherine."

Harvey, Turner and St. Laurent were replaced by J.C. Tremblay, Jean Gauthier and Lou Fontinato, all capable defencemen. A year later, Jacques Plante was traded and Bernie Geoffrion, often injured, retired in 1964.

If the Montreal Canadiens had a major weakness in the early 1960s, it was size. Too many times, it seemed, bigger clubs were battering the small Canadiens forwards along the boards and the playoffs became a grind. Frank Selke, and later Sam Pollock, set about remedying that problem in a hurry.

In 1963 the airlift began. Three huge defencemen (especially for that time) joined the team: Jacques Laperriere, Terry Harper and Ted Harris. Bryan Watson, a fourth defenceman who occasionally played forward, also signed on. The Montreal Canadiens would be pushed around no more. Just to make sure, Frank Selke reached into the American Hockey League for a player everyone said would garner instant respect for his teammates.

Gilles Tremblay remembers the new policeman's arrival.

"He showed up in training camp with a reputation of a good hockey player and one who hadn't lost a fight in the AHL. A lot of teams wanted him and it wasn't hard to see why. In our first game in Boston, he got into a fight with Ted Green right off the opening faceoff, won the fight, and all of a sudden we had a lot more room to skate again."

John Ferguson had a mission. He was going to be the meanest son-of-a-bitch in the NHL and he would waste little time in delivering that message, in person, to the benches of the other five teams. Unlike many other players, he had chosen the Canadiens, and not vice versa.

"I was in the AHL with Cleveland and I made the all-star team in 1962. The New York Rangers had seriously scouted me and I had the chance to go to either the Boston Bruins or the Rangers but I had always been a

Canadiens fan. I told Jackie Gordon that I preferred to go
to Montreal and if I didn't make it there, I could always
make it in the other two cities."

As it was, Ferguson ended up in Montreal and his
fierce, fearsome grinding allowed the Canadiens to become the Flying Frenchmen again.

One thing that opponents of fighting in the NHL never
seem to understand, as is well evidenced by a 1985
campaign against hockey violence and so-called goons in
a major U.S. sports publication, is that it has been historically accepted as an integral part of the game. There is
no question that there is little room for brawling, which
is tedious, time-consuming and diminishes the game.
Former league president Clarence Campbell described
the place of fighting accurately, when interviewed on the
topic.

"They'll never take it out of the game because it is an
outlet, a safety valve, that allows players to get some
built-up tension out of the way and to continue on about
their business. If you tried to stop it, animosities would
grow and linger and they would eventually lead to some
very ugly stick incidents. I am convinced of that."

A large majority of players agrees with that statement. Several European players, Mats Naslund among
them, would smile quietly when questioned about the
big, bad NHL with all of its Rambos ready to let gloves
fly at a cross-eyed glance or any other such perceived
slight.

"Do you really think that there is no dirty work back
home? The Russians are the best in the world with their
sticks and skates and a kick in the back of the leg is more
dangerous than a punch on the nose. The strangest thing
is that more fuss is made about fighting here; back home
it is not much of a topic, maybe because the fans don't
really notice the stickwork."

Fighting has its historical place in the dynamics of the
hockey game. Few modern hockey fans are aware of the
sport's beginnings. Most expect perhaps that the game
just happened on some icy lake or river a century or so
ago and evolved from there. Nothing could be further

from the truth. Hockey began as a rough game and always has been.

A variety of stick and ball games were played on ice in northern England, Scotland, the Netherlands and North America in the nineteenth century. It is believed that the original version of ice hockey combined several of the European games, and was played for the first time in Canada, sometime in the early nineteenth century. The official history of the game is that variations of bandy (Russian) and shinty (later corrupted to shinny) were played by British soldiers in Halifax and Kingston around 1850 and hockey developed at the Lake Ontario garrison in the same period.

Says *The Canadian Encyclopedia*:

> In 1879 the first organized team, the McGill University Hockey Club, was formed, and with the advent of a basic set of rules the sport quickly spread across Canada . . .
>
> Early hockey was played in rudimentary conditions, mostly outdoors on patches of natural ice, with snowbanks for boards and wooden posts for goals. There were 9 players per side on the ice, and the puck could not be passed forward. The on-side rule and primitive face-off ("bully") were adapted from rugby. With speed and rough play the game had immediate attraction, and strong local rivalries developed.

Most of the sport's earliest stars were rugby players who were looking to stay in shape during the traditionally lazy winter months. Thus, the earliest version of ice hockey developed as rugby on ice. Contrary to popular belief, the rugby influence was not weaned early from the sport. The twenty-minute period surfaced in 1910 and the forward pass rule was softened in 1918 (the year the NHL was formed) to allow it in the neutral zone— between bluelines.

It was not until the 1930-31 season, the NHL's thirteenth, that the forward pass was allowed all over the ice. Players like Howie Morenz, Aurele Joliat, the Cleghorns, Frank Nighbor and the like played a game much closer to rugby than to modern hockey. Morenz was especially valuable because his speed allowed him to elude defencemen and either shoot directly on goal or leave drop passes or laterals for his wingers. He and other speedy forwards were not averse to "crashing" the opposition's defensive line, much like rugby ball carriers do, hoping to create an opening.

Defencemen, on the other hand, were free to practically tackle any fast forward aiming to advance the puck, also in the rugby manner, and most contact took place in the centre of the ice surface and not along the boards, as is the case today. All of that violent action in open ice, with its sticks, elbows, knees and skates, led to major league stickwork that would shock today's staid burghers, and some serious brawling that would occasionally spread into the spectator stands.

Accordingly, when John Ferguson, Ted Harris, Terry Harper, Jacques Laperriere and Bryan Watson showed up in 1963, everyone knew why they were there.

"We knew that we would have trouble winning until we could handle the rough going," said Gilles Tremblay.

"It was necessary to get players like these to let us play our game. On a hockey team with 18 to 20 players, there are role players. Guys like Yvan Cournoyer, Bobby Rousseau and myself were there for our speed on wing and ability to get scoring chances. Jean Beliveau, Henri Richard and Ralph Backstrom were there for their ability to set up scoring opportunities and Ted Harris, Jacques Laperriere and Terry Harper kept our defensive zone under control. Fergy, Claude Larose and players like that gave all of the rest of us room to manoeuvre, to do our jobs, while they kept the other team's heads up. No Stanley Cup winning team I can think of has ever done it without the tough players who keep the opposition honest."

Another aspect of the team dynamic that the novice might find curious is the place held by the so-called "team policeman". One would assume from the hue and cry in the stands that this player is a marginal one, forever banished to the fringes of the group, never to be discussed in polite company and never really accepted by his more honest teammates.

That is patently false. The player who fights for his teammates, or is at least willing to drop his gloves so that less pugilistic players are free to do what they do best, is as essential to a team as any other player. He is accepted as such, a full contributor.

"We all have our jobs on a hockey team," said Yvan Cournoyer. "And we respect a player who does his job because he is bringing something special to the team. John was a rough and hard hockey player because the Montreal Canadiens needed a player like that. Without him, and guys like Terry Harper and Ted Harris on defence, we would not have been as good as we became."

His teammates respected Ferguson and they let him know it.

"It was really important to me that the guys felt that way. One year the Canadiens veterans voted me the most valuable player and that was the year that Cournoyer led the team in scoring. What impressed me was the fact that in the Canadiens scheme of things you could be a leader not only as a goal scorer but also as an aggressor."

John Ferguson assumed a leadership role, but he was a special case. Ferguson lasted all of 12 seconds in his first game before he became embroiled in that first ice fight with Ted Green. What most denigrators of his style of hockey might not realize is that Ferguson also scored twice in that game, a 4-4 tie.

"Fergy disrupted the other team, all over the ice," said Jean Beliveau. "When he was in the other team's zone, the goalie had to keep an eye on him at all times and that helped the rest of us who were making plays and taking shots. But he was just as valuable off the ice. John hated to lose and players on his team were afraid of him a bit. With a guy like him on your team, you don't want to fool around. He doesn't have to say anything; all he has to do is look at you, like the Rocket used to. But he was the nicest man to his teammates."

Ferguson believed in more positive reinforcement in the room.

"In the dressing room, I assumed that it was my responsibility to get things going and to move on issues to help all the guys give their best. If someone was lethargic, I had a way to make them deal with the situation by feeling good about themselves and I told them they could always count on me."

His presence counted, and when the brash young Boston Bruins strutted into the Forum in April of 1968 for the first game of their Stanley Cup semi-final, it was Ferguson who took the situation in hand.

All pre-playoff talk had centred on intimidation; the only question was which team would wear out the other first. Halfway through the first period, Green and Ferguson came together. Ferguson got position on his adversary, pulled his jersey over his head, and whaled away at the Boston defenceman. He came away a clear-cut winner and Montreal blitzed the Bruins in four straight.

"When you get right down to it, I made it my business to be an absolutely miserable son-of-a-bitch on the ice all of the time. But in the room, we tried other methods. We were very close and it was a team composed of comedians who always knew how to deal with pressure, guys like Larose, Laperriere and Harper. Those guys never stopped and kept all of us loose."

Those who watched him on the ice, or saw him adamantly refuse to socialize with players from other teams even in the off-season, would be surprised to discover that Ferguson was one of the ringleaders when it came to Canadiens' high jinks and pranks. When the popular Bryan 'Bugsy' Watson was traded to the Chicago Black Hawks in 1965, he telephoned the Canadiens' dressing room about two weeks after his departure and asked the equipment manager to forward his favourite pair of skates. He received them about ten days later, painted bright pink. The two teams laughed about that one for weeks.

How important were Ferguson's leadership qualities? When Beliveau and Ferguson announced they were retiring in 1971, Sam Pollock called Ferguson and offered him the team captaincy if he would reconsider and play another season.

"I decided to stay retired but that was a very important

gesture by Sam," Ferguson said. "That told me that my contribution to the Montreal Canadiens had been noticed and appreciated."

If the Montreal Canadiens were a much tougher team in the 1960s, they were a little less gifted offensively than previous (or subsequent, for that matter) editions. The big scorers were in Boston, Detroit and Chicago. In 1965, the Canadiens won their first (true) Stanley Cup of the decade. The team's top scorer that year was Claude Provost, whose main claim to fame usually was his ability to stop Bobby Hull from scoring. Provost was sixth in the NHL scoring race and Ralph Backstrom was tied for ninth. Beliveau and Richard finished further down the list in a year when injuries struck hard.

In the four years that the 1960s Montreal Canadiens won the Stanley Cup, no Montreal player finished higher than third in scoring (Bobby Rousseau in 1966).

"That kind of statistic proves something that we players knew very well—the value of Toe Blake to the Montreal Canadiens," said Beliveau. "In the 1960s we had a very good team but we were not head and shoulders above the rest of the league as we had been in the 1950s. The difference was that we had the very best coach in hockey and a man who could get the best out of his players at all times."

The praise for Blake is unanimous.

"To me Toe was the greatest," says John Ferguson, currently the director of player personnel for the Ottawa Senators. "He is like my father. I look up to him and I think that he is the greatest coach of all time. Players performed for Toe. He was a great taskmaster and demanded and earned respect. But, most importantly, it was a two-way street. If you earned it, you got his respect too, and too few coaches know how to do that."

During the 1985-86 playoffs, Ferguson visited the Forum for the seventh game in the Adams Division final against Hartford.

"The first guy I searched out was Toe. Since I had recently gone behind the bench again, I wanted to make sure that I hadn't gone rusty, so we talked."

Tom Johnson, a member of the team of the 1950s and

current assistant GM with Boston Bruins, tells a story that shows his feelings for his former coach.

"About three or four years ago Gerry Cheevers was our coach and he came to me during the summer with a voucher for me to sign. I asked what it was and he told me it was for several hundred dollars so he could go to a special hockey coaching clinic run by Gary Green (former Washington Capitals' coach) in the Laurentians."

Johnson looked up at his coach and said, "I've got a better idea." He reached into his pocket and pulled out a twenty dollar bill.

"Take this and go to Toe Blake's Tavern in Montreal. You'll learn more about coaching there in an hour than in four days in the Laurentians."

The punch line?

"I wasn't kidding," said Johnson.

Terry Harper saw Blake's biggest contribution as his ability to meld different personalities into a distinct unit.

"There were so many types of personalities that made the Canadiens so successful. All the individual personalities of players were allowed to surface but they surfaced as a group, and Toe made a team of it. He didn't try to change everybody or make anybody the ideal Canadien. He tried to have everyone be what they were. He was above anybody else I ever played for or ever met. He was more interested in the mental aspect of a player."

Blake was strong in game preparation and even stronger during the game.

"Toe knew how to work the rest in between periods," said Harper. "Sometimes he would come in and say absolutely nothing, and other times he would give us hell straight through until it was time to go back on the ice. And yet other times he would come in and say something really hilarious and have us all laughing like crazy. The point is, he knew when to do any of the three. He could tell when we were too tight and needed to relax a bit, or when we were complacent and [he] needed to jump on us. He had a tremendous feel for where the team was.

"The best part was that he brought the whole team along, not just one or two fellows ... the whole team. He believed in the players and they, in turn, believed in him."

Blake's coaching, the inspiration of veteran leaders like Beliveau and Richard, the new toughness in the persons of Ferguson, Harris, Harper and Larose, staunch goaltending by Gump Worsley, Charlie Hodge and, later, Rogatien Vachon, characterized the team of the 1960s. If we count from 1963-64, by which time the transition from the 1950s edition had ended, the Canadiens won the Prince of Wales Trophy for finishing first four times and won the Stanley Cup five times in eight years.

But for some reason or other, they will always be the team that Montreal forgot.

An educated guess would be that Montreal fans missed the élan of the 1950s. For years the Forum crowd has been likened to that attending world figure skating championships. The fans in Montreal award points for both technical and artistic merit.

In Montreal, not only did you have to win, you had to win with style and panache. The team of the '60s did not fit that bill, even though it won consistently. In the early half of the decade, the flash in the NHL was provided by Chicago where Bobby Hull and Stan Mikita plied their trade. And toward the end of the decade, Bobby Orr, Phil Esposito, and friends captured the imagination of offence-minded hockey fans everywhere. The Canadiens were terrific defensively and competent up front, but despite a few exceptions, Yvan Cournoyer especially, they generally won in a workmanlike manner.

Players like Terry Harper and Jacques Laperriere, both tall and lanky, seemed to blanket the Canadiens' defensive zone, throwing arms, elbows, sticks and legs in the way of opposing forwards and pucks. As a result, Montreal won three Vezina trophies in that period.

Few Canadiens made the first all-star team in those days. From 1963 through 1971, Montreal had 5 First Team and 13 Second Team nominations. Chicago was 20 and 5, Toronto 3 and 8, New York 4 and 7, Detroit 6 and 7 and Boston 9 and 5 during the same period.

No player epitomized the Montreal Canadiens' work

ethic and sense of personal sacrifice more than Harper. Conversely, no player got less respect from the Forum fans, who have been overrated as hockey connoisseurs at certain times.

Harper, a Regina native, was twelve years old when he was severely burned in an accident. For a while it was uncertain that he would ever walk again, but with a quiet sense of self-confidence combined with hard work, Terry built himself up and became a stalwart defender for his hometown Regina Pats.

He arrived in Montreal late in the 1962-63 season and went on to play ten seasons for the Canadiens. A 6' 2", 195-pound defenceman, he was the antithesis of everything the Montreal fans had come to expect from the flashier side of the sport. Harper once scored as many as four goals in one season and even won a fight, a penalty box affair with Bob Pulford very early in his career. However, J.C. Tremblay or John Ferguson he wasn't when it came to offensive prowess or intimidation.

Derek Sanderson perhaps said it best in his autobiography, *I've Got To Be Me*: "Harper can't fight worth a damn but he's got a lot of guts and he keeps coming back, although he usually gets the hell beat out of him." Another thing Sanderson could have said, but didn't, was that his Bruins could never beat the Canadiens when it counted because of players like Harper.

During the 1960s, when he was at his peak, Bobby Hull was asked about the defencemen who were toughest on him, at a time when Hull was shredding defences every night.

"Terry Harper," he said, "plays me as well or better than any defenceman in the league. I can never seem to get around him."

One thing the so-called knowledgeable fans overlooked in their merciless treatment of Harper was his skating ability. He was gawky, all angles, elbows and knees. But the forwards on his team who went against him in practice knew one thing; you couldn't get around him. Skating backwards, he put his flashier defensive mates to shame. Add to that ability a reach that could flick a puck off an attacker's blade from a seemingly impossible long distance, and it is little wonder that Frank Selke and Sam Pollock ignored the braying of the red-seat cognoscenti for a decade.

Harper's abilities also led to one of the more dramatic moments in Stanley Cup history, especially at the Forum. It came on Sunday, May 9, 1971, the third game of the final series against Chicago. Montreal had lost the first two contests in Chicago, 2-1 and 5-3, despite the heroics of Ken Dryden, and were locked in a tight duel with the Black Hawks who knew they could wrap up the championship if they could steal a win at the Forum.

Harper had been the goat of an earlier Chicago score and was hearing the boos from a surly segment of the crowd whenever he went near the puck. Midway through the second period, he picked up the puck behind his net and skated up the left side.

"Booooooooooooooo!" came cascading down from the rafters.

Harper eluded a Chicago checker at the Canadiens' blueline and swung in toward centre ice.

"Booooooooooooooo!"

He cut back towards the left boards, evading another check, and moved towards the Black Hawks' blueline as his teammates all braked to avoid going offside.

"Booooooooooooooo!" There wasn't a fan left sitting.

Just inside the blueline, Harper slid off yet another bodycheck and carried the puck behind the Chicago net. As he skated directly behind the cage, two Black Hawks smashed into him simultaneously. Falling, he still had enough leverage to pass the puck out in front of the net where John Ferguson was all alone in front of Tony Esposito. Ferguson made no mistake and the Canadiens were on their way to a 4-2 win.

A teammate, who prefers to remain anonymous for obvious reasons, summed it up best: "That was the best 'Fuck You' play I've ever seen in hockey. It was all some of the players could do not to give the crowd the finger."

Harper disentangled himself from the two Chicago players and rose to the rare, for him, sound of a standing ovation as all of his teammates on the ice converged on him, rather than Ferguson the scorer. In the stands, fans were cheering wildly, if not looking out of the corners of their eyes in semi-accusation at all of their *confrères* who had had the temerity to boo such a wonderful hockey player.

Harper, Ferguson, Laperriere, Harris, Provost, Larose —they were Montreal's version of Boston's Lunch Pail Athletic Club—eminently forgettable but for one thing.

Nobody told them how to lose.

They won with improbable plays by Terry Harper and the battling of John Ferguson that could take the starch out of a cocky team like the 1968 Boston Bruins. They won with the finesse of Jean-Claude Tremblay who, unlike his defensive partners, did not like the heavy going but could make a puck dance.

They won when they shouldn't have, against Boston in 1969 and again in 1971. They won with veterans like Richard, Beliveau and Backstrom and kids like Mickey Redmond, Serge Savard, Guy Lapointe and Phil Roberto. They won with raw rookies like Rogatien Vachon and Ken Dryden tending goal. The only silverware they collected was the Stanley Cup.

Individual awards, it seems, were for other teams. In terms of league awards, Claude Provost won the Bill Masterton Trophy (1968), Jean Beliveau, Serge Savard and Ken Dryden won the Conn Smythe Trophy, Jacques Laperriere won the Norris Trophy (1966) as top defence-man in the league, Laperriere (1964) won the Calder Trophy as top rookie and Beliveau the Hart Trophy as league MVP.

Including the aforementioned three Vezina trophies, that made ten individual awards between 1964 and 1971. No Canadiens player won the Art Ross in the same period because no Montreal player won the scoring championship. However, nothing can be more patently ludicrous than the fact that the league's least penalized and highest scoring team, historically, has not won the Lady Byng Trophy since Toe Blake turned the trick in 1946. It is quite obvious that players such as Henri Richard, Jean Beliveau and Guy Lafleur were penalized for playing with a team that regularly won the Stanley Cup.

More ludicrous is the fact that the Canadiens are even penalized for their success in post-season play. The Conn Smythe Trophy, for most valuable player in the playoffs, has gone to a player on the losing team only three times since its inception in 1965. In each case the winning team was the Montreal Canadiens. The three years were 1966 (Roger Crozier, Detroit), 1968 (Glenn Hall, St. Louis), and 1976 (Reggie Leach, Philadelphia). Montreal won those final series 4-2, 4-0, 4-0 or an aggregate 12-2, yet the so-called experts could find no Montreal player deserving of the award.

To return to John Walcot, Lord Mayor of London in 1402, the Canadiens of the 1960s may have raised few expectations as individuals. As a team, however, they did not disappoint.

# 10

## Guy Lafleur
## The Lion in Flight

It is a typical early spring day in the working-class Montreal suburb of Verdun—grey, blustery and chilly enough to raise serious doubts about the impending arrival of warm weather. The only indication that winter's grip has been broken has nothing to do with temperature: it is 7 p.m. on this dreary Thursday in April, 1971, and it is still daylight. Panchromatic daylight perhaps, but daylight nonetheless, and the celebration of the relaxing of winter's grip is evident. Everywhere in the streets of Verdun, cars and buses must inch daintily around the hundreds of ball hockey games that infest the streets with ruddy-faced kids between the ages of five and fifteen. It may be only a windy 40 degrees Fahrenheit, but most of the players are in the uniform of the day: running shoes, battered jeans, hockey shirts. Their equipment runs the gamut from gleaming new fibreglass-wrapped hockey sticks to those on which the blade has been worn to a mere inch-wide sliver. Everywhere, soggy tennis balls are whizzing at the goal. Everywhere, too, bunches of kids do something the professionals could never master —they play with 100 percent effort for hours on end, and keep a simultaneous play-by-play going in the best traditions of René Lecavalier and Danny Gallivan. "He shoots, he scores!" warbles a red-haired ten year old in a battered Black Hawks sweater, as he picks the top corner. The goalie's reply is muffled, but you don't have to be near to know what he has just said. It is a truism of the streets that the first kids on the block to swear fluently are the goalies.

Shortly after 7 p.m., almost miraculously, the streets clear. On most nights, the games would have at least another thirty minutes to go, but not tonight. Moments later, troops of future stars, wearing ski jackets (a concession to Mom) and clutching a valuable dollar in their hands, emerge from the three-storey row houses and head for Church and LaSalle. There stands the Verdun Auditorium, a brown brick barn where the Verdun Maple Leafs of the Quebec junior league play. Tonight the Maple Leafs will face the storied Quebec Remparts in a playoff encounter. Tonight the local heroes will face off against some very well-known eighteen and nineteen year olds with names like Jacques Richard, André Savard and Guy Lafleur. The single greenback will take care of the 75 cents admission and a soft drink or bag of chips between periods.

The Montreal Canadiens and their wonderful new goaltender, a rangy scholastic type, have the night off in their playoff series with the powerful Boston Bruins. This is the only game in town.

Inside, a curiously mixed crowd of more than 5,000 people has packed the Auditorium to the rafters. The Maple Leaf regulars, Verdun residents and the kids are there and on this night they have been joined by hundreds of more well-heeled Montreal sports fans. National Hockey League scouts are everywhere in the joint and the noise and heat are almost unbearable. The visiting Remparts in their dark red and black are the first team to emerge and skate around leisurely, with the easy grace and confidence possessed by only the very best teams. The message seems to be: "We'll beat you here, we'll beat you anywhere you want to play."

In the middle of a group of four skaters lazily circling the defensive zone in the south end of the building,

Number 4 chats easily and moves effortlessly. Wearing the dark red uniform with the crenellated "R" on the crest, a tiny black helmet perched high on his head and long sweeping sideburns, Lafleur looks more like a bell-hop than a hockey player. Yet this is the player who has filled the Auditorium, an unparalleled scoring machine with 103 goals last year and an incredible 130 goals, 79 assists for 209 points this season. These feats are unheard of even in the frenetic world of junior hockey. His 135 minutes in penalties attest to the less-than-legal attempts of some teams in the Quebec Major Junior A Hockey League to stop him at all costs.

*"Il a compté cent buts deux fois? Pas possible!"* ("He scored 100 goals twice? Not possible!") Every eye in the joint is on him.

The microscopic examination ends when a blast of sound introduces the Maple Leafs and they skate out in their home whites with blue trim. All night long we will hear "Hey, Hey, Hey, Goodbye". Unlike the 1980s, when the derisive "Goodbye" will dismiss losing teams in the late stages of hockey games, here the accent is on the "Hey, Hey, Hey" and the hit parade favourite blares away *ad nauseam* at every stop in play and during each intermission.

Amid the fanfare, the game gets underway and, again, all eyes focus on the skinny six-footer in red. He patrols his wing easily, almost perfunctorily, and ten minutes into the period a man sitting to our right turns to his neighbour and says: "This is the great player that Sam Pollock is going to draft number one? You gotta be kidding!"

There is a wonderful Québécois expression that imbues high skepticism with an air of juridical finality. *"Il y a rien là!"* ("There's nothing there!")

His companion, a seasoned hockey observer, remains impassive. "What's the problem?"

"He's out for an afternoon skate. He hasn't done a damn thing and he certainly doesn't look interested. He scored all of those goals because this league thinks defence is a dirty word!"

The cooler head prevails. "Not moving, eh? Like Frank Mahovlich doesn't move. Who's checking him?"

"Normand Cournoyer." The *frère de l'autre* as they say locally. The Canadiens' Yvan is known as the Roadrunner; his kid brother with Verdun is a carbon copy and very quick on his skates.

"Watch Cournoyer and tell me if Lafleur is goofing off," he adds.

Two shifts later, the point has been made. Lafleur may not appear to be moving, but Cournoyer, who must check him, is constantly at top speed, his short but powerful legs churning like pistons. With all that he can barely keep up. When you look closely you notice that Lafleur has something Bobby Orr has, the ability to accelerate so quickly and effortlessly, and to move to either side at top speed without losing a step, that he forces the opposition to back off. No matter how good they are on their skates, most professionals are just like the kids who play shinny on a pond; they favour one leg and one side, and when they move to their weak side, they usually are doing it at a slower speed. Orr, Lafleur and few others can go both ways at top speed. As a result, for them the rink is much bigger.

Late in the first period, Lafleur casually picks up a loose puck along the right wing boards near the centre redline and skates into Verdun territory. A defenceman is backpedalling furiously to cut off the angle; Cournoyer got caught on a line change and is motoring hard to catch up. Five feet inside the blueline he takes a short wind-up and shoots on goal. The puck has hit the twine and rebounded six feet in front of the crease before the startled goalie can even react.

It takes even longer for the crowd to react; they seem stunned by the suddenness of it all. Then there is a collective "oh", a quick exhalation, and everyone seems to be talking at once. Nobody is really cheering or booing— 5,000 hockey fans seem to be analyzing the goal.

"Not bad, eh?" smiles the cooler head. "That one would have beaten most pros I've seen."

When the emotional contest is over, an inexorable 5-4 win for the Remparts, Lafleur has scored three times with almost surgical precision. Scouts from 13 of the 14 NHL teams leave the rink shaking their heads. The members of the Montreal brain trust can be seen smiling as they shrug into their overcoats and head for the exits in animated discussion.

The Verdun kids, their heartbreak behind them, return to their ball hockey the next day. And on a breakaway, more than one announces: "Here's Guy Lafleur going in on goal . . ." before the top corner is picked. They will be joined by kids from coast-to-coast in the coming years.

*   *   *

Guy Damien Lafleur, nineteen, of Thurso, Quebec, is not much older than many of the kids who will grow to idolize him during the next decade. But the age difference is deceptive. In many ways, Lafleur has been a professional hockey player since he was fourteen and that brings with it a certain maturity that goes far beyond his years. In other ways it produces a curious blend of sophistication and naïveté, as if some lessons were left out.

"When it came time to leave home for the first time, I don't know if I was ready," Lafleur smiles, remembering what it was like to be fourteen and preparing to leave the universe that was Thurso, a town in western Quebec closer to Ottawa than Montreal. Until then, the story is the familiar one: smalltown boy from rural Quebec grows up as an altar boy and terrific athlete and gets into all sorts of mischief whenever he can. A sort of francophone Huck Finn.

"There was nothing very special about being a kid," Lafleur recalls. "Like all the kids my age, I hung around with the gang from the neighbourhood and my cousins. Maybe I was a little wilder than some because I was the only boy in a family with four sisters, so I had all the trouble I could handle. My dad came from a large family, seven children, and most Sundays all of us would end up at my grandmother's for dinner. We were almost fifty people. The parents would be inside talking and a lot of us kids would be outside playing sports, cowboys, cops and robbers, you name it. And we could get into our share of trouble, hunting small birds and animals or even each other with our slingshots, and later BB guns."

Guy's biggest scare came when he threw a rock that broke the windshield of a police cruiser passing by. "The policeman was a friend of my dad and I was so scared I ran home and hid behind the fridge," he said.

Hockey started with his first pair of skates at age five. Rejean Lafleur, a welder by trade, built a rink behind the house every winter and welded some pipes into the framework of goals. Potato sacking replaced netting but the twenty or so kids who would play pick-up hockey every day until well beyond last light didn't care. "Nobody had specific positions but one thing was true ... I never once played goalie—you had to be crazy to do that."

Guy Lafleur was one of the crowd and quite unaware of his worth as a hockey player because the pick-up games featured boys of all ages. "All I know is that by the time I was seven or so, I was taking hockey more seriously than some of my friends. I was so bad that I used to sleep in my equipment so I could be ready to play the next morning. Quite often my dad would find me in bed fast asleep with everything on except my helmet and he'd undress me without waking me up.

"On weekdays, we'd start playing at seven in the morning and then we'd play the other classes at lunchtime. After school, we'd play against other teams in the area. It was hockey, hockey, hockey and we loved it."

As Guy got older, he spent more and more time practising with the teaching brothers at l'Ecole Ste. Famille. "I'll never forget my math teacher. He used to tell us that Paul Anka [from nearby Ottawa] had made a lot of sacrifices to make the big time and that if we wanted to be athletes, we would have to make the sacrifices, even at our young ages."

Those words struck home with Lafleur and he went into "serious training" when he was nine. That consisted of slopping out the pigsties at a friend's farm, and helping at milking time with thirty-five dairy cows. Perpetually jammed in high gear, Lafleur also made first contact with his passion for motor vehicles there. "I was nuts about driving their truck and tractor." To build up his legs and stamina, he also started running cross-country after finishing his work, quite often for ten miles or so. "A lot of the kids at school thought I was crazy."

All of Lafleur's ice time was spent outdoors, until school carnival, when he and his teammates played in the local arena for the first time. Afterwards, they couldn't keep him out of arenas. The Singer sewing machine company, Thurso's major employer, had built the indoor facility and later sold it to the town for a nominal one dollar. It was a ramshackle affair. "The boards were pretty far apart in some places and you could see sunlight right through them." But it was hockey heaven to the rising young star and very early each morning, he would sneak into the arena through a hole in the boards and skate leisurely by himself.

All of his ice time and off-ice training began to pay off. "I was nine when I began to break out in hockey," he recalls. "Our team went to the peewee tournament in Quebec City three times, in 1962, '63 and '64, and I won the scoring championship the first year. I'll never forget because Red Storey gave me the trophy. I had my name in the local paper a couple of times, too."

The young player's fame spread further than that. Paul Dumont, one of the top amateur hockey people in Quebec City was so impressed by Lafleur's play at the Quebec tournament that he phoned Rejean Lafleur and asked if his son could move to the provincial capital to play midget or Junior B hockey. Guy was twelve, going on thirteen that summer.

"My dad came up to me and asked me if I wanted to go and I said yes. I kept bothering my dad to go, even if I was twelve, but I didn't know what I was getting into at that age. He thought about it for a long time and then said no. I was too young. A year later, Mr. Dumont called again. This time my dad said okay."

As was the case with many young athletes approaching puberty in rural Quebec, another road beckoned. Guy had been an altar boy for about five years and "it must have seemed that I liked it a lot because the priests decided I should become one of them. The old priest came over to my house and wanted to be sure that my decision to play hockey was the right decision. Did going away to play hockey mean that I had decided against the priesthood?" With all of these weighty matters roiling around inside him, a very young, green kid took the fated bus ride to Quebec City to play for the Canadian Tire and Repair Junior B team.

"It was tough for a fourteen year old kid. I cried, every night it seemed, and several times I called my dad and said I wanted to come home. But my dad wasn't having any of it. He told me: 'You cried for a year to go there, you are going to stick it out. You're not coming back.' Now that I have two sons, I think of how it must have really hurt him to say those things; after all, I was his only son and no father wants to tell his son he can't come home. But he was strong for me."

Strong and supportive. Rejean Lafleur often would drive to Quebec twice a week—a notoriously treacherous drive—to watch Guy play, and hop right back in the car to drive more than two hundred miles straight home to make it just in time for work the next morning.

Guy's eldest son, Martin, is ten. Could he picture him in similar circumstances, leaving home to play hockey more than two hundred miles away, just four years from now? Could he adapt to the role of the anxious father?

"Not in a million years," Lafleur replies nervously.

"I really don't know how my father had the strength to let me go. As a father now, I know it would be more difficult on me than my son. Besides, the situation is quite different these days. Not too many fourteen year olds go away to play hockey any more. They usually find a place near home. Yet, if he had the talent and the desire to make it, I would have a hard time stopping him. But if he doesn't have the talent, I would have to tell him. I would never want my son to become a junior hockey bum, giving away five or six years of his life to hockey when there is no real future in it for him."

In his second year in Quebec City, Guy had made a few friends in school and on the hockey team and life away from home became more enjoyable. By his third year, all of his friends were in Quebec City and Thurso was somewhere he went after the hockey season ended. "By then I was fine. I didn't want to go back home."

The team policy of billeting out-of-town players with families also helped Guy to adjust. When Jean Beliveau had moved to Quebec from Victoriaville, he stayed with the three McKenna sisters. Guy stayed with the Baribeau family at 238 Boulevard Benoit XV in Limoilou, a stone's throw from the Colisée. For six years, Mrs. Eva Baribeau was his surrogate mother. When Lafleur officially retired, February 16, 1985, at the Forum, Mrs. Baribeau was part of the Lafleur family group at centre ice.

"Mrs. Baribeau is a wonderful lady and she became a second mother to me," he recalls. "This stable home life was important to me because it meant that I belonged, I was not a complete stranger in Quebec. But even with that, it wasn't easy. School was hard because we travelled a lot; I missed a lot of school because I was on the road." Lafleur was enrolled in Jean Brebeuf high school but each year, when hockey was over, would return to Thurso and finish the school year at Ecole Secondaire St. Michel in nearby Buckingham, Quebec.

Lafleur lived the standard junior hockey player's life in those days. Education was of secondary importance and some junior hockey operators, while paying lip service to the benefits of good schooling for their players, found that schooling disrupted the team and subtly encouraged players to quit.

All of that changed within a year or two of Lafleur's graduation from junior hockey. The right winger found himself surrounded by college-trained hockey players like Rod Langway, Brian Engblom, Craig Ludwig, Ken Dryden and Chris Nilan on the Montreal Canadiens.

"I can't say I'm all that disappointed that I didn't get a better education because it wasn't available back then. Had it been available, I don't know what I would have done; I probably would have gone the same route as I did. However, if I was about sixteen or seventeen today and getting serious about a hockey career, I would probably go the other way. I know I would strongly advise young guys today to do anything they can to get scholarships or find a way to marry the two, because education is very important. The numbers game is against you when you are moving up through hockey; only a very small group of players ever make it. If you can do both, you won't have lost X number of years and have to start all over again at twenty-one or twenty-two."

Lafleur played ten games of Junior A his first year with the Quebec Aces and scored two goals and seven assists. "Mr. Dumont did not want me to move up too quickly; I was much younger than the other guys and I weighed only 133 pounds at the time." Lafleur moved up the following year and would play three years for the Aces and another two for the Remparts following a name change for the team.

At sixteen, he was labelled "can't miss" by the NHL scouts. Three years later (players weren't drafted until they were twenty in those days) the tag had changed to "franchise player". Guy Lafleur was going to be something very special in professional ice hockey.

Canadiens' scouts were particularly interested in the player who wore Number 4 with the Remparts, in honour of his idol, Jean Beliveau. At the time, a banner crop of French Canadian talent was emerging. Players like Rejean Houle, Marc Tardif and Gilbert Perreault with the Junior Canadiens and Marcel Dionne of the St. Catharines Black Hawks of the OHA league were regularly making headlines. In 1969-70, Drummondville's Dionne scored 55 goals and added 77 assists for 132 points—league records in all three categories—in a 54-game season. Victoriaville's Perreault was just behind with 51-70-121 in a league which was recognized as Canada's best at the time. Lafleur's totals that season were an astounding 103-67-170 in 56 games (and 25-18-43 in 15 playoff games!). Many hockey observers discounted that performance, however, claiming that the QMJHL was weak in comparison with the OHA. That argument would retain some validity for only one more season, and then Lafleur would shatter it once and for all.

The question was: where would Montreal go? Would the Canadiens go after Perreault, an extremely popular player, superb playmaker and hard worker? Would they opt for Dionne, offensive machine with terrific puck sense? Or would it be the "quiet machine" Lafleur in the Quebec league?

"In a sense, the decision was out of our hands the moment the National Hockey League decided to expand by two more teams," Sam Pollock says. "Perreault was born in 1950, a year before the other two, so he was going to go in the 1970 draft. The first two positions in the draft would be decided by a coin toss between the two new teams, Buffalo Sabres and Vancouver Canucks, and the best two players in the country, Gilbert Perreault and Dale Tallon with the Toronto Marlboros, were going to go 1-2. There was no question of trying to make a deal with Punch Imlach for the number one spot after he won the toss."

Punch knew his hockey players, especially since he had coached Jean Beliveau in Quebec in the early 1950s. Imlach was one of the few English Canadian hockey men who was comfortable with Quebec and Quebec-born hockey players. He built himself some powerhouses with the Maple Leafs and would have liked to take advantage of his contacts in the French-speaking province but was stymied by his boss, Stafford Smythe. "French Canadians do not represent Toronto or the Maple Leafs," Imlach was told virtually every time he broached the subject.

Now, however, Imlach was his own boss and he knew which of the two, Perreault and Tallon, would pan out. He chose Perreault and the quiet, unassuming superstar was Mr. Buffalo Sabre for his entire career. Tallon, a superb junior hockey player and junior golfer, was an above-average player with Vancouver, Chicago and Pittsburgh but never attained superstar status.

Montreal was shut out of the Perreault derby by expansion, but Trader Sam's machinations were still in evidence: the Canadiens drafted fifth and sixth and managed to secure goalie Ray Martiniuk from the Flin Flon Bombers and speedy winger Chuck Lefley from the

Canadian National Team in a draft that included such notables as Reg Leach, Darryl Sittler, Dan Maloney, Dan Bouchard and a centre with Ottawa 67s named Bill Clement, from Guy Lafleur's hometown of Thurso. Evidence that Sam Pollock is not infallible comes from the fact that Sittler was drafted number 8 that year.

"That draft made us redouble our efforts to secure Lafleur the following year," Pollock says. "1970 was a very good draft and 1971 looked like it might even be better. Lafleur and Dionne had a lot of company that year—the Junior Canadiens had Perreault's winger Richard Martin, centre Bobby Lalonde and defenceman Jocelyn Guevremont; there were players like Ron Jones, Chuck Arnason, Steve Vickers, Terry O'Reilly, Craig Ramsay, Larry Robinson and Rick Kehoe."

Lafleur's output that year was even more outstanding than in 1970; 130 goals, 79 assists, 209 points in 62 regular-season contests and 22-21-43 in 14 playoffs. In 76 games overall, Lafleur scored 152 goals, precisely two a game, and added exactly 100 assists. Dionne was no slouch either, with 62-81-143 in only 46 OHA season games, also more than 3 points a game.

The "good player, bad league" stigma was erased that spring when the Quebec Remparts met the St. Catharines Black Hawks in the final for the Memorial Cup. Quebec upset the Black Hawks in a riot-marred series and all doubts about the quality of the QMJHL were removed.

This is not to say that the Canadiens were unsure of their choice. "We had known for two years that we wanted Lafleur," Pollock says. "Had we not been able to get him, however, Dionne would have been a nice consolation."

On June 10, 1971, league president Clarence Campbell announced that the NHL draft was now in session and that the first pick was Montreal's. The room disintegrated when Trader Sam acknowledged that it was Montreal's pick then called time out. Three minutes later, with time in again and the room abuzz, Guy Damien Lafleur, nineteen years, nine months and twenty days old, became a Montreal Canadien. Marcel Dionne, who would be doomed to practise his sport in quasi-obscurity for most of his career in faraway California, was selected by the Detroit Red Wings moments later. About an hour later, a tall, gangling redhead named Larry Robinson joined Lafleur on his new team. Lafleur would go to Montreal right away and Robinson would join him two years later. More than any other players, these two would epitomize the Canadiens during the 1970s.

Years later, after having been selected by fans to the all-time Montreal Canadiens team (on defence with Doug Harvey), Robinson smiles and is thankful that he did not have the double pressure of being a Quebec-born hockey player and the number one NHL draft pick. "I was picked twentieth that year, in fact, fourth pick by the Canadiens (Chuck Arnason and Murray Wilson followed Lafleur) and there never was any question of being a member of the big team that fall. I went to training camp just hoping to play well and find a place in the organization."

The farm boy from Winchester, Ontario did just that, finding a place on the Nova Scotia Voyageurs where his crunching bodychecks raised eyebrows all over the league. He would play another half-season before being called up, and sticking with the parent club.

"Guy, on the other hand, was practically handed Jean Beliveau's sweater and told he was the replacement for the most popular Montreal Canadien ever. That kind of pressure would have destroyed a lot of players in any NHL city, let alone Montreal. It would have scared a couple of years growth out of me."

The shy blond with the immense sideburns who showed up at his first professional training camp that September agrees with Robinson. "I was very frightened and the stuff they were writing in the papers didn't help. They had me as some kind of saviour coming to a team that had just won the Stanley Cup and had players like Henri Richard, Yvan Cournoyer, Jean-Claude Tremblay and the Mahovlich brothers." Lafleur's first decision was a wise one; he turned down the offer of Beliveau's Number 4 sweater, opting instead for the Number 10 that Frank Mahovlich had worn for two road games after having been traded to Montreal from Detroit the previous year. "That kind of instant pressure I could do without," Lafleur says.

The quiet hockey player celebrated his twentieth birthday at the Canadiens' training camp, a first draft choice, secure in the knowledge that he would spend the coming year with the Montreal Canadiens. Some fifteen years later, retired from the game and President of the Longueuil Chevaliers of the Quebec Major Junior A Hockey League, he would say that he could not imagine how eighteen year olds could endure such pressure at an even younger age.

When Lafleur was drafted, the Entry Draft selected the best twenty year old players available. Considerable pressure was placed on the NHL by the WHA in the mid-'70s when that league, desperate for quality players, began drafting underage players at age eighteen. These included Wayne Gretzky, originally signed by the Indianapolis Racers and then transferred to the Edmonton Oilers when Nelson Skalbania's financial schemes began to collapse. The biggest dent was made by the Birmingham Bulls, who stocked their team with young players for the 1977-78 and 1978-79 seasons. The Baby Bulls included such current NHL stars as Toronto's Rick Vaive, Edmonton's Mark Napier, Washington's Rod Langway, Montreal's Gaston Gingras, St. Louis's Rob Ramage and Minnesota's Craig Hartsburg.

In 1980, the NHL began drafting eighteen year olds (they had selected occasional underage players in the past such as Bobby Orr in 1968 and Mario Tremblay in 1974). There have been complaints that this advanced age has especially harmed junior hockey in Canada.

"The eighteen year old draft by the NHL teams is a veritable disaster," says Lafleur. "This has hurt the entire system of hockey, but the worst affected are the young players who are drafted. When I was twenty years old, I got pretty homesick that first year in professional hockey. It has to be worse for a lot of these players, they haven't matured yet." The young players are hurt in several ways, he adds.

"A lot of these guys are drafted, go to the NHL team's training camp, and then are sent back to junior for a year or two to mature. But it is almost impossible for these guys to come back down to earth. They come back to their junior team, where guys might make $100 a week, with contracts for $75,000 or $100,000 in their pockets. They lose all motivation and quite often their progress stops dead. And there isn't a junior hockey coach who knows more than this kid's agent. Junior hockey and the team become a pastime for these guys; they are just marking time until they go up to the NHL."

Lafleur has lived the uncertainty of the NHL rookie season. In his case it was doubly hard, because he was the heir apparent to Jean Beliveau, the most beloved hockey player in Quebec, and was going to play in the Forum Fish Bowl.

One Saturday night in February, 1972, many in attendance at the International Peewee Tournament in Quebec City, where he had starred just a decade before, were surprised to see Lafleur in the press room. Nattily attired in a dark blue velvet sports jacket, grey slacks and tie, the rising young hockey star chatted easily with friends like *Le Soleil* columnist Roland Sabourin and other journalists. He paused only to sign autographs for the young hockey players who gathered up their courage to invade the press room.

Earlier that day, the Canadiens had played the Chicago Black Hawks in a rare afternoon game.

"Guy's here all the time," Sabourin said quietly, telling the Quebec media's big secret. Montreal writers who might be seeking the rookie's time and attention for interviews and feature stories would have a hard time finding him at his Longueuil apartment; whenever Montreal was home, Guy went home, to Quebec City, making the 300-mile round-trip at every available opportunity.

"I had been in Quebec City for six years and I would head up there regularly because I knew Quebec and I didn't know Montreal," he recalls.

"When I got to Montreal, just about all the players were married. I think the only bachelor was Pierre Bouchard, for all the obvious reasons," he laughs. "He still is single today and hasn't changed." Lafleur turns serious again and the pain of that first year returns.

"I had all of my friends in Quebec and I would head back there constantly. I really missed it. In Montreal I was lost. Even though Quebec was a pretty big place, it just was not Montreal." All of those sports and entertainment editors with the big Montreal dailies who sought "Rookie captures the Big City" features, with Lafleur flashing his sideburns and flowered shirts to the beautiful ladies in Crescent Street or Rue Saint-Denis discos would be disappointed. Lafleur was not averse to doing the town; it just wasn't the same town that the locals thought.

When there wasn't enough time to get away to Quebec, Lafleur would prowl his Longueuil apartment like a caged lion. Yet this was not a case of a terribly introverted young man hiding out. Rather, Lafleur was the type of person who preferred to scout the terrain first, then make a sortie. After years of headlines and adulation in Quebec, Lafleur had a cocky ingenuousness that was attractive to many. He wanted to be in control of situations, not vice versa.

The Huck Finn of Thurso would surface in the weirdest ways. A combination of his self-imposed incarceration in his apartment and his natural insouciance resulted in a strange introduction to the future Mrs. Lafleur.

Lafleur, perhaps a bit desperate for company, befriended the janitor in his apartment building and the two would often share short conversations. "Why doesn't a good-looking guy like you go out more often?" the janitor ventured, asking the most obvious question in Lafleur's world. "Montreal has some of the best-looking women in the world; downtown is crawling with them." A touch embarrassed at the turn in the badinage, Lafleur made some quick excuses about being on the road with the team a lot and not having the time to meet a lot of women.

"Have I got the answer for you!" replied the janitor. "There's a gorgeous stewardess on the eleventh floor you should meet. She's even from Quebec City." Pushed and prodded, Lafleur found himself in the girl's apartment where she was discovered on her hands and knees, scrubbing her kitchen floor.

After the basic introductions were dispensed with, he endeared himself to her forever by blurting tactlessly: "If you want to go out with me, you'll have to lose about fifty pounds."

Lise Barre was equal to the challenge: "Get out!"

On to Chapter Two of the Hockey Star and the Stewardess. Lafleur's janitor buddy had given him a master key so that he could use the sauna at all hours. One morning at about three a.m. and about three months later, Lafleur returned to her eleventh-floor apartment and let himself in. The coast was clear, she was away on flight duty, the janitor had said.

"I don't know what I had in mind," Lafleur recalls. "Maybe I thought I could find out what she was like by looking around her place. I had not seen her up close since she kicked me out and it seemed like she *was* losing weight." The amateur anthropologist prowled the apartment, checking out the furniture, the record collection and the stereo. He found a bottle of cognac by the sofa, poured himself a drink, turned on the stereo and sat back. He was on his second drink when the lessee walked in at about four a.m.

Mr. Smooth proved how quickly he could react; after all, this is a man whose lightning reflexes would terrorize the opposition for a decade.

"What are you doing back a day early?" he demanded to know.

The future Mrs. Lafleur had seen all the Rock Hudson-Doris Day pictures too.

"Get out," she said, in a touching replay of their previous farewell of three months past. "Or I'll call the police," she added, grateful for the extra line of dialogue. And then to avoid more early morning surprises, she moved out and returned home to Quebec City, breaking her lease and telling management that their building was not big enough to share with that hockey player who lived on the first floor.

"Who does he think he is? Maurice Richard?"

Lafleur used his connections to discover her address in Quebec. He drove there and contritely mumbled something about love at first sight and his overall weirdness. When he returned to Montreal, the girl he would marry a year later was in the car with him.

On the ice, life was just as eventful. Lafleur was not as shy but still was being worked gently into a team that, while rebuilding, had all the elements necessary to re-emerge as champions. That year, the Canadiens finished third in the East Division standings with 108 points, behind Boston's 119 and New York Rangers' 109, a repeat of the previous regular season. The Bruins' Phil Esposito and Bobby Orr finished 1-2 in the scoring race ahead of the Rangers' GAG (goal-a-game) line of Jean Ratelle, Rod Gilbert and Vic Hadfield. The Canadiens were ably represented in the top ten scorers by Frank Mahovlich, Yvan Cournoyer and Jacques Lemaire.

While Lafleur would not have to wait two full years before cracking the regular line-up as had Cournoyer in the mid-60s, he spent most of the season on the third and fourth lines, ending 1971-72 with 29 goals and 35 assists for 64 points, respectable totals. But that was 13 points behind Marcel Dionne of the Red Wings 28-49-77 and 10 points behind Sabres' rookie Rick Martin, with 44-30-74, and some grumblings were being heard in the reds.

Lafleur did not win the Calder Trophy as best rookie for 1971-72, but neither did Dionne or Martin. Canadiens fans were mollified when it was announced that Ken Dryden was the top newcomer, and especially gratified considering the fact that it was the rangy goaltender's second major award, following the Conn Smythe trophy he had won as best player of the previous year's Stanley Cup playoffs. They were not so happy when the New York Rangers bumped off the Canadiens in the playoffs, before losing to the Bruins in the final.

Montreal recaptured first place in the East Division the

next year, finishing 13 points ahead of Boston on the strength of 52 wins, 10 losses and 16 ties and went on to win the Stanley Cup by beating Chicago in the final. Despite the championship, more grumblings were heard about the number 1 draft as Lafleur's production dropped marginally to 28 goals, 27 assists for 55 points in 69 games. The right winger added 3 goals and 5 assists in 17 playoff games but the natives were restless . . . Dionne had turned in 40 goals and 50 assists and Martin scored another 44 goals.

A year later it was even worse. Rick Martin reached the 50-goal plateau, finishing sixth in the league scoring race with 52 goals and 34 assists for 86 points. Dionne was just behind with 78 points and young stars like Bobby Clarke and Darryl Sittler were emerging in Philadelphia and Toronto. For the first time in four years, the Canadiens had no players in the top ten scorers and were eliminated by the New York Rangers in the playoffs. Lafleur slipped to 21 goals and 35 assists for 56 points, a full 30 points behind Martin, a statistic thrown up time and time again by the cognoscenti on the hotlines. Worse than that, all he could produce in the six-game quarterfinal loss to the Rangers was a single, measly assist.

The consensus was the Canadiens had blown it. Sam Pollock was fallible. Imagine what a pure shooter like Martin would have done in his hometown, they speculated, conveniently forgetting that Martin was doing so well because his centre from the Junior Canadiens days, Gilbert Perreault, was playing with him. Would it not be great to have such a playmaker as Dionne on the Canadiens, they wondered aloud, forgetting, too, how easy it was to concentrate on individual stats when a team was going nowhere.

If anything positive could be said about the playoff loss to the Rangers, it was that another rookie, Steve Shutt, who had scored all of 15 goals and 20 assists in 70 regular-season games, had come alive during the playoffs with 5 goals and 3 assists in 6 games.

Claude Ruel, who had briefly coached the Canadiens

after Toe Blake's retirement, and would do so again after Bernie Geoffrion's resignation, was the man who worked with the young players.

"We selected Guy Lafleur number one because he was the best player available in the draft in 1971," he says. "We knew that Dionne was a very good hockey player; and certainly so was Martin—we did not have to go very far to see that, he played in our own building. But Lafleur was the best of the three and the only question was when he would begin to show it in the NHL. It was a question of confidence, for sure; somebody with his speed and shot, who scored all of those goals in junior, does not suddenly lose that ability. Especially not when he's twenty-two or twenty-three years old. It was a matter of time and when he would start putting them in."

Another factor that hampered Lafleur's development was that he played out of position for long periods of time during those first three seasons. The Canadiens had a rich harvest of wingers—Yvan Cournoyer, Claude Larose, Reggie Houle (although he was a left-hand shot), Phil Roberto, Chuck Arnason and Jim Roberts on the right side and Marc Tardif, Frank Mahovlich, Chuck Lefley, Houle, and three rookies—Murray Wilson, Steve Shutt and Yvon Lambert on the left.

With the retirement of Jean Beliveau and the trade of Ralph Backstrom to Los Angeles to set up the Lafleur draft, the Montreal team considered itself shorthanded at centre. "Considered itself" is the operative phrase; Jacques Lemaire and Pete Mahovlich would settle into those positions and carry the team through the rest of the decade. However, when Lafleur joined the Canadiens, the team noted his skating ability, size and speed, and pencilled him into the line-up as a centre.

"A lot of people look at Guy Lafleur's first three years and forget that," Ruel says. "He was playing out of position, and not complaining. Centre demands a lot more than the wing and it is quite a change for a player coming off the wing. Going from centre to wing is much easier. One good thing that came out of it was the fact that Guy really improved his passing game during those three years and that would really help him during his big scoring years later on. He was a great scorer, that was obvious to everyone. But he was also the best passing winger in the league when he was at the top." Not too many wingers have ever chalked up 80 assists in a season, as Lafleur did in 1976-77.

After three years of unfair comparisons with players who had been able to step into the lineups of their new teams and play thirty minutes or more a game without pressure, was the Flower ready to bloom?

That question was answered in Lafleur's fourth season. Several events conspired to help Lafleur break out. The WHA had lured away Rejean Houle and Marc Tardif the previous season and Frank Mahovlich left to join the Toronto Toros after the 1973-74 season ended. Veteran defenceman Jacques Laperriere retired, Chuck Lefley was traded and suddenly the Canadiens included names like Van Boxmeer, Risebrough, Tremblay and Chartraw. Lafleur was a veteran and, in the tradition of the Canadiens, was expected to lead rather than follow.

In training camp that fall, off came the helmet and *le Démon Blond* was born. Lafleur was teamed with veteran Pete Mahovlich and Shutt, the chubby Toronto sniper who had shown a very nice touch around the net in the previous playoff round, and all three took off.

Maurice Richard and Bernie Geoffrion had been the first two National Hockey League players to score 50 goals in a season. That they were francophones and Canadiens was a source of immense pride for Montreal fans.

Since then, it seemed, 50-goal scorers belonged to everyone else. Montreal might win Stanley Cups but other teams had the glamour boys who filled the nets, players like Bobby Hull, Phil Esposito and Johnny Bucyk. That rankled in a city where the fans award points for artistic and technical merit. At the Forum, the home team not only had to win, it had to win with style.

When players with names like Vic Hadfield (a journeyman to Montreal fans) and Mickey Redmond—a player

traded away by the Canadiens to obtain Frank Mahovlich
—began to reach the sacred plateau, Montreal fans could
not hide their frustration. Before Boom Boom beat
Toronto's Cesare Maniago on the last weekend in the
season in 1960-61, Jean Beliveau had flirted with immor-
tality with 47 and 45 goals in 1955-56 and 1958-59. Yvan
Cournoyer titillated them in 1968-69 with 43, and came
even closer in 1972-73 with 47, while his linemate Jacques Lemaire chipped in 44 the same year. Frank
Mahovlich, who would get as close to the magic mark as
48 goals with Toronto Maple Leafs and 49 with Detroit
Red Wings, would net 43 in 1971-72.

But that was as close as it got. The Flying Frenchmen
were not reaching the heights of goal scoring. Even
worse, the last time a Canadien had won the league
scoring title was way back in Geoffrion's 50-goal season,
1960-61, when he and Beliveau finished 1-2 with 95 and
90 points respectively. Since then, the scoring title was a
consolation prize for the perennial also-rans, the Chicago
Black Hawks (Bobby Hull twice, Stan Mikita four times)
and the Boston Bruins (Phil Esposito five times, Bobby
Orr twice) with Gordie Howe capturing the other title in
that fourteen-year period.

That all changed on March 29, 1975. Denis Herron
wore the blue, red and gold of the Kansas City Scouts
and his white fibreglass goalie's mask was painted with
warstripes. A ferocious countenance perhaps, but not
enough to deter Guy Damien Lafleur. Despite missing
ten games because of a fractured thumb, broken by a
vicious slash in a game against the fledgling Washington
Capitals, Lafleur went into Montreal's 76th game with
49 goals. Early in the game he teamed up with Mahovlich
to score Number 50 and the Forum went crazy.

Poor Denis Herron would become Lafleur's personal
property after that, giving up the Flower's 50th goal in
1977, again with the Scouts, and also in 1979, after
moving to Pittsburgh Penguins. Shortly thereafter, the
Chambly, Quebec native caught a break; he was traded
to Montreal, where he could watch as Richard Sevigny
gave up the 50th goals of the season to St. Louis's Wayne

*Toe Blake, David Molson and Sam Pollock celebrate a Rite of Spring in Montreal; another Stanley Cup parade.*

J. M°KENNA.    C. HART.    P LEPINE.    G. RIVERS.    A. LEDUC.    W. LAROCHELLE.    A. MONDOU.    N. WASNIE.    A. JOLIA

*1930-31 Montreal Canadiens Team Picture: Aurele Joliat appears ninth from the left, Howie Morenz appears two to the right of him and Owner Leo Dandurand appears at the far right of the photograph.*

*Coach Dick Irvin expresses his feelings and a beaming Frank Selke looks on as Jean Beliveau signs his first National Hockey League contract in October, 1953, after two years of wooing by the Canadiens. How did Selke pull it off? "It's simple. I just opened the Forum vault and said 'help yourself, Jean'."*

*Stalwarts of the Sixties: John Ferguson (top), Yvan Cournoyer, goalie Charlie Hodge and Claude Provost (after a 1964 playoff victory) didn't get an advertising contract for this picture. But they won the game. . . .*

WORTH.  H. MORENZ.  J. GAGNON.  M. BURKE.  S. MANTHA.  G. MANTHA.  A. LESIEUR.  E. DUFOUR.  L. DANDURA

Scotty Bowman, then coach of the St. Louis Blues, captain Jean Beliveau, and Montreal coach Claude Ruel pose after Montreal won the 1969 Stanley Cup in St. Louis. It was Montreal's sixteenth. Three years later, Bowman was head coach of the Canadiens.

The Forum, circa 1966. The hockey shrine was looking seedy before a major renovation was undertaken in 1968.

Maurice Richard scores on Sugar Jim Henry in the 1953 playoffs. The Canadiens won the Stanley Cup that year.

Jean Beliveau slides the puck past Gilles Gilbert of Minnesota as Frank Mahovlich looks on. The date: February 11, 1971. The time: 6:42 of the second period. The occasion: Beliveau's third goal in a 5-3 win and the five hundredth of his illustrious career.

Guy Lafleur scores a playoff goal against Philadelphia in 1976.

*The generations meet: Jean Beliveau, Guy Lafleur, and Maurice Richard.*

*Ken Dryden. Stops like this one put the lawyer/goaltender in the N.H.L. Hall of Fame before he was 35.*

*Lise Lafleur, son Martin, and "stepmother" Mrs. Eva Baribeau look on as Guy Lafleur acknowledges the cheers of the Forum Faithful, February 16, 1985, during his official retirement night.*

Mats Naslund, 5, always knew he would be a Montreal Canadien. This photo was taken in March, 1967, or about 20 years and 2 months before the Little Viking celebrated his first Stanley Cup with the real Canadiens.

Jacques Demers. Serge Savard believed in him and Demers made believers out of the hockey world.

*In a class all their own: Patrick Roy and Kirk Muller in the Stanley Cup Finals. Serge Savard brought Muller over from New Jersey in what may prove his best-ever trade.*

*Hockey's best goaltender hoists the Cup for the twenty-fourth time in the club's history. No other sports franchise can boast of a record like this one.*

*Beach party at 30,000 feet. Claude Lemieux, Gaston Gingras and Serge Boisvert (with a rose behind his ear) celebrate the Stanley Cup Championship high above Canada on the flight home.*

Babych and Quebec's Jacques Richard. Upon leaving Montreal for Pittsburgh in 1982, Herron's semi-centennial bad luck would return and he would be the victim of Michel Goulet's and Tim Kerr's 50th goals in 1984 and Wayne Gretzky's in 1985.

The renewed Lafleur, playing ten fewer games than the rest of the competition, finished fourth in the NHL scoring list in 1974-75, with 53 goals and 66 assists for 119 points, behind Bobby Orr, Phil Esposito and Marcel Dionne. Mahovlich was fifth, two points behind Lafleur, and Montreal finished the season in a three-way tie with Philadelphia and Buffalo for overall first place with 113 points. More importantly in the eyes of Montreal fans, Lafleur was 24 points ahead of Martin. The latter would get some measure of revenge when the Buffalo Sabres edged out the Canadiens in the playoffs that year.

That would be the last playoff disappointment of the decade. For the next three years, Lafleur owned the league and Montreal was on the way to four straight Stanley Cups. The young man who had imposed a rigid self-exile to his Longueuil apartment just three years before would begin to fully understand what life in the Forum Fish Bowl was really all about.

In the first years of their marriage, the Lafleurs set up housekeeping in Vercheres, a francophone community on the South Shore of the St. Lawrence across from Montreal. It was a nice neighbourhood, but "too nice", recalls Lafleur. "There were too many 'fans' in the area and we were looking for peace and quiet." One thing they weren't looking for was danger, for themselves or baby Martin, born in 1975.

During the quarterfinals of the 1976 playoffs, knowledgeable observers noted that Lafleur was skittish and seemed even more frenetic than usual on the ice, passing when he should shoot, shooting when he should pass. Management knew what was behind the erratic behaviour but was not talking. Halfway through the playoffs, the Flower seemed to blossom anew and Montreal ended the two-year reign of the defending champion Flyers in four straight to win the Cup, Lafleur wrapping up the post-season tournament with 7 goals and 10 assists in 13 games, including the winning goal in the 5-3 clincher over the Broad Street Bullies on May 16.

Ten days later, the real story surfaced. Montreal police, investigating a spectacular $2.8 million Brink's robbery that had taken place in March, received a tip from an informant that Lafleur would be kidnapped and held for a very large ransom during the playoffs. This was reported to Sam Pollock, and the managing director immediately hired private security guards to accompany his star everywhere he went, at home and on the road. At home, Lafleur was under close police surveillance for three weeks until the same informant contacted the Brink's investigators.

"It's okay, the heat's off," he told the police. "The guys who were going to pull this off were picked up on something else and they won't be going anywhere for a long time."

Jean Beliveau handled the affair for the club and was in constant contact with the police. "I had to devote almost all of my time to the affair. Guy's home was under constant surveillance and he was always under guard." Beliveau knew what it was like to be a target. He hadn't forgotten the night that burglars had cleaned out his Longueuil home while he was playing a televised game at the Forum.

What really hurt Lafleur was that his erratic performances in the first two series against Chicago Black Hawks and New York Islanders had led to a lot of booing from the home fans.

Lise Lafleur was quick to rise to the defence of her husband. "If they only knew what he was going through, they would have been less unjust toward him. It is unbelievable how these events tortured him; he lost about a dozen pounds in three weeks." For the Lafleurs, the ordeal lasted the full three weeks. During the first, Mrs. Lafleur and her infant son moved into the Bonaventure Hotel, where the team was staying during the playoffs. A week later, she returned to her parents' home in Quebec City.

Such is the size of the Canadiens' entourage that few of his teammates suspected that anything untoward was happening, even with extra private security guards around the team.

"It was quite common for the team to hire people to ensure that we had a quiet time during the playoffs," says Pete Mahovlich. "Most of us just assumed that these guys were there for the whole team. Guy never mentioned a thing to us at all about the kidnapping threat."

That was virtually the only secret in the superstar's life in the late 1970s.

The young man who spent much of his first season escaping down Highway 40 to Quebec City at every opportunity became Montreal's latest matinee idol. Lafleur's sharp-chiselled features adorned the covers of sports, gossip, fashion and news weeklies and monthlies as he moved into the fast lane lifestyle of the national superstar. He flew to exotic Monaco to film commercials for General Motors' Monte Carlo sedans ... but drove a Ferrari in real life. The young man who had once sequestered himself in his Longueuil apartment now owned Crescent Street and had a regular table at trendy places like Thursday's and the Auberge Saint-Tropez— pronounced the "Sane-Tro" by Montreal's In Crowd. Lafleur's new business agent, Jerry Petrie, entertained offers from all sectors, accepting some, turning down many, many more.

Lafleur may not have been more popular than Maurice Richard or Jean Beliveau in their day, and like them he had to share the glory of the Canadiens with a raft of superstars like Shutt, Dryden, Lemaire and the Big Three. But his timing was the best. This was the television age, the era of McLuhan's Global Village, and more people were able to witness, and appreciate, his wizardry on the ice. Just as important, French Quebec was exploding politically, socially and economically, with a proud new Parti Québécois government in office in Quebec City. People such as racing's Gilles Villeneuve, singers Robert Charlebois and Diane Dufresne, financier Paul Desmarais and Lafleur himself were symbols of the new vibrancy. A new pantheon of native idols had emerged, to be worshipped avidly by most Québécois.

Style took on a new importance as Quebec looked at itself in the collective mirror with new eyes, and liked what it saw. Guy Lafleur was part of Quebec's emerging élan. He had moved to centre stage when he shucked his helmet and began scoring goals with panache, his blond hair trailing behind him like the tail of Halley's Comet.

Others were filling the net in the NHL: Phil Esposito, Rick Martin, Reggie Leach, Jean Pronovost, Danny Grant, Marcel Dionne and Pierre Larouche. Only Larouche could match Lafleur for style and he laboured in near anonymity in Pittsburgh. As far as Montreal was concerned, the others were plodders, possessors of big shots, cannons which simply blasted the rubber into the net. Lafleur was *un artiste*, a magician who could lift 18,000 people from their seats with his end-to-end rushes. At home, Lafleur's linemate Steve Shutt increased his scoring in increments of 15, with consecutive years of 15, 30, 45 and 60 goals, but was never considered a threat to Lafleur's deity. A very smart man who often hid his intellect behind a ready smile and constant kidding, Shutt took the pressure off the fans by describing himself as a "garbageman"—someone who "just hangs around and picks up the leftovers of Lafleur, Lemaire or Mahovlich."

Conversely, while the Québécois love-in was in full swing, Lafleur quietly moved to an English West Island suburb called Baie d'Urfe. He would not discuss politics in public but quietly let the PQ and others know that he was not enamoured of their policies. He was once (a rare occasion) quoted on the subject in an English Canadian magazine:

> I try to understand the Parti Québécois, but so far it's not very good. I live in an English suburb of Montreal, I want my son to go to English school. I want him to learn English. I had to, to play hockey in Montreal. Some of my best friends are English. On the team we get about half and half. It's a family, we work together and for each other. I'm not taking a public political question, but I've got my own idea

about the way it goes. And I would say that I am an anti-separatist.

That comment helps to explain why, when Lafleur became involved in a noisy contract squabble in 1982, Premier René Levesque, who made notably less money, was quick to criticize the superstar. The fact that the PQ honeymoon was over and that one of Lafleur's reasons for his threatened holdout was Quebec's onerous tax system, (attributed by many to PQ financial ineptitude) seemed secondary.

By then, Guy Lafleur could practically do or say anything at all with impunity in Montreal. The French Canadian Huck Finn had emerged and was thriving in the fantasyland of the Montreal Canadiens. All the glitzy new magazines that had sprung up clamoured excitedly for his every word. "What does Mr. Lafleur think about this spring's fashion statement? Which car does Mr. Lafleur drive? Is it difficult to live the life of a highly paid athlete in the 1970s? Is all well in the Lafleur household?"

Guy loved the lifestyle and was not afraid to say so, with a characteristic combination of sophisticated naïveté and disarming honesty. "Hockey is number one in my life," he proclaimed. "I must be truthful and say that it even comes ahead of wife and family," he added, in a tone which implied: "I worked all those years as a kid and teenager to become a hockey player, not a husband and father. The other two were incidental." At home, Lise Lafleur, a remarkably strong young woman, turned the other cheek. She would occasionally put her foot down, like the time Lafleur and son Martin posed for a magazine cover photo. Guy was reminded, none too gently, that, in the real world, the family had gone through hell for three weeks during the 1976 kidnap scare. "I don't want the crazies knowing what Martin looks like," she said. There were no more cover shots.

Guy spent a lot of time with his teammates on Crescent Street. Steve Shutt fondly reminisces, "We played hard and we partied hard." Lise Lafleur stayed home.

Guy explained his philosophy to *Weekend Magazine* in 1978:

> She knew what the situation was before she married me, and understood. It's tough for me and tough for her to accept. Lise is not really a hockey fan, but she is, I think, my biggest supporter. I want her to be happy. We both pursue separate activities by mutual agreement. If I'm home one night a week and that's the night she usually goes out, that's fine. At heart I am a family man, but when I'm home I can't sit still. So after I wash the car and play with Martin, I drive Lise crazy sometimes.
>
> Sometimes, I think she is glad to be rid of me. We are discussing more children, but I don't want them right now. I don't want to father them and then hit the road; that's not right.

Lafleur gave that interview many times, seemingly oblivious to the divorce rumours. Quebec truly had changed; had Beliveau or Richard before him ever uttered such statements, both would have been roundly denounced from every pulpit in the land.

In 1982, his on-ice fortunes waning, Guy Lafleur had a conversation with a man he admired and respected, Roger Barre, his father-in-law. Roger Barre was dying.

"Guy, you are getting older and the hockey days are getting shorter," he told the thirty-one year old superstar. "You owe it to yourself, Lise and Martin to settle down for a while."

There was a reason for the conversation. One March night a year before, Lafleur had eaten dinner at Thursday's with teammate Robert Picard. Guy was mentally tired, in the middle of an ongoing battle with the tax man and at a rocky time in his marriage. There was wine with dinner and a couple of liqueurs afterwards, then the two players moved on to a nearby disco for a nightcap. At two a.m., Lafleur hopped into his Cadillac (the club had asked him to part with his Ferrari) for the drive home to Baie d'Urfe, about twenty-five miles up Highway 20. Picard suggested that Lafleur not drive. "I'm okay," Lafleur retorted.

Columnist Ted Blackman of *The Gazette* had written:

Lafleur had been known as a chain smoker, but not much of a capacity drinker. It's an industry gag that *La Presse* always gets its annual scoop ("Lafleur Blasts Coach, Teammates, Mom, Apple Pie") during a long team flight from Los Angeles, when he's had the time for a third cocktail and pours out his frustrations.

About twenty minutes after Lafleur left Crescent Street, the Cadillac swerved off the highway, sideswiping a light standard and ripping out about twenty yards of Frost fence. A fence post came through the windshield, gouging the star's right ear. He missed decapitation by millimetres. The accident occurred because Lafleur had fallen asleep at the wheel. Ironically, dozing off may also have saved his life.

All of this was part of the emotional baggage Lafleur carried into the meeting with his father-in-law. Mr. Barre also had some sensible financial advice. "He told me this would be the best time for me to get a better contract." Lafleur still had four years remaining on his current deal, which called for $375,000 a year. He went to Larry Robinson, who already was renegotiating his contract, and suggested the two combine forces. They did, and both got their raises. However, they scored few points with fans (or the Quebec premier) with their public complaints about the Quebec and Canadian tax situations. Lafleur's remark that it would be better to play for an American team was particularly tactless.

Veneration of the superstar was still high in 1982, but his popularity had begun to wane. The celebrated outbursts that grew out of his on-ice frustration disillusioned some fans. The first such explosion had come four years before, in 1978, when Lafleur suddenly demanded a renegotiated contract.

The 1978 contract hassle was a precursor to other public disagreements Lafleur was to have with management. The fact that management no longer included Sam Pollock, who had left the club in September, after the Molson sale, is significant.

Most hockey fans and the Forum's second floor were equally at sea when a French newspaper reported out of the blue that Lafleur had been distressed to discover in a Toronto newspaper that, while he was earning only $180,000 a year, Canadiens' goalie Ken Dryden was reportedly pulling down somewhere between $325,000 and $350,000.

The fabled Forum press corps swooped down on this story like angry paratroopers and Jerry Petrie was called to a hurriedly scheduled meeting with the club's new managing director, Irving Grundman. The latter had to act fast to head off trouble, because he still was defending himself for having lost the popular Pierre Bouchard in the league's waiver draft a month before.

Three facts were significant in the Lafleur situation. He was far off base with his claims about the salaries earned by Dryden and other Canadiens veterans. As well, the media reported that Lafleur had delivered an ultimatum to the team, threatening to sit out upcoming games if nothing was done about his salary demands. (As a result, the crowd of reporters outside the Canadiens' dressing room at Maple Leaf Gardens for the October 25 game almost outnumbered the fans in the paying seats.) This was later denied by both Grundman and Petrie. Finally, Lafleur eventually won the showdown and was given a renegotiated contract by Grundman, something insiders say would never have happened during Sam Pollock's tenure.

Lafleur played in that lacklustre 4-4 tie and tried to back away graciously from what had become an incendiary situation. Just before the game began, Petrie read a prepared statement, purportedly prepared by Lafleur, to the press: "Certain remarks have been made to certain members of the press which are regrettable, and as a result the matter has been blown slightly out of proportion. I just want to devote my full time and energy to playing hockey for the Canadiens and helping our team win another Stanley Cup."

He did just that, scoring 52 goals and adding 77 assists for 129 points to finish third in the league scoring race behind Bryan Trottier and Marcel Dionne. He added another 10 goals and 13 assists in 16 playoff games as the Canadiens won their fourth straight Stanley Cup. But something had changed. It was impossible to define, but somehow the Lafleur holdout had struck a nerve with the Canadiens; after all, Richard and Beliveau never had threatened to sit out during their careers. Something was irretrievably lost, but it was difficult to say exactly what. Before Lafleur would retire, there would be other interviews, some on salary matters, others on the weaknesses of management. There were also whispers about complaints by Lafleur of the linemates he had been saddled with, hints that Steve Shutt had slowed down, that newcomer Keith Acton wasn't getting him the puck enough.

There were other factors contributing to the change. Guy Lafleur was about to get more competition on the ice for the unofficial title of most spectacular player in the NHL.

The 1979-80 season was special. The Nordiques had joined the league, along with the Winnipeg Jets, Hartford Whalers and Edmonton Oilers with their young new scoring sensation, Wayne Gretzky. Over the past several seasons, Montreal had become very aware of the rising power of the New York Islanders and their emerging stars like Bryan Trottier, Mike Bossy, Denis Potvin and Clark Gillies. In 1978-79, the Islanders had edged out the Canadiens, 116 to 115 points, for the overall league championship, only to be ambushed by their cross-town rival, the Rangers, in the playoffs.

In 1979-80, Lafleur again would attain the 50-goal mark, scoring exactly that many and adding 75 assists for 125 points, but some of the magic was disappearing. Gretzky tied Dionne for the league leadership in points with 137 and Bossy scored 51 goals for the Islanders. The latter was a Montreal native who had escaped the Canadiens' talent net, despite a pro-Bossy clamour in the Montreal newspapers—proof that the club shared the opinion that scoring feats in Quebec junior hockey were overvalued. As a result, Bossy was Bill Torrey's first draft pick in 1977, but the fifteenth overall, after such players as Dale McCourt, Barry Beck, Robert Picard, Jere Gillis and Lucien Deblois. Selecting tenth, Montreal picked Mark Napier, who had scored 60 goals for Birmingham of the WHA the previous season, after 156 goals in three excellent years with the Toronto Marlboros of the OHA.

Bossy, meanwhile, had scored 308 goals in four seasons of junior with Laval Nationals and was considered a pure shooter. However, there was a *caveat emptor* as to his ability to play defence.

"Get me the scorer," Al Arbour told Torrey. "We'll teach him to play defence."

Bossy was an immediate hit in the NHL, winning the Calder Trophy as Rookie of the Year, setting a rookie scoring mark of 53 goals and earning a spot on the league's second all-star team behind Lafleur. That same year, Lafleur scored 60 goals, but it was the only time that he ever outscored Bossy.

Every year thereafter, Bossy scored more goals than Lafleur and whispers were heard even in Montreal as to who the real best right winger in the NHL might be. Lafleur was the first player to have six consecutive 50-goal seasons before that string was broken in 1980-81. Bossy has never had a sub-50-goal season to date in his nine-year career.

Montreal was still a powerhouse in 1979-80, finishing third overall with 107 points, behind Philadelphia's 116 and Buffalo's 110. Yet that result was somewhat inflated, since the Habs played in the notoriously weak Norris Division with Los Angeles Kings, Pittsburgh Penguins, Hartford Whalers and Detroit Red Wings, while Buffalo was in the tough Adams with Boston, Minnesota, Toronto and Quebec. The Flyers fought it out with the Islanders, Rangers, Atlanta Flames and Washington.

That spring, Montreal entered the best-of-five quarterfinal against the Whalers with a good shot at their fifth straight Stanley Cup, a challenge to the powerhouse history of the late '50s. The Habs swept the Whalers 3-0, but late in the third period of the third game, a journeyman player named Pat Boutette kneed Lafleur as he was skating past.

Lafleur was out for the rest of the playoffs, joining fellow 50-goal scorer Pierre Larouche on the sidelines. With 100 goals out of the line-up, the Canadiens went down in seven games to the rising Minnesota North Stars, something which never would have happened with Lafleur and Larouche playing, and the dream for five straight ended. Later that spring, the Islanders launched their four-year conquest of the Stanley Cup.

Contrary to the popular mythology of the mid-1980s, the Montreal Canadiens did not roll over and die in the ensuing years. The team maintained its position in the upper echelons of the NHL, especially during regular-season play, with first-place finishes in 1980-81 in the Norris Division and 1981-82 in the revamped Adams Division, before slipping to second place behind Boston in 1982-83. Popular mythology, created daily in the local media, painted the so-called "Grundman years" as a total failure, a damning canvas of Forum futility. That, of course, is not true.

However, two factors combined to attach a label of ineptitude to the once-proud franchise. The first was Montreal's poor playoff record; they were embarrassed 3-0 by the upstart Edmonton Oilers in 1980-81, and then lost a heartbreaking series to the dreaded Nordiques in overtime in the fifth game of 1981-82 divisional semi-final. The following year, the Sabres blew out Montreal in three straight, once again in the opening series.

The second, and most important, factor was that Guy Lafleur had plunged into a precipitous decline and was not producing as he once had. An injury in 1980-81 caused him to miss 29 games and *le Démon Blond* scored 27 goals and 43 assists for a mere 70 points. He would remain stuck at the 27-goal level for the next two years, breaking loose with only 30 goals in 1983-84. What frustrated Lafleur, and Montreal fans, during this period was that just about every scorer worth his shot was popping in 50; people like Rick Kehoe, Dennis Maruk, Dino Ciccarelli and Al Secord. Bossy was still Bossy, averaging 60 goals a season and 20 in the playoffs while Gretzky was sublime, scoring 55-92-71-74 to Lafleur's 27-27-27-30.

Whether or not Lafleur himself made conscious comparisons with Gretzky we will never know. The two played together for Team Canada in 1981 and got along well, with Edmonton fans chanting "Guy! Guy! Guy!" whenever Lafleur carried the puck. Unfortunately, Team Canada was humbled by the Soviet Union in that competition.

Worse still, the two played against each other in the 1980-81 quarterfinal and Gretzky owned the ice in their first head-to-head confrontation. It really stung when Canadiens' goalie Richard Sevigny showed that even if the Flower didn't, his teammates did make such individual comparisons, vowing on the eve of the first game that "Guy will put him [Gretzky] in his pocket before the series is over." All Lafleur had to show for the series was a single assist and one minor penalty. His nemesis ended the playoffs with 7 goals and 14 assists for 21 points.

Nobody could foretell that Lafleur would score only two more Stanley Cup playoff goals in his career, both in the 1981-82 series loss to the Nordiques. The last came April 10, 1982, a power play goal at 19:34 of the third period that allowed Montreal to escape the ignominy of a shutout.

A year later, after the Canadiens' worst season in living memory—35 wins, 40 losses and 5 ties in 80 games —the team would rise up and smite the Bruins and Nordiques in the playoffs and take a 2-0 lead on the defending champion Islanders before succumbing in six games. Lafleur's contribution in the 12 games would be three assists. His 30 goals and 40 assists in the regular season would be deceiving, too. Most of those were scored in the first half of the season.

In late February, with Montreal's record at 28-30-5, Bob Berry was fired as coach and replaced by Lafleur's former linemate, Jacques Lemaire. In the remaining 17 regular-season games and 12 playoff games, Lafleur would only score twice, ending the 1983-84 season and playoffs mired in the 26-game scoring slump.

In the 1984 off-season, as he had the year before, Lafleur worked hard to keep in shape and reported to training camp in top condition. But the magic was irretrievably gone. In 19 games, he scored just two goals, one each against Buffalo and Philadelphia, and both in October. Added to that were three assists, the last on a Mark Hunter goal on November 1 in a 6-5 win over the Islanders. The Flower spent long stretches of games rivetted to the team bench, kept there by Lemaire, a stickler for defence. Yet, Lafleur's skating and defensive play were better than they had been in several years.

He was skating well, as even the opposition would admit. Craig Ramsay, Larry Playfair and several other Sabres discussed Lafleur's last season on the afternoon of the Flower's public retirement ceremony.

"The strange thing was that he was skating much better this year than the last two seasons," said Ramsay, who would win the Frank Selke trophy as top defensive forward in the NHL that season. "He wasn't putting it in the net like he had before, but I always had the impression than when he got a couple, he would return to normal. Before every game, our coach would say something like: 'Let some other team wake him up, don't let Lafleur kill us.'"

Playfair agreed: "Say what you want in the press box; when you're down here on the ice, you see a different Lafleur and this guy can still play hockey."

On Saturday, November 24, Montreal beat the Detroit Red Wings 6-4 in a lacklustre game at the Forum. The win gave the surging Canadiens a 13-4-2 record and the club was playing superbly under Lemaire's defensively oriented system. So far in the young season, they had defeated the challengers in their division: Buffalo, Boston, and Quebec (twice). The Canadiens had also logged wins over the cream of the rest of the NHL—New York Islanders, Philadelphia Flyers, Edmonton Oilers and Chicago Black Hawks. Strangely enough, three of their four losses had come at the hands of the league's have-nots—Detroit, Toronto Maple Leafs and Pittsburgh Penguins.

When the team skated off the ice after the game, few

fans suspected that Guy Lafleur had played his 961st, and last, hockey game with the Montreal Canadiens.

Even though Guy Lafleur had not been scoring, his teammates and the fans were still rooting for him. But he was an open, festering wound that club management strove to cauterize. Shift after frustrating shift, Lafleur skated through his slump, seemingly a shell of the player who had terrorized a generation of NHL teams. As the Sabres said, his skating was still there, but every time he touched the puck it seemed he would instinctively make the wrong move. Each time he skated to the bench at the end of a shift, a collective sigh would float down from the seats. Everyone ached to see the Lion in pain, unable to shake it off. Forum games became group empathy sessions.

As well, although club management would not admit it, Lafleur posed too much of a challenge to the authority of Lemaire. A still-young thirty-three, Lafleur should have had several good years ahead of him. After all, his predecessors, Richard and Beliveau, had played to the ages of thirty-nine and forty-one respectively. They, too, had endured late-career slumps, only to finish strongly. Most importantly, both had finished their careers on Stanley Cup winners.

However, neither had railed against the team or management during their careers. The club feared another Lafleur outburst; they felt it would be devastating to a young, new team in full reconstruction. Ever since Henri Richard's celebrated criticism of Al MacNeil during the 1971 playoffs, management was hypersensitive to the slightest rumblings of a veteran.

The Friday before the Detroit game, and the day after a 3-2 home win over Chicago in which Lafleur hardly saw any action, the player held a long meeting with Lemaire. They discussed his contribution to the team.

"Before I retired, I was skating very well but they weren't letting me play," Guy says. "I was getting eight or nine minutes a game on the ice and that wasn't enough—I couldn't build up my confidence that way. And they knew that I was losing my confidence. There was a psychological war going on." Lafleur asked Savard several times for a trade but the general manager refused. "We can't trade you; you're part of the building," Savard told him.

"Then Serge would say to me: 'Go talk to Jacques,' which was his way of washing his hands of the affair. I spoke with Jacques but he had his own style. I respected that. On the Friday before I retired, I sat down with him and said, 'Listen, Jacques, we played together and had a lot of success and I was getting about 25 minutes a game. If you think at my age I'm not capable, say so, but I know I can still play if you give me the chance to prove myself.' There didn't seem to be a problem. We were scheduled against Detroit the next night and he said I was going to play on a regular line, I was going to play on the power plays and I might play on another line or kill penalties. I wanted to play 17 or 18 minutes, not 25 or 30—so I could get my confidence back."

Lafleur returned home and told his wife about the meeting. "She didn't believe a word of it; she said I was deluding myself if I thought Lemaire was going to do that for me. I told her I thought things would be fine."

On Saturday morning, Lafleur showed up for the team skate and was in high spirits. He was so keyed up, he returned to the rink at three p.m., surprising club president Ronald Corey who was in the team's exercise room.

"What are you doing here?" he asked Lafleur.

"I'm getting ready," Lafleur replied. "I spoke with Lemaire and I'm going to get some ice time tonight."

"Perfect," said Corey. "I hope things will go well and you pop a couple."

Lafleur was on the ice once in the first period, and twice in the second.

"After the second period, I asked Mr. Charest [the Forum policeman stationed just outside the team dressing room] to get Serge Savard, it was urgent. Savard didn't come downstairs because he knew. When he came down after the game, I said to him: 'It's over. You got what you wanted. It's over.'"

Just two weeks before Lafleur retired, Steve Shutt had been traded to Los Angeles Kings.

"It was all part of the plan. Mr. Corey had come in with a five-year plan to rebuild the Canadiens and I always thought that this attitude made a lot of sense. And when Serge became general manager in 1983, I thought they had picked somebody who would know what to do. But a little while after he took over, I found out from somebody with impeccable contacts—he had the scoop, as they say—that Savard had said he would get rid of all the players who had played with him and Lemaire over a period of three years. I didn't believe it at first but this person told me this was the mandate.

"When Steve left, I knew I was next."

A little under three months later, with the crowd chanting "Guy! Guy! Guy!" for five full minutes before he appeared, Lafleur skated onto the Forum ice for the last time. The Canadiens wore their home whites, the Sabres their distinctive blue-and-gold. Guy was in road red, the uniform of fable.

Standing at centre ice, awaiting him, were Guy's parents, Rejean and Pierrette, Madame Baribeau, his second mother from Quebec City, Lise Lafleur, and son Martin. For the first time in her life, it seemed, Mrs. Lafleur got a real look at her husband's world. She stood in her chic blue dress, a gold corsage above her right breast, and appeared overwhelmed by the ovation, looking on uncomprehendingly as Guy Lafleur drank from the heady wine of the fans' cheers for a last time. It was as if the fans were saying: "Guy's fantasy land is as much a real world as any other. This ovation is real. His special career and what it meant to all of us is real."

There were more than 18,000 paying customers, 200 journalists and media technicians and some 40 professional hockey players in the building and all unabashedly took part in a standing ovation that lasted a shade under five minutes. There were few dry eyes in the house, Lise Lafleur's included. In front of her, Martin bravely bit his lower lip throughout the special ceremonies.

Buffalo Sabres' assistant coach Joe Crozier stood on

the visitors' bench, clapping steadily, and forcing some of his players off the bench and onto the ice. There they clustered with a phalanx of photographers. "Guy! Guy! Guy!" cascaded down from the rafters. The Sabres and Canadiens banged their sticks on the ice and the boards in the kind of tribute accorded only to Morenz, Richard and Beliveau in this building.

Guy skated over to his former teammates, going down the bench shaking hands, stopping here for a word with Mario Tremblay, there for a joke with Larry Robinson. Then, to tumultuous cheering, he skated to the Sabres' bench and repeated the process. Tough hockey players like Larry Playfair and Mike Foligno were beaming ear-to-ear, past animosities and ice battles forgotten. They would admit later to being thrilled. With electronic flashes bouncing lightning bolts off the protective glass over the boards just behind them, Lafleur stopped and shared a quiet moment with Gilbert Perreault. A couple of Sabres players were on the other side of the mob of photographers and Lafleur couldn't see them; thinking he had pressed the flesh with the whole team, he shook hands with Foligno and returned to centre ice after a parting word to Perreault. You could see the disappointment on Paul Cyr's face all the way up in the press box.

As the great Bobby Clark once said: "There are players in this league that make fans of the rest of us. Lafleur was like that. He was the kind of player you not only played against, but you watched when he was on the ice."

After the emotional press conference on November 26, 1984, during which a distraught Lafleur announced his retirement, the Canadiens' management apparatus went into high gear. Guy was quietly enrolled in business courses and became a member of the second floor team.

For a while, it seemed to work. The shaken warrior who announced his retirement in late November was gone when Lafleur stepped to the microphone at an Ad and Sales Executives Club luncheon in early February, a week before his on-ice good-bye.

Tanned from a southern holiday, he was relaxed and

his pinstripes fit. The three hundred businessmen in the room cheered "Guy! Guy! Guy" as Lafleur made his way to the podium.

"The difference between my new life and my life three months ago is that I didn't have to carry a piece of paper on the ice with me," he joked, referring to his speaking notes. "I am no longer a hockey player. I am embarking on a new career and I intend to work as hard at it as I did hockey. For those of you who keep mentioning rumours of me returning for the playoffs, I must say that I won't be back this season." He paused. "I won't be back forever."

He made a passing reference to his past differences with management. "Now I can understand how they think upstairs. Now they're on my level ... the second floor."

Forever is a very long time, especially if you are a thirty-three year old man who has been in the limelight for two decades. In Lafleur's case, forever on the second floor was less than a year. In mid-September, the *Journal de Montréal* reported that Lafleur was locked in yet another salary conflict, this time over his future salary as a public relations representative with Montreal. With still one year to run on his $400,000-plus playing salary, Lafleur was offered a very generous $75,000 a year, with a liberal expense account and ten percent increases each year, to start in 1987.

The Flower's response was predictable. He suggested that a move to Quebec City might result in him working in the automobile industry and doing some public relations for the Nordiques.

This time, however, the second floor was firm. "I am saddened by Guy's decision to resign," said Corey. "In view of what he said publicly about a private matter, I had no alternative but to accept it, effective immediately."

"I was told I was resigning," says Lafleur. A few days later, Lafleur speculated on a possible return to a playing career, and got Serge Savard's permission to speak with other teams in the league. There were talks with the

New York Rangers, Pittsburgh Penguins and Los Angeles Kings, but all eventually fell through.

"Rogatien Vachon [Kings' GM] is Serge's biggest chum so there was little real chance there. The Rangers were in the process of dropping all of their veterans, like Mike Rogers and Pierre Larouche, so little happened there, too. Pittsburgh was a real possibility because Eddie Johnston liked the idea of teaming me up with Mario Lemieux but he had to clear it with Eddie deBartolo, the owner."

Lafleur gave all teams a deadline of 5 p.m. EDT on Friday, October 11, to come to some agreement, but Pittsburgh could not meet it. Later that day, he announced that he would not return to action. If there was a measure of revenge it came when the Canadiens included him among the eighteen players protected by the club in the waiver draft earlier that week.

Serge Savard did not see it that way: "We protected Guy so that he would retain his choice of team if he decided to return to action. If he had been unprotected, he might not want to go to the team that claimed him and after all he meant to Montreal for so long, it would be unfair to leave him in that situation."

What if Lafleur wanted to return to Montreal?

"Not a chance," Savard said.

\* \* \*

There was only one thing wrong with Lafleur's retirement — a minor thing really. He never should have retired; there was a lot of hockey left in the player.

Looking back now at his complete hockey record, with the ominous "DID NOT PLAY" entry for the years 1985-86, 1986-87 and 1987-88, the occasional fan would confess to being mystified by the events that befell The Flower. How, indeed, could a player who was washed up at 33 return for three final seasons, starting at age 37? How could the NHL turn its collective back on a player who still had so much to give his sport? How could all of these things happen, especially after many teammates and adversaries had insisted that Lafleur, as far as they were concerned, was far from finished?

Most of the answers lie within Lafleur, physically and mentally. Others lay within the hallowed halls of the second floor at the Forum.

Lafleur's greatness stemmed from many factors, but there was an overriding one that set him apart from most athletes — indeed, from most humans. Unlike his idol and mentor, Jean Beliveau, whose cardiomyopathy once prompted journalists to write of a Cadillac with a Volkswagen engine, Lafleur had a coronary muscle described by doctors as a "one in a million."

On September 11, 1971, three months and a day after being drafted by the Canadiens, Lafleur reported to the Montreal Canadiens' training camp and the opening-day physical. What the club doctors saw astounded them: Lafleur's resting heart rate was an incredible forty beats a minute, the same rate found in only the very best of Olympic and endurance athletes, among them famed cyclist Eddie Merckx of Belgium. His recuperative powers were amazing: after Herculean physical effort at maximum effort for lengthy periods of time, Lafleur was able to recover quickly, with only the minimum of rest. This wasn't a man; it was a machine.

Doctors will tell you that a physical specimen like this would not tend to run down prematurely at age 33. Other athletes famed for their longevity in the sport, Gordie Howe, Beliveau, Frank Mahovlich, Jacques Plante and Tim Horton, were not blessed with the internal combustion engine that drove The Flower, and even though in mid-career he had driven himself hard in extra-curricular activities, he had never run down his body like other athletes who were shells of what they had been in their prime. As mentioned earlier in this chapter, we met with several Buffalo Sabres on the eve of Lafleur's official retirement from Montreal and to a man they marvelled at his speed on the ice, and even more at the fact that he would even contemplate quitting.

"It isn't the wheels," insisted Larry Playfair, who on his best days would be lost in The Flower's wake, and knew it. "It has to be something else." To a man, too, the Sabres were concerned that the Canadiens were giving their former superstar the bum's rush.

The other part of the internal equation was The Flower's head, the fragile psyche that had betrayed him for so long and a reason why many of his teammates would not publicly contest his decision to leave the game. Over the years, they had borne witness to the manic depression, the incredibly high highs that fuelled the greatness, interspersed with nadirs of lows that brought the greatness plunging to the depths of mere competence. Nothing or no one could reduce Lafleur to a shell of the great player than himself and his doubts.

This had been most evident right from the beginning if you cared to look. When he starred for the Remparts, the Canadiens would often send scouts to evaluate his performances. When a more anonymous scout was in attendance at whatever Quebec rink the Remparts were playing in, Lafleur was head and shoulders above everyone. When he was aware that a bird dog of such stature as Claude Ruel was in the stands, Lafleur would almost shun the puck and attempt to crawl under the blueline and hide.

The same thing happened in his first three years with Montreal. There definitely was something to say for the fact that the Canadiens had a history of breaking rookies and young players into the system by making them spend long periods in the practice rink and on the bench during games. That was not true for Lafleur. He spent most of his first two seasons playing out of position at centre, but he received much more icetime than had illustrious predecessors like Jacques Lemaire, Yvan Cournoyer and Mickey Redmond. Most of his early problems were internal, and dealt with his inability to adapt to Montreal, the team, and Montreal, the city, and the weighty expectations of hockey fans in Quebec.

Even during the most successful years with the Canadiens, the exhaustion and insecurity would flare up. One classic and hushed-up example came in Philadelphia on the night of May 16, 1976, moments after Montreal had won its twentieth Stanley Cup and what would turn out to be first of four straight. While his teammates were drunkenly regaling reporters with champagne showers and slurred versions of "God Bless America," some players and journalists suddenly noted the absence of The Flower. In *Overtime, The Legend of Guy Lafleur,* Georges-Hébert Germain, writes:

*"Pete Mahovlich, Jim Roberts, the trainer Eddy Palchak and a few journalists, including Claude Larochelle of the Quebec newspaper* Le Soleil, *set out to look for him. They finally found him at the far end of the Spectrum. He had shut himself into a small, poorly lit room, and was sitting on a stool, a Coke in his hand, clearly unhappy to see them.*

*"The overly exuberant Pete Mahovlich shook him like a rag doll trying to get him to be happy. But Guy had only one desire: to be alone, not to have to speak or even listen to anything from anyone, to be left in peace for once.*

*"For years it had never, never stopped. The whole world was always running after him. He was always having to explain himself and give his opinion on every subject, whether things were going well or badly. He felt empty, and at the same time, brimming with tears. He would have liked to be left in peace to cry alone. He didn't have the strength to respond to Mahovlich and to tell them all to go away. Fortunately, Larochelle and Palchak, more sensitive than Pete Mahovlich, understood his feelings and tried to talk to him gently, the way you talk to a sick person, so sweetly and softly that he almost bursts into tears."*

That night Lafleur avoided the official team celebration and went to a quiet restaurant in Philadelphia with Larochelle, ironically a teammate of Jean Beliveau in junior hockey, and the two spent a quiet night talking about Quebec City and all of the people they knew in common "back home." For Guy Lafleur, this was catharsis, and he felt the tension and pressures oozing away in nostalgic conversation with the dean of Quebec City's hockey writers.

The next year, an almost identical scene happened after the Canadiens won the Cup in Boston: Lafleur emerged from the shower, sat down at his locker stall, and burst into tears. Larry Robinson, Steve Shutt and Réjean Houle surrounded The Flower to keep him from prying eyes. Despair in his face, trembling uncontrollably, he complained of lost sensation in his legs. His three teammates spoke to him softly, much like Palchak and Larochelle had the previous year, and with concern for the obvious physical and mental exhaustion they were witnessing. Practical players who shared Lafleur's predicament of impossibly high expectations in the hockey capital of the world, they prescribed two cures: one short-term and one long-term. The first was downing a bottle or so of victory champagne to banish the shakes and melancholy so he could emerge and face the media in the next room; the second was a long vacation away from it all, to recharge head and body for the next season.

Lafleur followed both prescriptions and the freshly dressed player who accepted the congratulations of the media that night was half in the bag. The long-term solution was a shared vacation in France with Lise Lafleur and Steve and Ninon Shutt.

The manifestations of Lafleur's fragile psyche when his career was in apogee were precursors of problems to come. When his career appeared to begin a perilous slide in 1980, those close to The Flower knew that things could get very bad before they got better. They were right.

After a series of injuries in the 1980, 1981 and 1982 seasons cost him 55 games of playing time, and much more in recuperation, Lafleur's goal totals started to shrink and he began to feel he was finished.

It proved to be self-fulfilling prophesy.

It did not take long for The Flower to regret a move made prematurely; the major problem was he had been neatly finessed by Ronald Corey and Serge Savard and there seemed to be no way out. Guy Lafleur was retired, the Canadiens had offered him what he felt was a meaningless job in public relations, the job description for which could be summed up in four words: "Smile for the birdie." And when a proud athlete began to chafe under the altogether different but not less consequential pressures of being a "second-floor suit," the second part of the job description kicked in: "Shut up and like it." However, any complaint he might make would sound like sour grapes; the P.R. job was for ten years and fully indexed so it would pay him as much as $175,000 a year by the tenth year of the contract.

In management terms, it was a seamless deal that allowed the team to save face, removed a thorn from the side of Jacques Lemaire, and pleased the fans who otherwise might have seen the boot that was being applied to The Flower's rear end. As well, it was a no-brainer; Corey and Savard knew that Lafleur was more Richard than Beliveau, and that he would eventually talk himself out of a job, under circumstances which would leave them blameless should The Flower be terminated.

Without knowing it, Lafleur had followed the script to the letter. And even though observers such as Jean Beliveau, Maurice Richard and Sam Pollock supported him, he found himself on the outside looking in. At age 34.

Now what to do?

First things first, Lafleur did something that he needed almost as much as oxygen. He took time off, resting up from the pressures of the game, upstairs and downstairs, and getting out of the public limelight for a while. There was no danger of his name being forgotten and, thus, his market-ability would be intact for a long time to come. He, like Richard and Beliveau before him, had transcended the game and the Montreal Canadiens. He, like Richard and Beliveau before him, had become a cultural icon in Quebec, and would remain so for the rest of his life. His popularity even extended far beyond Quebec, as he would discover.

In December 1985, The Flower surfaced on a hockey rink once again. What was most unusual about the end of his retirement was that the ice surface onto which he skated for the first time since retiring was in Paris, France. His new team was called the Français Volants, and included several former pros from Canada and some members of the French national team, and it would face off in a four-team Christmas tournament against Riga Dynamo of the Soviet Elite League, a Czech team from Brno and the Granby Bisons of the Quebec Major Junior Hockey League. Some top Soviets and Czechs, including Helmut Balderis of Riga and Jiri Lala of the Czech team, were surprised to see how strong Lafleur was skating, especially since they knew he had not laced up skates in thirteen months.

"If this is how he plays when he has not been on the ice in a year, I would pay money to see him in top shape," Lala said, through an interpreter. "He could play for any team in the world."

But, hours later at the Intercontinental Hotel, a disconsolate Lafleur doubted that such an opportunity would ever present itself.

"To tell the truth, I regret leaving when I did, but my retirement only partially was about hockey," he said. "I couldn't play for Montreal any more under the circumstances and Serge let it be known that he would never trade me."

Lafleur did play, but only for a Petro-Canada touring team of former NHL stars. On many occasions, he found himself reunited with former teammates Shutt and Lemaire, the latter having also walked away from the ferocious media blast furnace at the Forum. Slowly, and very carefully, Lemaire and Lafleur regained most of the friendship they had shared as roommates in their playing days.

On the ice, the trio dazzled, especially Lemaire and Lafleur, and there wasn't a hockey observer who saw them who didn't question their decisions both to quit at 33. Although five years older, Lemaire still had the smarts, speed and moves that had characterized his game. And Lafleur still had the instincts and the sublime talent, even though he could only show it against former pros and semi-pros.

For two more years, Lafleur made the most of his image in the business world, getting involved in many non-profit and for-profit ventures that kept him firmly in the consciousness of hockey fans in Quebec. The NHL contributed too, when in 1988 he joined players Tony Esposito, Brad Park and Buddy O'Connor, Philadelphia owner Ed Snider, and former referee/linesman George Hayes, as the newest inductees into the NHL Hall of Fame.

Little did anyone know on Hall of Fame night that this player had three more seasons in him.

In May, 1988, Lafleur watched the last game of the Boston-Edmonton final series, a rarity because he had shunned the game since his departure. As recounted by Georges-Hébert

Germain, he turned to friend and business partner Yves (Kid) Tremblay: *"You know, Kid, the more I watch them play, the more I think I could play just as well. Apart from Gretzky, of course, and two or three others."*

This was a conversation that had come up occasionally over three years, and each time Tremblay's answer was the same: "Talk to some people. You might be surprised by their reaction." And each time Lafleur would scoff, or simply do nothing. This time was different, and the conversation stayed with Lafleur for the rest of the spring and most of the following summer. When he heard that the Los Angeles Kings had made a lucrative offer to Mike Bossy, whose bad back led to his premature retirement from the New York Islanders, he had Tremblay call the team.

That effort was wasted; after all, Rogatien Vachon and Serge Savard were still bosom buddies. However, this time, Lafleur gave Tremblay the go-ahead to approach other teams and see if there might be a nibble.

Both Tremblay and Savard were quite surprised when Phil Esposito almost bit the fishing pole right out of their hands. Forever the showman, Esposito wanted someone to add a bit of spice to the transition Blueshirts, a team he knew was two or three years away from challenging the best in the league. Standing behind him and rooting loudly for The Flower was a very familiar face, Michel Bergeron, the former Nordiques coach.

Tremblay and Lafleur flew to New York and met with Bergeron, Esposito and Rangers' money-man Joe Bokino. It soon became obvious that the Rangers were very interested, but they wouldn't be forthcoming with a contract unless Lafleur could show them something.

Bergeron noted that Lafleur could make his comeback "at home," the Rangers' training camp that year would take place in Trois-Rivières, where "Le Tigre" Bergeron had launched his junior coaching career. He had greeted Lafleur warmly, as had Esposito, a former adversary and teammate on Canada Cup and All-Star teams. But, Bergeron was also a realist and he warned Lafleur that the players in the NHL had become a lot bigger and faster in the short four years

since he had stopped playing. If The Flower was not prepared, he could be in for a big surprise.

This was the challenge Lafleur needed and he was gal-
vanized into action. Upon his return to Montreal, he sought
out the best physical trainers because he was prepared to
suffer to get into the best shape his 37 years could support.
He knew that physically, returning to the NHL would be
less of a challenge than anyone else expected. His physical
training, however, would have to contain a huge component
of psychological reinforcement.

*La Presse* columnist Réjean Tremblay hit on the best man as
the two were sharing a drink in a Montreal bar on the Friday
night after the return from Manhattan. Lafleur should put himself in the hands of George Cherry, a boxing trainer who was
handling the Hilton family and many other pro fighters. Yves
Tremblay made a few telephone calls, and returned.

"He's expecting you tomorrow morning at nine."

"But tomorrow is Saturday."

"There aren't any days off in your program."

For three weeks, with many interested sports fans watching, Lafleur went through gruelling ninety-minute boxing
workouts under the watchful eye of Cherry. It was exactly
what he needed, physically and mentally preparing him to
withstand the rigors and pain of training camp.

When Lafleur got to Trois-Rivières, it was all downhill.

A few minutes after the last intra-squad game, The Flower
was summoned to a small room in the arena; he was a New
York Ranger.

Perhaps the least significant aspect of the final three seasons played by The Flower, was the statistics. With New
York, and the subsequent two seasons with the Nordiques,
he scored a total of 42 goals and 65 assists for 107 points, and
added a single playoff goal in four games with the Rangers
in 1989.

However, his return was a boon to the game, and allowed
hockey fans everywhere to revel at the career of a hockey
great who had brought much artistry to the sport.

Montreal fans will never forget February 4, 1989, and The
Flower's return as a Broadway Blueshirt. This was the second

scheduled visit to Montreal by the Rangers that season, but Lafleur had sat out the previous encounter on December 17, 1988 with an ankle injury. However, that did not prevent him from stealing the show in pre-game ceremonies. Dressed in civvies, Lafleur was to be introduced to the crowd, come out and say a few words, and then the hockey game would commence.

The Canadiens' hierarchy was still in control; Lafleur would not alienate an adoring crowd with poorly chosen words, they reasoned, and they could not ignore him. So the invitation was safe.

They forgot, of course, the most Gallic of statements, *le grand geste*, and when New York captain Kelly Kisio skated up to Lafleur and presented him with his No. 10 in visiting blue, Lafleur shrugged himself into the sweater and raised his arms heavenward, looking directly at the Canadiens' box upstairs. There, standing together, Corey, Savard and Lemaire were forced to join the tumultuous standing ovation that rocked the building.

If that was a great moment in Montreal sports history, it was easily eclipsed six weeks later when the Rangers returned to the Forum. On that night, the fans wanted two things only . . . a Montreal victory and a trip in a time machine, to once again savour the artistry and sheer ability of Lafleur. They got both; the Canadiens outlasted the Rangers 7-5, and The Flower played spectacularly, putting two goals behind Patrick Roy.

At season's end, after firing Bergeron and taking over his team as coach for the playoffs, Phil Esposito himself was fired. When Lafleur spoke to the new management group, he was told he could stay on as a player, but he wanted more. His original agreement with Esposito had included a position with the team after his playing days were over, but that was now out of the question. He was given permission to negotiate a deal with another team, and eventually signed with the Nordiques, following Bergeron back to Le Tigre's original club.

This was to be the culmination of a career; one or two years on the ice, and then a lifetime of building hockey and representing the Nordiques in Quebec. For two years, it worked.

However, when the time came to move upstairs, Lafleur found himself in the same predicament he had faced in Montreal six years earlier, "Smile for the birdie." Lafleur wanted a hockey job, contributing to the team on the ice and working with Pierre Pagé, Pierre Gauthier and the scouts.

He lasted a year as vice-president of public relations for the Nordiques, and left his position in August, 1993, ironically within a few days of Jean Beliveau's retirement from the same position with the Canadiens. The ironies were everywhere that month; Jacques Lemaire had been hired as head coach of the New Jersey Devils, taking Larry Robinson along with him as his defensive coach, and Steve Shutt was the newest member of the Montreal Canadiens' coaching staff.

"Marcel Aubut probably didn't think my job was worth much," he said after leaving. "He wanted to keep me, but he wanted Molson-O'Keefe Breweries and Rona Hardware stores to help pay for my salary . . . to match my salary from last year."

Lafleur saw this as a snub, and was gone. This time to a steady position as vice-president of public relations for Titrex, a company that markets natural food-based products, including Flower Power, a health drink originally marketed by Lafleur.

The biggest difference in his departure from the Forum, and his subsequent leaving of the Nordiques, is that the latter did not cause a scandal. Neither was Lafleur's personality assailed. There are no more stories about an egocentric player, unable to live in the real world.

Everyone, including Guy Lafleur, is comfortable with his retirement this time around.

# 11

## The Seventies

In Philadelphia, on a warm September Sunday in 1975, the 21st it was, their minds were on The Bull, Lefty, Mike "The Hammer" Schmidt and the Philly juggernaut that was thick in the fight for the National League's East Division crown. As well, a young coach from the West Coast named Dick Vermeil was proving that fanatical dedication to the work ethic would soon forge championship contenders of his National Football League Eagles, and the improving 76ers were readying for another National Basketball Association season.

In the Spectrum, across the street from Veteran's Stadium, the Stanley Cup champion Philadelphia Flyers, a.k.a. the Broad Street Bullies, were warming up for a season of mayhem on the ice and a run at a third straight championship. Tonight's exhibition game would be the return engagement of a weekend home-and-home series with the Montreal Canadiens, a powerhouse-in-the-making which just might be ready to challenge their supremacy.

Accordingly, the Flyers had bumped and battered the Habs during a 5-4 win at the Forum in the Saturday night encounter. There were 21 penalties handed out, including majors to Dave "The Hammer" Schultz and Montreal's feisty sophomore Doug Risebrough. Schultz added insult to injury when he scored the winning goal, tipping in an Ed Van Impe shot with less than three minutes remaining.

Exhibition game notwithstanding, a message had been
.delivered: "The Cup is ours; if you want it, you'll have to
take it away from us. Love, The Philadelphia Flyers, R. E.
Clarke, captain."

Risebrough became embroiled with Schultz after the
Philadelphia winger had abused newly appointed team
captain Yvan Cournoyer (Henri Richard had retired in
the off-season) with a crosscheck that reinforced the
message on a more personal note. Guy Lapointe read it
loud and clear ... the heavyweight rearguard came to his
captain's rescue with some of the nastiest threats against
The Hammer's personal wellbeing one might ever hear,
from a distance of twenty feet or so and over the heads
of two linesmen and referee Bryan Lewis.

After the game, William Scott Bowman congratulated
his young centreman for his temerity and his good sense
—Risebrough had tackled Schultz from behind, secured a
solid headlock and hung on for dear life—and then began
making clucking noises at some of the larger physical
specimens filling the Canadiens' home whites.

What follows is a re-creation of Scotty's lecture:
"Young Douglas weighs only 177 pounds soaking wet
and the trainer suspects he has batteries in his pockets
when he climbs on the scales," he said, his voice deceptively soft.

"There are others in this room who, in the interests of
team unity, will remain nameless, but who tend to be a
lot larger than six feet tall and 200 pounds in weight—
without batteries in their pockets. Again, to protect the
innocent, I must point out to these same anonymous
types that the gentlemen from Philadelphia love it when
someone like Mr. Schultz crosschecks our captain into
the ice and our people waggle warning fingers at said
honoured opponent. I wish to leave you with this question to ponder as we fly south to the wonderful state of
Pennsylvania. What do you think the Flyers would have
done if one of our players, heaven forbid, dared to re-
serve such treatment for their captain, a certain Robert
Earle Clarke?"

That evening at the Spectrum, the Canadiens team that skated out in road reds for the warmup was noticeably larger than the team that had worn the home whites the night before. In the lineup were healthy young red-meat-eaters with names like Sean Bryan Shanahan (6'3", 205 lbs.) Glenn Michael Goldup (6', 187 lbs.) Pierre "Butch Jr." Bouchard (6'2", 202 lbs.) and Rick Raymond Chartraw (6'2", 210 lbs).

Late in the third period, Montreal led 6-2 when young Mr. Risebrough pondered the question posed by his coach at the end of the previous evening's meeting. As he and Mr. Clarke skated back to their respective benches, they began exchanging pleasantries. Not content with simple expression of intent, they dropped their gloves and had at each other. As the two young men tussled, the answer to Mr. Bowman's question was delivered in the person of Schultz vaulting the boards and racing into the melée. He was joined by all of his teammates and Risebrough was joined by all of his.

In the words of Stephen John Shutt, a much better goal scorer than historian: "We kicked the living daylights out of them."

Schultz, who would end the evening with trios of penalties (three each of minors, majors and misconducts), was intercepted by Chartraw and the two replayed a first-period set-to, Chartraw 2, Schultz 0. Mr. Jack McIlhargey was thoroughly drubbed by Mr. Bouchard and left to sputter: "I'll get you for that next game!" Never at a loss for words in Canada's two official languages, Bouchard opined as to the low probability of such an encounter. "I'm not worried, you'll be in the minors by then."

Mr. Gary Dornhoefer, a.k.a. High Cheeks for his habit of obscuring the vision of opposing goaltenders in the crease—in all senses of this word—was being throttled by a large Canadien in front of the Montreal bench. "For Pete's sake, Scotty," he implored, "call him off. I can't breathe!" Meanwhile, the aforementioned McIlhargey had separated himself from Bouchard, with the help of overtaxed linesmen, and encountered Mr. Goldup. Alas, it was not be McIlhargey's night. Even notorious non-combatants were involved, including Jim Roberts and Bill Barber, Guy Lafleur and Mel Bridgman (Guy, of course, discovered he was a lover and not a fighter), Mario Tremblay and the same Mr. Bridgman (who, in turn, discovered to his chagrin that young Mario was a lover ... of fighting) and all the way back to the original twosome, Messrs. Clarke and Risebrough.

The referee for the encounter, Mr. Bruce Hood, assessed some 322 minutes in penalties for the entire contest, 250 of which were the result of the bench-clearing festivities. Five of those went to Andre "Moose" Dupont, the former Jr. Canadien who thumped William Scott Bowman during the melée. "I figured this was Scotty's idea all along," he fumed after the "pretend game" was over.

Mr. Shutt, the amateur historian, reflected on that innocuous encounter a decade later: "We won the Stanley Cup that night. It just wasn't official until next May. If you are going to beat the Stanley Cup champions, you have to beat them at their style because they dictate the game. Philadelphia was a tough team so we had to prove that we were tougher, to break them mentally. And even if we didn't win all of the fights, which we did anyhow, they knew that fighting us was not going to help them.

"Sitting in the dressing room after the game, a lot of guys were smiling. We knew we had them. Better still, they knew it, too. And once you beat them at their style, you could impose your style on them and we knew they could never skate with us."

Scotty Bowman, also assessing the impact of that exhibition game played ten years earlier, agreed.

"The Broad Street Bullies played their style of game and used it effectively. I would never think of criticizing their team make-up or the job Fred Shero did, because as a coach, you go with what you have. And although Dave Schultz and I have had our disagreements over the years, I could not criticize his style of play. You had to give him credit ... he played nine years in this league and came out of it with two Stanley Cup rings. He did what he had to do.

"We just had to find a way of countering what the Flyers had going for them." Eight months later, spotting Rick Chartraw and Pierre Bouchard as forwards, the Canadiens swept the Flyers four straight in a relatively tame series. Sam Pollock's team of the '70s had arrived and was on its way to four straight championships and a raft of league records.

If ever Sam Pollock's draft movement bore fruit, it was with the team he assembled in the 1970s. The 1968 and 1969 drafts ended an era, with the disappearance of territorial protection. However, that did not prevent Sam Pollock from assembling an impressive cast of home-brews.

The 1975-76 team comprised the following players:

Goal: Michel Larocque, Ken Dryden.

Defence: John Van Boxmeer, Guy Lapointe, Serge Savard, Larry Robinson, Don Awrey, Pierre Bouchard, Rick Chartraw.

Forwards: Jim Roberts, Doug Risebrough, Guy Lafleur, Yvon Lambert, Yvan Cournoyer, Mario Tremblay, Glenn Goldup, Ron Andruff, Murray Wilson, Pete Mahovlich, Doug Jarvis, Steve Shutt, Bob Gainey, Jacques Lemaire, Sean Shanahan.

All but Dryden, Awrey, Lambert, Mahovlich and Jarvis were obtained in the draft or, in the case of some of the veterans, came up through the ranks of team-sponsored junior franchises. Dryden was originally drafted by Boston, Awrey was obtained in a trade from St. Louis, Lambert was originally a Detroit draft pick, Mahovlich was obtained in a trade from Detroit and Jarvis from Toronto.

In the four-year Cup sweep, players would come and go. Additions who would wear at least one Stanley Cup ring included Bill Nyrop, Brian Engblom, Rejean Houle (back from the WHA), Pierre Mondou, Gilles Lupien, Pierre Larouche, Pat Hughes, Rod Langway, Cam Connor and Mark Napier. Nyrop was drafted in 1972, Connor and Lupien in 1974, Mondou, Engblom and Hughes in 1975, Napier and Langway in 1977. Only Larouche came in a trade.

In all, that meant that sixteen players who had been draft choices would play for at least one Stanley Cup winning team in the four-straight streak from 1975 through 1979. It also meant that the Canadiens did something few teams have ever accomplished—they managed to rebuild and rejuvenate while they were winning championships.

The 1970s Canadiens started a year late. Very few Canadiens fans expected the team to win the 1970-71 Stanley Cup and they were properly thankful for the championship. They were not too happy, however, with the spate of defections after the season. Gone through retirement were Jean Beliveau and John Ferguson, the latter to attend to his burgeoning business interests. Ralph Backstrom had been traded to secure the Lafleur draft and Rogatien Vachon followed him west in 1972. A year later, more changes were made with the departure to the World Hockey Association of Houle, Tardif and J.C. Tremblay, and the trades of Terry Harper and Chuck Lefley.

The team which had won in May, 1971 was the 1960s edition of the Canadiens. By 1975-76, the Stanley Cup winning team of '70-'71 was a faint memory as only Lapointe, Cournoyer, Savard, Peter Mahovlich, Lemaire, Bouchard and Dryden remained, and of those players only Cournoyer, Savard and Lemaire were real '60s vintage—the rest were transition era and soon-to-be '70s bedrock. Despite such a talent drain in a short four-year period, Montreal managed an interim Stanley Cup in 1972-73.

You did not have to travel far in 1970 to know how good the 1970s Canadiens were going to be. Playing for the Montreal Voyageurs of the American Hockey League at one time or another that season were Peter Mahovlich, Bouchard, Dryden, Lapointe, Dennis Hextall, Jude Drouin, Guy Charron, Chuck Lefley, Bob Murdoch, Phil Roberto, Reynald Comeau and Bobby Sheehan. They made a shambles of the AHL and some knowledgeable hockey people, noting the weakness of several franchises in the Western Division, felt that if the Voyageurs played in that NHL division, they would have made the playoffs.

A year later, the Voyageurs franchise would move to Halifax and continue its domination of the AHL, becoming a first professional home to future Canadiens named Gainey, Tremblay, Risebrough, Chartraw, Lambert, Guy Carbonneau and Keith Acton.

As mentioned earlier, the Canadiens of the 1960s carried over into the spring of 1971 and the surprise victory over the Bruins that paved the way for Stanley Cup Number 17. The Shot Heard Round the Dressing Room —Henri Richard's blast at interim coach Al MacNeil after the latter benched him in Chicago in the fifth game of the series—was to have long-term repercussions that would shape the team for the rest of the decade. Henri picked up his pride, scored the tying and winning goals in a 3-2 win over the Black Hawks and embraced MacNeil at centre ice.

Yet his tirade could not be undone. Someone had to go. Would it be the French Canadian team captain, bearer of that proud name Richard, which meant so much to the Canadiens? A fierce competitor who never gave quarter nor asked for the same from opponents much larger than he, Henri was a fixture in Montreal.

It was MacNeil who left, and of his own volition. The Richard criticism had resulted in death threats against the soft-spoken coach and his young family.

"There were many things involved in me finding myself as head coach of the Canadiens," said MacNeil. "I had known Sam Pollock for many years, well before he became GM of the Canadiens. I was captain of his club in Hull-Ottawa and he asked me to stay there and coach the team. I said no because I wanted a shot at playing in the National Hockey League."

MacNeil started out with Montreal and spent eight years in the NHL, most of them with the Chicago Black Hawks. When he retired, Pollock came calling and offered him a choice of two Canadiens farm teams, Cleveland and Houston. MacNeil opted for Houston and coached some impressive young talent, including such future stars as Guy Lapointe, Jude Drouin and Tony Esposito. A year later he ended up in Montreal coaching the AHL Voyageurs.

Pollock did not have to go far to find a coach for the Montreal Canadiens when Claude Ruel decided the pressure was too much for him in December, 1970.

"I took over and looked forward to a good long run behind the Montreal bench," said MacNeil. "I felt I was a career coach and I got along with a lot of the younger players like Tardif, Houle and Lapointe. But I ran into problems with some veterans. The team was pretty established and they balked at some of the things I wanted to do."

It was an up-and-down year for Montreal, thanks to mediocre goaltending, but Ken Dryden was called up and was brilliant in a seven-game defeat of Boston and a six-game triumph over Minnesota. MacNeil found himself coaching the Canadiens in the Stanley Cup final.

"I was playing the kids a lot and after game five Henri, who had been sitting on the bench a lot, blasted me. He said I was a bad coach. Then the Forum started getting phone calls with bomb threats. Remember, this was just after the Kidnap Crisis and the *War Measures Act* and French-English relations were not so good."

When MacNeil coached the next two games, a special bodyguard stood behind him at the Forum and in Chicago, and others were posted at home with Mrs. MacNeil and the couple's young daughter.

The MacNeil family took a Florida vacation after the Stanley Cup was clinched and when the Maritimer returned to Montreal, he told Pollock he no longer wished to coach the Canadiens.

Fifteen years later, Henri still regrets that the incident had French-English overtones. "This was a player-coach situation, nothing more. I meant what I said when I said it, and regretted it two minutes after because of the way it came out. Al and I made friends when it was over but his wife wouldn't speak to me after that and to tell you the truth, I don't blame her."

The soothing balm of another Stanley Cup notwithstanding, it was much easier to quietly promote the English-speaking interim coach to General-Manager of the new Nova Scotia Voyageurs and seek a replacement behind the bench. Sam Pollock was criticized in some quarters for not backing his coach, but the decision was MacNeil's. Pollock agreed with his former coach because he was a skillful player of the percentages. There was no percentage whatsoever in management coming down on a consummate professional like Richard, the man who had won the Cup for the Canadiens and whose ferocious competitive drive was an asset 99.9 percent of the time.

As well, finding a coach was not likely to prove difficult. One of Sam's protégés, Scotty Bowman, had accomplished miracles with trades and veterans on their last legs and had carried the St. Louis Blues to the NHL final three years running. However, the Blues' owners, the Solomon brothers, were upset because Scotty would not let them play with their new toy, and life was becoming tense in the Missouri metropolis.

Sam and Scotty went back a long way with the Montreal organization. Bowman, a Verdun boy from the neighbourhood which had spawned Donnie Marshall and Buddy O'Connor, played for the Junior Canadiens until a head injury in 1951-52 ended his playing career. In the third period of a game, Bowman got a breakaway and was chopped down by a vicious two-hander to the head wielded by Jean-Guy Talbot.

"That was it for me. I never was the same player afterward. I just didn't have the confidence. I had a lot of headaches and blurred vision and things like that in the off-season and the club recommended that I quit as an active player."

The club paid Bowman's tuition for business courses at Sir George Williams College and he began coaching for them at midget level. Two years later he was coaching in the Canadiens system and in 1957, became Pollock's assistant with the Hull-Ottawa Junior Canadiens, who would win a Memorial Cup.

The rich benefits of Canadiens' tradition were quite evident when Bowman went to St. Louis in 1967 and wrote his own ticket.

"Frank Selke and Sam Pollock had put together the biggest system out there and coaches and general-managers in the Canadiens' system were coveted by the new teams. After all, we knew where all the good players were and the new guys wanted that knowledge."

Bowman made immediate good use of his Canadiens' contacts and stocked his team with former Montreal players and farmhands. It paid off right away and the Blues were the toast of St. Louis. In the West Division final, spurred by such stalwarts as Dickie Moore, Noel Picard and Bill McCreary, the Blues led the Philadelphia Flyers 1-0 and three games to two, late in the sixth game. The Flyers scored a lucky goal to tie it and won it with an even flukier score in overtime. The Blues were down and the Flyers looked to win game seven on momentum alone.

During the playoffs, Bowman had been keeping close tabs on the Blues' farm team in Kansas City, player-managed by one Doug Harvey.

"I really thought Doug would be able to help us but league rules stipulated I couldn't bring him up until their playoffs were over. After our sixth game, he called me and said his team had been eliminated. I told him: 'Come on up, we need you!'" Harvey was the first star in the Blues 3-1 series clincher.

Montreal defeated St. Louis 4-0 in the Stanley Cup final that May, but that statement does no justice to the task accomplished by Bowman. The scores were 3-2, 1-0, 4-3 and 3-2, as a patchwork quilt of over-the-hill veterans and the rawest of raw rookies fought the Canadiens tooth and nail. A year later, the teams met again in another 4-0 whitewash and again the scores were respectable. In 1969-70, the Blues appeared in their third straight final, against the Bruins this time, succumbing in four games once more.

Sam Pollock watched and waited as his former assistant wrung superb results from the Blues. When the Richard-MacNeil affair became front page news, Pollock was determined to hire Bowman.

That decision proved as important as the acquisition of any player who played for the Canadiens during the rest of the decade. Bowman led the transition Canadiens to a respectable third-place finish in the East Division in 1971-72, one point behind New York Rangers and 11 behind Boston.

A few off-season player moves later, the Canadiens led their division in 1972-73 and captured the Stanley Cup. It was to be Bowman's first of five in eight years of coaching in Montreal, a winning percentage which would challenge the numbers turned in by the immortal Toe Blake in the 1950s and 60s.

However, there was a world of difference in their coaching styles. Peter Mahovlich smiles as he recalls the man who coached him to three of his four Cups with Montreal.

"First off, you have to start with the premise that Scotty is a liar. He would say and do anything to you so that the team would win. Some people would say we won despite Scotty, or even in spite of Scotty, but that isn't true either. He was an excellent coach, especially in game situations. He was terrible when it came to personal relationships . . . he didn't have any."

Players like Shutt, Henri Richard and Lafleur recall one of Bowman's quirks. Says Shutt:

"The strangest thing with Scotty would be that the farther ahead we were in a game, the more agitated he'd become. If we were playing a tight 2-1 game, he kept quiet and didn't say anything. But if we were up four or five goals, he'd go crazy . . . he'd be screaming at us to stay on them, not to goof off and let the other team into the game."

What do players talk about in those mini-huddles before a face-off? The ensuing tableau is fictional, but not too far from the truth.

(Montreal is leading 8-3 over some expansion team and has a powerplay late in the game.)

GUY LAFLEUR (looking over at the Canadiens' bench where an agitated Bowman is pacing nervously, chomping ice cubes like a Cuisinart) Come on, Shuttie, let's pop a couple more.

STEVE SHUTT: Jeez, I dunno. It would be really rubbing it in. The game's almost over.

LAFLEUR: I wanna see if we can give 'im a heart attack.

SHUTT: There isn't a guy on the bench who'll give him mouth-to-mouth.

LAFLEUR: I know. I wanna see which guys jump on the St. John's Ambulance crew to stop them.

SHUTT: You're on!

Toe Blake's style was to talk to players individually and privately, even though he was not beyond chewing out the entire dressing room when he felt it was warranted. Bowman chose to castigate his miscreants in front of their teammates, and even players who did not get along took exception.

Henri Richard became involved in a celebrated slapping incident with Serge Savard in Vancouver in November, 1972. The team had just skated to the dressing room after a 9-1 humiliation of the Canucks when Jacques Laperriere, seething over something written the day before, yelled: "Let's keep the goddamn newspaper guys out of the room!" The team, from the highest levels of management down, was in one of its periodic kill the messenger moods.

Some players were steaming about a humorous road trip story that had appeared in a Montreal newspaper and which had been read over the telephone to them but that none had read personally. Others were under instructions to act angry. Management wanted to put the media on notice.

"That's a good idea," Savard chimed in. A superb defenceman who had overcome broken legs in consecutive seasons to win the Conn Smythe Trophy in the 1969 Stanley Cup series, he had become a leader of a vocal faction of Young Turks that had been feuding with the press since the Canada-Soviet Union series two months earlier.

Richard, in his second season as team captain and very much Old School, intervened.

"Cut the crap. They have their job to do just like anyone else."

After a heated exchange, Savard challenged the team captain.

"If you like them so much, why don't you sleep with them?"

Many teammates and opponents will tell you that of the famous brothers, it was Henri and not Maurice who had the shorter fuse. Livid, the 5'7" captain strode over to the 6'2" defenceman and slapped him hard across the face ("I opened my fist at the last second") with a crack that could be heard outside the room. Players jumped in to separate the two and it was agreed that what had happened would "stay in the dressing room." It didn't, because several players were quite shaken by the incident. Richard and Savard hardly spoke for a long time afterward.

A year later, Savard missed a practice and Scotty Bowman railed about it during a team practice, upsetting Richard.

"It was near the end of the practice and we were all down at one goal, leaning on our sticks, when Scotty began calling Savard all sorts of names and talking about a guy he was hanging out with. Scotty said things like the guy was just divorced and him and Serge were in all the bars and hockey players shouldn't be so dumb as to be in such situations because they hurt the team," says Richard.

The diminutive team captain interjected.

"Scotty, if you have something to tell Serge, tell Serge. He isn't here now." The coach got the hint.

"Scotty played favourites, no doubt about it, and he loved playing one guy against another," adds Mahovlich, who was immersed in a classic feud with Bowman in 1977 when he was traded to Pittsburgh. Bowman was not often happy with his big centre and said so to the press. Peter had his own friends with the media and matched Bowman headline for headline before Pollock did everyone a favour and arranged a deal with Pittsburgh.

"The important thing is, Scotty's way worked. His teams might have hated him, but he got them to play to their capabilities and not too many coaches can say that. Agree or disagree, love him or hate him, he won and that's all people remember now."

That comment is heartily endorsed by Al Strachan, hockey writer for Toronto's *Globe and Mail*, who then was covering the Canadiens for the *Gazette*.

"The players hated Scotty 364 days a year. On the other day, they cashed their Stanley Cup cheques. Scotty played the media like a fine violinist and that upset his players to no end. But his attitude was win at all costs and the players trusted him behind the bench. He was a bit of a loner but he would often take the writers out to dinner and answer any and all questions we had."

Strachan remembered an incident that was classic Bowman.

"The team flew into Minnesota and was on a pretty good streak when Scotty called in the press and announced that he was benching Steve Shutt that night. This was the year Shutt ended up with 60 goals so he was really pissed off. Shutt told Lafleur, who wasn't too happy to be losing his left winger, and the veterans' committee called a meeting. They then took the grievance to Bowman who let them talk him into reinstating Shutt, who played that night as the Canadiens bombed the North Stars."

It worked. Bowman refused to let his team get complacent. He was always a step ahead of his players and they knew it.

Internal conflicts notwithstanding, the Canadiens team that emerged in the 1975-76 season was formidable. Shutt and Lafleur, who had played alongside Henri Richard two seasons before, now were paired with Mahovlich on the "doughnut line", a term coined by Pierre Bouchard ("a hole in the centre").

Veterans Jacques Lemaire and Yvan Cournoyer were an entry and played with left wingers like the smooth-skating Murray Wilson on a second line. The checking line was the best in the business, centred by Doug Jarvis, a rookie from the Peterborough Petes School of Higher Defence, and one of the best face-off men in the league. He was teamed with veteran Jim Roberts and the incomparable Bob Gainey, a player who was to defence what Lafleur was to offence.

The fourth line comprised "Piton's Raiders"—Doug Risebrough, Mario Tremblay and Yvon Lambert—three young players who hit anything that moved, scored important goals and wreaked havoc in the opposition's zone. "Piton" was Claude Ruel's nickname—he often remained late after practice working with the rookies.

"And then if you could take care of that group of forwards," says former Bruins coach Don Cherry, "you came up against the Big Three at the blueline and Dryden in net. The 75-76 and 76-77 Canadiens teams may have been the best ever in the NHL. They were certainly better than the 1980s Oilers because of the defence."

Boston had Bobby Orr. The Flyers had a staunch defensive corps of Tom Bladon, Ed Van Impe, the Watson brothers and Moose Dupont. But Montreal had Serge Savard, Guy Lapointe and Larry Robinson. All three could skate, shoot and hit with authority. Any of the three had the ability to break a game wide open with a pass, a rush or a bodycheck. Savard and Robinson were two of the best at "head-manning the puck"—spotting a streaking winger at centre ice and hitting him in full stride on the blade of the stick with a long pass.

Lapointe was a good passer as well, but his strengths were skilled skating, joining forwards on rushes, and playing the point on a power play. His prowess at the blueline, especially his devastating slapshot which he kept low and on net, was second only to Orr's and just ahead of another superb defenceman in New York named Brad Park.

Teamed with the Big Three were two quality defensive defencemen—Bill Nyrop and Brian Engblom—and an all-purpose backup, Pierre Bouchard, who played an important role in heavy traffic.

Ken Dryden is uncomfortable with long-winded or romanticized descriptions of his talent. Suffice it to say, therefore, that he is one of the very few members of the NHL Hall of Fame selected before his thirty-fifth birthday. In a little more than seven years with the Canadiens, he had a 2.24 lifetime goals-against average and 46 shutouts.

In post-season play, he played every minute of every game in leading Montreal to six Stanley Cups, or a Stanley Cup winning percentage of .750, highest ever in the NHL for a player who played five seasons or more. There are many who feel that Montreal would have won one of the Flyers' championships had Dryden not elected to sit out the 1973-74 season in a salary dispute. He is also the only player ever in NHL history to win a major NHL award a year before winning the Calder Trophy as top rookie. (He won the Conn Smythe Trophy for best performer in the 1970-71 playoffs, and won the Calder in 1971-72.)

This team would provide Montreal fans with the Firewagon Hockey to which they had become accustomed. In 1975-76, the Canadiens finished the regular season with 58 wins, 11 losses and 11 ties for 127 points, breaking the record of 57 wins and 124 points set by the Boston Bruins in 1970-71. If it was possible, the 1976-77 version was even better, setting records which still stand for most wins—60, fewest losses— 8 (80-game schedule) and most points—132. A year later, the Habs "slipped" to 59-10-11 for 129 points.

In these days of the one-way Edmonton Oilers and the Disappearing Veteran, in which thirty year old veterans with big contracts who have learned a few things about defence mysteriously lose a step so that cheaper non-defensive nineteen year olds can take their place, the scoring feats of the Canadiens might not be considered prodigious. Boston Bruins scored an incredible 399 goals in the 1970-71 regular season and that total was not surpassed until 1981-82, when the Edmonton Oilers net-ted 417 goals, and then added 424, 446 and 401 in the next three seasons.

However, Edmonton would allow 295, 315, 314 and 298 goals against. That meant that the Oilers finished those seasons with plus-minus figures of +122, +109, +132 and +103, about 1.25 to 1.5 goals a game more than their opponents.

Montreal was a better-balanced and much more devastating team. The 1970s Canadiens established league records in points, wins and losses, because while goals poured in at one end, they stayed out at the other. From 1974-75 through 1978-79, Montreal's plus-minus figures were 374-225 (+149), 337-174 (+163), 387-171 (+216!), 359-183 (+176) and 337-204 (+133). In that five-year stretch, Montreal outscored the opposition by 837 goals in 400 regular-season games, or 2.09 goals a game. In 1976-77, the per game differential was a phenomenal 2.76 goals a game! That team never could have been defeated 11-0 by Hartford Whalers or 11-9 by Toronto Maple Leafs, off-night or not, as were the Oilers.

1971 was a pivotal year in yet another way for the fortunes of the Canadiens. On December 31 of that year, scant hours before new capital gains tax provisions were to take effect, the Molson family sold the Canadian Arena Company (the Montreal Canadiens and the Forum) to a consortium of Edward and Peter Bronfman, the Bank of Nova Scotia and John Bassett's Baton Broadcasting of Toronto for about 15 million dollars. The new group was called *Placement Rondelle* (literally, "Puck Investment"). In 1958, Peter, David and William Molson had purchased the team for 5 million dollars from cousins Hartland and Tom, who in turn had bought the Canadian Arena Company in 1957 from Senator Raymond.

The Molsons had proven beneficial for the Montreal Canadiens. They allowed Frank Selke and Sam Pollock all the room necessary to manage the dynasty and underwrote the $9.5 million renovations that took place in 1968 which made the Forum one of the best rinks anywhere to watch a hockey game.

Jacques Courtois, a well-known Tory lawyer from

Montreal, was appointed president, while Bassett and the brothers Bronfman were named to the new board of directors. Along with the Bronfmans came financial adviser Irving Grundman, who would become involved in the business side of the Canadian Arena Company operations. All the other vice-presidents, Pollock, Toe Blake and Jean Beliveau, remained in their posts and little changed over the next seven years.

In 1978, the team was sold yet again. This sale had repercussions in the front office that eventually reached ice level.

Oddly enough, the deal began on a baseball field—the most uncomfortable, god-awful baseball field ever to plague the major leagues in a modern era—Exhibition Stadium in Toronto. In 1976, John Labatt Ltd. of London, Ontario became the majority owner of the expansion Toronto Blue Jays and watched in amazement as the baseball team tie-in boosted the company's share of the lucrative Ontario beer market by two percentage points, a major gain in the cutthroat beer wars.

Labatt's marketers immediately twigged to the sports connection and looked around for other vehicles. A purchase of the Canadiens, it was decided, would be a two-edged sword. Not only would Labatt become associated with the best club team in the sport, it could excise Molson beer from the high-profile Canadiens' TV broadcasts.

Strolling happily along a sunny Montreal sidewalk with a company lawyer, in search of a cab after leaving the press conference at the rue Notre-Dame headquarters of Molson's brewery where the sale of the hockey team just had been announced, Peter Bronfman answered the journalist's question with canary feathers in his mouth: "It was a seller's market."

Very aware of the Labatt interest, and very anxious to maintain a television partnership of more than a quarter century's standing, Molson Breweries of Canada Ltd. had just paid 20 million dollars for the Montreal Canadiens. However, the building and the team were separated this time which would explain Peter Bronfman's good humour. The separation was worth a 30 million dollar long-term lease, which is still in effect today.

The sale reached into the Canadiens "upstairs dressing room" in the departure of Sam Pollock. During the seven-year ownership of the club by Peter and Edward Bronfman's Edper Investments, Pollock had acquired an equity interest in the company. When the sale took place, he was deeply involved in the Edper scheme of things and reluctant to divest.

"I had been involved in hockey and the Montreal Canadiens ever since I had left high school. It was time to go. I never for a moment doubted that I would miss it, but I had a unique opportunity with Edper and I wanted to take advantage of it."

The Pollock departure had immediate repercussions. Scotty Bowman fully expected to be named general manager in his place, but when the 1978-79 season got under way, Irving Grundman had inherited the new title of Managing Director.

Grundman had joined the Canadiens with Edper in January, 1972, and had taken an advanced course in Sam Pollock 101. The two worked side-by-side for six years, eating lunch together almost every day and discussing the intricacies of the business and hockey aspects of the Montreal Canadiens. Whether or not it ever came to annointing a successor, the coach was to eventually find himself on the outside looking in.

"Scotty and I always had gotten along and we didn't have what you might call a personality problem. But when we talked that summer, he laid it on the line. 'I won't work for you', he told me. I told him that was too bad because I thought he was the best hockey coach available, I still think he is, and I would like him around."

Grundman tried to persuade Bowman to stay with the team: "Scotty, I don't see myself doing this job more than two, three years at the outside. I wouldn't have any problems nominating you for it when I step down. All you have to do is wait a little."

Bowman couldn't wait, but remained behind the bench

for the next season and the team's fourth-straight Stanley Cup. While he did not sulk in public, he was abnormally quiet with the team.

"It wasn't vintage Scotty," says Steve Shutt. "It was a strange year. We did all right in the standings even though we weren't steamrolling teams like we had in the past. We still would win the big games against most teams, although the Islanders played us very tough. And all through this Scotty was really calm. Like he was somewhere else."

Irving Grundman received a hot-and-cold reception as new head man for the Canadiens. The hot came when he showed his straight-A marks in Pollock 101 when three WHA grads, Mark Napier, Cam Connor and Rod Langway, joined the team. The three were officially signed to contracts and attended camp, but Grundman kept saying that some technicalities had to be worked out and that their contracts could not be registered with the league office. Until they were registered, their status was that of unsigned draft choices and Montreal had three fewer players to protect in the new league waiver draft on Thanksgiving Day.

The cold came when the Canadiens allowed the very popular Pierre Bouchard to be drafted by the Washington Capitals in that same waiver draft. The way the clubs had worked it was that Washington would claim Bouchard, place the defenceman on their protected list, and trade him back to Montreal after the draft—a standard Pollock-Macchiavelli scenario. However, the league ruled that this process contradicted the waiver draft rules and that Bouchard would have to stay with Washington.

"I went to lawyers and I showed the rule to Sam and everybody agreed that our trade agreement should have been okay the way the rule was worded," Grundman said many years later. "John Ziegler chose to rule against us."

As it turned out, Ziegler was worried about a player strike. Player union head Allan Eagleson had threatened a strike when all parties came to the conclusion that free agency in the NHL was a paper tiger. The waiver draft gave a semblance of mobility to the players.

The incident was an embarrassment for Grundman and the club which had been the class act of the league for so long. Even within the front office all sorts of rumours flew. One story claimed that Scotty Bowman was the real Macchiavelli in the affair. That version said Bowman had sat on the committee that drafted the wording of the waiver re-trade rule and had told Grundman it was all right to make the deal with Washington, knowing, of course, that it wasn't, only to go whistling loudly and innocently by the distraught general manager's office after the situation backfired. Both Bowman and Grundman deny the story. Since coaches rarely get involved on league rule committees, their denials are credible.

Sam was gone, the fans lamented. Would the winning teams follow him into retirement?

One winning team stuck around. On May 21, 1979, at approximately 10:45 p.m., team captain Serge Savard skated around the Forum ice with the 22nd Stanley Cup in the club's history. A few moments later, Bob Gainey was hoisted on his teammates' shoulders when it was announced that he had won the Conn Smythe Trophy as best individual performer in the playoffs. The Canadiens defeated the New York Rangers 4-1 in the final game, holding the Broadway Blueshirts to three shots in the second and four shots in the third period. Gainey was a huge part of the Grand Suffocation.

Sam Pollock and Frank Selke might be on the sidelines, and maybe Scotty Bowman's victorious smile was a wee bit thin-lipped, but this team on the ice was only the second-ever to win four straight Cups. In a few months they would embark on a quest for their fifth.

Bob Gainey was 25, Guy Lafleur, 27, Steve Shutt, 26, Larry Robinson, 27 and Pierre Larouche, 23. They had been joined by some terrific young players like Mark Napier, Rod Langway, Brian Engblom and Cam Connor in the last year. The transition to the team of the '80s should be smooth and uneventful. The drive for five should be quite interesting. And the spirit of Sam still lived!

The Canadiens and the rest of the NHL teams would return to the Forum in three weeks, June 11, for the NHL Entry Draft. This year, Montreal would not enjoy the greatest position, their first pick being Number 27 overall, a young defenceman named Gaston Gingras. Still, a diminutive Swede named Naslund would be found as the 37th pick overall, a high-scoring Chicoutimi centre named Guy Carbonneau would be 44th and goalie Rick Wamsley of Brantford Alexanders would be number 58.

Better still, Montreal had the number 1 pick all locked up for the following year, and every scout in the league was predicting a bumper crop in '80.

# 12

## La Guerre

In May, 1979, the Montreal Canadiens won their 22nd Stanley Cup and the province of Quebec was their oyster. Four and a half months later, they were involved in a dire struggle with a new challenger, the Quebec Nordiques.

Things would never be the same again for the Canadiens.

*     *     *     *     *     *

*Images of la Guerre . . . Part 1*

The Quebec Nordiques and the Calgary Flames have finished their pre-game skate and are back in their dressing rooms, and the attention of the full house at the Colisée on this chilly November evening in 1985 turns to a weird device suspended about twenty feet above the ice, right beside the scoreboard.

The four-sided black-and-silver contraption hovers over the rink like a shroud. *"Qu'est ce que c'est?"* ("What is it?") The question travels around the Colisée like the ubiquitous Wave.

Moments before the teams are to come onto the ice for the start of their National Hockey League contest, the house lights dim, then are extinguished. A single spot illuminates a portable lectern at centre ice, where the house announcer begins his spiel. "Tonight the Nordi-

ques would like to honour one of our own . . ." He introduces André-Philippe Gagnon, a remarkable Québécois
performer who has recently wowed audiences in Paris
and Burbank, Ca., with his imitations of Joe Cocker and
the entire "We are the World" aggregation, with the
accent on Kenny Rogers, Willie Nelson, Bruce Springs-
teen and Bob Dylan.

Then while the mostly unilingual (French) audience
holds its collective breath, the mysterious black-and-silver device is transformed into a rear-projection screen
and the silence in the arena is broken by the ever-familiar
"He-e-e-e-r-r-r-e-e's Johnnnnnnnnnnny!" A video of
Gagnon's recent seven-minute appearance on the Johnny
Carson show is played back to a standing ovation.

Gagnon is the hottest ticket in French Canadian entertainment after his triumph on the Carson show—he sells
out two weeks of performances at Montreal's Place des
Arts in two days—and is *un petit gars de chez nous*, hailing
from just outside Quebec in Loretteville.

The video extinguished, he is introduced to a standing
ovation and escorted on the ice by Mr. Everywhere, team
president Marcel Aubut. Gagnon receives a complete
Nordiques outfit, sweater, pants, socks, pads. He has the
crowd in stitches with his imitations of Aubut, coach
Michel "Tigre" Bergeron and Peter Stastny.

As everyone knows in these parts, everything is fair in
*l'amour et la guerre* and the Nordiques have scored an office win over their arch (in all senses of the word) rival
Montreal Canadiens. Johnny, Ed and Doc are the latest
*fleur-de-lys* conscripts in their perpetual struggle against
the *bleu-blanc-rouge*.

This game transcends a mere sixty minutes of body
contact on a 200 by 85 foot ice sheet. Any popular Que-
becer can expect to take part at any time.

After the 1984 winter and summer Olympic Games,
both the Nordiques and Canadiens almost drew and
quartered Québécois gold medalists Gaetan Boucher
(speedskating) and Sylvie Bernier (diving) in their frenzy
to "honour" them first. The internecine struggle between the two franchises reaches into every nook and

cranny of North America's French collectivity. Picture Kojak in a Nordiques or Canadiens sweater saying "Who loves ya, baby!" with a Québécois accent.

The on-ice activities of two of the NHL's most talented and colourful teams often pale in comparison with the marketing war being waged on all fronts.

\* \* \* \* \* \*

*Images of la Guerre . . . Part 2*

Defenceman Brad Maxwell sprawls exhaustedly in the visitors' dressing room of the Forum, the most famous hockey rink in the world. His shoulder pads and blue-and-white sweater lie in a crumpled heap at his feet. He is still wearing one elbow pad and has only loosened his skate laces. He is surrounded by a solid phalanx of hockey beat reporters, print and electronic. There is an angry red welt across his right arm, in the very spot where the shoulder pad ends and the elbow pad begins.

Quebec and Montreal have tied 4-4 in this New Year's Eve 1984 matchup, the teams' second game in four days.

"These guys really hate each other," he says in a dull monotone, equal parts amazement and fatigue. Nothing has prepared him for *la Guerre*; after all, he had only eight years and 450 NHL games under his belt before he was traded to the Nordiques by Minnesota North Stars two weeks earlier.

"Minnesota and Chicago, and Minnesota and St. Louis always have been good rivalries but nothing like this. In four days, we have just played *two* seventh games of the Stanley Cup final."

In the 1984-85 season, the Canadiens and Nordiques met for an incredible 17 games, 2 exhibition, 8 regular season and 7 in their seesaw Adams Division final, won in overtime by Peter Stastny. With the exception of the first game of the playoffs in which both teams came up flat two days after thrilling last-minute wins over Adams Division rivals Boston Bruins and Buffalo Sabres, all games were emotional rollercoasters, fraught with intensity rarely seen since the old six-team NHL.

"There is no such thing as an exhibition game between Montreal and Quebec," Stastny says with a grim smile. That is because the Montreal Canadiens and the Quebec Nordiques conduct their war on many planes, from the ice to the front office, from Abitibi to the Gaspé, in public relations, advertising, marketing, the newspapers, on radio and television, in the NHL boardroom and in courtrooms.

Who would have figured it as recently as seven years ago?

In 1976, with the upstart World Hockey Association failing on most fronts, a thirty year old Quebec City lawyer named Marcel Aubut was appointed president of the Nordiques and given a single mandate. "Get the Nordiques into the NHL," he was told. Otherwise there will be no Nordiques, was the unspoken corollary.

A tall order in most situations, it was virtually impossible in the world of Quebec hockey. After all, Aubut had everything going against him; *la Métropole*, as Montreal is known even in Quebec City, was 142 miles upriver. The Canadiens were in the midst of a four-year Stanley Cup reign. Sam Pollock, acknowledged as the model for the current generation of NHL hockey executives, was in charge of the Canadiens.

Pollock, although he will modestly deny it, was the most influential man in NHL boardrooms. As a hockey fan, he respected Quebec's aspirations for admission to the NHL. As a businessman, he considered Quebec City as little more than a daycare centre for rising stars like Jean Beliveau and Guy Lafleur. Quebec City was Montreal turf and it was inconceivable that it be surrendered to a rival team.

Nobody could reckon with the chutzpah of Aubut, a cross between Rimbaud and Rambo. While the three-piece pinstriped suit is his uniform, it would not be too difficult to picture him in jungle fatigues, carrying an AK-47 with bandoliers of ammo crisscrossing his chest. The only way to describe Aubut's eventual impact is to say that he methodically blew away all opposition.

"Marcel is nothing like most people from Quebec City," says veteran *Le Soleil* columnist Claude Larochelle. "This is very much a closed town, a civil service town, and we don't seem to develop the go-getter type of person." Some outsiders might go further in their descriptions of attitudes of North America's most picturesque and only walled city, perched high on bluffs above the St. Lawrence River.

"It's not closed, it's cloistered," says one French-speaking journalist from Montreal, who begs anonymity. "There's an old joke that goes like this: 'What do you call a seventy-five year old man who was born in Sherbrooke, moved to Quebec City when he was a baby and has lived there all his life? Answer: The Sherbrooker.'"

The difference between Quebec City (half a million people, almost totally French-speaking) and Montreal (just under three million, a cosmopolitan mix with hundreds of thousands of Jews, Greeks, Italians, Portuguese and yes, *les anglais*) are a lot more profound than just size and language spoken in the street.

Historically, the two cities have banged heads for nigh on four hundred years, going back to the time when Samuel de Champlain and the *coureurs de bois* started blazing trails in the northern woods on both sides of the St. Lawrence. The fur trade opened the way for farming, which in turn led to settlements. Montreal and Quebec began as fur trade depots and grew in importance as hardy Bretons and French soldiers began hacking out farms in the wilderness and raising families.

By 1759, when Wolfe's British troops snuck past sentries in the dead of night at Cape Diamond and routed Montcalm's French army on the Plains of Abraham, the competition between the two cities was well ingrained in the collective psyches of all denizens of New France. It would be only a mild exaggeration to say that Montrealers laughed at Quebecers for being caught asleep at the switch. Fifteen years later the catcalls were reversed when an American Revolutionary army under General Robert Montgomery marched out of New England, up the Richelieu River and captured Montreal, only to be stopped at the walls of Quebec City on New Year's Eve.

That's how far back this rivalry goes.

(Incidentally, both Montcalm and Wolfe died of battle-field wounds that day, a lesson not lost on the current belligerents.)

Both cities took turns moving to the fore in economic, social and political importance until Montreal finally gained the upper hand in the late 19th century. Montreal became the economic engine of the province of Quebec, a vibrant metropolis that was propelled to international prominence by its public relations-conscious mayor, Jean Drapeau. The Main, Peel and St. Catherine, Mount Royal, the Metro, Place Ville-Marie, Central Station ... all were known across Canada and received some recognition outside Canada's borders.

When Quebec abandoned its rural roots after the Second World War, its young men and women went to Montreal to find jobs in factories and plants owned by companies with names like Northern Electric, Canadian National Railways, Steinberg's, Dominion Engineering and Canadair. There a cosmopolitan mix of Jew, Italian, Greek, German, *Canadien français* and English Canadian lived in fragile harmony and learned to work together at building one of Canada's two major metropolises.

Eventually, economic inequity and social unbalance gave birth to *la Révolution tranquille*. In Montreal, young *Canadiens français* students became *québécois*, started the first demonstrations against restaurants like Murray's that provided English-only menus, and sunk the roots of modern Quebec. There, a new nationalism, founded by young revolutionaries and nurtured by an emerging phalanx of artists, songwriters, actors and playwrights, gave rise to a new pride and new sense of accomplishment.

While all the action and innovation was taking place in *la Métropole*, Quebec City was becoming more of a walled city than ever. Home to *l'Assemblée nationale*, the provincial legislature, it seemed caught in a time bubble, perpetually five years behind the rapid changes wrought in Montreal. It gave the impression of a city under siege, its self-satisfied bourgeois citizens standing smugly on the ramparts and staring down curiously at the rabble trying to swim the moat far below. Quebec was a civil service paradise, forever middle class and comfortable. It was also terribly jealous of the excitement in Montreal.

Such a background produced Marcel Aubut. It shouldn't have; his demeanor was more that of a hustler on Montreal's Main than a good *bourgeois* from the genteel *Grande Allée*. While Aubut lives there now, a dues-paid member of Quebec City's elite, he started out as a farmer's son from a tiny hamlet outside Rivière-du-loup. He left the farm at age twelve to go to school at the Quebec Academy but he never forgot his roots. There are three vehicles parked in the Aubut driveway, two luxury cars and a black four-wheel drive Toyota. Guess which one Aubut drives at breakneck speed along Quebec City's precipitous slopes?

Graduating at the top of his class at Université de Laval in suburban Ste. Foy, Aubut made his reputation with the ink barely dry on his law degree.

In a civil action, Aubut found himself staring down a lawyer with a reputation, Jean Lesage, a pillar of Quebec society, who as Quebec's premier from 1960 to 1966 was the acknowledged Father of the Quiet Revolution. Had Aubut been from a proper Quebec City family, he would have known his place—which definitely was not facing a living legend in a Quebec courtroom at age twenty-five.

"I was scared shitless for about two minutes," he admits with characteristic candour. "Then I sat down and went to work. I realized quickly that I was in a no-lose situation: a loss to Jean Lesage for a young lawyer was no disgrace."

Aubut never had a chance to test that hypothesis; he won his case. He also won a new important friend. Lesage did not sulk; instead, he adopted Aubut as his protégé and the young advocate's career surged forward. There are many Quebecers today who feel that one day Aubut will follow in Lesage's footsteps as premier of the province.

"Jean Lesage had a reputation of a winner when he left

politics and he didn't like to lose," Aubut recalls. "But he said he saw something in me that he liked, even though I beat him."

What the late premier saw was straight-ahead drive and frankness, a combination he felt could be useful in many situations. A member of the Board of Directors of the Nordiques, he knew that the team could benefit from somebody like the brash young lawyer he had faced in court.

Aubut joined the club in 1976, the same year that the separatist Parti Québécois government of René Levesque was first elected. Aubut was to represent the Nordiques in the first round of merger negotiations with the National Hockey League. He faced an impossible task—NHL President Clarence Campbell, by no coincidence a Montrealer, had been quoted as saying that it would be "unthinkable that Quebec would be accepted into the league." So Aubut targetted Campbell and worked on him mercilessly. He failed miserably.

Their desperation for a chance to play the Montreal Canadiens on any terms grew to a frenzy in 1977 when the Nordiques won the WHA championship, the Avco Cup, and the Habs captured their second straight Stanley Cup.

Aubut rolled up his sleeves and worked even harder. In 1979, with the WHA teetering on the brink of dissolution, he was 0 for 2.

"We just couldn't get past their conditions for entry into the league," Aubut recalls. "They kept saying that Quebec City was too small and there wasn't enough money in the area to support a team. We said they shouldn't worry, Carling O'Keefe brewery was prepared to spend a lot of money. We also argued that being so close to Montreal would be good for a natural rivalry to build, not bad. They kept saying that our rink (the old Colisée) was substandard and that they would consider us if we built a better one.

"And when we'd go to the City of Quebec for financial support they would tell us to get a franchise first, then they would find money for the rink. It was a vicious circle."

Aubut and two other WHA team representatives, Michael Gobuty of Winnipeg and New England's (Hartford) Howard Baldwin, took to flying into Chicago regularly for strategy sessions that would last long into the night. They split the 17-team NHL in three, and began an intensive lobbying campaign to get enough votes from the NHL Board of Governors.

Aubut kept losing, even though several auspicious events had occurred. First, Clarence Campbell retired and was replaced by a Detroit lawyer named John Ziegler. Then Sam Pollock left the Montreal Canadiens when the Bronfmans, Peter and Edgar, sold the team. The latter event had a catch; the Bronfmans sold to Molson Breweries and the Nordiques were owned by a rival brewery.

The Quebec representative spent months on a private jet canvassing his group—Boston, Detroit, Montreal and Toronto—and turned on the pressure. But he couldn't get over the arena stumbling block and when NHL president Ziegler gave the WHA trio a February, 1979 deadline, even Aubut lost hope.

Yet politics and sports make strange bedfellows in more places than Texas football and the South West Athletic Conference (SWAC). Guy Bertrand, a prominent separatist lawyer who was also player-agent for some Nordiques players (he prompted some nervous giggles for his suggestion in 1976 that a Team Quebec be formed to compete in the first Canada Cup) called Aubut, a well-known federalist. Quebec had not yet held its May, 1980 referendum on separation and the phone call was the equivalent of a Castroite volunteering to work on the Committee to Re-elect Ronald Reagan.

Bertrand offered a meeting with René Levesque and Aubut was sitting in the premier's office a few days later.

At the time, the PQ government could only watch helplessly as scores of multinationals left the province, unwilling to chance separation from the rest of Canada. A wary premier said he could not come up with any money without some sort of guarantee that big business would be onside.

"I told him I would be back with a Carling O'Keefe director and we met again a couple of days later," Aubut smiles.

Striding into the meeting with Aubut was Lesage, who was Levesque's boss in the 1960 Liberal government before Levesque renounced a united Canada, a man still very much respected by Levesque and many of his ministers and backbenchers. An hour later, Aubut and Lesage left the meeting with five million dollars in provincial government money. The federal government, matching Quebec dollar for dollar in a pre-referendum spending competition, chipped in another five million, as did the city.

The NHL could no longer refuse, even though the next vote saw the Molson bloc (several Canadian teams including Montreal) turning thumbs down.

The Canadiens capitulated when large parts of the province suddenly began boycotting Molson's beer in favour of O'Keefe. Aubut smiles smugly when asked about his part in the anti-Molson campaign that "miraculously sprung up", as he put it. "I don't sell beer," he laughs.

When the first puck was dropped to start the 1979-80 NHL season, the Edmonton Oilers, Winnipeg Jets, Hartford Whalers and Quebec Nordiques were proud new members of the club.

In Quebec's case, however, the cost was steep and they were practically secret new members. Part of the price the Nordiques had to pay for admission to the NHL, and to recognize Montreal's original territorial imperative, was a five-year moratorium on sharing TV revenues in Canada. Time passed and Montreal and Quebec (read Molson's and O'Keefe's) began readying plans for the upcoming TV rights negotiations.

Molson's moved first and in 1982 offered to buy Quebec's rights for Hockey Night in Canada. Aubut said they would have a deal, if O'Keefe would be given the opportunity to sponsor some playoff games. Molson said no and made a very, very expensive mistake.

Aubut did not get mad, he got even. He started by

buying the rights to a few NHL games played in the U.S. and selling them to a French pay TV station in Montreal. Molson immediately challenged the move, claiming that it contravened the league's broadcasting agreement.

"There wasn't a word about pay TV in the agreement," says Aubut. "They also specified Canadian games."

Ziegler ruled in Aubut's favour.

Not satisfied with occasional Nordiques away games on pay TV, Aubut then went for the jugular. He had accurately read the currents in the league boardrooms. Many American owners were tired of being treated as parvenus and weak sisters by Montreal and Toronto and Aubut found a receptive audience when he started touring the U.S. with the idea of a new TV agreement in Canada.

He went to the New York Islanders first, convinced that if he could deliver the Stanley Cup champions, other teams would follow. The Islanders agreed and so did the other American owners. A long court fight ensued and Aubut won again. Every Friday night and on occasional Sunday afternoons during the last two hockey seasons, CTV has broadcast an NHL game. The CBC maintains its traditional Hockey Night in Canada telecasts on Saturdays. The cherry on the sundae was the fact that Molson's had to spend 26 million dollars to secure its Saturday night position, only to have Aubut and O'Keefe undermine it by putting together its Friday night package for a mere 10 million dollars.

"I did it team-by-team because I knew the American owners were fed up by the Montreal-Toronto axis," he says. "Each time before they had signed with Molson, they weren't given a choice. This deal gave them a choice, and more power in the league, too. They liked that, and the million dollars or so each team got in the new deal."

Aubut liked the new recognition and power the TV deal gave Quebec in the NHL executive suites. All that remained was to carry over the newfound power onto the ice.

Not everything worked out in the long run, however. By the end of the 1985-86 season, the CTV deal was falling through. The network was not happy with the broadcast schedule for the regular season and the playoffs and threatened to pull the plug.

The Nordiques could not match Montreal when they first joined the NHL. Facing them was a juggernaut with four straight Stanley Cup championships in its trophy case, and names such as Lafleur, Steve Shutt and Lemaire up front and Lapointe, Robinson and Savard on defence.

Eventually, circumstances began to work in Quebec's favour. After winning their fourth Cup that May, a year after Pollock had left and named Irving Grundman as GM, the Canadiens' brass watched in quiet horror as perennial all-stars Dryden and Lemaire retired, the latter to accept a playing-coach position in Europe. Then Bowman, smarting over the Pollock snub, left for Buffalo.

The Nordiques could not ice a team strong enough to compete with Montreal, yet they managed to acquit themselves quite nicely in head-to-head competition, even though Quebec would not make the playoffs that year and the Canadiens would battle Buffalo and New York Islanders for the top three spots in the regular season.

The early NHL Nordiques contented themselves with winning off the ice. The original team that had played in the World Hockey Association in 1974 wore a dark blue uniform with red shoulder stripes. The team that joined the NHL essentially wore a Quebec flag with a Nordiques crest slapped on it. The Nordiques were blatantly marketed as Quebec's team, *l'équipe des Québécois*, and they stocked the line-up with native-born French Quebecers. The Canadiens, their *bleu-blanc-rouge*, and their English front office were snidely referred to as *"l'équipe des anglais"*.

Remembers Steve Shutt: "It was a disgusting piece of crap for them to pull and the kind of problems it caused weren't worth it. First, it really upset the French players on our team because they were not used to being called *les anglais* by people in their own hometowns. We had worked through the nationalism of the late 1970s without any of that stuff working its way into the game and all of a sudden, the sports pages looked like the op-ed pages. If the Nordiques wanted to get us emotional about them, they succeeded. We hated them and the crap they were pulling and a guy like Lafleur who practically grew up in Quebec City was in an impossible situation."

These subtleties were not lost on the voracious press corps in both cities. Dailies commissioned polls to determine the popularity of both teams and published maps of a Quebec divided into "Quebec blue" and "Montreal red". Emotions rose to fever pitch in *tavernes* all across the province, spread to the Forum and the Colisée, and finally onto the ice.

Lafleur, who like Beliveau had played his junior hockey in Quebec City before moving up to Montreal, began hearing boos when he returned to his second home. Games took on a chippy nature. Montreal fans in Quebec and Nordiques fans at the Forum, gently tolerated before, became the targets of verbal and occasional physical abuse.

"I think we went through a period of adolescence," Aubut recalls. "And a lot of things happened that I would rather have not happened." One of those came during what should have been Quebec's proudest moment—their defeat of the Canadiens in the best-of-five opening round in the 1981-82 NHL playoffs. Montreal GM Grundman, Mrs. Grundman and Montreal players' wives were spat upon by Colisée fans. Grundman was subjected to anti-Semitic insults, and the Canadiens demanded extra security from the Nordiques.

That incident overshadowed some brilliant manoeuvering by Aubut within a year of his team's entry into the NHL that would drastically alter his on-ice product. In the late spring of 1980, he launched Operation Europe and stage-managed the defections of brothers Peter and Anton Stastny from Czechoslovakia.

In an operation worthy of spy thrillers, the brothers were spirited away from their Innsbruck hotel in a red

Mercedes and taken at high speed through the Tyrolean Alps to Vienna, where they received visas at the Canadian embassy and then boarded a plane for Canada.

The next season, Peter scored 39 goals and added 70 assists to set a record points total for an NHL rookie. Anton chipped in 85 points on 39 goals and 46 assists and the Nordiques had instant respectability. Ever since the arrival of the Stastnys, the Nordiques have been a competitive team.

"It was like getting two number one draft choices," Aubut cackles, adding that the whole story of the defection would make a great book someday.

"They added stability to our team, and a tremendous amount of discipline and dedication. Our Québécois players tend to get too emotional out there and lose their tempers. Peter, especially, showed our guys how to keep their minds on the game."

That was a tall order for Stastny—now the team captain—who spoke little English and no French when he defected. He occasionally had to work on the coach, too, a banty rooster named Michel Bergeron, who had a reputation for chewing gum at 5000 rpms behind the bench and taunting opposition players in pre-game warmups in Quebec's junior league. Bergeron also was known as a winner, an intense, emotional guy who would torment officials and the opposition.

Bergeron proved to be Aubut's second major coup of 1980. He had found a coach with the same otherworldly drive that he possessed and Quebec began its serious love affair with the Nordiques.

The fiery Bergeron, five-feet, six-inches of scrap and yap who looks like he should be throwing dice in an alley (while Aubut hangs out around the corner holding the money), hides a shrewd hockey mind behind his explosive exterior. He is lovingly called *"le Tigre"* in Quebec and he will do anything to win.

After defeating the first-place Canadiens on a Dale Hunter goal in overtime of the fifth game of the 1981-82 series, the Nordiques polished off the second-place Boston Bruins in the division final before succumbing to the Islanders in the conference final.

A lot of the success for the playoff performance went to Bergeron, who thoroughly outcoached Montreal's Bob Berry and Boston's Gerry Cheevers.

"I have two major priorities in my life," says the youthful Bergeron, "my family and coaching the Nordiques." Those close to him might question that order, remembering his daily round trips of 180 miles when he coached junior hockey at Trois-Rivières. After running his team's practice, Bergeron would hop into his car and drive to Montreal, where he would watch Canadiens' practices run by Bowman. Afterwards he would sit and talk hockey with his guru, assailing him with question after question.

"How else do you learn? Scotty was nice enough to talk to me and help me and I was serious enough about being a hockey coach to go out of my way to learn." In 1985, after Bergeron's Nordiques eliminated Bowman's Sabres in the first round of the playoffs, Bowman said some derogatory things about his former star pupil. "That's hockey," Bergeron laughs.

Bergeron wasn't laughing in November, 1985 when he started suffering from headaches and double vision. After a week in hospital, his condition was diagnosed as post-viral encephalitis and he travelled to Minnesota's famed Mayo Clinic for treatment.

He was still suffering blurred vision when he returned behind the bench in late November. The players, relieved to have him back because the team was 3-8-1 under assistant coach Simon Nolet and 13-2 under Bergeron, were merciless. "I hear the Flames are going to play nine guys tonight because Michel can't tell the difference," said one. "That's nothing, I hear he's going back to the Quebec junior league to coach the Shawinigan Cataractes," retorted another. This is the terrible humour found in winning dressing rooms.

Coincidental with a winning record were several quiet changes. First, all vestiges of nationalistic marketing quietly disappeared, as Aubut and the Nordiques were genuinely embarrassed by the events in their rink during the Canadiens' playoff. Secondly, the team also quietly dropped their "francophone first" policy, opting for the best players they could find to play the roles defined by management. When hometown boy Réal Cloutier, who had scored 283 goals in five years with the WHA Nordiques and another 122 in three-and-a-half NHL seasons, began making impossible salary demands and undermining Bergeron, management was strong enough to trade him to Buffalo for Tony McKegney, André Savard and Jean-Francois Sauvé. The most surprised person in Quebec was Cloutier, who had gambled that the Nordiques were afraid to trade a homebrew superstar.

It was the first of several brilliant deals for Quebec GM Maurice Filion. McKegney and Savard contributed handsomely to the team until an injury ended Savard's career. McKegney was later traded to Minnesota for Maxwell and Brent Ashton. The diminutive "Tattoo" Sauvé anchored the team's power play before going to Europe and Ashton has been a 30-goal-a-year power forward, adding muscle to the Stastny line.

The Nordiques, like the Canadiens' "French Foreign Legion" of eight Americans, two Swedes and a Czech, have a core of players with names like Shaw, Price, Mann, Hunter, Siltanen, Kumpel, Moller, Gillis and Malarchuk.

In the team's early days, there was the "Farrish factor", named after journeyman defenceman Dave Farrish (NY Rangers, Toronto and a variety of stops in the American Hockey League). After a trade from Quebec City, the English Canadian complained that anglophones did not get a fair shake with the team. The report was widely circulated across North America and there was little the Nordiques could do or say to refute the charges. In truth, the universal equation of sports grousing could have been applied to identify the root causes of Farrish's discontent: the vehemence of sour grapes is always inversely proportional to time played.

The team's non-French players would scoff at any suggestion of language favouritism by the club, or of problems of settling into a city that is 95 percent French-speaking.

Dale Hunter of Petrolia, Ontario parades in his long underwear under the stands before a game with the Gretzky Oilers and kibbitzes easily, in English, with two Colisée security guards. He grabs a peaked hat from one and goosesteps a few feet down the corridor to the general mirth of all.

"Anybody who says anything bad about this city is nuts," he states with the trademark pugnacity that has earned him both the respect and enmity of opponents around the league. "This city is tremendous. It is not too big, so you don't fight the rat race, and it's not too small, so you can get all the services you'd find in other places around the league. There is an English community here and they help out with things like babysitting services, schools and helping wives and families getting settled. And the French people are wonderful, too, especially if they recognize you as a Nordique."

"This is the major leagues," says Mark Kumpel of Wakefield, Massachusetts, a member of the 1984 U.S. Olympic team. "No hockey player in his right mind would worry about coming here and not being able to speak English. Could you imagine some guy choosing to stay in the AHL because his team was in the States or English Canada? That's insane."

Quebec City is also popular with hockey beat writers and players for other teams. During the 1984-85 Campbell Conference final playoff, the late Pelle Lindbergh treated several of his Philadelphia teammates to *calèche* (horse and buggy) rides in and out of some of the older town's tiny, cobblestoned streets. He wanted to show North American-raised Flyers what it was like back home in Sweden.

This is not to suggest there were no French Quebeckers playing for the Nordiques in the mid-'80s. Far from it, with goalies Mario "Goose" Gosselin and Richard Sevigny, Gilbert Delorme, Norman Rochefort, Robert Picard, Alain Côté and Michel Goulet.

Goulet, whose aristocratic bearing evokes the *sieurs* of

New France, was arguably one of the best four left wingers in the game at the time — comfortable in a group which included Montreal's Mats Naslund, Philadelphia's Brian Propp and Edmonton's Jari Kurri — a tall, smooth-skating sniper who averaged 56 goals a year between 1982-83 and 1984-85 and totalled 509 goals in the span of his career with Quebec and Chicago.

Soft-spoken by temperament, he was ice to coach Bergeron's fire and sometimes the combination set off explosions in the Nordiques' camp. Early in 1985-86, when the Nordiques were struggling with only three wins in fourteen games, it was Goulet who was singled out by Bergeron for lackadaisical play.

"I don't accept that kind of criticism," Goulet says. "If we are a team, we are playing badly as a team, not because somebody thinks one or two individuals are letting the team down." Of course, it made headlines.

Goulet, who evokes cheers of "Goo! Goo!" in the Colisée when he sweeps down ice, was a natural target after his celebrated 1985 training camp salary holdout. Three months later, he still was not talking to GM Filion.

Is it harder for a French player to play in Quebec City?

"I can't really say, although it seems that players from Quebec are expected to produce more by the fans. I like it here and I like this kind of pressure. I don't spend too much time worrying about whether or not this market is big enough for me to get off-ice work making commercials, or whether or not I get a lot of attention like I might in the bigger media centres."

Besides, Goulet gets all the media attention he wants during playoff time as the Nordiques and Canadiens wage their little war *en famille.* Suddenly, as the snows recede and warming breezes waft down the rue St. Catherine and the Grande Allée, young men from Timra, Sweden; Bratislava, Czechoslovakia; San Diego, California and Red Deer, Alberta discover the true meaning of a Québécois family feud.

"The strangest thing," says Hunter, "is that we probably respect them (Montreal) more than any team in the league. I don't think we hate them or they hate us (although both teams will admit to loathing Boston) but the circumstances dictate that the series becomes a war."

The animosity came to a head during the sixth game of the Adams Division final, Good Friday, April 20, 1984. Late in the second period of the game in Montreal, Quebec led 2-0 but trailed 3-2 in the series. A series of fights broke out and just when it appeared that order was about to be restored, Quebec's Louis Sleigher sucker-punched Montreal's Jean Hamel, a former Nordique, along the boards.

When the teams emerged for the third period, the Canadiens went after Sleigher, who received a thorough correction from Chris Nilan and another bench-clearing brawl erupted. During the festivities, Peter Stastny had his nose broken by Montreal's fiery Mario Tremblay and entered the team dressing room for repairs.

"Fix it so I can play," he told a club doctor, who advised him that the procedure could be excruciating. "I don't care," Stastny retorted and the doctor did as obliged. Only then did Stastny discover that he had been assessed a game misconduct and could not return. Montreal poured in five straight goals and won the series 4-2.

A year later, his oft-fractured proboscis long repaired, Stastny got a measure of revenge with an overtime goal in the seventh game of the Adams final to eliminate Montreal.

That series, chippy and emotional, was quieter than the preceding one and play in the 1985-86 season showed that the teams have left a lot of the vindictiveness behind.

One reason is that—and one might earn the wrath of dyed-in-the-wool fans for saying it—the Nordiques and the Canadiens have come to resemble each other. Quebec has built a tougher defence and the Canadiens a more prolific offence. Both teams feature a pair of explosive European snipers, Quebec's Stastnys and Montreal's Swedish pair of Naslund and Kjell Dahlin. Both have strong defensive forwards (Quebec's Paul Gillis, Ashton and Alain Côté; Montreal's Bob Gainey, Guy Carbonneau and Mike McPhee). Add to that such top talents as

Montreal's Bobby Smith and Quebec's Goulet, and two exciting young Quebec-born goalies in Gosselin and Patrick Roy, and the family feud could go on for years.

The Nordiques, through other intermediaries, have strengthened their defence with former Canadiens Robert Picard and Gilbert Delorme. Neither will admit it, but their presence in the Quebec dressing room and on the ice tends to cool certain situations.

"You cannot forget that you played with people like Larry Robinson, Craig Ludwig and Gaston Gingras on defence and behind guys like Tremblay, Gainey and Nilan," says Delorme. "These guys were and are my friends, but there are no friends on the ice, just guys in the other uniform."

Picard, acquired in a mid-season trade for Mario Marois, parrots the same cliché. "When you're playing a game, there are no friends—even if you played with them before."

Nevertheless, one cannot help but notice that when Delorme and Picard are in the thick of the action against former teammates, a corner altercation or a slashing incident in front of the net cools off with only a few harsh words spent. The gloves usually stay on.

All bets are off where Dale Hunter is concerned. "You can't help but feel you are always fighting an uphill battle against them," he says. "Everything about playing in Quebec is reflected in Montreal because of what Montreal has always meant to hockey. It upsets us because we don't get a lot of respect, even though we have been fighting those guys even-up for five years. We can't even go on a road trip without passing through Montreal airport."

It has gotten so that the Nordiques are wondering if the stylized "N" on their crest stands for Rodney Dangerfield's "no respect". A classic example of what it means to be a Quebec Nordique came at Christmas, 1985. During the holidays two Soviet teams—Central Red Army and Moscow Dynamo—toured North America and played various NHL teams in a 10-game series. The Aeroflot jet carrying the Red Army, in reality the

Soviet national team, had barely touched down when the Russians had swished by the Los Angeles Kings and Edmonton Oilers in one-sided victories.

Soviet coach Viktor Tikhonov, a veteran of many North American exhibitions, told reporters in post-game interviews in Edmonton that he was "really looking forward to our New Year's Eve match at the Forum against Montreal."

He wasn't kidding. The Red Army dismantled the Habs 6-1 in a one-sided contest. Late in the third period, the knowledgeable Forum crowd admitted defeat and accorded the Soviets a standing ovation. Even the stone-faced Tikhonov allowed himself a gold-toothed smile.

So what does this have to do with lack of respect for the Nordiques? In between shellackings of the Oilers and the Habs, the Soviets "passed through Quebec" en route to Montreal and were thoroughly thrashed, 5-1. The victory ignited Quebec, sending the team on a third seven-game winning streak of the year and into first place in the Adams Division. No one noticed.

"You figure it out," growls Bergeron. "We have the Stastnys, two of the best players in hockey; we have Michel Goulet who scores 50 goals a year, every year; we have a good defence and terrific goaltending and we play well on the road. We are very tough at the Colisée. We beat all of the contenders—Edmonton, Philadelphia, Edmonton, Montreal and Washington. And still they put us down."

He stops dead in mid-diatribe, and smiles broadly. "That's good. It makes my job a lot easier because I don't have to waste a lot of time trying to motivate this team. They do it themselves."

\* \* \* \* \*

*Images of la Guerre . . . Part 3*

And finally, to la guerre, comes a real bunker and a real war-room and a group of strategists and generals most definitely under siege. No more metaphor, this is the *real* McCoy.

All that is missing as we get off the elevator on the fifth floor of the Radisson Hotel in downtown Montreal is sandbags by the entrance, and a sentry with a rifle on his shoulder. As the mirror-glass doors separate and we step into the corridor, we are met by the next best thing: three uniformed security people, who wear their wariness and quasi-military bearing as comfortably as their large, police-issue flashlights and walkie-talkies. A desk has been set up in the corridor, with a modular room divider behind it, preventing a beeline to the rooms on the floor. Is that barbed wire atop the divider, or just a curiously shaped shadow? Several other team officials are gathered here as well, and any journalist or similar ne'er-do-well who might try to crash this party will be politely, but very firmly, repulsed and escorted to the elevator for deportation without a hearing.

This is Day Three of La crise Lindros, and the Nordiques are under siege. While French Quebec continues to sputter in futile rage, a time bomb that could bring the league down has continued to tick, and all of the Emergency Ordnance Demolition experts in the world can do nothing to stop the explosion.

As well, this is June 24, la fête nationale as Saint-Jean-Baptiste day has come to be called in a province that cannot decide if it is one or not. The week, which culminates with the Canada Day holiday on July 1, is Quebec's second Christmas break at the other end of the calendar; the summer solstice is solemnly celebrated for a week with barbecues, family gatherings, golf, swimming, tennis and pure relaxation with maybe an Expos game on the tube and a cold one close at hand.

But the goût de la fête is nowhere to be found here at the Radisson, home of the entire Quebec Nordiques' front office during the recently concluded NHL meetings. They are all here — hockey people, front-office staff, secretaries — Marcel Aubut, Pierre Pagé, Pierre Gauthier, Jean-D Legault and Jean Martineau, and a phalanx of lawyers.

They are here because, for the second time in twelve months, the roof seemingly has caved in on the Nordiques, and one of the league's proudest franchises is being held up to public ridicule. They are here because the time has come to stop the bleeding.

The first cave-in took place in Buffalo's Memorial Auditorium on June 9, 1991. At approximately 12:15 p.m. EDT, Chief Scout Pierre Gauthier and General Manager Pierre Pagé made their way to the stage on the floor at rink level in the Aud and ended months of speculation by announcing to the hockey world that the team had drafted Eric Lindros, universally proclaimed as the Next One. This was to be the Second Coming, the selection of a hockey Messiah and the culmination of several years of suffering by the Nordiques and their fans. The favourite sport in sports bars and other watering holes in La Vieille Capitale that spring was The Line-up Game as the Nordiques' faithful amused themselves for hours on end by drawing up mock line-ups for the *fleurs de lysés* home opener on October 5 against Hartford. "Okay, Lindros, Owen Nolan and Mats Sundin on the first line; Joe Sakic, Valery Kamensky and René Corbet on the second; and then any six plumbers on the next two lines because these guys are going to go crazy. . . ." It was beautiful to be able to *rever en couleurs* (dream in technicolour) like this, after years of drought.

High in the stands at the Aud sat several impatient Nordiques' fans dressed in the club's powder blue road jersey, with 88 Lindros on the back. The words ". . . from the Oshawa Generals of the OHL, Eric Lindros . . ." were barely out of Pierre Pagé's mouth when they were on their feet, clapping and yelling wildly, hoping that the sheer enthusiasm and volume of their cheers would be enough to convince the recalcitrant giant that Quebec would be a great hockey home.

At the press conference of the projected top players the day prior to the draft, Lindros had been subjected to a veritable barrage of questions, both hostile and friendly, and had steadfastly maintained that he would not play for the Nordiques if drafted by the club. Jean Perron, now a broadcaster in Quebec City, got up and accused Lindros of breaking up Canada if he did not sign with the Nordiques. As silly as that sounds, he was only reflecting the opinions of his radio audience.

It was difficult not to be sensitive to the plight of the Quebec Nordiques at that moment. Lindros approached the stage, shook hands with the Pierres, clasped the proferred Nordiques hat and sweater in his giant paws and pointedly refused to don either article. The gigantic hockey player squirmed and fidgeted while the photographers did their work, passed quickly by the Nordiques' table to desultorily press the flesh, followed that with a series of quick interviews with journalists and then, poof!, right out the door.

It didn't quite match the dramatic impact of Mario Lemieux refusing to acknowledge the Pittsburgh Penguins on draft day in Montreal in 1984, but neither was it a ringing endorsement for Quebec's refusal to trade the selection to another team. In recent days Lindros and his family had given increasingly clear indications that he would never play for the Nordiques; and, soon thereafter, these would graduate to categorical refusal.

Thus began a proud franchise's great trial.

In the days and weeks prior to the draft, the Lindros camp suggested to the Nordiques that the team hold an auction for the right to draft Lindros, figuring that this would prove ample overcompensation for the loss of his services. The Nordiques might be offered a quality forward, a top-notch defenseman, draft choices and even cash by one or several teams which felt they were just one impact player away from winning it all.

As well, player agent Rick Curran had done his homework. His analysis concluded that Quebec's small marketplace simply could not afford Lindros, who even before joining the NHL was making as much in endorsement income as all but five or six of the league's top stars. Curran argued that Lindros would make only 40 percent after taxes of what he could receive for a similar salary in another market, and if the Nordiques were forced to compensate him for the economic disadvantage of earning his wage in that market, it would most probably throw their entire team salary scale out of whack. And, it followed logically, this would prevent Quebec from icing a competitive team, and that was a priority for the young giant who had been a winner wherever he had played.

There was some suggestion of a deal whereby Lindros would sign for Quebec for one or two years and, if still dissatisfied, then would move on elsewhere. That was as transparent as it was stupid; Lindros knew the trouble other Curran clients had encountered in trying to exercise their "free-agency rights" and move to teams of their choice. Free agency did not exist in the National Hockey League, especially for quality players.

No one, not the Lindros family, the league, Quebec (city and province) and the sport were served by the soap opera that developed in the ensuing twelve months, much of which was exacerbated by the ill-considered and ill-timed comments emanating from the Lindros camp that once again pitted English Canada against French Canada in what should have been a simple story of employment rights. Adding gasoline to the blaze was the xenophobic media reaction in Quebec to a hockey player's decision to decide where he would ply his trade.

The Nordiques' hierarchy trusted Marcel Aubut to bring home the bacon, at whatever cost, but he ran into a severe clash of cultures. This had nothing to do with French or English; it centred more on the Lindros family's poor homework in Marcel Aubut 101. When they said "no," the lawyer translated that to "now negotiations will start." The word "impossible" meant "negotiations will take a little longer," while "never" signified "these people sure know how to bargain."

Eventually, however, it dawned on all concerned that this was not to be. As the situation developed, several constant negative themes emerged. Eric Lindros would not play for Quebec because 1) the small, francophone market would not be able to support the extracurricular marketing and sponsorship opportunities that should be his due; 2) playing, working and living in the Other Solitude was not something an 18-year-old English-speaking Canadian kid from southwestern Ontario particularly wanted to do, especially since so many Quebec anglophones of his age were also turning their back on the province and seeking employment in Ontario; 3) this was the 20th century and people had a right to pick and choose where and by whom

they would be employed; 4) he could not play for a team
that was not dedicated to winning; 5) the Lindros clan did
not and could never trust Marcel Aubut; 6) the Lindros family was unhappy with the character assassination plot
against Bonnie Lindros that had been launched by the
Quebec media; and 7) all of the above.

It did not help that Quebec hockey fans, both in Montreal
and Quebec City, attempted to make the young star's life
miserable during an event that should have been the crown-
ing glory of his still very young career as a hockey player —
the Canada Cup.

It upset many Quebecers when they heard that Lindros, a
mere junior star, had been invited to join the Canada Cup
team in its Toronto training camp. Many fans and several
prominent commentators dusted off their "Canadian citizen-
ship," something kept under the rug 99 percent of the time,
and demanded that their MPs and the Mulroney government intercede with Hockey Canada and the National
Hockey League to prevent Lindros from playing, unless he
saw the light and signed with the Nordiques.

What they failed to realize, as most nationalist Quebecers
who only gaze curiously at the goings-on in the rest of the
country when it suits them, therefore operating from a
quasi-permanent base of erroneous assumption about the
rest of Canada, was that Hockey Canada was a convenient
shell for this country's forays into international hockey competition, especially the Canada Cup. After years of steward-
ship under Alan Eagleson, it was obvious to all that the
Canada Cup, or the true world championship, was the
NHL's baby, signed, sealed and delivered, and hell could
freeze over more solidly that the Colisée ice surface before a
politician would get his say. (The same people would also
fail to get Lindros barred from the Canadian Olympic team
at Albertville, even though this time Hockey Canada would
have a say.)

If Lindros could earn a spot on the Canada Cup team,
he would play against the Swedes, Finns, Americans, Ger-
mans and Soviets. Little did Quebecers realize that Eagleson
was determined to have Lindros play on the team because he
had let the management group of the 1984 Canada Cup

squad talk him out of allowing another 18-year-old prodigy, Mario Lemieux, from joining the team. Seven years later, Eagleson still regrettes that decision, and he was determined not to repeat the mistake, political hot potato or not.

Lindros was to be tested, both on and off the ice, by his Canada Cup experience.

As he wrote with Randy Starkman in Fire on Ice:

*(Pat) Burns and I had a pretty interesting introduction. I was going up the elevator with him on the second day of training camp and he just gave me a look. It wasn't a cold look, but then it wasn't warm, either. And then he spoke to me.*

*"I really think you should go to Quebec."*

*I think he was was just trying to see what kind of reaction he could get out of me. The Nordiques are the Canadiens' hated division rivals, so Burns and I would be seeing a lot of each other if I were to take his advice. But I knew then that there was no way I was ever going to be suiting up for the Nordiques.*

*"I don't think that's ever going to happen," I told him.*

*Burns looked at me deadpan, and then shrugged his shoulders.*

*"Well, if you don't go, it's not going to hurt me, because I don't want to see you eight times a year."*

*We both laughed. We got on really well after that.*

After the first practise, the four coaches of Team Canada very quietly pencilled in the Incredible Hulk into the starting line-up, and there never was any question of him not playing . . . especially after he ran over Al MacInnis and Luc Robitaille and received the endorsement of no less an interested observer than Wayne Gretzky. The Quebec media went ballistic when one of the first players cut from the team was Nordiques' star centre, Joe Sakic.

Prior to the tournament's official start, the Canadian team played a pair of exhibitions, against the Czechs in Montreal and the Soviets in Quebec City two days later. In Montreal, fans booed Lindros in the pre-game warmups and during his first few shifts in the initial period. By the end of the game when he was awarded the game star award for an eye-popping display of raw talent and power, they were on their feet cheering.

Two nights later, after an incredible ordeal with the media, Lindros scored his team's opening goal in a 3-3 tie. It was the first and last time No. 88 would play for the home team in the Colisée. Team Canada easily won the Canada Cup in 1991, despite losing Wayne Gretzky to injury and playing without Mario Lemieux; and Lindros was a major contributor. That heightened the sting of rejection for Quebec fans.

During the ensuing 1991-92 season, it became apparent that both sides would never get together and the franchise began to suffer from a group psychosis. Everywhere the Nordiques went during the 1991-92 season the Lindros Question overwhelmed them, and a team that had confidently expected to soar in the Adams Division and end a playoff hiatus of four years, found itself once again in the nether regions of the league, able only to surpass the freshman San Jose Sharks (52 points to San Jose's 39) in the standings.

Everywhere the LQ arose, the local media experts counselled a trade, usually to the local team. Everyone had an opinion, reasoned or otherwise. Early on in the piece, and despite the suspicions of others, the Nordiques came to the disquieting conclusion that Lindros would never play for the team. In fact, he had made it impossible for himself to ever play in Quebec because of his intemperate statements and accusations. Never mind the money issues, and the exposure and commercial issues, Eric Lindros would not come to Quebec because he expressed a strong aversion to Marcel Aubut, and he was convinced the Nordiques had cheated to make sure they could draft him.

The Lindros clan made much of two transactions by the team during the 1990-91 season that they claim were made to ensure a last-place finish and first choice in the draft. On November 17, Quebec traded Aaron Broten, Lucien Deblois and Michel Petit to the Toronto Maple Leafs, their most immediate competition in the depths of the NHL standings, in return for prospect Scott Pearson and two second-round draft picks. Pearson played one game for the Nordiques and scored a goal, and then was banished to the AHL.

Two months later, to the day, the Nordiques traded veteran defenseman Joe Cirella to the New York Rangers for a college player and a draft choice. In other words, four experienced regulars had been moved and not replaced in the daily line-up. Whether these players were stars or plumbers, no team can afford to lose that many experienced bodies over an extended period of time without suffering in the standings.

When Quebec and Toronto completed their transaction on November 17, their records were 3-16-3 (9 points) and 4-17-1 (9 points) respectively, including a loss each the night of the deal. When Cirella was dealt, Toronto was mired in another slump even after posting a very respectable December record of seven wins, four losses and a tie. The Leafs began January with two ties and five losses and both teams were once again deadlocked for last place in the overall league standings with 28 points, Toronto at 12-31-4 and Quebec at 10-30-8. At the end of January, the teams were again tied, this time at 31 points, but from that point on, the Nordiques "surged ahead" and had a comfortable 11-point margin, 46 points to the Leafs' 57, at season's end.

When the subject of tanking the season was brought up by the Lindros group at a secret meeting in Quebec six weeks after the draft, Marcel Aubut was alleged to have abruptly cut off the statement with a terse "I don't want to talk about that." Later, when Aubut suggested that the Nordiques had earned the rights to Eric Lindros, Carl Lindros retorted that the Nordiques had chosen to lose during the 1990-91 season, so Eric was not convinced that the team took winning seriously. The Lindros clan made much of a conversation agent Rick Curran had had with former Quebec coach Dave Chambers in New Jersey a week after the Cirella trade, and after the Nordiques had lost a game to the Devils 6-1. The team started Scott Gordon, arguably a fifth-string goaltender in the game, and when Curran asked Chambers why, the coach replied that he had been told not to worry too much about wins and losses.

Still, the Lindros negotiating team allegedly offered to sign a two-year deal with the Nordiques, as long as it contained an escape clause allowing Eric to move to another team afterwards, no strings attached outside of normal trade considerations. The Nordiques refused.

At the same time, the Lindros family was convinced that Aubut was fixating on the case, and that he had been on a mission to sign Eric since the player was sixteen years old. There was solid economic basis to this theory: the acquisition of such a high-profile star was necessary if the Nordiques were going to be able to finance Marcel's dream — a brand new, and much larger, Colisée.

A little more than a month after the Quebec City meeting, the Lindros family claimed that Marcel Aubut offered Eric a 10-year, $50-million contract, which they turned down.

As tension heightened between the two camps, Aubut went on to deny the offer and exhibited his mounting frustration in private. In late January, he met Lindros family legal adviser Gordon Kirke, at Mirabel Airport just outside Montreal, en route to the Olympic Games in Albertville, France.

*"When it became clear to him that I wasn't there to discuss a contract, he lost it. In Marcel's words: "There is no f_____ way an eighteen-year-old is going to tell me what to do! We are taking off the gloves!"*

That was all bluff and frustration, however. By that time the Nordiques' management team had privately admitted defeat in their attempts to sign the player and was quietly putting together a strategy for maximizing their returns in a trade. One thing was obvious throughout 1991-92: both sides blew smoke constantly and played their pet journalists like classic Stradivarius's. When all would be said and done, the true story had been replaced by at least two competing mythologies.

Everybody lied, all of the time.

One chapter in the Lindros Saga has ended; another was about to begin, and for a while it, too, would appear to be spawned by the pen of such giants of the horror genre as Stephen King or Clive Barker.

The strategy was simple; the NHL meetings around the 1992 draft in June in Montreal would present the best opportunity for a deal. The Nordiques would follow the Lindros clan's own advice, essentially letting the hockey world know that an auction for Eric's services would take place during the meetings. Those teams who might be anxious to get a head start on the competition by calling ahead, would not be discouraged, either.

And so the Nordiques set about trading Eric Lindros . . . from now on, the news could only be positive.

There is no French word for the expression "snakebit."

By the time the league's twenty-two teams congregated in Montreal for their annual meetings, the Lindros auction cast a huge shadow over the June 20 Entry Draft. By late Friday the 19th, all but three (Chicago, New York Rangers and Philadelphia Flyers) had fallen by the wayside, unable to meet the ante of many millions of dollars in cash compensation, a minimum of three starting players and two draft choices or top prospects. Even Montreal had expressed serious interest, with Serge Savard meeting Marcel Aubut on two occasions June 18 (7:30 a.m. and midnight) before deciding that a package that included Patrick Roy, Mathieu Schneider, Eric Desjardins and a lot of Molson money was too rich for his blood.

Regular visitors with Aubut on Thursday and Friday were Jay Snider of the Flyers, Neil Smith of the Rangers and Bill Wirtz and Mike Keenan of the Blackhawks. By late Friday, the most interest was being shown by the Flyers (three meetings and two telephone calls), the Rangers (one call) and Chicago (a meeting). Between 11 p.m. and midnight on Friday, both Montreal and Detroit officially withdrew from the Lindros sweeps and the Flyers-Hawks-Rangers negotiating continued in earnest.

What transpired in those hours, and the following (Saturday) morning, was the stuff of much speculation and several full days of testimony before an arbitrator the following week. We will never know the exact story.

In a nutshell, the Flyers' Jay Snider and General Manager Russ Farwell received permission from Marcel Aubut to speak with Rick Curran and the Lindros family and essentially pose one question. Would Eric Lindros play for the Flyers if they dealt for him? They felt that this stipulation was necessary because Curran had once said that Lindros would not play for Philadelphia.

Neil Smith apparently had made a similar demand of Aubut, but never really pursued the issue after an initial refusal.

The Flyers would later claim that once the Lindros family cleared the hurdle of not vetoing a deal, by telephone, the agreement with the Nordiques kicked in. Aubut would reply that he had only given the Flyers permission to sound out Lindros, but that did not constitute a deal, even though he had steadfastly refused the same courtesy to other teams in the league.

By 11:30 a.m. Saturday morning, the Flyers felt they had a deal and team spokespersons began to leak that word to the several hundred media types gathered at the Forum for the Entry Draft. That deal had been sealed by a handshake, Snider argued, a claim refuted outright by the Nordiques.

Between 11:30 and 11:55 a.m., the following events transpired, according to the Nordiques.

At 11:30, Aubut visited the Flyers' suite and talked with Snider and Farwell. A deal seemed imminent, and this is where and when the Flyers said a handshake sealed the issue. However, Aubut telephoned Stanley Jaffe of the Rangers at 11:40 and asked if the Rangers were ready to up the ante. Five minutes later, Aubut spoke by telephone with Philadelphia chairman Ed Snider, and Farwell also spoke with him just afterward. At 11:45, Aubut met again with Jay Snider and the team's chief operating officer, Ron Ryan, in the Nordiques suite.

After they left, he spoke once more by telephone with Stanley Jaffe of the Rangers and invited him to fly to Montreal. The Nordiques and Rangers had a deal: the rights to Eric Lindros would be transferred to New York for either goalie John Vanbiesbrouck or defenseman James Patrick, depending upon the netminder's free-agency status, Doug Weight, Tony Amonte, Soviet phenom Alexei Kovalev, the Rangers' first-round picks in 1993, 1994 and 1996, and U.S. $12 million.

Pagé, Gauthier and the Nordiques hockey people preferred the Rangers' trade. Aubut and others liked the proposed agreement with Philadelphia better — goaltender Ron Hextall, defensemen Steve Duchesne and Kerry Huffman, centre Mike Ricci, goaltender Ron Hextall, centre Peter Forsberg, and the Flyers' first-round draft choices in 1992 and 1993, and the sum of U.S. $15 million.

Aubut and the Nordiques raced across town to the Forum and had just taken their seats at the team's table when the telephone rang. Aubut answered and informed the caller, Jay Snider, that Quebec had accepted the New York offer. Snider responded by saying that in his opinion, the Nordiques and Flyers already had a done deal, and that he would protest to the league if the Rangers' deal was announced.

Shortly thereafter, a stunned NHL already trying valiantly to put a happy face on the league meetings, what with the impending departure of John Ziegler for botching the latest collective bargaining agreement, was smacked by a double whammy. A very cautious statement was released by the league later that afternoon:

"Two competing proposals for the services of Lindros will be submitted to arbitration for resolution. The issues in the arbitration will not be disclosed. The parties have agreed to use an independent arbitrator.

"A hearing will be held promptly, the exact time and location to be determined. No comment beyond this statement will be made by the parties or by the NHL."

As it turned out, arbitrator Larry Bertuzzi conducted four days of hearings with all parties, and ruled in favour of the Flyers the following week. There are many people in hockey who professed to smelling a rat when his decision came down. Most insiders felt that the Nordiques-Rangers claim would be upheld, and pointed towards the presence of interim president Gil Stein, a former Flyers' lawyer and a close friend and confidant of the Snider family, in the controversy.

Drafted by desperate league governors to keep the lid on the Lindros affair, considering John Ziegler's lame duck status, Stein immediately appointed the arbitrator and decreed a gag rule. Both the Rangers and Nordiques complied, and as the hearings began, so did the Flyers.

By the third day of testimony, it became very evident that the Flyers were very nervous about their chances. On more than one occasion, Jay Snider was seen and heard in loud exchanges in the Radisson corridors, especially after Eric Lindros had testified. Lindro testified that the Flyers had inquired about his willingness to go there if they traded for him and he had told them that he had no objections to playing in Philadelphia, but testified that never during the conversation did it sound to him that the Flyers had concluded a deal. That, in large part, was Philadelphia's case: the very phone call and Lindros's non-refusal (yes, a double negative) to go to Philadelphia, meant that a trade existed between the two teams. As far as they were concerned, all that remained were a few details.

That wasn't the case in Marcel Aubut's opinion; in fact, the Nordiques saw this version as the product of Jay Snider's wishful thinking. Insiders felt that Snider had every reason to desperately chase after rainbows. Bobby Clarke, whom Snider had forced out of Philadelphia three years prior when he had convinced his father that he could oversee the hockey side of the business, had returned to the team as a vice-president for hockey operations just ten days before the draft. The former team captain had shown his acumen by taking the Minnesota North Stars to the Stanley Cup final, while Philadelphia was missing the playoffs, and the contrast was glaring.

The Philadelphia story circulating was that if the younger Snider botched the Lindros deal as he had other hockey decisions, the senior Snyder would shunt him into the family's cable television business, and Clarke would take over all hockey decision-making for the club. As it turned out, Snyder won and Clarke was soon gone, this time to the expansion Miami Panthers.

None of this speculation surfaced at the time, however, because following the lead of the Toronto media, most beat reporters were homing in on Aubut and the Nordiques, a much easier target. Dumping on Quebecers always has sold newspapers in Toronto and points west. Moreover, there was no shortage of envious NHL executives prowling the hallways of the Radisson, wearing their opinions and jealousies on their sleeves.

Mike Kiley of the *Chicago Tribune* quoted one:

*"The Nordiques have been squeezing people all week, and it got ridiculous,"* one source said.

Scott Morrison of the *Toronto Sun* was relentless with his anti-Quebec diatribe . . . and too bad if his story, headlined

"The Game of Greed," was far off-base, par for the course for a Toronto newspaper trying to cover happenings in the neighbouring province to the east.

*"The word is greed. . . . And when the New York Rangers offered $5 million more than the Philadelphia Flyers had, maybe a player more or another pick, one done deal was summarily dismissed for another."* Morrison and others later would be stunned that their information was so wrong, and the more intelligent among them later discovered that they had been shamelessly abused by the Flyers. Only Al Strachan of *The Globe and Mail* dared to challenge the so-called conventional wisdom and laud the Nordiques for skilfully manoeuvring themselves into a win-win situation. Either deal, he said, was a masterpiece of bargaining by Aubut, Pagé et. al, and well worth the previous year's bad press. The rest, conversely, was sour grapes.

Just prior to announcing the arbitration agreement, Gil Stein asked that all three teams respect his request for silence on the affair. Two teams complied, and it soon became very evident which team leaked, because journalists all over North America had the details of the Flyers' deal exactly, but were far off in their Rangers-Nordiques speculation . . . often listing the wrong players, and a $20-million cash payment that was off by a mere $8 million. The reason was obvious; both the Rangers and Nordiques had stayed quiet, forcing journalists to make up their own trades.

And after Larry Bertuzzi's surprising decision was handed down, both the Rangers and Nordiques maintained league unanimity by accepting it without reservation, even though privately they were flabbergasted and dismayed by the Toronto lawyer's reasoning.

Some fourteen months later, Marcel Aubut cannot complain about the results of the deal. The ex-Flyers who joined his team — they would also include Chris Simon, a very large winger — combined with an international cast of names like Sakic, Kamensky, Sundin, Young and Kovalenko to turn in the team's best regular season record in almost a decade. Ron Hextall took the team to a second-place finish in the Adams Division and was a model citizen, while Huffman and Duchesne quarterbacked the team's offense from the blueline.

However, a proud man who is recognized by his peers as an innovator and forward-thinker, is still smarting about the treatment he received in the media.

The Flyers again finished out of the playoffs, but gave every indication that they will be in contention for many years to come. Surprisingly, the team joining them out of the playoff hunt in the Patrick Division was none other than the New York Rangers, the previous year's division leader in regular season. Stanley Jaffe was not amused, feeling that Eric Lindros would have put his team over the top.

Gi l Stein, who made two solid enemies in two very different cities, would overstep his bounds in a certain matter involving his induction into the NHL Hall of Fame, and be bounced from the league.

Aubut and the Nordiques will never openly question whether the arbitration decision was kosher, or if Stein influenced the arbitrator, but they will forever wonder.

As they will forever wonder what it might have been like to have No. 88 lead them onto the Forum ice against their archrivals.

# 13

## The Interregnum

Montreal, 10:20 p.m., April 27, 1980: A Runyonesque gathering is engrossed in the kaleidoscopic swirl of myriad television images in a store window on this chilly spring evening.

The Granada TV Rental outlet is about 200 yards east of the Forum. There, 18,000 hockey fans are sweating through what the National Hockey League calls Game 7 of Series K. Outside the Granada showroom, watching the five television sets with their multiple images of the seventh game of the semi-final involving Montreal Canadiens and the youthfully tenacious Minnesota North Stars, is our crowd. Official "paid" attendance: nine (we don't count the passersby).

Montreal Urban Community Police patrol car 25-4 is parked directly at the curb, about ten feet from the store window. Inside are four cops, the two regulars assigned to that car and two others from Car 25-31, which is parked across the street. Directly behind them is a Diamond Taxicab, its driver chewing on a cigar. At the corner sits an empty bus from Line 165. The bus driver is standing to the right of the storefront. He feels the cold and zips up his regulation grey sweater.

Two other players in this little vignette are feeling no cold at all. Fresh from a tavern just down St. Catherine Street, one of them lies sprawled against the rear fender of the patrol car. The other, much livelier, keeps up a lurching commentary while the silent ballet blinks before us in green, yellow, red, white and blue.

"Minnesota is gonna win it," he declares over and over again with the conviction of the truly inebriated. "No way they're gonna lose. The Canadiens are tired. Look at 'em, they're dragging their asses."

The driver's window in the patrol car rolls down.

"Shut the hell up or I'll kick yours!" says the cop.

"It's a free country," sniffs the wino, miffed that no one wants to listen to his colour commentary. The door is nudged open an inch and the wino takes the hint.

Back on television, the Habs are pressing. After opening the scoring on a Mark Napier power play goal at 9:12, they suffered the indignity of giving up a short-handed effort just five minutes later. It was pure fluke. Denis Herron went behind his net to clear a puck up the boards and launch another power-play rush, something a goalie does 500 times a year. The puck hit the side of the net and bounced out to checker Tom Younghans who was alone in front of a deserted cage. Late in the second period, defenceman Craig Hartsburg scored with a point blast on a North Stars' advantage and the Canadiens have trailed since.

Montreal is severely strapped in its drive for five. Late in the third game of the best-of-five opening round game against Hartford Whalers, winger Pat Boutette stuck out a knee and caught Guy Lafleur as he skated past. The blatant foul ended Lafleur's playoff series, but the Canadiens went ahead and won the game in overtime. Two NHL greats, Gordie Howe and Bobby Hull, retired after this game. Several years later, some Canadiens fans would say that this was the last game played by the real Flower.

Also sitting out is Pierre Larouche, Lafleur's linemate. The Canadiens scored 328 goals during the regular season. Larouche and Lafleur, with 50 each, accounted for almost one-third of them. Their linemate, Steve Shutt, who scored three goals in a 5-0 shutout of the North Stars earlier in the series, looks lost. In this game, he does not get a shot on goal.

Still, the game is close because the Canadiens have a rockribbed defence led by the Big Three and ably back-stopped by the Little Three, Brian Engblom, Gaston Gingras and Rod Langway. Serge Savard and Guy Lapointe are limping on leg and foot injuries, respectively, so the Little Three are in the thick of it.

Early in the third period, two veteran playoff campaigners—Mario Tremblay and Yvon Lambert—do what they do best. They "muck", banging and bouncing bodies against the boards, and the puck comes free. It is directed back to the point where Rod Langway lets it go. It eludes Gilles Meloche and the game is tied 2-2.

Inside 25-4, the cops are slapping each other on the back. The cabbie lays on the horn and the blare substitutes for the silent roar of the Forum fans we can see in standing ovation.

"Enough!" One of the cops has stepped out of the car and is glaring at the cabbie. Station 25 is just around the corner and this foursome wants to escape the notice of their watch commander.

The goal lifts the Canadiens and they start pressing the younger North Stars. We all have seen this happen many times before. The Lion Awakes.

But a strange thing happens. Even though the Canadiens have the better flow, they aren't getting the shots on net. The North Stars regroup at their blueline, stop the thrust and parry dangerously with several 2-on-1 and 3-on-2 breaks. Herron is called on to make several important saves.

The game ebbs and flows silently in front of us. We cannot hear the announcers in French or English, although the cabby has the game on radio, but we all know that each announcer is saying the same thing: overtime beckons.

There is a strange dynamic to a tight playoff hockey game. Play seems to become constipated as the clock winds down. Instead of pressing in the last five minutes of regulation time, and still having some time left to get even again if the opponent scores, the players all act as if overtime is the real goal, even though a mistake made then will have no redemption. They are avoiding defeat rather than striving to win. You can already hear the post-game interviews in the losing dressing room: "Well, we took 'em to overtime and they just got the break."

Players know they get special dispensation if they lose in overtime, and act accordingly.

As a result, there are weird gaps in the action. Instead of pressing to the advantage, players hesitate and drop back and the puck often just lies there with rival players avoiding it like the proverbial plague.

It is this kind of situation that confronts a Canadiens forward with 90 seconds left in regulation.

Instead of turning on the jets and racing a North Star to a loose puck in the neutral zone, he peels off and heads back to his end. Minnesota's Steve Payne pounces on the puck and relays it to centre Bobby Smith who carries it over the Canadiens' blue line. He "shoots-passes" it to streaking winger Al MacAdam who tips it over Herron's leg. Minnesota 3 Montreal 2. Time: 18:43 of the third period. Can the Forum be quieter than the Granada storefront?

"Nuts, Minnesota's gonna win."

The wino is brave again, and maybe a little surprised that his prediction may come to pass. This time the cop can only give him a hard stare and, forgetting the proximity of the station house, slams his hand down on the wheel, hitting the horn in a bleat of defeat.

"The Canadiens are jinxed. Christ, we didn't even have winter," adds the beery philosopher, invoking Montreal's lack of snow in the winter of 1979-80 as the true portent of the impending loss. Inside 25-4, one of the cops can't help but laugh.

Some 77 seconds remain in the dynasty. Can the Canadiens come back yet another time? Behind the Canadiens bench, coach Claude Ruel cannot hide his concern. Scotty Bowman is in Buffalo. Jacques Lemaire has spent the winter in Switzerland. If Ken Dryden is watching the game, it is on television from Toronto. Lafleur and Larouche are absent. Doug Risebrough is dressed but he's injured and he hasn't played a second in this crucial game. Lapointe and Savard are limping.

Play resumes, and with 40 seconds remaining Meloche stones Napier. The camera pans the Canadiens' bench and all players are watching the game intently. The only players with their heads down are those who have just come off the ice, gulping for air. The mental toughness is still there, these guys are not quitting.

Twenty seconds remain and Meloche gets his toe on a shot from the point. And then it is over. There will be no second "five straight".

You can't help but wonder if somewhere in the building, the Class of 1960 is heaving a sigh of relief. Their "five" is safe.

As the green-shirted North Stars mob Meloche and the white-shirted Canadiens console Herron, the bus driver shrugs, walks quickly to number 165 and drives off. The cabbie follows as the rear doors of Car 25-4 open and two officers cross the street to Car 25-31. The driver of 25-4 throws a last look at the two winos, one sleeping quietly on the sidewalk where his partner is trying to wake him, and drives off. Car 25-31 follows. The winos are still there when the Forum funeral procession comes down St. Catherine Street.

The thing about defeating a champion is the surprise that follows. No matter how battered and torn the champion may have been during the contest, the aura of invincibility is all-pervasive, and even the challenger can't believe it when the last siren, bell or gun is sounded.

At 10:44 p.m., with a minute left on the game clock, it was Minnesota that watched the scoreboard with trepidation. The mystique of the Habs worked two ways. It left Minnesota players asking themselves deep inside: "What are they going to do to win it this time?" Across the ice on the other bench, Habs were asking themselves: "I wonder who's going to pot the tying goal?"

At 10:50, both teams, still disbelieving, were in their dressing rooms. Minnesota's tiny cubicle under the reds on the east side of the Forum was inundated by media types: recorders and cameras thrust into the faces of young, exultant faces and all asking the rubberneck's big question: "How does it feel?"

In the home team's museum/dressing room, the same question is repeated, albeit more quietly. None of the players look up. The torch has been passed to them, and dropped. Tonight the pictures of the Hall of Famers which line the upper wall seem to stare down accusingly.

Off in a corner, Doug Jarvis sits quietly, uncomprehendingly. A superb defensive forward and product of the wonderful Peterborough Petes' training ground that has sent so many great players to Montreal and other NHL teams, this is the first time he must face a Stanley Cup loss in his NHL career. He joined the team in 1975-76 and in each year of his four-year career has returned home in the spring as a Stanley Cup champion.

The realization dawns: these guys don't know how to lose. The learning process is a painful and time-consuming one. For the Canadiens, it started a year earlier.

Shortly after the 1978-79 season ended, Al MacNeil announced he was leaving the organization to accept the coaching job with the Atlanta Flames. To some that was minor news. But to those who covered the Canadiens and knew how well MacNeil had done his job preparing young players in Nova Scotia for eight years, it was seen as an important defection. MacNeil made his announcement early because he wanted to be ready for the NHL draft.

His was not the only significant departure from the club that year. Few people close to the team doubted that the Stanley Cup-clinching game in May was Scotty Bowman's last behind the Canadiens' bench. He had brooded for a year over the appointment of Grundman as managing director and the creation of a hockey management board.

Bowman made his move one weekend in early June. He was locked into heavy negotiations with Buffalo Sabres and they were pressing for an answer.

"I was in constant communication with both teams and finally decided that I was going to meet with the

Canadiens' board on Monday. Buffalo started pressing because the draft was just around the corner and they wanted all of this resolved. I called Mr. [Seymour] Knox because he had given me a deadline of midnight Sunday. He was upset because this already was an extension of an earlier deadline."

Bowman did not want to coach any longer. He felt he had earned his promotion into the front office, whether with Montreal or another team, and was determined to obtain the front office position. Many years and many coaches later in Buffalo, he would discover that there was no coach good enough to work for Scotty Bowman, general manager—with the notable exception of Scotty Bowman, coach.

"Buffalo was worried about my decision. They wanted to know a week earlier and that's why I ended up coaching. I said to them: 'I'll come but I'm not going to coach.' That was the bottom line and finally they agreed to this. But I needed more time to meet with the Canadiens and probably, to really make up my mind.

"So I told them: 'Look, you've been fair with me, I'll be fair with you. I'll agree to coach for you for one year if you give me this one-day extension.' I didn't want to start off with them thinking that I was just trying to use them as a way of staying with Montreal."

Bowman decided that Sunday and phoned Knox and, later, Molson's president Morgan McCammon. He still wanted to meet with the Canadiens' board the following day, Bowman told them, but his mind was made up. That Monday Bowman met with Canadiens' president Jacques Courtois, Jean Beliveau and Irving Grundman to tell them of his decision.

"We had a good conversation and parted as friends. It was a good way to leave and I thanked them. There was no animosity."

When the draft meetings opened later that week, Scotty Bowman sat at the Buffalo table and MacNeil was with Cliff Fletcher's Flames.

After the management defections came the player moves. Less than a week after Bowman's announcement, thirty-three year old Jacques Lemaire joined the exodus. Lemaire still had several productive years ahead of him in the NHL; indeed, he had played better as he matured, replacing Peter Mahovlich between Shutt and Lafleur on the club's top scoring line and adding a component it had never possessed, defence. All this from a player of whom it was said in his earlier years: "He could go into a corner with eggs in his pockets and come out with all of them intact."

Lemaire, always a quiet and serious individual, was one hockey player who took his *métier* to heart. He worked hard and taught himself the defensive game in the NHL. He also was good with the younger forwards. His studious approach to the game left little doubt that he could turn to coaching after his playing days were over.

There was only one roadblock. Lemaire was a very shy, intensely private person who hated the Montreal Canadiens' fishbowl. He never begrudged the media people their jobs; he just didn't like the cameras pointed at him.

When the Swiss came calling for a player-coach who could speak French, Lemaire was the right man.

"I feel that at thirty-three, I am very fortunate to have this opportunity," he told a news conference, one of many which would keep the Montreal hockey writers away from their beloved golf courses during this summer of change. "After sitting back and analyzing everything, and considering the alternatives, I have decided to go over there as a playing-coach. I want to continue in hockey after my playing days are over and I think this will give me some experience in coaching and managing."

Lemaire would be taking a salary cut, but it was worth it, he said. He earned 150,000 dollars a year with Montreal in 1978-79 and the contract with Sierre was for 75,000 U.S. dollars a year. However, it was tax-free and the Lemaire family would be provided with a free house and automobile.

Three weeks later, and a scant six weeks after the last Stanley Cup parade, Ken Dryden announced his retirement. He had talked it over several times with Irving

Grundman during the preceding season and the Canadiens had ample warning. Despite his relatively young age, thirty-one, Dryden felt it was time to move on to other things. The hockey writers were reached at their respective golf courses July 8, a month before Dryden's birthday, and summoned to a hastily convened press conference.

"Retiring was a lot easier yesterday than it is today. But it is a decision that I've taken and will have to live with. To have lived in Montreal, to have played at the Forum, to have played before the people of Montreal and to have played with the kind of people I've had the opportunity to play with, makes for a truly remarkable experience."

Another player who had provided Montrealers with many remarkable experiences during his career would be third on the retirement match that summer. Yvan Cournoyer, the Road Runner, had missed much of the last season and the Stanley Cup playoffs after back surgery in January, his second such operation. The thirty-five year old right winger went to training camp that September and was flying, scoring two goals in a 3-3 tie with Philadelphia and another against Chicago.

However, he did not suit up for the two last exhibition games against Toronto and Boston and took his turn before the microphones October 10.

"I tried it and found out I just can't do it," he said. The back was too sore and, although Cournoyer had shown oldtime form, he knew that the wear-and-tear of a full season would be too much. He would hand the captain's "C" officially to Serge Savard. The rangy defenceman had worn it during the Stanley Cup conquest earlier in the spring and now it was his for good. In one summer, Montreal lost three players with twenty-five Cups among them.

"Talk about your house of cards," Grundman reminisced.

"We lost talent at every level that summer and those of us left had to work even harder to maintain our previous level. As much as the losses of the players hurt us, we felt that the nucleus of players who remained was good enough to keep us at the top of the standings. We still had the best defence in the league and we had players like Larouche, Shutt and Lafleur to put it in the net, and Jarvis and Gainey to check the other teams' forwards."

Bunny Larocque finally would get his wish to become number one goalie with the Canadiens, but Montreal needed a dependable back-up who could challenge Larocque for the top spot if necessary. Young forward Pat Hughes, Mark Napier's brother-in-law, was traded to Pittsburgh for Denis Herron, a smart move.

Not so smart a move was the appointment of Bowman's replacement. A variety of people had been considered for the post: Jacques Laperriere, Henri Richard, Dickie Moore, Gilles Tremblay and Claude Ruel. The summer rumour mill was hyperactive in the off-season but none of the guesses came close.

When Red Fisher of *The Montreal Star* scooped the world September 4 with the news that Bernard "Boom Boom" Geoffrion was Scotty Bowman's replacement, the hockey audience was stunned. Glib, funny in a beer commercial sort of way, Boom Boom had been instrumental in launching the Flames franchise in Atlanta. He had shown some talents as a coach, but his strength was public relations, which he was practising for Atlanta when Irving Grundman reached out for him.

"We made a mistake," Grundman admits several years later. "Bernie had coached twice so he had experience and he was a very popular man in this city in his playing days. And although he was famous for his craziness and sense of humour, he was a bright, intelligent man who could communicate. And the thing we needed with a veteran Stanley Cup team was communication."

It never happened.

Geoffrion blitzed into Montreal and immediately took over his press conference, cracking jokes in French and English, the latter a curious combination of French and Georgia Peach accents. His first coaching stint with New York Rangers in 1968-69 had lasted three months into the season before he was sidelined by ulcers. Four years later, he coached the brand new Flames into the Stanley Cup quarterfinals and again quit because of illness.

Montreal's hockey media asked the obvious question: What makes you think you can survive the real heat of coaching the Canadiens?

"I am the new, improved Bernard Geoffrion," he told the masses. "I can handle this. I am serious and I am going to prove it to you."

Both sides agreed to wait and see, especially the veteran journalists who had covered the Canadiens during the 1950s. They had Geoffrion tabbed as right winger on the NHL's all-time Team Strange, with Eddie Shack on left wing and Mike "Shakey" Walton at centre. Boom Boom earned his spot, scoring 393 goals in 16 NHL seasons and engaging in more fun than was legal for fifty people to enjoy.

This was the same Boomer who peered through the hole in his baseball glove in the famed Miller Lite beer commercials in the United States.

Indeed, some scribes remembered, "da Boomer's fun" almost killed him once. The incident occurred in practice. The Toe Blake Canadiens did not waste time on drills and weaves and repetitive "3-on-2s" during their ice training. The best way for the top players in the league to get better was to play against the top players in the league—themselves.

The players were skating hard and having fun in one such scrimmage when Geoffrion went down in a clump. His teammates gathered around and made their usual derogatory comments such as "Hey Boom, the scrimmage ain't on TV" until it was noticed that he was changing colour. Rushed to hospital by ambulance, Geoffrion spent several hours on the operating table as doctors worked hard to minimize the damage caused by a ruptured spleen.

This was the man who would guide the fortunes of a veteran team that had battled Scotty Bowman to a draw over the preceding eight seasons?

It was Boom Boom in the Lions' Den and it ended predictably. Three months and a week after Geoffrion entertained the media wretches at his inaugural press conference, he was in Irving Grundman's office.

Michael Dugas of *The Gazette* was sitting outside Grundman's office when Geoffrion stomped in December 12. He took notes.

"I'm sick and tired of them. They're not acting like professional players. Why should I get sick over a bunch of guys who won't listen to me. Guys are coming in at two or three in the morning [coach, meet Rick Chartraw] laughing and joking around. I'm not going to stick around and let everyone in Montreal blame me for what's happening ... because it's not my fault."

The coach went on to complain about Pierre Larouche strutting through an airport smoking a big cigar on the night of a loss. Captain Serge Savard was too interested in his horses to bother helping Geoffrion. The only player who seemed to care was Larry Robinson, he added.

"I had a dream to coach this team. This dream is a nightmare now. I don't care if you pay me a million dollars a year, I will not stay."

The next day, Claude Ruel began his second stint as head coach of the Montreal Canadiens. The club responded and their opening-game loss in Minnesota in their quarterfinal playoff was their first in 25 games.

There would be no second run of five consecutive championships. But unlike the impression that has been created since, there would be no precipitous plunge from the Olympian heights either.

If those time-bending journalistic historians like to compress Montreal's first forty years to make it seem that the Canadiens have always been the NHL's top franchise, which is not in the least true, the Montreal media, especially the French-language media, still give the impression today that the Irving Grundman years were the club's modern Dark Ages.

The truth is that under Grundman, Montreal finished first in their division three times and won one Stanley Cup. The Canadiens visited no Stygian depths in that era.

In 1979, they were second overall to the New York Islanders, but won the Cup. The Islanders would then win four in a row. However, lost in the shuffle was the fact that over this five-year period, Montreal Canadiens —the supposedly aging giant that stumbled geriatrically from NHL rink to NHL rink—scored 532 points to New York's 531. Other teams in the league, called challengers or up-and-coming at some time during that half-decade, included Philadelphia, Boston and Buffalo. They had 501, 498 and 479 points respectively.

In bottom-line conscious Montreal, however, the Stanley Cup was the only thing. Regular-season results and the fact that the team was perennially competitive meant nothing if the club failed in the playoffs. That the Canadiens were second in goals scored (360) and best in goals against (223) during the 1982 regular season would pale to insignificance after a fluke shot by Dale Hunter trickled behind Rick Wamsley in the first minute of overtime of the fifth and final game of the opening round of the playoffs.

The most unfortunate part of Irving Grundman's two last years as managing director of the Montreal Canadiens revolved about one player.

Montreal's normally demanding media looked at the elimination by Minnesota as pure luck, and with a lot of justification. The Canadiens went into the series without Larouche and Lafleur and with two of the Big Three, Lapointe and Savard, hurting. Doug Risebrough dislocated a shoulder and hardly played.

Going into the draft June 11 at the Forum, the Canadiens knew they were in a position to do themselves a lot of good. They had acquired first pick and the 1980 crop had one word stencilled across it: bumper.

The Central Scouting people, and Montreal's own scouts who had made the trip to Saskatchewan many times, were drooling over a big centreman with Regina Pats who was setting the Western Hockey League on its ear. His name was Douglas Peter Wickenheiser and he had been selected Canadian junior of the year on the basis of a 170-point season (89 goals, 81 assists). If that wasn't enough, he scored 14 more goals and added 26 assists in 18 playoff games.

But Wickenheiser was not alone. The Portland Winter Hawks had a strapping big defenceman named David Babych who was a franchise, the reports said. Not to be outdone by their western cousins, the Montreal Juniors were inspired by a pepperpot centreman from Verdun named Denis Savard. Lower down in the ratings was a huge crop of quality eighteen year olds, many of them defencemen like Larry Murphy, Darren Veitch, Paul Coffey, Rick Lanz, Jérôme Dupont, Normand Rochefort, Moe Mantha, Ric Nattress and Steve Konroyd. Forwards available included Jimmy Fox, Mike Bullard, Brent Sutter, Barry Pederson, Paul Gagné, Steve Patrick, Kevin Lavallee, Mike Moller and John Chabot.

There was a great deal of pressure in the French-language media to draft Savard. An exciting player, he was born with a CH tattooed on his chest and fit the mold of Montreal centres that went back to the Morenz days. He would be terrific with Lafleur and Shutt, they reasoned, and Larouche could form the lynchpin of a strong second scoring line.

But the Canadiens wanted a big centre, something they dearly missed since the Peter Mahovlich trade three years before.

"Although Pierre Larouche was hurt in the playoffs, all indications we had were that he would be all right and he could return between Guy Lafleur and Steve Shutt in the fall," Grundman recalled. "We also knew that Guy was going to be okay from his knee injury. We really studied this thing before the draft was held. All of our people said to go for Wickenheiser."

Montreal picked Wickenheiser, Winnipeg Jets drafted Babych and Chicago selected Savard. That day, Montreal reporters began marking their calendars. The NHL schedule had Chicago coming to the Forum October 11— exactly four months later—for the first Canadiens' home game of the 1980-81 season.

On that night Savard played and starred. The Canadiens, in their infinite wisdom, did not dress their number one pick. When Savard deked Larry Robinson out of his jockstrap and scored, the ovation was very loud. A lot of hockey people still feel that not dressing Wickenheiser for that game hurt the Regina native more than he will ever admit.

As it was, none of the heralded draft choices won the Calder Trophy as best rookie for that season. It was captured by a twenty-five year old veteran rookie named Peter Stastny. However, Savard was not far behind in the voting, thanks to his 28 goals and 47 assists. Babych also had a strong season with 6 goals and 38 assists for 44 points as a rookie rearguard. Montreal's "big centre" finished with 7 goals and 8 assists in 41 games.

The low point of his season came when the Canadiens made a mid-season swing through Alberta. In one of his infrequent outings, Wickenheiser had scored twice and added an assist in a Forum game against the Flames, who had moved to Calgary from Atlanta in the off-season. Yet, he was not dressed for the return game in Calgary, or two nights later for a game against the Oilers. Sitting in the press box was becoming a habit, so Wickenheiser was learning to swallow his disappointment quietly. However, his parents and a large number of friends from Regina drove to the two Alberta games and never got to see him play.

By the midway point of the season, Wickenheiser was a disillusioned nineteen year old.

It would be unfair to intimate that the Canadiens benched Wickenheiser with no reason or for spite. One thing that hurt him was the emergence of a feisty pivot who had spent two years maturing with the Nova Scotia Voyageurs. Keith Acton, a product of Peterborough, had scored 45 goals with the Voyageurs in 1979-80 and was promised a full shot at making the team. He delivered with 15 goals and 24 assists in 61 games.

Wickenheiser's real challenge came from without. As long as he played in Montreal, he would suffer the Savard comparisons and it would get worse as Savard proceeded to set all sorts of records for Black Hawks centremen.

Four years later, and a year after Wickenheiser would be traded to St. Louis Blues, Claude Ruel would admit that "Wickenheiser just wasn't the hockey player we thought he was. He just wasn't good enough and that's the real reason why he was not dressed for that first Chicago game."

Since he was always fiercely protective of the younger players on the Canadiens, Ruel's remark was uncharacteristic. It showed clearly how sensitive a nerve the Wickenheiser draft had become for the entire organization.

Was Wickenheiser a bad choice? Grundman denies it to this day.

"Every scout in the NHL had him listed as number one. Our own scouts had him listed as number one. Central Scouting had him as top pick. We made the right choice according to our own priorities and the information we had at the time. One major factor was temperament. We always tried to assess what kind of person a young player was. Wickenheiser checked out. He was one of the most popular guys in the dressing room here and all of his teammates were cheering for him. He is a class individual and it is unfortunate that it didn't work out for him in Montreal."

The big centre was not in the lineup when Montreal skated out against the Edmonton Oilers' "kiddie korps" in the opening round of the playoffs that spring. The Canadiens were swallowed in three straight and Ruel, a great sergeant, was chewed to bits by Glen Sather's generalship behind the bench.

Also out of the lineup for that series were two long-time veterans. In February, Rick Chartraw was dealt to Los Angeles Kings for a second-round draft choice. A month later, at the stroke of midnight with regard to the trading deadline, Michel Larocque was sent to Toronto for Robert Picard and an eighth-round draft choice.

The Canadiens faced a disturbing summer and this time the storm clouds were clearly evident on the horizon. Guy Lafleur thought Ruel was thoroughly outcoached in the playoffs and said so. Ruel thought Lafleur was thoroughly outplayed, by both Wayne

Gretzky and Lafleur's shadow, Dave Hunter, and said nothing. Others in the entourage hinted at the same problems and it was obvious that a new coach would have to be appointed.

In the summer of '82, Montreal went coach shopping and came up with Bob Berry, a native Montrealer and former Los Angeles Kings star and coach. In three years with Team Surfboard, Berry had managed a very respectable 107 wins, 94 losses and 39 ties. He was known as a strict coach who believed in a system of play. All of these qualities sounded good to the Canadiens' front office.

There would be a few differences in coaching the two teams, Berry acknowledged. "In Los Angeles we had a 500 dollar fine for anyone who showed up with a tan," Berry smiled. The Los Angeles Kings have always been known as the Hollywood Cabana Club by their envious NHL confrères from colder climes. It was always a little too easy to leave practice and head right for the beach.

"I guess we won't need it here. I'm going to give some thought to some new rules but I'm not going to change my coaching philosophy to please anybody. There will be curfews. People will be on time for everything. I don't think this is too much to ask of any professional athlete."

It was quite obvious that Grundman had taken Geoffrion's parting shots to heart, and that the message had been relayed to the incoming coach.

Geoffrion had talked tough and had been openly defied by his players. Claude Ruel, on the other hand, had tried to be more understanding and less demanding of his charges. As a result, they cut him to ribbons in the press. One of the worst culprits was Guy Lafleur, who suffered from a bad case of "diarrhea of the mouth" in the mind of the managing director.

Lafleur went through a frustrating season and this led to several tirades. After missing the previous playoffs with the knee injury, he worked hard to be in condition for training camp, only to be stricken with a hamstring injury. He missed 29 games during the season, scoring 27 goals and 43 assists in 51 games. The ultimate embarrassment came in the playoffs, after Richard Sevigny had announced to the world that the Flower would put Wayne Gretzky in his back pocket in any confrontation. Sevigny, of course, was dead wrong, but it was Lafleur who had to eat his words.

That summer, Lafleur worked very hard in preparation for Canada Cup II, and found himself playing on a line with Gretzky and Gilbert Perreault. Perreault, it turned out, was the best of the three before an ankle injury sidelined him for the final against the Soviet Union, an 8-1 loss. The experience, and the Edmonton and Calgary fans chanting "Guy, Guy" every time the Flower touched the puck, seemed to rejuvenate him and he reported to camp ready to play hard in 1981-82.

Little did Lafleur know how close he came to playing for Buffalo a year later. Tired of his public complaints, stories of his overnight escapades and lack of on-ice production, Grundman discreetly shopped him around.

"At the time, Buffalo was having a very hard time renegotiating Gilbert Perreault's contract and it looked like they weren't ever going to agree. I met their vice-president and lawyer Bob Swados, who was also their alternate governor, at a governor's meeting and we started talking. We had several conversations over a two-week period but the whole thing fell through when the Perreault contract was straightened out.

"Who knows? That deal might have turned things around for both clubs. The only thing I know is that Perreault was probably the only player Montreal fans would accept in a Lafleur trade."

Berry's appointment came a week before the draft and it was a quiet, almost timid contingent that sat at the Canadiens' table June 10. In the previous thirteen months, four men had called themselves Coach of the Montreal Canadiens, and other bodies had been shuffled hither and yon after a decade of almost boring but very successful sameness. The Canadiens had three draft picks of the 21 in the first round and another two in the second round, or five of the top 42. If Ron Caron's scouts had done their jobs, some talent would be found.

Drafting seventh, the Canadiens went for bloodlines and claimed Mark Hunter from the Brantford Alexanders of the Ontario junior league. The younger brother of Edmonton's Dave and Quebec's Dale, he was known as a tough, good skater with a very good shot. With choices 18 and 19 overall, the Canadiens went for Chicoutimi defenceman Gilbert Delorme and a Swedish forward named Jan Ingman.

However, the talent pool was already thinning out. Whereas 33 of 42 first and second round choices from the 1980 crop went on to play in the NHL, only 26 of the 1981 players would stick with an NHL team for longer than one season. Montreal went back to Sweden for choice number 32, drafting Lars Eriksson from Brynas, and turned to the University of Wisconsin for a defenceman named Chris Chelios as pick number 40.

Hunter and Delorme were in the lineup when Montreal opened the new season and would make decent contributions. Joining them was Craig Laughlin, a Toronto native who had been drafted four years before and who chose to finish his education at Colgate before reporting to the Voyageurs, where he played two seasons. The left winger showed promising qualities and scored 12 goals and added 11 assists in 36 games alongside Mario Tremblay and Pierre Mondou.

The team of the '70s was officially terminated during the 1981-82 season. First, Serge Savard retired, disgusted with the shabby treatment afforded him by Montreal fans during the last season. Savard may have lost a step, but he still had plenty of experience and could play on that alone. He proved it by anchoring the Winnipeg Jets defence and helping to break in Dave Babych and a bunch of fuzzy-cheeked rearguards after John Ferguson coaxed him out of retirement.

During the Edmonton series, Savard was booed mercilessly by Montreal's so-called class fans. A player who suffered two broken legs early in his career, who won the Conn Smythe and Bill Masterton trophies and probably should have been awarded the Norris Trophy at least once in his career, Savard had been a pillar on defence. He did not deserve this slap in the face.

After Edmonton humbled Montreal 6-2 to sweep the Canadiens 3-0, the veteran defenceman was in tears in the dressing room. He knew then that he had worn the Canadiens uniform for the last time, and retired in August.

Gone also was Yvon Lambert, for nine seasons the Canadiens' Gary Dornhoefer, a fearless player who would plant his rear end in a goalie's face and absorb what Danny Gallivan would call a "plethora of slashes and high sticks" so that the fleeter members of the Canadiens' power play could manoeuvre for goals. Lambert was yet another product of the rural Quebec work ethic, starting to skate in his teens and playing his first organized hockey game when he was fourteen. He would never have made it in the 1980s Quebec amateur hockey, where the so-called "Elite system" tells kids at seven and eight years of age that they are not good enough.

With the continued improvement of second-year players like Keith Acton, some rookies (Wickenheiser) and some veterans (Larouche) were being pressed. Both players experienced difficulties adapting to the defensive side of their roles. Wickenheiser took it well, but Larouche did not. As a result, he spent a lot of time on the bench, when he was allowed to wear the uniform.

Dressed for only 22 of Montreal's first 33 games, Lucky Pierre had 9 goals and 12 assists for 21 points and he was chafing at the bit. The crisis came on a New England swing just before Christmas. The Canadiens played a game in Hartford and then settled down for the 90-minute bus ride to Boston. Larouche had been benched for five straight games and spent most of his free time hollering loud and long for a trade.

Larouche became involved in a long and beery condemnation of management and coaching during the ride, even though Grundman, who was sitting up front, said he heard little of it.

"A lot has been made of the bus ride, but that was not what was wrong. Most clubs have a standard policy: players cannot drink in the bar of the hotel where they are staying. That's reserved for the coaches and management and avoids any run-ins. When we got to Boston, there was Pierre in the bar at the Sheraton." Larouche was asked to leave and refused. A little more than a week later, he was a Hartford Whaler and the happy-go-Lucky Pierre of old, scoring 25 goals and 25 assists in the 45 games remaining in the season. They loved him in Hartford, until about halfway through the next season.

They loved him in Montreal, especially when it was learned that Irving Grundman had shown a flash of Pollock brilliance in arranging the deal with Whalers' GM Larry Pleau. Larouche went to Hartford for the Whalers' number one pick in 1984, and if by some miracle Hartford would rise to the top of the rankings, thus inversely affecting the quality of that pick, Montreal had the option of flipping picks with Hartford.

"When I came here and saw that one, I almost fainted," says Emile Francis, the current Whalers' President and General Manager.

Irving Grundman and his chief hockey man, Ron Caron, were looking ahead three years. There was a tall rangy centre playing for Laval Nationals who looked very good and might be available in 1984 if the Whalers could remain near the lower echelons of the league for a few more years. His name: Mario Lemieux.

Buried in the everyday goings-on of the 1981-82 NHL season was a February 11 contest at Montreal against the Pittsburgh Penguins, a longtime league doormat. Montreal won 4-2 on goals by Gaston Gingras, Mario Tremblay, Steve Shutt (his 350th) and Doug Jarvis (into the empty net) to win their tenth straight, the first time in 14 years a Canadiens' team had accomplished this feat. More importantly, however, it was the Canadiens' 2,000th win in regular-season — a first for any NHL team.

Another event which was to have great bearing on the immediate future of the teams also took place during the 1981-82 season. The league realigned its divisions. Montreal, leader of the Norris Division which comprised Los

Angeles, Pittsburgh, Hartford and Detroit, now joined the Adams Division with Boston, Buffalo, Quebec and Hartford.

Moving from such a weak division to the league's most competitive was the tonic for the Canadiens. Whereas the Canadiens had fought the surprising Kings for the Norris championship in 1980-81, finishing with 103 points to the Kings 99, there were too many easy games with Pittsburgh, Hartford and Detroit on the schedule.

Adams Division competition with the hated Nordiques, the perennially competitive Bruins and the Scotty Bowman-led Sabres got the club going and the Canadiens finished the season with 46 wins, 17 losses and 17 ties for 109 points, third overall.

The new playoff format would have them playing the Quebec Nordiques, fourth-place finishers in the Adams with an excellent 82 points on 33 wins, 31 losses and 16 ties. The Canadiens were looking good going into the playoffs. They were getting scoring from two lines and defence was strong with the Jarvis-Gainey-Hunter line bottling up the opposition forwards and Robinson-Langway-Engblom-Picard-Delorme keeping the crease clear in front of rookie goalie Rick Wamsley.

The first series was eagerly anticipated and game one went according to form, an easy 5-1 win for the home team. Then things went sour. Quebec, led by the Stastny brothers, a scrappy centre named Dale Hunter and a born-again Dan Bouchard in goal, stunned the Canadiens 2-1 in the second and won the series' third game in Quebec.

Montreal stormed back to win the fourth game and both teams left Quebec City feeling that the Canadiens would correct things in game five. Quebec's defence was notoriously weak and the Nordiques lost two defencemen, Pierre Lacroix and Jean Hamel, to injury in the second period. However, the Nordiques entered the third period with a 2-0 lead, even though the Canadiens had carried the play from the start.

The normally reserved Forum crowd, whipped to a frenzy by this emotional confrontation with the country cousins from *la Vieille Capitale*, "oohed" and "aahed" every shot on net.

Finally, Bouchard caved in under the onslaught. Mario Tremblay, his eyes laser beams all evening, scored at 10:49 and the crowd erupted. Almost a half period remained and Montreal was coming on.

It didn't take long for the tying goal as the Canadiens pressed and Robert Picard scored at 12:14.

But Bouchard got right back up and held against the wave, stopping Mondou, Lafleur, Tremblay (twice) and Shutt as Montreal outshot the Nordiques 15-5 in the third period and the game went into overtime.

Bob Berry reminded his team that anything could happen in overtime. "We've got two jobs. We stop them, and we make sure we stop them, and then we exploit the opportunities."

With that in mind, he started a defensive alignment; Gainey, Jarvis and Hunter up front, Engblom and Langway on the blueline. And the defensive line went on the offence.

Right from the faceoff, Mark Hunter, Gainey and Jarvis carried the puck into the Nordiques zone and Engblom pitched in to trap it on the boards with Jarvis and gain a faceoff.

"Dougie and I were playing soccer with it along the boards and he yelled that it was still at my feet. I looked down, and I think it was Michel Goulet who kicked it up the boards."

The puck bounced to Dale Hunter and he sped off on a 2-on-1 break with sniper Réal Cloutier. Rod Langway was the only player back and he made the perfect play, preventing a clear pass and a clear shot. Hunter passed to Cloutier but the angle was bad and the puck rolled off Cloutier's stick and behind the net. Then it was just Dale Hunter and the puck behind the net in a mini time warp.

With everyone else in the building seemingly operating in slow motion, Hunter picked up the puck and tried to come around the goal to Wamsley's right side. The goalie slid across and the Nordiques centre tried to stuff it into the net. And then nothing . . . the crowd relaxed, Wamsley had it under him.

Still in slow motion, Dale Hunter raised his stick, the referee skated leisurely to the net and pointed to the puck and then at Hunter, the red light went on and the Nordiques were streaming off their bench. Outshot 35-19, outplayed by a large margin and with a defence that couldn't stop a good midget team, the Quebec Nordiques had defeated the Montreal Canadiens and NHL hockey in the province would never be the same again.

For the second straight year, the Canadiens had failed to emerge from the first round of the playoffs.

Fingers began pointing at Grundman, Caron, Ruel and the Canadiens' brain trust. The celebrated number one pick of 1980, Doug Wickenheiser, did not play in the Quebec series, just as he had sat out the Edmonton playoff debacle of the previous year. Worse still, his spot had been taken in the lineup by Jeff Brubaker, a tough winger who had been unable to crack the Hartford starting twenty.

Other draft choices were put on glass slides and examined under the microscope. Montreal's first pick in 1978 was Danny Geoffrion, Boomer's son, and he did not make it. Dave Hunter, picked later in the same draft, was allowed to go to Edmonton and responded by shutting down Guy Lafleur in the 1981 playoffs. Gaston Gingras, picked 27th overall in 1979, was the Canadiens' top pick and was in and out of the lineup in 1981-82. Dale Hunter, whose winning goal eliminated the Canadiens, was picked 41st the same year.

Some diehards went even farther back. Mike Bossy was selected 15th in 1977, five spots after Mark Napier of the Canadiens.

And then there was Wickenheiser. In two seasons of NHL play, Dave Babych anchored the Winnipeg defence and Denis Savard had scored 194 points on 60 goals and 134 assists. Wickenheiser's numbers were 19 goals and 31 assists in 97 games.

Where is *la relève*? The torch has been dropped! The Quebec Nordiques went on to defeat the Boston Bruins in the Adams Division final and eventually lost to the New York Islanders. Every game they played that May was a festering wound for Canadiens supporters and management.

The most persistent complaint, however, was the hardest to refute. The Nordiques' all-Québécois (read French-speaking) front office and coaching staff had proven they were as good as any English-speaking front office out there, especially the English-speaking head office at the Forum. They had gone out and found good Quebec-bred hockey players and turned an expansion team into a winner in two short years. Their hockey people were better, period.

As an indictment against the entire NHL, it was a fair criticism. For too many years, French-Canadian coaches and managers were effectively shut out of the highest echelons of professional hockey by an Old Boys Network that did not look kindly on non-English Canadians. They tended to justify their condescending attitude by explaining, "Some of those French boys can really play, but I doubt they can add two and two."

However, laying that rap at the doorstep of the Canadiens was unfair. No team had gone further in hiring French-Canadians at all levels over the almost three-quarters of a century of the club's existence. Owners with names like Letourneau, Dandurand, Raymond and coaches named Lepine, Lalonde, Mantha and Ruel were ample proof of that. Nevertheless, the complainers were unforgiving.

"We caught it all that summer," said Grundman. "Everything we had done was at fault. Ron Caron was taken to task because the French media didn't like him. He was an Ottawa boy and wasn't buddy-buddy with the writers, so he was fair game. All through this he kept his cool and did his work."

Caron and Grundman, ever mindful of the criticism, then proceeded to supervise Montreal's worst draft in years. The Canadiens had accumulated five choices in the first two rounds, their regular pick in the first round, number 19, and picks number 31, 32, 33 and 40 in the second round. The 1982 crop was notoriously thin after the top 10 picks, but even here the Canadiens went wrong.

The Canadiens were determined to shut up the critics and selected Quebec junior players with their first two picks—Alain Héroux of Chicoutimi and Jocelyn Gauvreau of Granby. Neither player would make it and Héroux was selected two spots ahead of Pat Flatley of the New York Islanders, a quality forward who would star for the Canadian Olympic team in 1984. The remaining three selections by Montreal came from the United States: defenceman Kent Carlson of St. Lawrence University, David Maley of Edina High School (University of Wisconsin) and Scott Sandelin of Hibbing High School (U. of North Dakota).

Quebec, on the other hand, completely free of any language stigma, was free to make its two selections in Ontario, for David Shaw of the Kitchener Rangers and Paul Gillis of the Niagara Falls Flyers. By the 1985-86 season, Gauvreau and Héroux were out of hockey, Carlson had played a few games with Montreal and then been traded to St. Louis, and Maley and Sandelin, both highly heralded in university play, were graduating. Gillis and Shaw were regulars with the Nordiques.

Montreal may still "win" the 1982 draft if Maley and Sandelin show well in coming seasons. But the Gauvreau-Héroux and Shaw-Gillis comparison serves to prove just how much influence one playoff win by Quebec had on the Montreal Canadiens, even four seasons later.

The short-term influence also proved staggering. The Canadiens returned to training camp that fall with question marks hanging above the team like the proverbial Sword of Damocles.

If Doug Wickenheiser had not yet panned out, Keith Acton had. The diminutive centreman from Stouffville, Ontario had scored 36 goals and 52 assists in 1981-82 to lead the Canadiens in scoring. Two quality centremen were due to move up from the Nova Scotia Voyageurs: Dan Daoust (25-40—65) and Guy Carbonneau (27-67—

94). Doug Jarvis was his regular steady self at the position and Pierre Mondou, a delightful free-form scooter, had shown well the year before with 35 goals and 33 assists in 73 games alongside veterans Mario Tremblay and Rejean Houle. There was also Doug Risebrough, who had struggled through an injury-ridden season the year before and looked ready to return.

The Canadiens were rich in centres and fairly deep in forwards and defencemen. The major problem, however, was still that the Canadiens forwards were small as a group and the club had been unable to fill the void with some board-pounding skaters up front. Montreal could afford to trade a centre or two, and maybe a defenceman, to obtain a larger forward. Names mentioned included Ryan Walter of Washington, Brent Ashton of Colorado (now New Jersey) and Curt Fraser of Vancouver Canucks.

It took no time at all to clear the logjam as Grundman pulled off the largest Canadiens' trade in a decade. Montreal obtained Ryan Walter and defenceman Rick Green from the Washington Capitals in return for Rod Langway, Brian Engblom, Craig Laughlin and Doug Jarvis.

The trade registered 7.0 on the open-ended Richter Scale, and the aftershocks were in the 5 to 5.5 range. Within seconds of the announcement, the Montreal media went to work. Engblom and Langway? Together? The best defensive pairing in the league last year? You can't be serious!

Most observers had expected some movement for Langway because the New Hampshire graduate had long been unhappy with his contract and wanted to play in the United States where a dollar is a dollar and not Canadian monopoly money.

"Rod made it clear to us that if he was not traded to an American team, he was going to retire," Grundman said. "There was no doubt in my mind that he would. Rod is the sole provider for his family and he was very concerned about his family's welfare. There never would have been a question of trading him if he hadn't been so adamant."

In the wake of Langway's consecutive Norris Trophy selections in 1983 and 1984 as the league's top defenceman, it is easy to forget that the Montreal criticism centred on the trade of Engblom, a Second Team All-Star in 1981-82, and the only Canadien to crack the elite squads that season. Few people mourned the losses of the fairly anonymous Laughlin, or Jarvis, a top-notch defensive centre.

Shortly after that deal was announced, the club dealt Risebrough to Calgary Flames.

"Mr. Grundman felt that I was not going to make the team that year because they were bringing up several young centres and couldn't leave them in Nova Scotia any more," Risebrough recalled. "He was very fair to me and arranged a move to a team I approved. He didn't have to do that."

Still, trading four Canadiens to any team in one deal and a fifth shortly afterwards was a shock that reverberated throughout the dressing room for the whole season. It did not help that the "Washington Canadiens" instantly transformed that franchise into a contender and that Risebrough became the team leader in Calgary, enjoying his best scoring year since 1976.

The shock of the trade was blunted because a young Swedish player named Mats Naslund strode into the training camp, took Reggie Houle's job away from him alongside Mondou and Tremblay and proceeded to make Montreal fans forget about Craig Laughlin. At the same time, Guy Carbonneau was playing on the defensive line and scoring a respectable 47 points on 18 goals and 29 assists and Walter scored 29 goals and played an aggressive game in the corners.

Rick Green, a very strong defensive defenceman who had been the number one pick overall in the 1976 draft, proved to be deceptively fragile, missing 18 games during the regular season, and only playing 7 games the following year. Larry Robinson, exhausted by mid-March because of the time logged earlier in the season, was not himself, and Gilbert Delorme, although scoring 12 goals, tended to sacrifice position to deliver thundering bodychecks and his defensive partners were exhausted by a steady stream of 2-on-1s and 3-on-2s.

Before the trade, Montreal had the "defence of the 1980s". After it, they struggled behind their own blue-line, giving up 63 more goals (almost one a game) in 1982-83 than in the previous year.

Montreal slipped to second place in the Adams Division that season with 98 points, 12 behind the Boston Bruins, and lined up against the Buffalo Sabres in the division semi-final.

Robert Sauvé, a goaltender from Ste. Genevieve, a village on the westernmost tip of Montreal Island across from Ile Bizard, came home and posted back-to-back shutouts over the Canadiens. Montreal managed two goals in the third game in Buffalo, but they were not enough to prolong the series. The team had been swept three straight and, worse still, Montreal had not escaped the first round of the playoffs in three years.

This time the house-clearing operation would take place on the Second Floor, not in the players' dressing room. Irving Grundman and Ron Caron were forewarned of the coming changes. The first sign had come the previous November when Morgan McCammon announced that Molson's had reached into the Carling O'Keefe-Nordiques empire and come up with Ronald Corey, a marketing and beer man who had once had a tryout with the Junior Canadiens.

The message? If the Canadiens could no longer be French downstairs, they were going to be French upstairs.

# 14

# The New Order

We were sitting in the stands, Section 36 in the west-side whites, and the oldtimer had tears in his eyes.

There below, wearing the road reds, were the original Lions in Winter, the Class of 1959, skating onto the ice surface with the familiar CH in the middle, for one more ovation.

Claude Mouton was at the microphone. *"Mesdames et messieurs: Le Rocket . . . Maurice Richard!"*

As the portly Rocket skated gingerly in on Jacques Plante, the Forum ovation rose to a crescendo. Standing at centre ice with their sticks raised in acknowledgement was a group of middle-aged athletes—Tom Johnson, Bob Turner, Jean-Guy Talbot, Doug Harvey—a defensive corps as hard to penetrate as the Wall of China. Don Marshall, Claude Provost, Dickie Moore: tough wingers who could shut you down at one end and cut you open at the other.

Finally, the Scoring Machines—Henri Richard, Boom Boom Geoffrion, Jean Beliveau and of course, the Rocket.

This was a night for older fans, the veterans of the 1950s and '60s who saw eleven Stanley Cup Champion teams in twenty years. It was also a night for *les Anciens*, the men who had hung the banners high in the Forum rafters. A team which had taken greatness in stride was beginning to publicly acknowledge a longstanding debt.

A special team luncheon the day before had left the 1984-85 edition in awe.

"These guys are an inspiration to us all," said Ottawa's Bobby Smith, transformed into a fan for a day. One of the older players on the current team, he was born in the "middle of it—February, 1958—"and thus had never seen many of *les Anciens* play. But he had heard the stories.

"They were true champions, my Dad tells me. When you see these guys, you know what the uniform means to us. It's like wearing Yankee pinstripes."

Back in the stands, the greying fan took a handkerchief from a jacket pocket and wiped away the excess moisture. He pointed to the Canadiens' bench where the current team players banged their sticks against the ice or along the boards.

"What makes it so sad is the fact that those guys don't seem to know what this all means. We wouldn't be having all of these ceremonies if those guys would win once in a while."

It was the best of times, it was the worst of times and, as the fan surmised, it was time for regular journeys down memory lane, because the 1983-84 Canadiens were living a nightmare.

Suffice it to say, the worst season in memory made everybody work harder, from management to the promotions department to the players. The new season had begun four days after the Sabres put the Canadiens away in the first round of the previous year's playoffs. Ronald Corey had given the regime a year to deliver, and then cleaned house.

Gone were Irving Grundman, Ron Caron and Bob Berry. It was the biggest corporate blood-letting ever in management ranks and an embarrassment to a once-proud organization.

"Corey met with me on Tuesday afternoon, said he wasn't renewing my contract, and said I could remain with the organization for two or three weeks," Grundman recalled.

The man Pierre Larouche had contemptuously called a "glorified bowling alley manager" did not linger. He cleared out his desk and departed the building three hours later. Few people realize that Grundman would have left of his own accord. The handwriting was on the wall when Corey was hired five months before. Hockey committee or no, you could not have two bosses and that was the situation when Corey joined the team. It left both men in an impossible situation.

"I was the managing director and that meant that I was in charge of the hockey operation. Mr. Corey came on board and persistently asked to attend our hockey decision meetings. I kept telling him: 'If you want to attend meetings, call your own.' Before his appointment, the club presidency was basically a ceremonial office and not tied in with the day-to-day operations. It was an impossible situation for both of us because Mr. Corey's mandate was unclear, officially, that is."

Unofficially, the mandate was crystal clear. Clean house. Get the fans and the players believing in the Second Floor again. Better still, let's make the Canadiens Quebec's favourite beer, oops, team.

When Corey was hired, his new bosses at Molson's spoke of his personality, his drive, his leadership and his strong attachment to Montreal and Quebec. The latter reference was a slap at Grundman, who had acquired a reputation for locking himself in a corporate ivory tower, far from the maddening crowds. It was also an indication that Quebec's internecine beer wars were in high gear. Molson's Quebec subsidiary had recently undergone a major management shakeup, an advertising agency had been dismissed, and Molson's stranglehold on beer sales had slipped. Part of the reason was a sports-led resurgence of the Carling-O'Keefe Nordiques.

When the reality of the situation dawned on Molson's, they went looking for O'Keefe president Corey, a graduate in marketing from the University of Western Ontario. After graduation and before joining O'Keefe, he had covered sports for several French-language newspapers, produced hockey telecasts for the Canadian Broadcasting Corporation, worked as public relations manager for Molson's and become executive vice-president of a small company.

Corey was a firm believer in the Global Village. The

Canadiens' management style of Frank Selke and Sam
Pollock and their philosophy of "listen attentively to the
fans and then go right ahead and do what you were
going to in the first place" was for another time. The new
Canadiens would become very familiar with the medium
and the message.

One message was that Canadiens' management had
become estranged from the people who paid the shot, the
fans. That was patently absurd, of course. Canadiens'
management had always maintained a healthy distance
from the people who lived and died with each win.

"A good businessman cannot be a cheerleader," Sam
Pollock once said. "Cheerleaders don't win anything."

The real changes, of course, lay in the great political
and social upheavals that were affecting Montreal and
Quebec. In every aspect of Québécois life, people at the
top were beginning to heed the masses. Previously anonymous business moguls and politicos alike welcomed the
new unveiling and cultivated the new image.

A similar transformation would have to be effected by
the Canadiens. With the major league public relations
effort launched by the Nordiques, and that team's recent
success on the ice, the Canadiens were being challenged
like never before.

The new Montreal Canadiens would be run like any
other major corporation. Organized under vice-
presidents of finance, marketing, hockey operations;
monitored in weekly management committee meetings
and evaluated according to a five-year plan, the team
would also become fully computerized. The Canadiens
would be actively marketed like any other company, and
a young man named Francois-Xavier Seigneur was hired
to do the job.

"No more cathedral, no more shrine at the Forum,"
Corey said. "We want the fans to feel that they are part
of the team, not people going to Mass. We want them to
have fun at hockey games."

That request posed some problems, however. The
players who wore the uniform could no longer be called
the Flying Frenchmen—they had not done much flying

in recent years, and a majority were non-francophones. A realistic appraisal of the situation by Canadiens' management and Molson's, showed clearly that Montreal no longer would be able to guarantee a majority French-speaking presence on the team. Even the Nordiques, who had actively pursued French players to the detriment of team strength in their first three NHL years, had discovered that the only way to success was to assemble the best team possible without language constraints.

If the Flying Frenchmen were to become the French Foreign Legion, a polyglot aggregation of mercenaries, their legacy at least could be kept alive in the front office.

On the day Grundman was dismissed, Corey fielded the question. "If you're asking whether I'm primarily looking for French-Canadian names to fill these positions, the answer is no. I want the best people available."

Nobody believed that for an instant.

Serge Savard became the automatic front-runner for the managing director's job, even though he still was a player and had an option year left with Winnipeg. That tidbit was published immediately, after some very broad hints were dropped by Canadiens' management.

Jacques Lemaire, who had returned from Switzerland to coach in American college ranks as an assistant at Plattsburgh, N.Y. and in the Quebec junior league with the Longueuil Chevaliers, was the front-runner for the coaching job. Another name mentioned was that of Orval Tessier, the coach of the Chicago Black Hawks. These rumours also arose after some name-dropping in high places.

Two weeks later, the thirty-five year old Savard was the Canadiens' managing director and the financially strapped Winnipeg Jets were richer by a third round draft choice and 50,000 dollars.

Grundman had complained that Corey wanted to run the team and was always underfoot in the hockey operations side of the front office. Would that be the case with Savard?

"Serge is in charge, complete charge," Corey told the press conference announcing Savard's appointment. "I feel he will be one of the great general managers in the NHL. Naturally, I would expect him to discuss his decisions with me, but he will make them. I have my own work, he has his."

Three weeks later, after Savard and Corey failed to convince Lemaire to take the top job, and thirty-eight days after he was fired, Berry was back as head coach of the Canadiens. Joining him as assistant coaches were Lemaire and Laperriere. It would prove to be an impossible situation for Berry.

The players were all in favour of the changes and Guy Lafleur was so moved that he promised a major concession in the coming season. "With the appointments that have taken place since the end of the season, I don't have to worry about management any more. I'm going to start a new career ... I'm going to keep my mouth shut." Little did he know how wrong he would be.

Savard's second order of business was the June draft at the Forum. There was no opportunity for Montreal to improve its drafting position, number 17, in the first round, because a lot of teams were watching the Canadiens' 1984 drafting position (Hartford's first-round pick) with a wary eye.

"There were quite a few good young hockey players available in the 1983 draft," said Savard. "Montrealers had watched Pat Lafontaine play for the Verdun Junior Canadiens all year and hoped he might still be around, but we didn't have a prayer." Lafontaine, a Detroit native, set records with 104 goals, 130 assists and 234 points in 70 games. He was selected third in the draft by the New York Islanders. Another top Quebec junior, Sylvain Turgeon of Hull Olympiques, was a Bossy-like sniper, and had parlayed quick hands into 54 goals and 109 assists in 67 games. He was selected second overall by Hartford, behind Minnesota schoolboy Brian Lawton.

When Montreal's turn came up, Alfie Turcotte, a blue chip centre and former team-mate of Lafontaine with

Detroit CompuWare midgets, was still available. He had been the MVP of the Memorial Cup championships, won by his Portland Winter Hawks team.

"We were lucky he was still around," Savard said.

In the second round, Montreal had three picks and went to the Quebec junior ranks twice. Claude Lemieux, a combative right winger with Trois-Rivières Draveurs, was pick number 26 and Sergio Momesso, a large left-winger with Shawinigan Cataractes was 27th. Eight picks later, Todd Francis of the OHA's Brantford Alexanders, Mark Hunter's former team, was selected. Later in the draft, Montreal selected Turcotte's team-mate John Kordic, a bruising right winger, Arto Javanainen, a right winger from Finland and Thomas Rundquist, a Swedish centreman. They also continued the practice begun by Caron and Ruel of drafting high school players who would go on to American colleges for four years. These included Rob Bryden, a left winger with Toronto's Henry Carr High School, Dan Wurst, and Jeff Perpick, Minnesota defenceman with Edina High School and Hibbing High School respectively.

The loudest cheer of the session came with pick number 143 in the seventh round. "Montreal Canadiens select, from the Central Red Army Team of Moscow, goaltender Vladislav Tretiak." Savard wasn't joking. "You never know what might happen. I would rather have him on my list than on someone else's."

The rest of the summer went quickly. Savard settled into his office and was very active, as were F.X. Seigneur and others. The managing director spent most of the off-season sounding out his NHL counterparts for possible deals, and ran into the Pollock Curse.

"So many of those guys want too much for what we want because they have been burned in Montreal deals before and don't want to repeat the mistake," Savard moaned, the sleepless nights beginning.

Irving Grundman returned to his bowling business and admitted he was sleeping better, and in August, Ron Caron bounced back as the new director for hockey operations with the St. Louis Blues. The only down note sounded during the dog days was the announcement by Rejean Houle that he was retiring after ten years with Montreal sandwiched around three in the World Hockey Association with Quebec Nordiques.

When training camp began in September, a larger-than-usual rookie crop was in attendance and there were some splendid specimens. Kent Carlson, Turcotte, Kordic, Momesso, Lemieux and Francis were recent draftees and were joined by a large contingent of Nova Scotia Voyageurs, among them John Newberry, Mike McPhee, Greg Paslawski and goalie Mark Holden. On the second day of camp, the boys showed their intensity with no fewer than six fights in scrimmage.

Doug Wickenheiser and Newberry got involved in the first preliminary and moments later, defenceman Bill Kitchen fought with John Lavers, a junior player from Newfoundland. Then Chris Nilan and Jeff Brubaker indulged in their fourth bout in two days. It got so that Berry had to intervene. Normally that would have been a good sign, an indication that the team was tired of complacency.

However, the exuberance of training camp was dampened ten days later when league president-in-absentia John Ziegler came out of the closet and dealt the Canadiens a blow. Young defenceman Ric Nattress, another former member of the Brantford Alexanders, had shown well in 40 games during the previous season. Montreal's second pick in the 1980 entry draft, he had dished out impressive open-ice bodychecks and was reliable in the tough going, as was fellow rookie Craig Ludwig.

In August, 1982, while still a member of the Brantford juniors, Nattress had been arrested for smoking marijuana and fined 150 dollars. On September 23, 1983, 13 months after the incident, Ziegler stepped in and suspended Nattress for the entire 1983-84 season, ostensibly after a "month-long investigation." Nattress had met with Ziegler for a grand total of fifteen minutes September 16. A week later, the boom was lowered.

"For many years, it has been a clear policy that no employee of the league is to be involved with illegal drugs. If you choose to be involved with illegal drugs, you will not be involved with the National Hockey League."

Then in a display of pomposity belying his stature, Ziegler continued: "I would hope that Mr. Nattress will seek to straighten out his character and self-discipline so that he realizes both on and off the ice the pride and achievement that have been the hallmark of the Montreal Canadiens." If Nattress could tread the straight and narrow during the first half of the season, Ziegler added, the suspension could be reviewed and set aside after 30 games.

Savard admitted that the suspension was unduly harsh and that the team might appeal. As it turned out, the club did nothing. Any good lawyer could have invoked the Canadian Charter of Rights and Freedoms and done a lot of damage to Ziegler's overly zealous ruling. For once, Lafleur's reaction was right on.

"What's he trying to prove? It's ridiculous. The kid isn't a pusher. All he did was smoke a joint"—before he joined the Montreal Canadiens. In 1977, when Don Murdoch of the New York Rangers was caught with 4.8 grams of cocaine in his luggage during a routine check at Toronto International Airport and suspended for 40 games, he already was in the NHL.

"Murder", a valuable addition to the Rangers as a rookie in 1976-77, was never the same after that. When Nattress returned to play in December, he too, was a much more tentative hockey player. Worse still was Savard's missed opportunity to make a gesture that would show his players he had their best interests at heart.

The scrappy camp was subdued by the Nattress suspension and the Canadiens got off to a bad start in the regular season. They were short on the blueline as Rick Green came down with a serious wrist injury that would sideline him for 73 regular-season games. The injury forced the Canadiens to claim Jean Hamel when he was left unprotected by Quebec Nordiques in the waiver draft. As well, Kent Carlson, a terrific scrapper but slow of foot, found himself as a regular on defence which comprised veterans Robinson, Picard and Hamel, third-year man Gilbert Delorme, and sophomores Bill Root and Ludwig.

It was not going to be a banner year back of the blue-line and the American-born defenceman everyone talked about, Chris Chelios, was touring Canada and the United States with the American Olympic team. He would not be available before late February or early March.

There were changes up front, too. Paslawski cracked the line-up after a good training camp, as did John Chabot, a slick-passing rookie centreman. The biggest disappointment was Turcotte, who showed up for camp grossly overweight after a summer of "pizza and ice cream" and would split the season between Portland and the Canadiens.

Doug Wickenheiser, who had started out the previous season so well alongside Lafleur and Walter, and then had been inexplicably taken off the line, was finished as a Montreal Canadien. The mind games and the pressure were too much for him to handle, even though the popular player had the full support of his team-mates. It got so bad that his parents visited Serge Savard on the sly.

"They came to me and begged me to trade him," Savard said. "The Montreal experience was hurting him deeply and he was being unjustly blamed for something he had no control over, being selected number one in the draft. I said I would do my best and hoped it would be the best for all concerned. I still don't know if Doug ever found out about his parents' visit."

The Wickenheiser family's wish would come true three days before Christmas when he was moved to St. Louis with Paslawski and Delorme for big winger Perry Turnbull.

However, that was not the major deal of the season for the Canadiens. As the team set out on the new schedule, there were problems. Mark Napier, a 40-goal scorer a year before, Wickenheiser, Chabot and Picard were not dressed for an early October game against Quebec. Two weeks later, Napier and Keith Acton were en route to Minnesota and lanky Bobby Smith, whose pass had ended the Canadiens' hopes of a fifth-straight Cup in 1980, was coming to Montreal.

Smith provided immediate dividends, 15 goals in his first 20 games with the Canadiens, but could not do it all himself. Lafleur was hot in the first half of the season, scoring the majority of his 30 goals before January, but Steve Shutt was not producing, and neither were many other forwards.

When Savard obtained Turnbull from St. Louis, it was expected that his addition would turn things around, make the club more aggressive in the corners. It never worked out; the number two choice in the 1979 draft and the Canadiens' system proved incompatible and he would score only 6 goals and 7 assists in 40 games.

Berry, a coach who was trying anything and everything to inspire his charges, was reduced to a chain-smoking wreck between periods. It was a common sight after games for reporters to happen upon the coach, his head down in a cloud of smoke, wondering where it all had gone wrong. It was becoming increasingly obvious that he would have to pay for the inadequacies of the Canadiens' system and his players.

That was the situation when the Montreal oldtimers skated out onto the Forum ice December 17, 1983 for their special ceremony. It had become a standard press box joke that the number of official ceremonies and tributes before Canadiens' games was inversely proportional to the number of victories won by the team. The oldtimer who had wiped the tears from his eyes that night cried for two teams, nostalgically for the team of the '50s and with sadness for the 1983-84 Canadiens.

Nine weeks later came the fourth coaching change in four years for Montreal. A thousand or so Montrealers will never forget that Bob Berry was fired February 24, 1984. They wear that date on the T-shirts they were given at a special CFCF-Radio 1960s bash at the Château Champlain. While they boogied to the Beatles, Rolling Stones and Wilson Pickett, Berry learned of his dismissal.

Most of the people milling around Berry at the hotel

that Friday night had not yet heard of the latest events and were still wishing him and the team luck. Berry spent a long time on a public telephone just off the main lobby and then did something he had probably ached to do on many nights during this nightmarish season—he went out and got sloshed. The Canadiens' record was 28 wins, 30 losses and 5 ties. They were in fourth place in the Adams Division, 9 points better than Hartford.

With the playoffs beckoning, Savard had been forced to act. "All season long I was hoping the team would get going but I couldn't wait any longer. We made deals to strengthen the team and it didn't happen. I don't hold Bob Berry personally responsible for everything that has gone wrong. I just hope Jacques Lemaire can turn it around."

It worked—for exactly two games, with wins over New York Rangers (7-4) and Detroit Red Wings (3-1). The Canadiens ended the season 7-10 under Lemaire for a final standing of 35 wins, 40 losses, 5 ties and 75 points in 80 games. It was Montreal's worst showing since 1950-51's 25-30-15 record. (In 1969-70 when the club failed to make the playoffs, they were 38-22-16 for 92 points.)

The last 17 games were deceptive, however. While *Gazette* columnist Tim Burke correctly described the fans' diminished expectations when he wrote on the eve of the playoffs that the "Canadiens stir a feeling of pity," three major changes that would transform the team had quietly taken place during the season's home stretch.

First, Rick Wamsley was injured and goalie Steve Penney was called up from Nova Scotia late in the season. He got into four games and lost all four but played well, especially in a 5-2 home loss to the Nordiques in the last week of the season.

The second change was in strategy. Lemaire worked hard at building a new system, defensively oriented, which had all five skaters controlling the neutral and defensive zones. A scoring centre like Bobby Smith suddenly became a soccer-style sweeper, covering the neutral zone like a vacuum cleaner while his linemates scrambled for position. Only then could he launch them on a counterattack.

In the Canadiens' end, the team began playing a modified zone defence, clogging up the middle in front of the net in a bid to nullify point shots and passes crossing through the slot.

The third major change was in personnel. Chris Chelios and Rick Green joined the team for the last 12 and 7 season games respectively. They represented an automatic forty percent improvement at the blueline. Although Chelios would post only two assists in his dozen games because he was nursing an injured ankle, he provided the Canadiens with something they had lacked all season, a rushing defenceman. Green was rock steady in front of the Montreal net, policing the area with grim determination. Robinson and Ludwig, tired due to the constant pounding they absorbed during the year, were rejuvenated. Suddenly, the Canadiens defence had regained its traditional concrete hardness.

Burke's "pity" column appeared March 29. On April 9, his column was titled: "Wins over Bruins revive a tradition." Boston had finished first in the Adams Division with 104 points, one more than Buffalo and 29 ahead of Montreal. But the Bruins had to go down to the final Sunday of the season to take first place. And in their 79th game, a Saturday afternoon contest against Montreal, they barely eked out a 2-1 victory in a fight-filled contest. The game was a preview of the playoffs.

Montreal had managed to rest a few veterans in the last week of the season and they were fresh when the playoffs began on Wednesday, April 4. The plan was simple: bottle up Bruin forwards Barry Pederson and Rick Middleton and have a skater in front of defenceman Ray Bourque at every turn. Match the Bruins hit for hit.

Terry O'Reilly, a splendid player whose courage and work ethic formed the heart of the Bruins lunchpail brigade, was called on to explain why, again, the Canadiens had eliminated the Bruins.

"We had a terrific streak at the end of the season but a

lot of those wins were against some pretty bad teams. So, we deluded ourselves a bit about how good we really were. On the other hand, the Canadiens' points total in no way reflected their true quality as a team. We depended too much on Middleton, Pederson and Bourque and the Canadiens knew it. Our guys were dead tired from playing 45 minutes a game and the Canadiens made sure they hit them every chance they got."

If there was any justice in the NHL, Terence Joseph James O'Reilly would have won at least one Stanley Cup in his 13-year NHL career. Less skilled than many of his counterparts, he worked and worked throughout his career and became the heart of the Bruins. Unfortunately, he joined Boston a year too late (although he played one game and scored a goal in the 1971-72 season, the last time Boston won the Cup). Four times in his career the Bruins came up against the Canadiens in post-season play; four times the Bruins were eliminated.

"He was my hero," Chris Nilan will unabashedly admit. "If I can improve my game to the point that I'm as valuable to my team as Terry was to the Bruins, I will consider my career a success."

While Montreal swept the Bruins, clinching the series with a 5-0 win at the Forum, Quebec Nordiques were turning the tables on the second-place Buffalo Sabres.

A second Quebec-Montreal confrontation loomed, this one with a difference. This time the Canadiens were the underdogs and the pressure was on the Nordiques.

Quebec responded well in the first game, peppering Penney with 32 shots en route to a 4-2 win. The second game at the Colisée was an entirely different matter. Montreal took a 1-0 lead on a Pierre Mondou goal in the second period and Penney held the fort against waves of Nordiques for the first 40 minutes of play. However, the third period was only 36 seconds old when Anton Statsny tied it up. The stage was set for a collapse by the Canadiens; after all, the strain of protecting such a fragile lead must have worn them down physically and psychologically.

Except that it was Quebec which collapsed.

Ryan Walter and Mats Naslund took a leaf from the Bruins' book and stormed the Nordiques net as John Chabot let fly. Naslund deflected the puck past Dan Bouchard and it was 2-1. Steve Shutt and then Perry Turnbull, who had struck two goalposts earlier in the game, finished off a 4-1 win and the Colisée fans went home grumbling.

The Canadiens won the third game and appeared ready to blow Quebec out of the Forum in game four when they took a 3-1 lead into the third period. That evaporated quickly and Quebec returned home with the series tied 2-2, on the strength of an overtime goal by Bo Berglund. Montreal was given yet another opportunity to collapse and return to the bad habits of the regular season.

Game five was a replay of game two. Pierre Mondou, once again, scored halfway through the second period to give the Canadiens a 1-0 lead which they nursed into the third period. Quebec pressed but a stonewall defence and the imperturbable Penney parried every thrust. Four minutes into the final period, Guy Carbonneau forced Bouchard to make a big save and the puck came to Mario Tremblay in the slot. Bouchard was down and out of the net when Tremblay directed his shot past defenceman Pat Price for a 2-0 Montreal lead.

It was a 3-0 eighty seconds later when Bouchard lost a race with Bobby Smith for a loose puck at the blueline. Steve Shutt kept the puck onside and picked the corner with a wrist shot. Barely 90 more seconds had elapsed when Naslund skated in on a rink-long breakaway and put the puck through Bouchard's legs. At the other end, Penney stopped all 24 shots directed at him.

The events of the final game of the series, the so-called Good Friday massacre, are described elsewhere in this book. Suffice it to say that Montreal won a fight-filled sixth game 5-3, after trailing 2-0 early in the third period.

The Canadiens followed that up with a pair of victories

over the New York Islanders before injuries and momentum caught up to them and they dropped the series 4-2 to the defending Stanley Cup champions.

It didn't matter, however, because the playoffs had rescued a season and the team was back. This was the first summer in four years that the players could return home with their heads high. The Nordiques' climb in popularity was arrested and *les Glorieux* were Number One in the hearts of most Quebec, and even most Canadian hockey fans. It didn't even hurt much when the team was shut out in post-season awards and all-star nominations.

A larger turnout than usual greeted the home team at the next Forum function, the 1984 entry draft, and management did not disappoint. Irving Grundman's gift to the new management, the Hartford first-round draft choice, number 5 overall, would not be good enough to secure Mario Lemieux, the tall centre the Canadiens had coveted for four years. Leading up to the draft, Savard tried desperately to arrange a deal with Pittsburgh's Eddie Johnston to no avail. Lemieux was going to be the Penguins' franchise and Johnston knew it.

Just before the draft began, Savard completed a deal with the man who was rapidly becoming his favourite trading partner, Ron Caron. Rick Wamsley went to St. Louis in return for the Blues first-round choice, number 8 overall, and other switched choices in later rounds.

After Lemieux, Kirk Muller, Ed Olczyk and Al Iafrate had been selected in the first four spots, Savard unveiled his draft secret.

"Montreal selects, from Czechoslovakia, Petr Svoboda," he announced. Moments later, a skinny kid who could speak neither English nor French was trotted out in a Canadiens' sweater that was ten sizes too large. Everywhere he went, an interpreter followed.

Nine short months later, a gifted Svoboda would demonstrate his mercurial temper and linguistic talents during the playoffs against Boston, standing at centre ice and screaming "Fuck you, Linseman, fuck you!" over the heads of two linesmen, the referee and several players, with the conviction and inflection of a native-born Canadien while Larry Robinson hid his laughter in his gloves. On this day however, he was a little boy lost, confused by foreign languages and customs.

He spent the summer with the Savard family in St. Bruno, learning to speak English.

"Hey, don't blame that on me," Savard smiled. "We taught him nice words like 'pass the bread'. We're a polite family."

Three spots later, Montreal reached for yet another Brantford Alexanders' player when rugged forward Shayne Corson was selected. Tall centreman Stéphane Richer of Granby was next, picked number 29, and his best friend, goalie Patrick Roy, followed as number 51.

By 1985-86, Svoboda, Richer and Roy would be regulars and Corson would be banging on the door. Management was back on track.

Under Jacques Lemaire, the 1984-85 Canadiens finished first in the Adams Division, eliminated Boston in the best-of-five opening round, and then fell to the Nordiques on an overtime goal by Peter Stastny in the seventh game of the Adams Division final.

That result hurt but the organization was strong enough to stand up to it, especially in this, its 75th anniversary year, and the 60th birthday of the Forum. During the season, Steve Shutt was traded to Los Angeles Kings, a team of his own choosing, and Guy Lafleur retired when he grew tired of riding the bench. John Chabot went to Pittsburgh in a trade for Ron Flockhart, and yet another American defenceman, Tom Kurvers, made the team with a display of pinpoint passing rarely seen in the Forum. In an exhibition game against Edmonton Oilers, won 5-4 by Montreal in overtime, Kurvers' passes led to four Canadiens' breakaways and two goals.

Mats Naslund became the new Guy Lafleur and the most popular Canadien. Stars like Guy Carbonneau and Chris Chelios were not far behind.

During the late fall, the team launched an "all-time dream team" contest, in which fans could select the very best players to ever wear the *bleu-blanc-rouge.* On January 13, 1985, more than 1,800 fans and members of the Canadiens' family gathered at the Queen Elizabeth Hotel.

In the presence of the Prime Minister of Canada and the Mayor of Montreal, the Fabulous Six took the stage: goalie Jacques Plante, defencemen Doug Harvey and Larry Robinson, left winger Dickie Moore, centre Jean Beliveau and right winger Maurice Richard.

It was the highlight of the hockey year. All of those in attendance were given a unique program, the cover of which was a reproduction of a very special painting commissioned from artist Michel Lapensée that captured 75 years of hockey history.

There, in living *bleu-blanc-rouge,* they were: Howie Morenz, Aurele Joliat, Harvey, Moore, Beliveau, Claude Provost, The Pocket, Guy, Bill Durnan, Elmer Lach, Toe, Serge, Fergy, Reggie, Jake the Snake, Ken Dryden (leaning on his stick), the Rocket, The Road Runner, Coco Lemaire, Shutty, Bob Gainey, Jacques Laperriere, Scotty, Butch Bouchard, the Boomer, Dick Irvin, Irving Grundman, Frank Selke, Tommy Gorman and Sam Pollock.

The picture said 75 years. The picture said class. The picture said dynasty. The Torch had been passed. And accepted.

# 15

## The Young Lions

Not *really* knowing has a delicious sense of anticipation to it, probably not too dissimilar from that delicate sensitivity one feels when a rap on the noggin is forthcoming. All the nerve endings seem to congregate in one place and, if the blow does not arrive, there is almost a palpable sense of disappointment.

For anyone closely watching the Montreal Canadiens, and especially for the Second Floor, the 1985-86 season was going to be a watershed. During the previous year, reports had come in from all over North America that the Kids Are All Right. Stéphane Richer, drafted from Granby in 1984, was traded to Chicoutimi and was leading the Sagueneens in scoring; Claude Lemieux and Sergio Momesso, the Class of '83, were the stars of the Verdun Junior Canadiens and the Shawinigan Cataractes respectively, two teams which would compete in the four-team Memorial Cup round-robin championship. The Ontario representative would be the Sault Ste. Marie Greyhounds, and their leading scorer, Graeme Bonar, belonged to guess who? Another top forward in the Ontario league was Shayne Corson of Brantford Alexanders, a forward who was a "Gainey who can score", the reports said.

In the American Hockey League, defenceman Mike Lalor and scrappy centreman Brian Skrudland valiantly struggled to inspire a Sherbrooke Canadiens team that would make the league playoffs on the last night of the regular season.

Back home in Quebec, Patrick Roy, the goalie who had looked so good against the Oilers in NHL exhibition, was being bombarded every night with the weak Granby Bisons and showed well, even though his goals-against average was high.

A sign that the near future was promising for the Canadiens came in September, 1984, when a special training camp was held to select the team that would represent Canada at the 1985 World Junior Championships during the Christmas holidays. No fewer than seven Montreal draft choices attended the selection camp and three, Richer, Corson and Lemieux, made the team that would return with the gold medal.

In the American college ranks, Canadiens' scouts were keeping a close eye on two players, Dave Maley, a rugged forward with the Wisconsin Badgers, and defenceman Scott Sandelin of the University of North Dakota Fighting Sioux, Craig Ludwig's alma mater. Sandelin's coach Gino Gasparidi let the world know how he felt about his defenceman when he said he was even better offensively than another UND alumnus named James Patrick, the top defenceman on Canada's 1984 Olympic team and a stalwart with the New York Rangers.

What it came down to was what scouts all over the hockey world were talking about: Everywhere you looked, Montreal had some good kids. If only half of them panned out, the Canadiens would be substantially improved over the coming years. The Canadiens were in year three of Ronald Corey's Five-Year Plan, and everything seemed to be on schedule.

While the Canadiens were losing in game seven overtime to the Quebec Nordiques in the 1985 playoffs, Bonar, Lemieux and Momesso were gathering in Shawinigan and Drummondville to show their stuff in the Memorial Cup. Lemieux's Verdun team had blitzed through the Quebec league playoffs, wiping out Hull, Shawinigan and Chicoutimi, the latter a series in which Richer had played poorly and fought often, spending more time in the penalty box than on the ice leading his teammates. His team eliminated, Richer joined his former Granby buddy Roy in Sherbrooke for the Calder Cup playoffs. He wasn't very pleased with his exit from the junior ranks and was thankful for the opportunity the American Hockey League playoffs represented.

"I had a pretty good year with Chicoutimi but the playoffs were different. I was not quite myself, I don't know what got into my head. I was dropping the gloves against everybody."

Richer, like Lemieux and Momesso before him, had discovered the new status of being a Montreal draftee in the Quebec Major Junior Hockey League.

"Players in the league seemed to be more interested in stopping me, so they could prove that they were good enough to stop a Montreal player. If they did that, maybe it would help their draft chances. I also noticed Lemieux and Momesso a lot and I'd watch them a lot more because I knew they were going through a lot of what was happening to me."

While Lemieux and Richer were born in western Quebec—the same area that had produced Guy Lafleur—they did not know each other well because Lemieux had moved north to Mont Laurier at a young age. However, they renewed acquaintances in junior, *à la* Beliveau-Moore.

"Stéphane and I had our run-ins in junior, maybe because we were probably both trying to prove that one of us was the best from our area. We're both very competitive. After I was drafted in 1983, I remember watching Momesso during games and wondering if we would both make the Canadiens. When Richer was drafted a year after us with Patrick Roy, I wondered the same about him. And I would try extra hard against Patrick when he was in nets for Granby," said Lemieux.

In the 1980s, Montreal's eighteen year old draftees more often than not were sent back to their respective junior teams for another season, or even two, of maturing.

This system, while far removed from the Selke junior hockey sponsorship era of the 1950s and '60s, where large numbers of seventeen and eighteen year olds congregated at a Montreal junior camp and were then shipped out to various teams in groups, had the same reasoning behind it.

"Unless an eighteen year old has something very special to offer the Montreal Canadiens, we are not going to put that player through the pressure-cooker of the Forum," said Serge Savard, whose son Serge Jr. played in the same league as Richer, Lemieux and Roy. "This is especially true for our junior selections from the Quebec league."

In the sociological terms introduced earlier in the book, therefore, the occupational culture for Richer, Roy, Lemieux and Momesso was quite similar to that of their many illustrious predecessors like Moore, Beliveau, Geoffrion and Plante, even though many operational changes had taken place in the Canadiens' hierarchy.

Whether they played on a team full of Montreal-sponsored junior players as in the 1950s, or as individual draft choices on an independent junior team of the 1980s, the young players grew to understand very quickly what the Montreal Canadiens meant to their lives and what the "big team" expected from them. In a 21-team league, and despite the universal draft, Montreal has managed to retain the positive aspects of the perceived familial obligations of another age: loyalty, dedication, purpose and sense of common direction.

In this way, people like Serge Savard, André Boudrias, Jacques Lemaire and Carol Vadnais passed on lessons they, themselves, had learned as juniors in Montreal and, later, as pros in such far-off places as Houston.

"After one Montreal rookie camp, you got a pretty good idea what to expect," said Lemieux. "You knew that they did not approach hockey like most organizations, and that they were looking for some specific type of individual. You also realized that they would probably make more demands on you, and could, simply because they were the Montreal Canadiens. I also got that message when I played almost a full season in Sherbrooke in the American Hockey League."

Like Steve Penney, the incumbent netminder when he

was drafted, Patrick Roy was a native of the upper-middle-class Quebec City suburb of Ste. Foy, the son of a high-ranking civil servant. His was no romantic story of a poor farm kid wearing Eaton's catalogues for shin pads and hand-me-down skates. However, the significance of making it with either the Canadiens or the Nordiques was not lost on him.

"I think you can say that once you became a Canadiens' draft pick, you had special status when you went back for another year of Quebec junior hockey. After the 1984 training camp, I thought I had done very well and might get invited to stay up. But Penney was still the number one goalie and when they got Doug Soetaert from Winnipeg, I knew they wanted me to go down to junior for one more season. After the experience of wearing the *bleu-blanc-rouge* even in training camp, it was hard to get my head into wearing the Granby uniform again. But I think Montreal Canadiens counted on that, they wanted to see how I reacted to returning to junior. It was like a test. We were a weaker team than most and I sometimes had a hard time staying in the game. I had to keep reminding myself that *they* were watching."

There was a lot more significance to the fact that the Canadiens suddenly had so many all-star draft selections in the Quebec Major Junior Hockey League. The league itself, for several years, had taken a back seat to the other two major junior leagues in Canada, the Ontario Hockey League and the Western Hockey League. Scouts and NHL general managers had fallen into the habit of routinely downgrading the Quebec league. The two most common complaints were that the league could not play defence and that the players were too small.

A detailed breakdown of the drafting practices of the National Hockey League teams shows clearly that the professional teams were not enamoured with the Quebec league and that this disaffection had festered over a long period of time.

Since the entry draft was instituted in 1969, up to the 1985 selection some 3,198 players were selected by the NHL teams. The majority, 903 or 28.2 percent came from the OHL; 699 or 21.9 percent from the WHL; 491 or 15.4 percent from U.S. colleges; 382 or 12 percent from the QMJHL; 232 or 7.2 percent from International teams; 198 or 6.2 percent from U.S. high schools and 293 or 9.1 percent "others".

Even those figures are flattering to the Quebec league because the first American high school player wasn't drafted until 1980 and international draft selections were in small handfuls until that same year. Since 1980, 198 players were drafted from American high schools, 184 from international hockey and 124 from Quebec. (The OHL had 363, the Western League 254 and American colleges 139 in the same period, the latter drop-off attributed to the increased activity in drafting eighteen year olds out of high school, before they went to college, giving them four " free", years to develop, so to speak.)

A majority of those players drafted in American college ranks after 1980 were Canadians; the good U.S. players were generally spotted in high school. A lot of those Canadians were Tier Two junior or high school players who earned hockey scholarships at sixteen or seventeen and then developed south of the border, such as Minnesota-Duluth's Brett Hull (the son of the Golden Jet) and Joe Nieuwendyck of Cornell, both drafted by Calgary Flames.

The defunct Quebec Remparts led their own league with 47 players drafted in the 1969-85 period, two ahead of Cornwall and three ahead of Sherbrooke. (The Sherbrooke Beavers moved to St. Jean in 1983 and Cornwall Royals joined the OHL a year before.)

However, the Remparts' performance would only be good for ninth place in the OHL, tied with the Kingston Canadians, who had five fewer years to provide players to the pros. The Peterborough Petes, once a Montreal-sponsored team, led the OHL with 92 players drafted in the same period, just ahead of the Toronto Marlboros with 88 and Kitchener Rangers and Ottawa 67s, both tied with 81.

The top source of WHL talent was Calgary (Centennials and Wranglers) with 64, two ahead of another former Montreal-sponsored team, the Regina Pats.

The draft pattern angered many Québécois hockey fans, to say nothing of the hockey writers who covered both the QMJHL and the Canadiens. What frustrated them most, however, was that their two teams, the Canadiens and the Nordiques, had begun to draft the same way as the other 19 teams; indeed the Canadiens seemed to do a majority of their scouting south of the border.

There were several reasons for this.

First, Sam Pollock was one of the first to enjoy success in drafting from American college ranks in the 1970s. In 1972, Bill Nyrop was found at Notre Dame and picked number 66; in 1975 Brian Engblom (Wisconsin) and Pat Hughes (Michigan) turned up. The list grew in the late '70s: Bill Baker of Minnesota ('76), Rod Langway of New Hampshire, Mark Holden of Brown and Craig Laughlin of Clarkson College ('77), Larry Landon of RPI, Chris Nilan of Northeastern and Rick Wilson of St. Lawrence ('78). Irving Grundman and Ron Caron followed up and picked Craig Ludwig of North Dakota and Mike McPhee of RPI in 1980.

Second, the college players were generally larger and better; larger—especially after the league began drafting eighteen year olds—because they were older, usually twenty-one or twenty-two when they graduated; better because the colleges might play 40 games a year and practise three times to every game played.

Chris Chelios, a notorious rink rat, played two years of Tier Two junior hockey with Moose Jaw from 1979-81 and then went to the University of Wisconsin for two more years, before joining the U.S. Olympic team in 1983.

"The major difference was that you had much more ice time at college to work on things," he said. "At Wisconsin, it was basically our rink and we didn't have to share it with many people. If you wanted to take the time, you could be on the ice working on parts of your game three or four hours a day. And the coaching staff, people like Bob Johnson, were always there to help."

In junior hockey, where small town businessmen were more concerned with their investment and the bottom line, nobody bought tickets to practice so the players slogged their way through 80-game seasons, travelling huge distances from town to town in what Dave "Tiger" Williams called The Iron Lung, subsisting on pizzas, McDonald's Quarter Pounders and beer. When they were home for a week or so, they often had to share the rink with everybody from figure skaters to nine-year-old ringette players and peewee hockey leagues.

Said one NHL general manager whose team had drafted college players almost exclusively: "At least you don't have to teach these kids how to eat, damn it! We had to bring in a nutritionist one year because we were losing a lot of games late in the third period. A number of our young guys were running out of gas and we finally figured out why—they didn't know how to eat. Guess who were the biggest culprits? That's right, the Juniors. It'd bad enough they don't get the book learning in junior, but when they can't develop common dietary sense on how to take care of their bodies. . ."

He had a point. During the 1985-86 season, the Canadiens also brought in a nutritionist to wean Richer and Roy (among others) of their hamburger road habit and teach them all about the wonderful world of pasta and complex carbohydrates. Patrick was so bad with his addiction to french fries and potato chips that his teammates nicknamed him Humpty Dumpty after a well-known potato chip brand or "casseau", after the French-Canadian word for the cardboard containers french fries come in.

When Pollock left Montreal, Ron Caron expanded the team's American scouting base, Ken Dryden was enlisted to help build a European network, and both delivered. Another factor that hurt the Quebec league was that many of the players drafted from there by Montreal could not make it with the talent-rich Canadiens, no matter where they were selected in the draft order. They might have been successful with weaker NHL teams, but could not crack the strong line-up at the Forum.

From 1975 to 1980, Montreal drafted 24 players from the Quebec League. Only seven went on to play in the

NHL: Pierre Mondou, Normand Dupont, Richard Sevigny, Alain Côté, Louis Sleigher, John Chabot, Robbie Holland and Guy Carbonneau. Of these, only Mondou, Chabot and Carbonneau played for Montreal for any length of time. The only Quebec league player drafted in the top 10, Danny Geoffrion, the number 8 pick in 1978, never made it.

With the arrival of the Nordiques and their "draft French" policy (which was immediately revoked once the Nordiques began winning and felt they had a chance to challenge for the top), Montreal was forced to look at the Quebec league in a new light. The Nordiques took Canadiens drafts like Alain Côté and Louis Sleigher and gave them a chance to prove they belonged in the NHL. The Nordiques found Normand Rochefort, a steady defensive defenceman, in the Quebec league. They turned up a scoring jewel in Michel Goulet and a quality goaltender in Mario Gosselin, who backstopped Canada at the 1984 Olympic Games. Players like André Savard and Jacques Richard, former Remparts, were reclamation projects from other teams and became successful with Quebec, if only for a season or two. All of this left the Canadiens behind the eight ball in their own backyard.

It did not help the "shop in Quebec" cause when the Canadiens' first two choices in 1982, Jocelyn Gauvreau and Alain Héroux, did not make the grade.

When Serge Savard took over, and brought in people like André Boudrias as Director of Scouting, the drafting policy remained the same as in Sam Pollock's prime: go for the character player.

"But if we could find two players of equal ability and size and one who was from Quebec, there certainly was nothing wrong with leaning to the Quebec player," Savard said.

"The funny thing is, it's only here that this can sometimes be taken the wrong way. Anywhere else in hockey, it is considered a terrific idea to go for a hometown boy if possible. Calgary and Edmonton would love to have more Albertans playing for them and Boston and Hartford love to draft boys from New England. Here we often get criticized, even in the French press, for drafting local boys or French players, and it is the dumbest criticism I have ever heard."

The Canadiens redoubled their efforts in scouting Quebec and superscout Claude Ruel, one of the best judges of hockey talent in the NHL, paid special attention to the QMJHL.

In 1983, Claude Lemieux and Sergio Momesso were drafted and Stéphane Richer and Patrick Roy came along a year later. In all cases, the so-called reputation of the Quebec league worked in favour of the Canadiens: all four players were still available after other choices were made. In 1983, Montreal drafted centre Alfie Turcotte in the first round and was able to claim both Momesso and Lemieux in the second round. In 1984, Richer was Montreal's third pick behind Petr Svoboda and Shayne Corson and number 29 overall. Roy was even more of a find in the third round, number 51 overall.

Montreal's scouting tentacles also found other players whom the universal draft ignored.

In late 1983, Jean Perron was an assistant to Coach Dave King with the Calgary-based Canadian Olympic Team. One of the team's last cuts before it headed to Sarajevo for the Winter Games was an Alberta-born centre named Brian Skrudland.

"Dave thought he was too slow, but I liked him," said Perron, who joined the Canadiens the following year. Shortly thereafter, Skrudland was signed as a free agent and sent to Nova Scotia in the AHL where he joined another free agent, Mike Lalor.

By late 1984 and early 1985, a large number of young future Canadiens were scattered throughout junior hockey and collegiate ranks. As mentioned earlier in this chapter, when the Team Canada juniors met in a special training/tryout camp in late summer 1984, seven Canadiens draftees were invited and three, Corson, Richer and Lemieux played on a line on the team that won the world championship that December.

The Memorial Cup was another indication that the 1985 Canadiens' training camp would be something special, with Lemieux, Momesso and Bonar lining up against each other. It did not help Lemieux's cause when he and his Verdun teammates showed poorly at the Memorial Cup tournament. Momesso, on the other hand, shone and his stock rose accordingly while Bonar was somewhere in the middle, playing well in some spots, and not so well in others.

The revelations of the spring were Richer and Roy, longtime friends, who found themselves in the thick of the American Hockey League playoffs with Sherbrooke. There they joined Skrudland, Lalor and Serge Boisvert, yet another free agent signing, who had ended the Montreal season in the NHL before returning to the AHL.

After the third game of the playoffs, first-string goalie Paul Pageau returned home to be with his wife who was about to deliver a child and Greg Moffett, his backup, had equipment problems.

"We put Patrick in nets and he immediately showed that he was a money player," said coach Pierre Creamer. "And Stéphane gave us a quality play-making centre who could score. Both of these players made all the difference in the world to our team."

The Sherbrooke Canadiens, a joint Montreal Canadiens-Winnipeg Jets enterprise, won the Calder Cup. Better still, they won it in front of the entire Canadiens' hierarchy. With Montreal eliminated by the Nordiques, people like Corey, Savard, and Boudrias began making the 90-minute drive to Sherbrooke to watch the American Hockey League playoffs.

The stock of Richer, Roy, Skrudland and Lalor soared.

"When I saw Patrick play in the Calder Cup playoffs, I knew he would be good enough to play for Montreal the next year," said then assistant coach Jean Perron.

Montreal had every reason to look forward to 1985-86. The team had played well and captured first place in the 1984-85 season—despite the departures of Steve Shutt and Guy Lafleur—only to lose to Quebec in overtime of a seventh game. Rookies like Chris Chelios, Tom Kurvers and Svoboda showed they belonged and mixed well with veterans like Rick Green, Ryan Walter, Larry Robinson and Guy Carbonneau. The rookie crop coming up was a winner, in junior hockey and in the AHL. If only half of the eight to ten blue chippers could crack the Canadiens' lineup, the team would be a solid challenger.

With that in mind, and any trepidation felt by managing director Savard (and Boudrias) moderated by sheer numbers, the Canadiens went to Toronto in June, 1985 for the NHL draft. There they quickly manufactured a deal with Ron Caron that sent Mark Hunter to St. Louis in exchange for St. Louis's first-round pick, number 12 and other later-round considerations. The advanced drafting position allowed Montreal to pick ahead of (number 15) Quebec Nordiques and they selected José Charbonneau, a six-foot, 195-pound right winger with Drummondville, the highest-rated Quebec junior in the draft. The Canadiens also retained their regular number 16 position and opted for Tom Chorske, a Minnesota high schooler.

By the end of the 1985-86 season, it looked like Savard had gotten too cute with that particular draft manoeuvre, especially since Hunter scored 44 goals for the Blues. The younger brother of the Oilers' Dave and the Nordiques' Dale, Mark had been an oft-injured but very popular member of the Canadiens whom Larry Robinson described as possessing the three prime requisites of an NHL hockey player: "head, heart and balls." His opinion was shared by many team veterans.

However, Charbonneau showed well on offence with Drummondville in 1985-86 and is considered a serious candidate for a regular spot on the club in the late '80s.

The questions began to be answered at training camp in September, 1985, baptized by one veteran as "The Invasion of the Killer Tomato Cheeks."

Everywhere there were good young players and many surprises. The positives included Momesso, Richer, Lalor, Skrudland and Roy, all of whom made the team on the effort they showed in camp. Other young players like John Kordic, a bruiser picked from the same Memorial Cup-winning Portland Winter Hawks team that supplied Alfie Turcotte, and Domenic Campedelli, plus Kjell Dahlin, from Mats Naslund's hometown of Timra, Sweden, all showed promise as good role players. Dahlin stayed with the team, inheriting Mark Hunter's Number 20 while Campedelli and Kordic were late cuts and went to Sherbrooke.

The negatives were Lemieux, Bonar, Corson (to a lesser degree) Steve Rooney and Charbonneau. Lemieux went through the motions in camp and was quickly despatched to Sherbrooke. Bonar, Corson and Charbonneau returned to their junior teams for another year of seasoning while Rooney, playing with a shoulder injury that would necessitate surgery in mid-season, remained with the parent club.

There was, of course, one more rookie of note. On Monday, July 29, the authors spent most of the morning interviewing Canadiens' president Corey in his Forum office. At the same time, right next door in Savard's office, F.X. Seigneur, Savard and others were hard at work on a press release and plans for an early afternoon press conference.

Several times during the interview, the team president excused himself to take "important" telephone calls. He wasn't kidding. While Corey was describing his team's makeup, Jacques Lemaire had quietly resigned as coach of the Montreal Canadiens. Always an intensely private individual who valued highly his family's privacy, he was not comfortable with life under the media microscope.

"It was a good time for me to make this decision," he said. "I felt very confident that Jean Perron could do the job; he is an excellent coach with a good background and he is well known to the players after a year as my assistant."

When the new season got under way at Pittsburgh on October 10, Perron was behind the bench. Just five days over thirty-nine years of age, he now would be the most second-guessed sports coach in Quebec.

"If I knew then that I would be starting my season with injuries to Mario Tremblay, Lucien Deblois, Ryan Walter and Steve Penney, and that Chris Nilan would get a 10-game suspension, I would have turned down the job right then and there," he said half-jokingly the following May while basking in the afterglow of the Stanley Cup.

During the 1985-86 season, Jean Perron would have many occasions to make that same remark, with a lot less levity.

The season got underway with a whimper in Montreal. With as many as eight rookies in the lineup for games, the Canadiens lurched through October and early November. The team started with a victory in Pittsburgh and a home opener win over Chicago Black Hawks before travelling to Boston on the season's first Sunday.

It is not necessary to describe in detail the emotional state of affairs that exists between the Bruins and the Canadiens. Suffice it to say the teams do not like each other. Montreal and Quebec fight a war for their province every winter, but the players respect each other. There is little admiration or respect for the Bruins, a feud whose origins go back a long, long way.

Thus, when Chris Nilan butt-ended Boston's Rick Middleton in the mouth on that October Sunday, earning an extremely rare 10-minute deliberate injury penalty (a 10-minute power play), and a subsequent 10-game suspension, those feelings were exacerbated.

Nilan was not openly apologetic about the incident, but he quietly regretted it. One reason was that 1985-86 was finally going to be the season where the ebullient right winger from West Roxbury, Massachusetts, shed his goon image and received credit for his hockey skills. In 1984, the *Boston Globe Magazine* published a long feature on Nilan titled "Toughing it Out."

Writer Charles Kenney was bang on when he began:

> It is amazing, really. Nobody ever thought Chris Nilan was anything special when he played hockey at Catholic Memorial High School in West Roxbury, nor were there great expectations when Nilan went off to play at Northeastern. And certainly nobody—but nobody—ever could have believed Nilan would make it in professional hockey.

But looking back on the years of turbulence—the times when it seemed Nilan defied the odds almost daily—looking back, the absolute craziest thing about it all is that after his first full professional hockey season with the Montreal Canadiens, Chris Nilan returned home to West Roxbury with all of his teeth.

Nilan was a gregarious kid who grew up in the Boston area in the age of Bobby Orr and the Big Bad Bruins. He idolized the Bruins and a young forward named Terry O'Reilly who came along in 1972, because he saw something of himself in both.

"Chris was never a natural hockey player," said his father, Henry Nilan, during the first period intermission at a Bruins-Canadiens game at the Garden. "He always had to fight for what he got, in all meanings of the word. He always seemed to be willing to work harder, fight more and push more for what he wanted. He came to me when he was about sixteen years old and announced he was going to play in the National Hockey League someday. I told him not to put all of his eggs in one basket, especially since I didn't think he was all that good. We always were able to talk with each other like that. Chris has always respected people who aren't afraid to say what they think."

When Nilan graduated from high school, he was neither the athlete nor the scholar to advance to collegiate ranks and he applied to a prep school, Northwood School in Lake Placid, New York for the 1975-76 school year. There he bettered his grades and worked hard on his hockey, garnering the school's award for most improved player, and was rewarded with a scholarship to Northeastern University where former Bruin Fern Flaman coached. He played rarely in his freshman year but saw a lot more ice time as a sophomore, "trying to knock everybody all over the ice." He was still the farthest thing from a star and when Chris told his father that he was going to be drafted by an NHL team, even he knew that chance was remote.

On May 25, 1978, Nilan mourned as his beloved

Bruins went down 4-1 to Montreal Canadiens in the sixth, and last, game of the Stanley Cup final.

Two weeks later his lifelong allegiance changed; he was the fourth-last pick (number 231) of the NHL draft, all by the Canadiens who used their thorough scouting system to advantage, picking numbers 229 through 234. Nilan and Louis Sleigher, number 233, both made the NHL. Ironically, the top two draft choices of that year, Bobby Smith (Minnesota) and Ryan Walter (Washington), would team up with Nilan in Montreal. The Canadiens had four picks in the first two rounds in 1978. Only one player, Dave Hunter, number 17 in the first round, made it to the NHL with the Edmonton Oilers. Danny Geoffrion, number 8, Dale Yakiwchuk, number 30 and Ron Carter, number 36 were less fortunate and only Keith Acton, number 103, made the Canadiens from the 1978 draft above Nilan.

"I always knew I would make it," Nilan says in his seventh NHL season. "I didn't know *how*. I just knew I would. I was going to do anything to get there, anything at all."

Making it meant a return to Northeastern for his junior year and continuation of his studies in criminal law. The following summer, however, Nilan decided to leave school. In August, 1979, a scant three months after the Canadiens had won their fourth straight Stanley Cup, the brash young kid from West Roxbury attended his first professional training camp.

"No matter what kind of self-confidence you have, or how you motivate yourself, that first camp is one of the scariest things in your life. Here I was trying to skate with Guy Lafleur, Larry Robinson and players like that. I threw my weight around but in a lot of cases I just bounced off guys.

"I found out what the pros and the Montreal Canadiens were all about. The players up here were bigger, faster and stronger, a lot stronger. They did not seem at all impressed by a college kid from Boston who liked to throw his weight around."

Nilan was clearly deficient in skating and offensive skills, but people like Claude Ruel and Ron Caron saw something they liked. He was assigned to the Nova Scotia Voyageurs of the American Hockey League. In the first minute of his first game with the Voyageurs, he "pulled a John Ferguson", getting into a fight with Glen Cochrane, a tough defenceman with Maine Mariners, a Philadelphia Flyers' farm team. After 49 AHL games and 307 minutes in penalties, Nilan was called up to Montreal temporarily as the Canadiens underwent a rash of injuries. He never returned to the AHL.

In his second NHL game, Nilan and Philadelphia's Bob "Hound Dog" Kelly—an original Broad Street Bully—went into a corner after the puck and the sticks went up. The gloves went off and Kelly went down, the victim of a couple of crisp right hands. The next year, Nilan became the first Montreal Canadien ever to eclipse the 200-minute mark in penalties for a season. He has never fallen below that mark since, and has outlasted a phalanx of right wingers at that position on the club, including the immortal Guy Lafleur.

"The Chris Nilan who has been my teammate has been two different players," says Larry Robinson. "The Chris Nilan who was up here his first three seasons did not play regularly and nowhere near as well as he does now. He wasn't a bad skater but it took him a long time to get going, and he had no confidence with the puck.

"The Chris Nilan who is playing with us now is very different. He is one of the best checking right wingers in the league and plays on the best checking line in hockey with Guy Carbonneau and Bob Gainey. He is a much better skater and a much better stickhandler and that shows in the statistics. A checking winger who can score more than 20 goals a year is a valuable commodity. He accomplished that with years of extra work up here. There were times when he might not have been as good as a lot of other players with Montreal, but the coaches kept him around because he worked so hard and improved every day."

When the Year of the Rookie rolled around in Montreal, Nilan was an even more valuable commodity to the Canadiens, a veteran who was not afraid to shake up some rookies. He was the catalyst in an incident that started to bring the club together in mid-season.

When the season started, several of the newcomers were greeted with the traditional "rookies haircut", although one veteran complained that "these kids are so green, they don't have hair to shave." Where illustrious names like Lafleur and Shutt had worn the familiar Numbers 10 and 22 just a short time before, unfamiliar rookies like Skrudland, Momesso, Lalor and Richer wore numbers in the 30s and 40s. Instead of being weaned slowly, a game here, a game there, in traditional Canadiens style, seven or eight of these kids were pouring over the boards every night. The man patting them on the back and telling them to go was a rookie, too.

The loss in Boston started an October tailspin that left the club in last place in the Adams Division. Never did the club look worse than in an 11-6 thrashing in Hartford where the Whalers led 7-2 after one period. The principal architect for that debacle was 1984 playoff hero Steve Penney who let in five goals on three shots (the other two goals went in after Hartford forwards actually lost the puck on their own stickhandle and it trickled under a goalie who was flopping worse than a walrus in mating season) before he was replaced by Roy halfway through the initial period.

Then something strange started to happen. Even in the Hartford game, you could see that some of the kids could play. Richer scored a goal after beating five Whalers inside their own blueline. Momesso popped one from in-close when the defencemen could not move his bulk from the crease. And Kjell Dahlin scored on the prettiest breakaway goal never seen by Montreal fans (a power failure interrupted the Saturday night telecast) in the second period.

As the rookies gained confidence, the team began to win and move up in the standings. Richer led all rookie scorers with ten goals when an ankle injury put him on the disabled list in November. The first sign of his fragile mental condition came the next day when he worried openly about getting back into the lineup. To that point, he had been one of the top four or five Canadiens forwards.

Momesso and Dahlin settled in very well and both showed a good touch around the net, to the point that for the greater part of the season the Canadiens would be the second highest scoring team in the entire league, trailing only the Edmonton Oilers.

However, Momesso did not stay past December, suffering what doctors at first feared was a career-ending knee injury and was out for the season. His loss loomed larger than just that of a big, tough scoring rookie. On a team rapidly polarizing into two major groups—not cliques—an unusually large rookie class and a solid core of veterans, Momesso was popular with both.

"The veterans all liked Sergio," said Larry Robinson. "He is a quiet, hard-working player who does his job without a whole lot of fanfare. We miss him."

His loss was offset by the performance of Kjell Dahlin, a wraithlike right winger who settled in comfortably on the right wing with Bobby Smith and fellow compatriot Mats Naslund and ran away with the rookie scoring race in the first half of the season. A left-handed shot with good speed and a deft stickhandler, Dahlin fit in well with Smith and Naslund and the three anchored the league's best powerplay throughout the season, working the puck skillfully.

"Kjell's contribution to that line and the powerplay is his ability to work the puck around with the other two," said Jean Perron. "Other teams are afraid to pressure those three because of their stickhandling and passing ability; make one mistake and it's in the net. The major reason is Kjell Dahlin. He has brought an added dimension to the line and makes it even more dangerous than it was before."

As the season moved into the second half, the Canadiens were in first place, trying to hold off the Nordiques. While the kids were playing well, and veterans like Carbonneau, Gainey, Robinson and Nilan were at peak form, the club could never show the kind of consistency that would make it a solid contender in the post-season tournament.

The major problem was goaltending. Steve Penney reported to camp overweight and immediately developed a serious groin injury. Patrick Roy would play some of the best 58 or 59 minutes of hockey seen at the Forum since the heyday of Ken Dryden. But the other one or two minutes would be a horror show, shots going in from terrible angles outside the blueline, rebounds the size of beach balls and uncertainty when clearing the puck in front and behind the net.

Doug Soetaert, the most consistent of the three goalies, rarely got to play. Before the season, Savard took a long time to sign the former Ranger and Jet while he courted Gilles Meloche, who had been traded late the previous season to Edmonton. Oilers' GM Glen Sather was adamant: "Give us Brian Skrudland for Meloche straight up." Savard had also seen the AHL playoffs and refused point blank. A week later, Soetaert was signed to another contract by Montreal.

The three-goalie system caused problems for the principals until they took time to sort out their emotional baggage themselves.

"It was so silly in practice that we were almost fighting each other to get in and out of goal," says Penney, who was traded to Winnipeg in the off-season.

"Normally, with two goalies one would take a goal at either end of the rink and that's that. With three we had to rotate, and quite often a goalie didn't want to leave the cage so the other guy could go in. The other players noticed this and, although they thought it was quite funny, they knew it was a serious situation, too."

The netminders had a heart-to-heart just before Christmas and sorted out their misunderstandings. It wasn't quite the Three Musketeers, but they saw that they shared the same predicament and it was best to talk out their problems.

Things were not that simple for the rest of the team.

Roy's inconsistency, the Momesso injury, the benching of Brian Skrudland and Dahlin's sudden slump all brought matters to a head during a West Coast swing in late February.

After a poor Forum performance against Hartford on Saturday, February 22, the Canadiens headed west for a week and games against Edmonton, Vancouver and Los Angeles, with a stop in Long Island before returning to Montreal for a four-game homestand. The team that flew west was playing strange hockey, losing a pair of Monday night home games in overtime to the Los Angeles Kings (and Soetaert to injury) and Minnesota North Stars and to the hapless New Jersey Devils at the Meadowlands, before reviving and thumping the Philadelphia Flyers and tying Washington Capitals in two of their best efforts of the year.

Montreal dropped their first game 3-2 to Edmonton in a lacklustre effort by both teams, then flew on to Vancouver for a Wednesday game with the Canucks. On Tuesday, the team held a full-scale workout at the Pacific Coliseum. On Wednesday, the Montreal papers were full of headlines about a Nilan-Richer fight in practice.

The two players came together during a drill, exchanged words, and Nilan connected with a few punches before other teammates intervened. Six weeks later, as the post-season playoffs got under way, Larry Robinson remarked that "there is no such thing as rookie and veteran in the dressing room. We're all in this together as players. We all wear the same shirt."

Another six weeks after that, the cheers of a half million Stanley Cup-happy Montrealers numbing his ears, Bob Gainey was asked by a reporter for a community TV channel how "the rookies and veterans managed to resolve their differences and come together as a team."

"There was no dissension or rookie-veteran split," he replied, very mindful of the new harmony that had guided the team to Montreal's 23rd Stanley Cup.

There was some division. Coach Jean Perron is the first to admit that the Nilan-Richer fight started the reunification of the team. "The bubble burst between the youngsters and the veterans. That's where the guys began to realize that they better pull together before it was too late."

It also helped a rookie coach deal with his own differences with veterans. Perron decided that the best strategy was to play it cool, and let the players sort it out among themselves. He knew he could not be caught favouring one side or the other. Some veterans admitted afterwards that they had expected an overreaction, especially after the French papers in Montreal played up the incident, and began to see their coach in a new light when he let the players sort out their differences among themselves.

With Soetaert hurt and Roy blowing hot and cold, Steve Penney was pressed into action in the next two games with Vancouver and Los Angeles. He acquitted himself well as the team won both, the second on a three-goal explosion in the last three minutes of play. Trailing L.A. 4-3, Montreal tied it when Nilan set up Richer with a perfect pass at 16:46 and won it on goals by Dahlin and Gainey.

Nilan and Richer made such a show of public emotion after the tying goal that a teammate on the bench quipped: "They better knock that off. This is a family arena!"

The team flew back east in a better frame of mind, and promptly got thumped by the resurgent Islanders. St. Louis Blues, also known as Montreal West or "The B Team" because of the nine former Canadiens in their lineup, waltzed into the Forum two nights later and thrashed "The A Team" 7-4 on Thursday as very little went right for the Canadiens. Boston followed and Montreal took out its frustrations on the hated black-and-gold with an 8-3 bashing Saturday night and then went flat again the following Monday and lost 5-2 to Hartford, that club's first-ever win at the Forum.

Vancouver Canucks were the next visitors and the Canadiens were hard-pressed to win 3-2. The following night the team travelled to Boston where they lost 3-2.

The slump was on again. First Calgary, then Quebec, skated away with Forum wins and Montreal slunk out of town with its tail wrapped firmly around a collective hind leg.

For four of the previous five months, the Canadiens had been the league's second-best scoring team and featured its best power play. Lately, however, the offence had ground to a halt and the power play was a poor comedy of Alphonse and Gaston indecision. Where short, sharp passes to the open man and multiple shots on goal had characterized the power play before, it was now an exhibition of uncertainty—bad passes, bad shots, blocked point drives and missed open nets.

On the team's top scoring line, Bobby Smith found himself alone more often than not . . . and for his trouble got the lion's share of the blame from the hometown faithful.

During one three-week stretch, neither Naslund nor Dahlin were skating well and Smith would often break into the offensive zone and have to pull up because his wingers were nowhere to be found. His ability earned him the Peter Mahovlich treatment from some fans. On many occasions during his career, Big Peter was castigated for passing too late or not getting the puck to swift linemates like Steve Shutt and Guy Lafleur. Strangely enough, he still holds the club's assists record with 82.

*"Maudit mangeur de puck* (puck eater)!" the fans would rail at Peter as he headed up-ice, cradling the vulcanized rubber disk on his stick.

Bobby Smith started hearing *"mangeur de puck"* too, as the fans blamed his reticence to pass on him rather than his nonexistent linemates. At six-feet five-inches, he was a large target. In early February, it appeared that Naslund and Dahlin would score 100 goals between them, but those predictions went out the window by mid-March. Naslund finished with 42, Dahlin with 31. In a 5-3 win over Philadelphia on February 16, Naslund and Dahlin scored their 37th and 27th goals respectively. In the remaining 22 games, they scored 5 and 4 goals.

To add to the team's problems, the defence was spotty.

Chris Chelios and Rick Green, one-third of the starting blue-line corps, were injured so long that everyone seemed to forget that they were still on the team. Gaston Gingras, a major reclamation project of Pierre Creamer in Sherbrooke, was called up in mid-season for spot duty on the power play. The possessor of one of the hardest slapshots in the league, he immediately paid off with several booming goals, including a howitzer that almost decapitated Philadelphia goalie Bob Froese.

Gingras' quick insertion into the lineup and the immediate dividends provide a classic example of the benefits of employing identical coaching methods and playing style on the farm team as on the big club. During a season where the Canadiens lost many players to injury, Alfie Turcotte, Randy Bucyk, John Kordic, Kent Carlson, Serge Boisvert and Gingras could move up without suffering culture shock.

"We may not have had a great many high-quality players in Sherbrooke this season," said Creamer, "but they were coached to play the same way as the Montreal Canadiens. When Gaston moved up to Montreal, he went on a power play that worked exactly the same as ours, so he fit in right away and was comfortable."

In the post-draft era, most NHL teams feature a full roster of 30 to 35 players, 22 with the big club and 10 to 13 playing for a minor league team that is operated jointly with another NHL team. For example, the Fredericton Express of the American Hockey League was stocked with players belonging to the Quebec Nordiques and the Vancouver Canucks. What system of play did coach André Savard employ? Did the former Nordiques player's hockey strategies meet with Tom Watt's approval in Vancouver? Were the players who were called up to Quebec City able to fit in comfortably and quickly with the style of coach Michel Bergeron?

In Montreal, in 1986, these questions were being considered. Was it worth the extra investment for Montreal to operate under the old farm system concept? Would it be impossible to put into practice any lessons learned in the days of Father Frank and Trader Sam? "Not at all," said Savard.

Although it is almost economically impossible for a National Hockey League team to afford a full farm team these days, the Montreal Canadiens feel strongly that their community includes the AHL roster, and that players there must learn the Montreal Canadiens way of doing things. Savard is a strong believer in "Selkeism".

"We know that the main word is farm. That word means you eventually get back what you put into the ground. The harder you work on cultivating, the better the produce will be when it comes time to harvest. It was worth the money and the time invested."

Thus, Gingras paid instant dividends when he drove up the Eastern Townships Autoroute and reported to the Forum.

However, the absence of Chelios and Green, a later injury to Tom Kurvers and the erratic play of Petr Svoboda, meant that Gingras played more than the Canadiens had originally intended. On some nights, he was a major contributor; on others, he had problems.

Svoboda was a more worrisome case for the team. Young Petr, who when drafted less than 700 days earlier could not speak English or French and was munching on his very first hot dog, sparkled during his rookie season and won many admirers for his skating ability and the pounding he took from opposition forwards. He spent his first Montreal summer in the suburbs living with the Savard family and the first season boarding with another family.

In his second year he lived in his own apartment a short distance from the Forum. As a rookie, Svoboda was the team's unofficial mascot, and was taken under wing by Larry Robinson. Like many teenagers, he occasionally slept in and was late for practice and would receive a gentle slap on the wrist.

In his second year, the tardiness became a disease and when Svoboda announced that he had bought a house in the far suburbs to share with his newfound love, a stunning Parisienne, his teammates immediately took bets on how soon it would be before he would erase the legendary tardiness exploits of Rick Chartraw from the club record books.

"Jeez, he was always late when he lived up the street. Now he has to get up 90 minutes earlier just to be as late as he used to," said one player. "This might be awesome."

Sure enough, Petr was late for practice and this time there were no slaps on the wrist. Instead he was benched and he brooded.

Other problems surfaced on the ice. Over the previous year, Svoboda had put on 12 pounds and now weighed a respectable 172. He felt a little cockier at the higher weight and began to show signs of temper. When opponents crashed into him with the same enthusiasm as they had during his rookie season, he began to lose his cool and developed the bad habit of taking retaliation penalties.

The whole affair reached a head March 10 in the 5-2 loss to Hartford. In the third period, with the game still up for grabs and the Canadiens pressing in the Whalers zone, Svoboda was caught up-ice as Hartford broke away 2-on-1. He coasted back to the Canadiens' zone, a third Whaler forward sped by him into the play and scored and the Canadiens lost the game.

His fellow players, management and the fans were upset: one never quits on the play in the Forum. Ever. He saw very little ice time for the rest of the year. A month later, when announcer Claude Mouton would read out the list of Canadiens not dressed for a playoff game, a large cheer would go up when he read: "Number 25, Petr Svoboda."

When the Canadiens embarked on their last major road trip of the season, which included stops in Winnipeg and St. Louis, three days off in Montreal, and then back-to-back encounters at Hartford and Boston, the team was down. Blueline Fever had struck most members of the defensive corps and that was never better highlighted than in a 6-4 loss to the Jets. Doug Soetaert returned from a double knee injury to face his former team and played strongly for the first two periods as Montreal took a 3-1 first period lead and led 3-2 going into the third period. But his knees were still fragile.

The best player on the ice for Montreal was Chelios,

who also was recovering from a knee injury that had sidelined him since December.

The third period was a comedy of errors. Just 19 seconds into the period, Rick Green chased Winnipeg's Brian Mullen behind the Montreal net and the latter flipped the puck into the goal crease. It hit Gingras' skate and deflected into the goal.

A minute and three seconds after that, Thomas Steen directed an off-balance shot towards the Montreal net. This time Craig Ludwig redirected the puck past Soetaert. In just under ninety seconds, the Canadiens had scored two goals and found themselves trailing in the game for the first time. The Jets got two more without assistance from the Montreal defence and coasted.

That was it, as far as Perron was concerned. The team returned to boot camp drills. The Canadiens flew into St. Louis and were put through strenuous skating drills for ninety-minute sessions on Thursday and Friday.

It was time for the coach to deliver a message, one that many of the players didn't much care to hear. "The first message was simple. 'I'm the boss and you are going to do it my way.' Nobody was going to argue with that part of it."

Part two of the message was that the team had no intensity and that was unforgivable. Perron reminded his charges that the designation Flying Frenchmen belonged to history; this team was decidedly less spectacular, which is not to say less talented in its own way.

"I told them that all you need to inspire you when you play in Montreal is to look down at your chest and look at the crest. I also said that the work ethic had been set aside and that the only way this team was going to win was with a concerted team effort. We didn't have the superstars who were capable of doing it by themselves."

Some of the veterans were not pleased and Larry Robinson told Red Fisher of the *Gazette*:

> If he skated the hell out of us because he was unhappy with our performance against Winnipeg, why didn't he start doing it after St. Louis beat us in Montreal? Or after Hartford beat us in Montreal? Or a month and a half ago? Is he telling us we're out of condition after the 73rd game of the regular season?

In 11 games, the Canadiens had gone from first place in the Adams Division, four points ahead of Quebec, to fighting for their playoff lives with Boston, Buffalo and Hartford.

"Losing games is a problem," Robinson told the *Gazette.*

> We've got lots of problems. And the only way of solving problems is to get some discipline on the ice. Discipline is not to give up three-on-twos or two-on-ones to the other team—and making the most of ours. I don't know how many of them we've had in the last few games, and each time the pucks seem to be going into our net. On the other hand, I don't know how many times we had them on the other teams with nothing happening.

This outburst was a departure for the normally placid Robinson. His remarks and others by Guy Carbonneau caused many journalists to speculate that Perron's days behind the Canadiens' bench were numbered.

The first in a series of team meetings was called and it was attended by the managing director. His message was simple. "Jean Perron is the coach of this team. What he says, goes. End of story."

That Saturday, the Canadiens played a solid game, only to be undone by a couple of players who wore the CH on their hearts, even though their jerseys said Blues. Rick Wamsley stoned his former teammates and Doug Wickenheiser scored the game winner in a 3-2 victory.

Although they were sluggish on offence, the Canadiens enjoyed a good effort, especially from Steve Penney in nets. The constant criticism about Montreal's season had everyone in the league maligning the goaltending, sometimes with justification. Patrick Roy was too adventurous and tended to fall asleep in games and give away bad goals. Doug Soetaert was a journeyman. Steve Penney was poor technically. Yet both Penney and Soetaert were outstanding in what turned out to be their last appearances of the season.

Despite the criticism, Montreal was in the chase for the Jennings and Vezina trophies most of the season. Soetaert did not remotely resemble a journeyman when

Perron let him play, contributing three shutouts and a very steady presence in goal. Many team veterans openly questioned Perron's underutilization of the former Ranger and Jet, especially during Roy's more erratic periods.

Penney was terrible at the beginning of the year and had only himself to blame. He reported to camp overweight, suffered a bad groin injury, and managed to misplace the steely confidence that had made him such a formidable competitor during the 1983-84 playoffs. Nonetheless, the St. Louis game was his best of the season and followed solid performances in Vancouver and Los Angeles. He appeared ready to make the goaltending position a three-man fight again until sidelined by a sprained knee.

After the St. Louis loss, the Canadiens returned home for two days of workouts before they embarked on their last road trip of the year. The practice pattern was repeated with painful monotony—90 minutes of skate, skate, skate.

Here were no more complaints, private or public. Instead, the players began to admit their shortcomings. "Sometimes we're the last to know that we aren't doing it as individuals or a group," said defenceman Craig Ludwig.

"You don't have a meter that tells you when you're not going all out. You might think you are, except that there's no bounce in your legs and you're not taking out other players like you should. And our team is eighty percent work ethic—we beat the other guys because we outwork them. We aren't going to improve our game skills by skating like this, but our attitude will improve." Ludwig would be prophetic, although events would unwind slowly.

On Wednesday, the Canadiens met the Hartford Whalers. All day long the players prowled the Hartford Sheraton like caged tigers. Perron made the pre-game skate optional and only Randy Bucyk and Soetaert took advantage, skating alongside assistant coach Jacques Laperriere and assistant trainer Gaetan Lefebvre. The play-

ers attended a meeting in the morning, slept in the afternoon, and walked across the street to the Civic Center at
5 p.m.

Going into the contest, Montreal was in second place
with 80 points, two better than Boston, four up on
Buffalo and five up on Hartford. Whereas the Canadiens
had been fighting the Nordiques for first place two
weeks before, they now cast nervous glances in the rear-
view mirror.

Before the contest, Chris Nilan paced quietly outside
the Canadiens' dressing room in his underwear, quietly
putting on his game face and chatting amiably with
Canadiens' equipment manager Eddy Pelchak and some
of his Hartford counterparts. Not so popular on the ice,
he is an off-ice favourite around the league, always ready
with an autograph or conversation for fans and hockey
hangers-on.

Just around the corner, Whalers Ulf Samuelsson and
Kevin Dineen were also in their underwear, enjoying a
game of basketball one-on-one in the cavernous Civic
Center garage area. Samuelsson was in a particularly
frisky mood, it was his 22nd birthday and he had enjoyed
a good season with the Whalers, a team clearly heading
for the upper echelons of the NHL.

Hartford was loose. Montreal wasn't. After the game,
the standings read:

|          | GP | W  | L  | T  | Pts. |
|----------|----|----|----|----|------|
| Quebec   | 75 | 41 | 29 | 5  | 87   |
| Montreal | 75 | 37 | 32 | 6  | 80   |
| Boston   | 74 | 34 | 30 | 10 | 78   |
| Hartford | 75 | 37 | 35 | 3  | 77   |
| Buffalo  | 74 | 35 | 33 | 6  | 76   |

The Canadiens played well but could not get untracked
on offence. Dahlin, Walter, Smith and Richer missed
glittering scoring opportunities early in the game as
Mike Liut turned in a solid performance behind a stingy
Whalers defence.

There is a special dynamic to a slump—or prolonged
negative performance—in sports. Once acknowledged,
and players and coaches will go out of their way to deny

its existence, the slump takes on a life of its own. Everything negative is magnified a thousand times while even positive efforts and results are doubted.

Pete Rose, who has known more success than adversity in his long baseball career, says a slump can get a player believing in a malevolent supernatural force.

"You might not be concentrating as well as you normally would because you are always thinking about how things are going. And even when you can win the battle inside your head and regain your confidence and concentration, you bang line drives right at people. You want to throw your bat at the sky and yell: 'Why are you doing this to me?' That is exactly the wrong attitude, but you can't help it."

Rose's point is that a slump is more of a mental condition than a physical one. When athletes are performing well, they don't think about what they are doing, they just do it. Conversely, when it seems that adversity is overwhelming them, it is all they can do *not* to think about it.

"When we are going well and a goalie stops me on a breakaway, I skate away thinking, 'All right, I'll get him next time'," Bobby Smith said after the game, reflecting on his confrontation with Liut. "When we're in a slump, I skate away thinking, 'How could I blow that?' In one case, your mind is where it should be directed, forward, because that is what you can do something about. In the other case, all you think about is the past, which you can do nothing about."

The game was scoreless late in the second period when the Canadiens made a poor line change. With four Canadiens racing desperately off their bench to head him off, Dineen picked up the puck along the left-wing boards and skated in on Roy. Gainey made a superhuman effort to overtake him and hooked the winger's stick as Dineen was about to shoot. Somehow, Dineen mustered the strength for a second effort, freed his stick and lifted a one-handed shot past a startled Roy.

The game was over early in the third period. Hartford pressed quickly and scored at 15 and 47 seconds to put the game out of reach. The first was a blueline "seeing-

eye" dribbler off the stick of defenceman Scot Kleinendorst which took most of the period's first 15 seconds to
skitter through a forest of skates and sticks and into the
corner past a thoroughly screened Roy. The second was a
flip shot by Ron Francis from a scramble just outside the
crease.

The Canadiens' defence played well in front of Roy,
despite missing both Robinson who had been left home
with a sinus condition and Svoboda who was not dressed
because of yet another tardy arrival at practice two days
before.

"We played well and we weren't very nervous," said
Mats Naslund. "The most important thing for us to
remember is that we shouldn't panic; if we continue to
work hard, this will turn around."

That night, the team bused to Boston, while Savard
drove in a rented car. When he arrived, Lemaire, Savard
and Perron burned the midnight oil in the coach's hotel
room at the Boston Sheraton.

At 7:30 the same morning, the telephone rang in Sherbrooke and Claude Lemieux picked it up.

"Claude, it's Pierre Creamer. You've been called up.
You have to report to Boston for the game tonight." Six
months after his poor training camp relegated him to the
minors, and three months after he finally accepted that
fact and began to play like he could, Lemieux was a
Montreal Canadien again.

Boston, like the rest of the Northeast, was enjoying an
early spring heat wave, but leadbelly clouds threatened
thunderstorms. The players and Montreal media
prowled the spacious lobby, their moods matching the
elements. Savard and Lemaire seemed to be everywhere
while Perron stayed out of sight, fuelling speculation
that his job was in jeopardy. The scene recalled the situation two years earlier when Bob Berry was struggling
through the team's most difficult regular season in 30
years. Everybody noted the presence of assistant coach
Jacques Lemaire and predicted "any time now."

In Perron's case, Lemaire was above him, not below,
on the corporate ladder, but the speculation was the

same. Nobody believed Savard when he said that Perron was his coach, no matter what.

Savard meant it.

"This team had five coaches in forty years and now we've had five in six years," he said. "We have had a different coach at the last three training camps. When I hired Jean Perron, I had the long term in mind. And don't forget, we set up a five-year plan for this club; this is only Year Three."

Perron, not as shy around the press as Lemaire had been, but also not a coach who courted publicity like Scotty Bowman, kept his own counsel. He was, however, feeling the frustrations.

"It is very, very hard to be head coach of the Montreal Canadiens. You can't begin to understand the pressures that go with this job. I was assistant coach for a year and thought I had a good line on how it would be to coach Montreal, but even I underestimated it. In this town, as the joke goes, the media and the fans are with you win or tie, but don't tie too often."

Downstairs in the lobby on this steamy Thursday, Richer, Gingras and Roy were the only players in sight as Bertrand Raymond and Yvon Pedneault of *Le Journal de Montréal* prowled, looking for material to fill their daily four pages. The next day was Good Friday and only *Le Journal* was publishing. The rest of Team Tandy, nicknamed for the portable computers used by the press, had the day off. "They've gone from a zone defence to a man-to-man," quipped another reporter, as Pedneault and Raymond squeezed Gingras and the two rookies for every last drop of copy.

And then Lemieux walked into the lobby, nattily attired in a blue velvet sports jacket and flannel trousers and carrying his equipment bag and hockey sticks. Both Raymond and Pedneault were seen looking skyward and mouthing a silent *"merci"* as they converged on the rookie and the official greeting committee of Lemaire and Savard.

That night, Lemieux played on a line with Walter and Richer and the trio was the team's best against the

Bruins in a 3-3 tie. In the dressing room after the game, Naslund summed up the performance for all concerned: "Big win."

The tie pretty much ensured Montreal's participation in the playoffs and the Canadiens went on to win three of their last four games, although not as convincingly as they might have hoped, particularly against Pittsburgh and Detroit.

In the team's last regular-season game against Buffalo at the Forum, a victory, Roy played well overall but let in two long shots, one from outside the blueline when he went down on his knees for no discernible reason while trying to catch an eye-high puck. He received a chorus of boos for the faux pas.

The playoffs and the hated Bruins beckoned and the Canadiens were still not firing on all cylinders. A team with eight rookies might be fodder for an aroused team from Beantown.

There was one piece of good news, however. Chelios and Green were back from long injury layoffs and both were playing inspired hockey. Robinson was enjoying his best season in a long while and Ludwig was steady as well. Better still, rookie Mike Lalor had proved that he belonged and Gingras was doing everything asked of him by scaring goalies to death with his shot.

With a five-day layoff, the defence rested. After all, didn't all the experts say during the season that it was defence that decided the Stanley Cup playoffs?

*Cherchez le gardien. . . .*

# 16

# The Lions Fly

*"If two stand shoulder to shoulder against the gods,
Happy together, the gods themselves are helpless,
Against them while they stand so."*
Maxwell Anderson, *Elizabeth the Queen*

Unity of purpose, they say, is everything. It can defeat armies, spread ideas and philosophies, and stir the placid and sedentary to heroic action. Rare is the leader who does not try to promote this unity by any and all means at his disposal.

In Jean Perron's case, the process of uniting the Montreal Canadiens into a cohesive unit began in late season on the Winnipeg-St. Louis road trip and ended sometime during the Adams Division final against the Hartford Whalers.

Little did he know that this process would have a distinctly avian theme . . .

### The Birdman of Alcatraz, Part Two

(A struggle in four acts)

Species represented

Patrick Roy (*Rouahis nervosus*)—A long-legged non-flyer with a wide wingspan; what it doesn't knock down with its wings, it falls on.

Claude Lemieux (*Tombus constantus*)—A notorious ocean diver which keeps coming up with pearls. Gets nasty when provoked.

Brian Skrudland (*Yappus scrappus*)—A combative cousin of the myna, pecks away constantly at enemies and can strike with lightning speed.

Larry Robinson (*Aquila chrysaetos*)—The illustrious Golden Eagle, once said to be battling extinction.

Bob Gainey (*Buteo jamaicensis*)—The classic Canadian red-tailed hawk, swoops down on anything that dares move in its territory. An older relative of the Mike McPhee, is known to favour the left wing.

Chris Chelios (*Sterna paradisaea*)—Also known as the Arctic Turn, for his manoeuverability in heavy traffic.

Chris Nilan, John Kordic, Steve Rooney and David Maley (*Pestus controlus*)-The Harriers, the reasons why most teams prefer to exhibit their most dove-like nature when confronting this quartet in their natural habitat.

Craig Ludwig, Rick Green, Mike Lalor and Gaston Gingras (*Katyus Doorbarrus*)—The reason why, as the play moves into its fourth act, Patrick Roy became *Rouahis* less *nervosus*.

Bobby Smith, Mats Naslund and Kjell Dahlin (*Snipus offensis*)—Given room to display their manoeuverability by the presence of the *Pestus controlis* quartet, proven dangerous to enemies.

Jean Perron as the Birdman.

And a cast of various other contributors.

If anything characterized the difference between the two teams that were the Montreal Canadiens during the 1985-86 regular season and then during the playoffs, it was unity. The team that blew hot and cold during the regular season bore little resemblance to that which suffocated all opposition during the playoffs en route to the franchise's twenty-third Stanley Cup championship.

As we mentioned in the previous chapter, there was friction in the ranks during the regular season. Not out-and-out dissension, that the coaching staff and upper management could quell with a series of concrete actions, but rather a lack of closeness that was hard to identify and harder to deal with.

The most obvious reason for the disunity was the onslaught of rookies: eight made the team and several others almost joined them. Veteran players became nervous when close friends were in danger of losing their jobs, a fairly standard group reaction anywhere in sports. On their side, the rookies hung together for mutual support.

Another difference was cultural, but not in the sense of language or ethnic background. Several veterans, Chris Nilan, Mario Tremblay and Guy Carbonneau, were convinced that some rookies simply did not believe in the kind of full commitment they had been reared to expect. The occupational culture was threatened, they felt, if the next generation of torch bearers could not understand that the Montreal Canadiens were not just another hockey team.

As well, the Five Year Plan hung over the heads of the veterans like a black cloud. When team management speaks of a long-term strategy to rejuvenate the team and bring it back to the league's upper echelons, veterans, quite rightfully, feel threatened. Many feel that "long-term" excludes them, especially as they see a steady stream of teammates come and go.

It took a long time for the Canadiens to coalesce. Isolation was the key factor.

For the members of the Montreal media brigade, the appearance of the Canadiens in the Stanley Cup final can most easily be described as incredible. For local fans, it might be most accurate to say that they willingly suspended their disbelief. Yet, by the time the team got there, it was a logical extension or conclusion of the natural order of things for the players whose playoff road was characterized by an intense commitment to both hard work and team discipline.

When does a working team finally come together to function as a winning team? For many social scientists, a team is best understood as a group of individuals who cooperate in the staging and execution of a set of routines. To perform efficiently, that group must exhibit such characteristics as enthusiasm, high group solidarity, unanimity of purpose and a strong shared set of beliefs and attitudes which highlight common goals.

The theory looks great on paper, but in reality we know little about exactly how and when players transform teams into united entities prepared to sacrifice for one another to achieve common goals. We have seen the cohesion manifested in a variety of winning combinations: Vince Lombardi's Green Bay Packers, the family atmosphere fostered for decades by the Los Angeles Dodgers and especially in the 1973 and 1974 editions of the Philadelphia Flyers.

Everyone remembers the brawling from coast-to-coast of the Broad Street Bullies but they forget that the Flyers were by far the most cohesive unit in the league in those two seasons. Fred Shero and team captain Bobby Clarke made sure that every player knew his place and responsibilities in the organization, even, as Dave Schultz says, to the exclusion of the players' wives and families on certain occasions.

Fight one Flyer, you fought them all, a philosophy right out of Dumas' *The Three Musketeers*. The Montreal Canadiens, and especially Scotty Bowman, knew that the only chink in the Flyers' suit of armour was the fighting side of the Philadelphia game. That is why a simple exhibition hockey game in late-September 1975 (described earlier) took on such importance.

"When that game was over, they had beaten us on the scoreboard and in the fights," said Schultz. "I sat in the dressing room and I said, 'Oh-oh! They know they can beat us at this game too.' You got the feeling that they were as together as we were." That game launched the Montreal powerhouse of the 1970s and Schultz would be out of hockey before Montreal lost another Stanley Cup.

E. Wright Bakke describes the team unification process as follows:

The agents acting for the formal organization ... and the individual acting for himself will simultaneously seek to make agents out of each other for the self-actualization of the formal organization ... and the individual himself ... The tendency of any individual toward co-operation or conflict with other participants in the organization ... will be proportional to his estimate of how much they help him or hinder him (to achieve his goals) ... The effectiveness of this *fusion* process is a function of the degree of compatibility of behaviour demanded and expected of the individual by the agents of the organization ... and by himself ...

This analysis of group integration helps explain the emergence of the *Club de Hockey Canadien* during the latter half of the 1985-86 season and in the playoffs. In discussions, the agents of formal organization impose their expectations and values on the young athletes and the set of strong commitments begins to appear within the ranks. The Canadiens spent a lot of time in group meetings during this period.

How does this influence emerge? It is everywhere at the Forum, and epitomized by people like Toe Blake, Jean Beliveau, Serge Savard, Jacques Lemaire and Jacques Laperriere.

The belief in a meaningful and constructive occupational culture, developed by Frank Selke Sr. and nurtured by Sam Pollock, provides the Montreal Canadiens with a special framework on which to build their expectations and values. It is quite similar to the process of acculturation undergone by a young recruit to a major corporation like IBM, Exxon or Xerox, or even the U.S. Marine Corps —recruits must learn to think, act, sleep and walk like "IBM people" or "Marines". They must find personal definition within the definition of group.

As Orville Brim and Stanton Wheeler explain:

A primary feature of the work setting that may aid the recruit in developing a meaningful definition of it is the extent to which others in the setting are or have been in his position and can aid his adaptation ... much adult socialization is organized so that a large number of persons are introduced to the new setting simultaneously . . . adaptation is likely to proceed much differently from the case where one person enters alone, since the recruits can arrive at a collective solution to the problems they face.

So while many teams faced with the rookie-veteran division might have been unable to deal with such a rift, real or perceived, Montreal had the wherewithal to use the rookies' group dynamic to reach each individual within that subgroup, and teach him about the benefits of contributing as part of a larger group—the whole team.

People who had "been there before", the veterans, were made to understand that it was in everyone's interest to develop unity. The rookies, at the same time, were made to see the benefits of learning from those who had experienced what they were going through. The process all came together in group isolation.

In past years, especially during the Pollock era, the "playoff" Canadiens were sequestered in hotels in downtown Montreal or the nearby Laurentians. The reasoning was fairly straightforward: playoff pressures are such that players need all of their physical and mental energy directed to the task at hand. This focus might not be possible if the players are at home, constantly harassed by friends for tickets and gossip while trying to maintain domestic harmony in homes that usually include several small children. In the case of young bachelors, it was a good idea to get them away from the temptations of Montreal's renowned night life.

The team attended meetings and practice as a group, ate meals as a group and spent spare time quietly watching television, reading, or playing backgammon and cards. It was forced socialization and players got to know their teammates better at this late date in the season.

Another school of thought believed that the players were being overly regimented and deprived of family and home for an unduly long period—up to two months if the club advanced to the Stanley Cup final series. The frustrations of wives and girlfriends became keen late in the playoffs and some domestic telephone calls were fraught with tension on both sides.

The case against domestic deprivation was made most clearly by Chris Nilan on the Saturday night the Canadiens won the Cup in Calgary. Injured in the third game of the series with damaged ankle ligaments suffered during a fight with burly Tim Hunter, Nilan was out of the series, even if it went seven games, so his conjugal rights were restored.

During the second intermission of the final game, he was interviewed (and kissed) by The Coach, Don Cherry, on the CBC broadcast. Later that evening, a journalist prodded him. "So what was your biggest thrill today, Chris? Winning the Cup or getting kissed on national TV by Don Cherry?"

"Neither. It was Mrs. Nilan showing up on the 11th floor of the Westin Hotel this afternoon after two months on Alcatraz!"

Alcatraz, in the real world, is a rock in the middle of San Francisco Bay. It was originally fortified by the Spanish, and then used by the U.S. as a military prison after 1859 and a federal penitentiary between 1933 and 1963. Also known as The Rock, the prison was home to some of the most incorrigible criminals in the United States and Robert Stroud, the legendary Birdman who made a name for himself as an ornithologist during his almost 60 years of incarceration there.

Alcatraz, 1986, was where the Canadiens found themselves in early April as the playoffs beckoned. In this case the surroundings were a touch less spartan than Stroud's —the Sheraton Hotel on Ile Charron, an island in the St. Lawrence River between Montreal and south shore Boucherville. The team stayed there for the duration.

It was here that the team dynamic really developed for the Canadiens. There might be two schools of thought about team isolation during the playoffs but for the Canadiens' brain trust there was no doubt. Perron was adamant. "There was no question with our team. There was one way to go and that was the hotel. With the large group of youngsters on our team, we had to bring everybody together. They don't know what it takes to win—things like concentration, relaxation . . . away from the traffic. Montreal is not like any other hockey city. There is no other place in the National Hockey League where you would get that kind of attention and we had to make sure that the only thing in their minds was hockey."

What the Sheraton Ile Charron did for the 1986 Canadiens was evoke the train travel of the 1950s and the close-knit unity of the 1970s teams. Jean Beliveau and his team-mates would spend long hours discussing games, situations and individuals on eighteen-hour train rides to Chicago; Guy Lafleur, Steve Shutt and their cronies would get together in a bar and do the same as a team, and, suddenly, so did the 1986 Canadiens.

It was not only management deciding, "Let's put them all together in isolation and hope something good comes out of it." There was, as Jacques Lemaire explained, an evolutionary process involved. "Winning in team sports is a process. You just don't draft the best talent and leave it to their creativity. You have to build up a team identity and work ethic where every individual knows his role and what is expected of him.

"The first step of the process was to get the rookies to work together with the rest of the team. Once these people believe in each other, they begin to make sacrifices. They will do a little more whenever possible. That couldn't and didn't happen overnight; it was a season-long process.

"The next step was to get them to work well together and that came about in late season. That was when you got the feeling they could become a winner. I saw it during the last six to eight games of the year." This statement might amaze outsiders who only noticed one thing during that time: the slump that threatened the team's presence in the playoffs.

But Lemaire saw more during this period. "The players were doing more for each other, supporting one another on and off the ice and beginning to believe in the team's potential. The final step was to get everybody to win together and that happened during the playoffs. It was an A-B-C progression and the Stanley Cup was the result."

Two of the biggest role players were Bob Gainey and Larry Robinson, and had he not been injured, Mario Tremblay would have joined them. They were the three survivors of the previous Stanley Cup teams of the '70s and, as the team drew together during April and May, were a source of inspiration for the younger players.

Reading constantly during the two months of playoffs that the Canadiens had no superstars, that they were a generic version of the once-fabled teams who swept all before them, was a persistent thorn in the sides of many Montreal players. To a man they looked to veterans like Bob Gainey and Larry Robinson for leadership and inspiration. "When you are in the room between periods of a very tough game and you look up and Larry and Bob are sitting across from you, it builds up your confidence," said Skrudland.

"When we'd get too hyper, Larry and Bob could calm us down. When we got a little low, they'd get us up. And it didn't take a lot of talking on their part to do it. Best of all, though, was the fact that when we were out on the ice, Bob Gainey and Larry Robinson were on our side. We might have been in awe of them in the room; the other teams were in awe of them on the ice."

Other veterans helped as well, among them the three players who came in the "big trades", Bobby Smith, Ryan Walter (although out with a broken ankle until the final series) and Rick Green, not to mention Nilan.

The atmosphere was 100 percent hockey. In early April, with playoff games on television every night, the Canadiens would get together as a team to watch other series when they were not playing themselves. Perron watched the team come together.

"We had a TV set, coffee, milk or soft drinks and the guys could watch the games together. Other nights we brought in video cassettes of movies for entertainment. I didn't hear the guys talking about how boring it was, or what a sentence they were suffering through."

None of this means, though, that natural instincts were totally suppressed. "When we won the fifth game against New York on a Friday night and the guys found out we were going right back to the hotel, some of them didn't like it. We knew that there would be a layoff of at least five days because of the way the Calgary-St. Louis series was going, and some of the players thought they might get a day or two off. I said no way. We've got to win and that's it. We aren't doing this to punish anybody ... we just wanted to make sure that we kept the guys under control."

As the playoff series went on, the players drew closer and closer together. One of them nicknamed their hotel Alcatraz, and the name spread from there. It was an in-joke that was originally kept very quiet, and only surfaced during the final series.

On road trips during the season, the Canadiens are models of decorum. Each player must wear a jacket and tie and be clean-shaven, alien behaviour for San Diego-bred beach boys like Chelios, but the rule nonetheless. In fact, the club not so gently insists that the travelling media respect this rule and it is not unusual to see writers and broadcasters quickly slapping on ties in airports as they prepare to board the team flight.

Ile Charron was off limits to the media horde that swelled with each series but a large number of press people were aboard the team charter that flew back to Montreal on Monday morning, May 19, with the series tied 1-1. The plane had hardly finished its banking ascent when off came the jackets and ties and out came the Alcatraz '86 shirts, the shorts and sandals. The white jerseys with Beach Boy cutoff sleeves, and accessories such as shades and sandals gave the Air Canada flight a definitely laid-back look as the Canadiens flew home for games three and four of the final.

On the front in bold black letters was the word Alcatraz and the small S symbol of Sheraton hotels, compliments of the staff of the team's home away from home. On the back, a stark black 86. The statement was "Us Against The World"; no media, hangers-on or team management need apply.

Rookies and veterans wore them proudly and tried to maintain an air of high nonchalance. Unity of purpose had been achieved and, better still, the team believed in it. One writer turned to another and said, "They've won it. They aren't going to lose another game and they know it."

Up front, team management knew it too, but they contented themselves with thin smiles. "I knew the guys were getting closer and I knew they were getting more demanding towards their teammates," said Perron.

"They didn't like a guy not doing his share. They wanted to win at all costs. They wanted to go home after the third game against Calgary and I wasn't sure. Then I decided that we'd return to the hotel and there was some grumbling." Bob Gainey stood up and said, "If we're going to win, we'll have to pay the price." At that point the Canadiens led Calgary 2-1, but a loss in the upcoming fourth game would have evened the series and returned home-ice advantage to the Flames.

"When the captain stands up and says these things, especially when the players know that he's got four Stanley Cup rings, they shut up and listen. Bob Gainey's got a lot of respect in the room and he did what a captain's supposed to do: he took charge," noted Perron.

The twenty-third Stanley Cup was a genuine team effort for Montreal, which is not to say that individuals were not outstanding. By the final series, many Habs were being touted for the Conn Smythe Trophy, given to the best performer in the playoff season.

Patrick Roy and Claude Lemieux emerged as the front-runners—Roy for his spectacular goaltending and Lemieux for his four game-winning goals and two overtime tallies.

Most importantly, the defensive players who shut down the opposition (Montreal would allow their opponents 30 or more shots only four times in 19 games, an amazing statistic in this so-called era of free-flow "Europeanized" hockey) began to receive their due as well. Guy Carbonneau and Bob Gainey on the first checking line, and Brian Skrudland and Mike McPhee of the second defensive trio, had done such a thorough job in Montreal's full-court press that even occasional hockey viewers sat up and took notice.

If the Bruins, Whalers, Rangers or Flames got past those four players, they ran into "the forest" as one NHL GM described the Montreal defence. Larry Robinson, Rick Green and Craig Ludwig, giants all, dealt out punishment to smaller opposition forwards and were strong enough to move the bigger bruisers out of the slot when necessary. Mike Lalor, a stay-at-home defenceman who played several inches bigger than his 6 feet, 195 pounds, and the fleet-footed duo of Chris Chelios and Gaston Gingras, gave opposition coaches fits.

"Nobody in the league has the combination of size, strength and mobility that the Canadiens have behind their blueline," said a discouraged Bob Johnson in a subdued Calgary dressing room while the Canadiens celebrated 40 feet away. "Some teams are big and slow back there and you dump the puck in and beat their defencemen to it or skate it past them. Others are smaller and more mobile and you can body them off the puck or crowd the net with big forwards. We tried both against the Canadiens and they were ready. Ludwig, Robinson and Green were quite prepared to use their bodies if we tried skating it in and Chelios and Gingras did an excellent job skating to the puck when we threw it in."

The best way for the Flames to defeat the Canadiens, beyond outscoring them in every game, of course, would be to overwhelm them physically and psychologically. Had they met the Canadiens team of mid-season, they might have been successful. After all, Calgary was the team that had slain Wayne Gretzky and the defending champion Oilers; if that wasn't good for a few psychological points, nothing was. They had a big team, powered by veterans like Doug Risebrough, Lanny McDonald (and even in Montreal they sympathized with the fact that likeable Lanny had never won the Stanley Cup in his thirteen-year career) and John Tonelli, the workaholic former New York Islander who led Team Canada to the Canada Cup win in 1984.

But by the time Calgary faced off against the Canadiens in the Saddledome, Friday, May 16, they were up against a team that was equal parts folklore, tradition and hard work.

They could not psyche out the Canadiens with tales of the fabulous exploits of rookie goalie Mike Vernon because Patrick Roy was on another planet in post-season play. And Claude Lemieux had come out of nowhere and played a Rocket Richard-like right wing, with the notable exception of his propensity for diving at the least provocation.

The playoff road had many important milestones. It all started in the first period of the first playoff game against Boston at the Forum, Wednesday, April 9.

You could sense something was going to happen in the game because the pre-game skate was somewhat unusual. Normally teams ignore each other in the warm-up, content to work out quietly and limber up for the contest that will follow in about 30 minutes. In the past, the pre-game warm-up would see NHL players blasting slapshots at their goalies and practising breakaways.

The modern day warm-up is much more elaborate. After an initial skate to get the muscles working, teams work on 2-on-1 and 3-on-2 drills inside the bluelines and players who are not involved stay out of the way by skating lazily in the rectangle between the blue and centre red lines.

The only people usually watching the pre-game warm-up are the standing room customers and a few early birds. The writers and broadcasters are having dinner in the press lounge upstairs and trading notes on players and coaches. So few witnessed the "pinball ballet" in warm-up that set the tone for Game 1. While their teammates went through their drills, Chris Nilan and Ken Linseman started "talking". Nilan, skating clockwise, and Linseman, counterclockwise, timed their rectangular skate so that they were side-by-side along the centre red line.

It went like this: Nilan and Linseman both made their turns in unison to find each other shoulder-to-shoulder along the redline. Yap yap yap, turn (skate along one's blueline) turn, yap yap yap, turn, skate, turn, yap yap yap. This intriguing little tableau played for approximately ten minutes, a good half of the pre-game skate.

After the game, Nilan was asked what they were discussing. "He kept telling me how I was going to eat his stick and I kept calling him a little faggot," replied West Roxbury's finest.

However, when the game got underway, Nilan and Linseman were not the main card. That was provided by a Bruin who was no stranger to playoff rumbles in the Forum and a Canadiens defenceman who hadn't been called upon to drop the gloves in a very long time.

Boston reported for work early in the first period and the Canadiens were nowhere to be seen. The Bruins had the better of the play and Roy was forced into good saves on Linseman and Simmer early on. There were a few roughing minors, not unusual when these teams meet, and Boston was much better than the 11-7 shots on goal totals indicated when the teams went to their dressing rooms at intermission, tied 0-0.

The second period started much the same way, quietly aggressive, when Boston's Louis Sleigher pulled what commentator Don Cherry called the "dumbest play I've seen in a long time." The puck was loose in front of the Boston bench and Larry Robinson was trying to play it with his skate when Sleigher charged the big defenceman, elbow raised high. This was the same Sleigher who had set off the Good Friday brawl with the Nordiques in 1984 when he sucker-punched defenceman Jean Hamel.

Fortunately or unfortunately, depending on your point of view, Robinson saw Sleigher out of the corner of his eye and was able to avoid most of the elbow. Sleigher, on the other hand, was unable to avoid an aroused Robinson who hammered him to the ice and fell on him, flailing away.

"The stupidest thing in the world when you play Montreal is to wake up Larry Robinson," said Cherry. "I used to tell my players not to wake him up because, if you do, he'll kill you."

After the dust had settled, Robinson and Sleigher were in the penalty box with majors and Sleigher's minor for elbowing gave Montreal a power play. By the time the pair emerged, the Canadiens led 2-0 on a pair of goals by Bobby Smith. Mike McPhee made it 3-0, tipping in a Robinson shot before the period ended.

Montreal was ready to be challenged on that night, and Boston would have to win a game in the Forum if they wanted their first post-season triumph over the Canadiens in 20 tries. Almost as if Sleigher refused to absorb the lesson he should have learned in the second period, the Bruins winger smashed into Roy behind the Canadiens net at 13:22 of the final period, Robinson immediately raced after him and thumped him once more.

Shortly thereafter, a typical Montreal-Boston melée broke out and several players squared off. McPhee and Stéphane Richer showed it would be a long series for Boston if they wanted to fight, winning clear-cut victories over Keith Crowder and Mike Milbury while Nilan and Linseman flirted with each other for 10 minutes, with a linesman hanging onto Nilan all the way. In all, 207 minutes in penalties were assessed by referee Bryan Lewis, and Jean Perron came close to thanking his counterpart, Butch Goring, for waking up the Canadiens.

Montreal would need no further wake-up calls in the series.

Game two was a strange game, especially when compared with the previous contest. Fans were still talking about the Jay Miller-John Kordic confrontation weeks later, giving the impression that the contest was as brawl-filled as its predecessor, but this was not the case.

The pre-game warm-up was as spirited as that of the first game and this time the hockey writers were in their seats, pens in hand. Nilan and Miller, then Nilan and Brian Curren, the king-sized Boston defenceman, spent a long time talking during the skate. Nilan and Miller were smiling ferociously during the badinage and all in attendance expected a fight-filled rematch.

Referee Bob Myers had other ideas, and quickly despatched players for any infraction. Defenceman Gord Kluzak was whistled down for hooking at 6:13 and when he and Nilan began yapping, joined the Montreal right winger for a ten-minute rest.

The teams once again emerged from the first period in a scoreless draw but Montreal drew first blood midway through the second period when Stéphane Richer beat rookie goalie Bill Ranford in close. With a little less than four minutes remaining in the period, Goring sent Jay Miller onto the ice for a faceoff. As Miller was skating to the Boston zone, Goring called him back and said a few words to him. Miller nodded and skated to the play.

Jean Perron tapped John Kordic on the shoulder and the Montreal rookie lined up beside Miller, a bruiser who was called up after Nilan butt-ended Rick Middleton in the mouth in October and who had participated in several confrontations with Nilan during the season.

Miller and Kordic had flirted during the first game but little else happened. "So, you here to play hockey or go?" Kordic asked as both players leaned forward for the face-off.

Miller grunted something unintelligible and Kordic turned to watch the linesman drop the puck. At that precise moment, Miller yelled, "Go!" and began flailing away at Kordic. The attack drove the Montreal winger back a few feet and he stumbled. However, he regained his balance and unleashed a barrage of devastating left hands that hammered Miller to the ice. Once again, the Bruins lost the fight, and to add insult to injury, Montreal scored a powerplay goal on the extra minor assessed Miller for instigating the fight.

Miller was not through, however. He brought thousands of Canadiens supporters to their feet when he stormed into the Bruins' dressing room and attacked the door. With everyone in the upper blues and many fans in the whites watching on extra-large TV screens installed to show replays, Miller was KO'd by the folding door.

That was the only fight that night and a theory of some hockey observers was proven right during the third period. During the 1985-86 season, and in previous years, whenever the Bruins discarded their so-called Big Bad Bruins roughhouse tactics, they beat the Canadiens.

One Montreal broadcaster said they suffered from the "Harry Sinden-Boston Garden" disease. The theory had it that Boston drafted big bruisers because of the small size of the Boston rink, euphemistically called an "arena with character" by supporters and "urban blight" by its detractors. Small players would get killed in the Garden and wouldn't have the room to put their skating skills to advantage on a rink with the smallest neutral zone in pro hockey.

When Sinden took over the coaching reins in Boston in 1966, the Bruins went for big players. The trouble was, big often also meant slow, and those players were at a disadvantage against good skating teams in the regulation-size rinks (200 feet long by 85 feet wide).

Thus for years, the Bruins would skate into the Forum and suffer defeat at the hands of better skating teams. Even during the fabulous Bobby Orr-Phil Esposito era, the Bruins could never beat Montreal in post-season play. When they tried intimidation, the Canadiens found bigger, rougher players who could skate. John Ferguson neutralized Ted Green; Rick Chartraw, Gilles Lupien and Pierre Bouchard cancelled out Stan Jonathan, Terry O'Reilly and John Wensink (despite a Jonathan-Wensink tag-team win over Lupien-Bouchard at Boston in the 1978 playoffs) and Mario Tremblay, Chris Nilan and John Kordic nullified the likes of Bobby Schmautz, Jay Miller and Brian Curren in the 1970s and 1980s.

One of the most enduring pictures of Boston playoff frustration against the Canadians is a montage of the team's last four coaches (Don Cherry, Gerry Cheevers, Harry Sinden and Butch Goring) standing on the visitor's bench at the Forum and screaming at the referee while dejected Bruins skate around listlessly, their moods blacker than their uniforms.

The repeated intimation that the Bruins could always count on being cheated out of a game by a combination of bad refereeing and the Forum crowd has been a standard Sinden complaint for almost two decades. He even has an ironic phrase for it: "The Ghosts of the Forum."

A psychologist would call this complaining negative reinforcement. Unintentional or not, Boston management has given the players an out, a subconscious excuse for losing their games in Montreal. In 1985-86, the Canadiens beat Boston six straight at the Forum—four during the season and twice during the playoffs.

Boston could easily have won two of those games: a 2-1 setback on February 1 in which they held the Canadiens to 14 shots in the whole game, and the first game of the Adams Division semi-final.

As it was, they came pretty close to winning the second contest, a game in which the Canadiens played much better than the first and held a seemingly insurmountable 2-0 lead with less than half a period to go. After the Kordic-Miller confrontation at 16:06 of the second, the teams settled down to play serious and clean hockey. At 12:15, Barry Pederson struck, converting a pass from Linseman and the Bruins were back in the game. The Canadiens sagged and 41 seconds later Crowder tied it from a scramble in front of the net.

Patrick Roy and Claude Lemieux chose this game to begin their climb to prominence. Roy was forced to make several good saves as Boston roared to life and his favourite conversational companions, his two goalposts, saved him late in the period. With five minutes remaining in the game, defenceman Ray Bourque sped out of his zone and over the Canadiens' blueline and unleashed a blistering slapshot from the face-off circle to Roy's right. The goalie was beaten cleanly, but the puck struck the post dead-on.

Less than a minute later, Lemieux suckered Boston winger Kraig Nienhuis into doing what the Bruins do best at the Forum, taking a stupid penalty.

A desultory scrum took place to the right of the Boston goal at 15:44 and Lemieux prolonged it just enough so that Nienhuis could skate up to him and crosscheck him to the ice, right in front of Myers. The Bruin winger was still in the penalty box when Lemieux rubbed salt in the wound with the game-winning goal at 17:33.

The teams travelled to Boston and this time the pregame skate got serious, as Kluzak and Nilan almost came to blows. Alternate referee Terry Gregson and Serge Savard got in between the belligerents and were reinforced when game referee Don Koharski and his two linesmen came running out of their dressing room in their underwear.

Although there was a spate of minor penalties and misconducts in the first period, there were no fights and the Bruins led 1-0 when the teams skated off for intermission. Lemieux and Mats Naslund gave Montreal a 2-1 lead by the halfway point of the second period but goals 14 seconds apart by Reed Larson and Crowder gave Boston a 3-2 lead with one period remaining.

If the theory that the Bruins have better success against Montreal when there is less fighting is valid, so is another. The second theory says a strong skating winger who can hit will do well in the Garden.

This idea was proven barely a minute into the third period when Guy Carbonneau sped into the Bruins' zone and dropped a pass to Bob Gainey. The latter whipped it by Ranford before the Boston goalie could move.

Seven minutes later, Rick Green was whistled off for tripping and the Bruins pressed on the powerplay. Forty seconds into his penalty-killing shift, Gainey picked up the puck along the right boards in his own zone, avoided a Boston checker and sped away into the Boston zone with defenceman Craig Ludwig to his left and Bruins rearguard Ray Bourque trying to head him off.

About thirty feet away from the Boston net, Gainey, on his off-wing, looked across to Ludwig and simultaneously fired a wrist shot in the opposite direction past a surprised Ranford. The series was over and Montreal would face Hartford in the division final, following that team's rout of the Quebec Nordiques.

If the Montreal-Boston series was characterized by barely concealed hostility and pugnacity, the Canadiens-Whalers confrontation was just the opposite. Both teams had four days off to prepare and the truce period gave them plenty of time to throw bouquets at each other.

Nilan had been particularly rough on the Bruins, telling all who would listen that Boston coach Butch Goring was "yellow" and that the Bruins were cheap-shot artists and cement-footed goons. Now he was all flowers—the Whalers were a good team and even their tough guy, winger Torrie Robertson, was a quality player, he purred.

"He really said that?" glowed Robertson when Nilan's compliment was delivered. "Tell him thanks for me."

Robertson and his mates also said thanks three nights later as they skated off the Forum ice with a 4-1 win over the Canadiens. Robertson had a confrontation with Kordic and came out second best, but Hartford won the war, breaking the game wide open with goals by Stewart Gavin, Sylvain Turgeon and John Anderson in the second period.

The Canadiens and Whalers went on to play a defensive series that was characterized by hard and clean bodychecks in every zone and goaltending that scaled new heights. When Patrick Roy wasn't stoning superlative forwards like Kevin Dineen, Ron Francis, Ray Ferraro, Anderson and Dean Evason, Mike Liut was picking the pockets of Bobby Smith, Mats Naslund, Lemieux and Richer.

The Hartford Whalers, quietly assembled through a series of astute regular-season moves that earned Emile Francis the admiration of his peers, would prove to be the best team the Canadiens faced in the playoffs. "I am not putting down the Rangers or the Flames but the Whalers were a lot better team than anyone gave them credit for," said Jean Perron. "And Jack Evans coached them beautifully. They played within their system the whole way and it showed; it took an overtime goal by Claude Lemieux in the seventh game for us to beat them. They could easily have won and gone all the way like we did."

The undisputed leaders of the Whalers were the forward line of Dineen, Francis and Anderson, goalie Liut and defenceman David Babych. Defensively, Doug Jarvis and Stewart Gavin pressed the Canadiens forwards at every opportunity.

Anderson was a late-season acquisition from Quebec, in a trade for Risto Siltanen, and had played very well for the Nordiques during the first six months of the season. After the Nordiques bowed out in three straight, observers said that GM Maurice Filion had outsmarted himself with the Anderson-Siltanen trade.

Babych was acquired early in the season from Winnipeg for forward Ray Neufeld, a deal only John Ferguson thinks went the Jets' way and Gavin was a steal from Toronto Maple Leafs in a swap for defenceman Chris Kotsopoulos. Last but not least, Jarvis, Gainey's linemate in Montreal for seven years and four Stanley Cups, came over from Washington for Jorgen Petterson in mid-season, a trade that helped both teams despite commentator Howie Meeker's low opinion of Jarvis.

"That team took us right down to the wire," said Larry Robinson. "They deserve all the credit in the world for what they accomplished. Players like Scot Kleinendorst, Joel Quenneville and Ulf Samuelsson did a hell of a job in their zone and even when Liut was out for two games, Steve Weeks played very well in nets."

The series was tied 3-3 when the teams returned to the Forum for game seven on Tuesday, April 29. At 1:19 of the first period, Guy Carbonneau stole the puck at the Hartford blueline and walked in on Liut. The Hartford goalie slammed the door and set the pattern for 66 minutes of heart-stopping hockey. Six minutes in, Liut stopped Skrudland and McPhee on a 2-on-1 and 30 seconds after that, Roy stopped Gavin on his doorstep. Then Richer and Lemieux combined for a stellar scoring opportunity, only to be foiled by Liut yet again.

This scenario played over and over until late in the first period with Montreal killing a penalty. Mike McPhee rushed Francis, playing the right point for the Whalers, when the puck got trapped in the latter's skates. The left-winger muscled Francis off the puck and sped away on a breakaway. He beat Liut low to the stick side.

The score remained 1-0 very late in the game and it appeared the Canadiens would win their second straight series on a short-handed goal. But late in the third, Dean Evason raced up the left-wing boards with a defenceman in front of him. Babych, who had not been pressing offensively because a bad groin injury hampered his skating, was trailing. Evason crossed the Montreal line and dropped the puck to Babych who "first-timed" it past a partially screened and very surprised Roy with 2:48 remaining. The Forum went deathly quiet. The Canadiens should have been leading by several goals by then and instead were deadlocked when the siren sounded, simultaneously announcing the end of regulation play and the onset of sudden death overtime.

A year before, the Montreal Canadiens had blown game six in Quebec and then lost game seven at the forum on an overtime goal by Peter Stastny. During the regular season, the Canadiens turned in one of the worst overtime records in the league while Hartford already had two overtime victories in the 1986 playoffs, against Quebec and Montreal in game one and game four of their respective series.

How would the Canadiens react this time?

They stormed the Hartford net with little result for the first five minutes of play. At 5:12, Nilan and Kleinendorst got their sticks up in the Hartford zone and, after belabouring the issue, were assessed misconducts by referee Andy Van Hellemond.

Montreal gained a face-off to Liut's left shortly thereafter and the puck skittered behind the Whaler net. Skrudland mucked furiously along the boards and kicked it to Lemieux who moved out in front of the goal and lifted a sharply angled backhand over a surprised Liut's shoulder as he skated by. The Forum exploded.

Lemieux, meanwhile, skated towards the Canadiens bench and saw his teammates storming towards him. He did what came naturally—he took a dive and covered his head. "I scored a goal like that in junior last year and my teammates almost killed me," he explained afterward. "I don't want to get hurt by my own guys."

Three eventful weeks into the playoffs, Lemieux and Roy were folk heroes in Quebec, and their fellow inmates on Alcatraz were starting to believe. Roy admitted that he spoke with his goalposts before every game and there he was, shortly after the national anthems, about 40 feet away from his net and bent over in deep conversation.

"I started in the last regular-season game in Hartford

and I do it every night," he explained to a growing media throng. His words and delightful flakiness were the stuff of headlines all over North America and he received prominent play in *Time, Sports Illustrated* and *The Sporting News.*

Lemieux wasn't far behind when he confessed to "going off quietly in a corner "and having a private conversation with his teenaged brother Serge, who is severely retarded and has spent his life in institutions. "Whenever I am in a tight spot I talk to him," Lemieux said.

The press gobbled it up. In an age of terse "how-I-did-it" quotes, usually blamed on "dumb hockey players" but really the result of stupid and lazy post-game questions by a large number of hockey reporters, Roy and Lemieux were deemed more colourful than anyone around. When one night later, the Calgary Flames eliminated the Edmonton Oilers, everyone began to believe.

If anything, the five-game series with the New York Rangers propelled the two young players even more into prominence. The Canadiens and Rangers slept through the first game, a 2-1 win by Montreal, and the Habs bombed John Vanbiesbrouck for four goals in the middle period of the second game to take a 2-0 series lead going into Madison Square Garden.

The Rangers had 27 shots in the first game and 21 in the second and winger Wilf Paiement was not convinced by Roy. "I'd like to see how he would play if he had to face 35 or 40 shots a game. We'll try to do that back home." Other Rangers concurred.

Paiement and his teammates would get their answer the very next game.

Before the Monday night contest started, the New York faithful began chanting derisively, "Roo-Ah! Roo-Ah! Roo-Ah!", a Manhattan distortion of Roy's name. His name had been explained to them by ESPN broadcasters who couldn't even come close to the real French pronunciation "Rwah". (They, and their English Canadian counterparts were even further off on Lemieux, in the best tradition of mangled French surnames perfected by that master of foreign elocution, Foster Hewitt.)

Little did they know Roy loved the special attention

and he showed it by turning in what Jean Beliveau later described as "the best playoff game I've ever seen a goalie play."

The Rangers took the lead early in the first but Richer tied it at 6:00 when his clearing pass banked in off Vanbiesbrouck's skate. After one period it was still 1-1, despite a 16-7 New York advantage in shots on goal and a dozen clear scoring chances.

In the middle period, it was the Ranger goalie's turn to shine as Montreal outshot New York 15-6. Nevertheless, the Rangers scored the only goal. Mats Naslund tied the game at 5:06 of the third, but it looked like New York had the victory wrapped up when Bob Brooke climaxed a furious siege in Montreal territory with a shot along the ice that beat Roy at 12:54 and made the score 3-2.

It was not to be for the Blueshirts. Brian MacLellan, who was acquired early in the season to add muscle to the diminutive Rangers, took a bad late penalty at 16:04, *à la* Boston's Nienhuis, and Bobby Smith tied the game on a backhand from the slot at 17:56.

It was Montreal's third overtime of the playoff season. The question again was, how would they perform?

The answer? Spectators and the players watched in amazement as Roy kicked out thirteen New York shots, including an incredible four in a row after New York won a face-off in the Canadiens' end. In all, the Rangers took 47 shots on goal during the game, or about two games' worth for Montreal, and Roy stopped 44.

For nine-and-a-half minutes, Roy robbed the Rangers blind. With 9:30 gone in the overtime period, the teams faced off in Montreal territory. The puck was passed to the right point. Defenceman Willie Huber fanned on his attempted shot and Mike McPhee broke away down the left wing. Across the ice, Huber's defence partner James Patrick was far out of position, almost against the left point boards when McPhee broke out and Lemieux streaked up the middle. As he went to turn and head off Lemieux, Patrick tripped over linesman Ray Scapinello's skate and fell to the ice.

McPhee and Lemieux raced in alone on Vanbiesbrouck and the left winger passed to the rookie who lifted it into the Rangers net over Vanbiesbrouck's shoulder. The New York papers were full of Roy and Ray (Scapinello) the next day. TV replays show that Patrick was too far removed from the play to catch Lemieux, a good skater. Still, even the Canadiens admitted that the old intangible, luck, was on their side so far this playoff year.

After all, this was the team that had entered the playoffs with a 24-square foot question mark in goal. "Everybody else might have been worried about our goaltending but Jean Perron wasn't and neither was I," said Francois Allaire, the former Quebec university coach and the team's goaltending coach. "People said Patrick had technical weaknesses but there weren't very many. He came to the organization as a very sound goalie whose special strengths were his incredible quickness and a very good glove. He worked hard at Sherbrooke a year ago and did most of his learning there."

Allaire admitted that Roy improved his concentration during the playoffs, and that the Canadiens worked many special drills to help him improve his positioning in the crease, cutting down angles on shooters and taking away the strengths of other teams.

"By the time the playoffs came around, our work with Patrick was about the book we had on each team. For instance, Boston was very good at getting the puck in from the boards into the crease and slot so Jean improvised drills that had Patrick and the defenceman working on this.

"Hartford, on the other hand, took a lot of shots from far out so we had our players doing the same thing. New York tried a lot of European-type motion and weaves so we had him drill with our forwards a lot. Finally, Calgary liked jamming the crease with big forwards so our defencemen did the same thing in practice, forcing Patrick up against the screening player to cut down the possibility of deflections." The latter drill paid dividends in the second game of the final series when Roy got his left leg on a close-in deflection by the Flames' Tim Hunter.

If this chapter has given the impression that a set Montreal line-up played so well that all Jean Perron had to do was open and shut the doors at the team bench, nothing could be further from the truth. With the early elimination of the Sherbrooke Canadiens—they did not make the AHL playoffs—Kordic, Serge Boisvert and Scott Sandelin (who played for the U.S. national team in the World Championships) joined the team. Goalie Vincent Riendeau and forward Shayne Corson, who was still nursing an injury, also moved up after their junior seasons.

The additional players meant Montreal was carrying some thirty hockey players and Perron divided the practice sessions in two. The A group comprised those players who could be called upon for playoff action and the B group was made up of those players who probably would not play unless an injury or illness felled a regular. Several players moved from A to B, and back again, as a result of their game performances, among them Lucien Deblois, Petr Svoboda, Steve Rooney and David Maley.

Maley joined the Canadiens in late March after Wisconsin was eliminated from the NCAA championships and spent most of what remained of the regular season trying to shed a few pounds and find a place on the team. A rugged 6' 2" forward, he skated well and possessed good hockey sense. He was finally dressed for the Pittsburgh game on the penultimate Saturday of the season and played all of two shifts. He played another couple of shifts against Detroit four days later and then was relegated to the B team for what appeared to be the duration.

But as was the case with all players in the organization, people were watching him closely, whether he sensed it or not. Coach Perron was one who paid special attention to the youngster. "I could see in practice that he didn't like other players taking the body against him and that he was really anxious to get playing. He is a big boy and he showed me some very good skills and soon we decided he was ready."

New York blanked the Canadiens 2-0 in the fourth game of their series and the teams returned to Montreal for game five. Midway through the third period, with the Canadiens leading 2-1, Maley, the big Minnesotan, knocked down a clearing pass at the Ranger blueline and shot at the net. Vanbiesbrouck made the save but lost the rebound. Gainey scored an insurance goal and Montreal was in its first final in seven years.

Maley's first playoff point was a big one, and he would loom large against the Calgary Flames.

Montreal had to wait a week for Calgary to finally eliminate the stubborn St. Louis Blues as Jacques Demers' unlikely alliance of former Canadiens, Flames, and a few Blues left over from the 1983 near-move to Saskatoon took Calgary to the wire, rebounding from a three-goal deficit late in the third period of game six to score an overtime win and force a seventh game.

Calgary finally subdued the Blues 2-1 in the seventh game, and the question going into the final series was, "Would fatigue bother the Flames more than the week-long layoff would affect Montreal?"

Late in the first period of the first game, the teams were tied 1-1 when Calgary defenceman Paul Baxter flipped a puck high into the Canadiens' end. Jim Peplinski flicked it out of the air with a high stick and scored. Referee Kerry Fraser conferred with his linesmen and the goal stood, enraging Roy. He slashed Ron Finn across the back of his legs to earn a 10-minute misconduct, and then gave Ray Scapinello a two-handed shove, something which should have earned him an early shower and a date with NHL vice-president Brian O'Neill.

But this is the era of the instant replay and Fraser, like any of his counterparts faced with the situation, pretended not to see the second infraction. Imagine the uproar if, first, the goal proved to be an integral part of the final result (it was), second, he kicked out the Montreal goalie who had the hockey world abuzz, and third, the videotape showed the goal was no good (which it did).

Calgary went onto win 5-2, becoming the first team to score four goals against Roy in one game (Hartford had scored an empty-net goal in their 4-1 series opener) and five against the Canadiens (another empty net tally).

But that victory was it for the Flames. Two nights later Calgary took a 2-0 lead at 0:15 of the second period but the Flames would score only seven more goals in the next

430 Lions In Winter

11 periods, two of these coming with a little more than three minutes remaining in the third period of the fifth and final game.

The Canadiens won game two with three improbable heroes all scoring their first goals of the playoffs—Gingras, Maley and Skrudland—and the latter set a playoff record for fastest overtime goal, 0:09.

From then on, Montreal methodically shut down the Flames, stifling them at every opportunity. In the 1-0 Forum victory that gave Montreal an insurmountable 3-1 lead heading back west, the Flames were held to 15 shots over all, including only two in the second period and six in the third. Lemieux scored his fourth game-winner of the playoffs, pouncing on an errant clearing pass by Doug Risebrough and blasting it through a surprised Vernon at 11:10 of the third period.

Gingras and Skrudland also scored in the Cup-clincher while Maley set up Rick Green for the third-period goal that made it 3-1 and dashed Calgary's hopes. At 10:30 of the final period, 19 seconds after Green beat Vernon with a wrist shot, Naslund fed Bobby Smith for Montreal's fourth goal. It was delicious irony that the tall centre whose pass had ended Montreal's hopes of a second Drive for Five on a brisk April Sunday in 1980, scored the goal that won the Canadiens' twenty-third Cup in 1986.

Smith's Cup winner was his seventh of the series and his strong two-way play was important to the team's success. His linemate Naslund ended the playoffs with eight goals, including a pair in Montreal's 5-3 win in game three in which the Canadiens blitzed the Flames for three goals in 68 seconds late in the first period.

Larry Robinson and Bob Gainey led both on the ice and in the dressing room. Gainey scored five goals and added five assists while shutting down the best forwards the opposition could muster. His linemate Guy Carbonneau scored seven goals while Skrudland and McPhee combined for another five goals between them.

Green, Lalor and Ludwig played strong physical games in front of the Canadiens' net while Chelios and Gingras moved the puck quickly out of danger with their good skating and stickhandling.

Forgotten in the shuffle because they rarely played (one not at all) were two former Winnipeg teammates, Soetaert and Deblois. The former could have infected his team with complaints about his lot, but chose instead to show full support for his goalkeeping partner. Soetaert and Deblois accepted their lot with grace and aplomb and, as a result, showed the non-playing rookies how to behave. Their contribution was an important one.

All that said, the 1986 playoffs belonged to Patrick Roy and Claude Lemieux and it was Roy who was awarded the Conn Smythe for top playoff performer after the last siren had sounded.

*Cherchez le gardien, trouvez la Coupe Stanley!*

Montreal Canadiens found both in the spring of 1986. The Torch had been passed, taken up and held firmly aloft.

In a year where Jack Nicklaus won the Masters, Willie Shoemaker the Kentucky Derby and the Boston Celtics the NBA Championship, it appeared that order had returned to the universe of sports.

The Montreal Canadiens could return to their mausoleum the following September and look the Forum ghosts right in the eye.

# 17

# The Seven-Year Itch

## Part I — Upstairs

*Saturday, August 14, 1993 dawns hazy and humid in southern Quebec and upstate Vermont. The ice is already down on Rink Three at the Dollard-des-Ormeaux Civic Centre and well marked with skate tracks as the tryouts for the Atom, Peewee and Bantam AA North Shore Pirates are nearing the end of their first week.*

*One of the surest signs of the insanity of hockey at the minor level is the fact that dozens of young players are competing for the highest levels of hockey during the dog days of summer while baseball is going full tilt, and even before the minor league football season starts. The Canadian Amateur Hockey Association thinks it is a terrific idea — and the Quebec Amateur Ice Hockey Federation concurs — that double letter or rep teams start their season weeks well before Canadian Thanksgiving, ergo the need for mid-summer tryouts.*

*About 120 kilometres to the southeast, just on the other side of the Vermont border, there is no ice at the Collins-Perley Sports Complex just outside St. Alban's, Vermont. There will be soon enough, and some of the boys who wear the blue, red and white of North Shore will play here during the winter against the boys in Vermont colours of green and gold, as they have for many years.*

*While Dollard's Rink 3 is an icebox on this day, its Vermont counterpart is an oven, yet all talk at both rinks is about hockey.*

*Hundreds will visit the suburban rink in Montreal's West Island on this day to watch young pre-National Hockey League hopefuls place a tentative foot on a higher rung of the ladder.*

*Meanwhile, at Collins-Perley, thousands of Vermonters and New Yorkers, and the occasional Quebecker, will visit for a chance to touch hockey's greatest prize, the Stanley Cup.*

*Herb Zurkowsky, a hockey reporter with Montreal's English-language daily* The Gazette, *is surprised to see what the visit of Lord Stanley's trophy means just the other side of the border. He is typical of Montreal sports media and the majority of Quebeckers. To him, and them, the sport ends at the border, and even though Vermont's own John LeClair is finally having his turn with the silverware in this summer of endless show-and-tell, he has a hard time fathoming the response.*

*If the Great White North is the blind spot of the United States of America, and don't we have a doozy of an inferiority complex to attest to that lack of affect, then the North Country is the blind spot of southern Quebec. Northern Vermont and Upstate New York conjure up very few images for Quebeckers beyond the Pyramid Mall (Plattsburgh) and the University Street Mall (South Burlington), pleasure domes of cross-border shopping, and the beaches of Lake Champlain, ironically referred to as Quebec's Riviera. Quite often the names are the same — Malboeuf, Gagné, Benoît, Rousseau — but they speak different languages and usually only over a cash register.*

*If they play our game on the other side of the border, it must be a pretty basic game, Montrealers seem to think. After all, we've never heard of anybody from around there making good.*

*Minor hockey teams, located primarily in the predominantly English-speaking areas of the province are not surprised in the least. They know that the kids in the border towns from Plattsburgh, Potsdam and Massena (New York) and east through St. Alban's, Essex Junction and Chittenden-South Burlington (Vermont), are as hockey-mad, and as competent, as they.*

*And because Montreal loves to ignore its cross-border neighbours, thousands of people who live an hour away from the Forum have grown up generally as Bruins fans, stretching their New England affiliation to its very limits.*

*LeClair may have been a new name to most Montrealers two seasons ago, but some had followed the hockey progress of the big*

*galoot his Canadiens team-mates called "Marmaduke" for many*
*years — from his first games with St. Alban's tykes, squirts and*
*peewees, through high school with Bellows Free Academy, and*
*up to ECAC competition with the University of Vermont*
*Catamounts.*

*These few observers have also witnessed the exploits of the next*
*generation of North Country hockey stars with names like Glenn*
*Coupal, Brad Shroyer, Chris Line, Peter Bay, Nate Finucine and*
*Brian Ramsay, many of whom are already household names many*
*miles south in Boston or Troy, N.Y., but unknown just one hour*
*away in hockey-rich Montreal.*

*And for those with little memory, Montreal's Eric Desjardins*
*was captain of the Canadian junior team that lost to the Soviet*
*Union, led by phenoms Pavel Buré and Alexander Mogilny, at the*
*1989 Junior World Championships in Alaska. A tall robust for-*
*ward named LeClair was the best player on the U.S. team in that*
*tournament, many observers felt — even better than the much-her-*
*alded Mike Modano.*

*That was four years, many degrees cooler, and many thousands*
*of miles away. Today, oppressive heat sucks the strength out of all*
*objects, animate or not, on this second day of the Vermont tour.*
*Yesterday, the shy behemoth who broke Hollywood's back with*
*overtime goals in the third and fourth games of the Stanley Cup*
*final, proudly presented Montreal's Stanley Cup to Vermont gov-*
*ernor Howard Dean in a special ceremony in the state's metropo-*
*lis, Burlington, and then toured two hospitals and a special camp*
*for children suffering with cancer. Earlier today, senior Vermont*
*senator Patrick Leahy presented LeClair with a special letter from*
*President Bill Clinton, the closest the Canadiens will get to a trip*
*to the White House. . . .*

It has been that kind of a summer for the Canadiens and
the Stanley Cup as the Habs push back the borders of their
territory in several directions; east and north into Nordiques-
land and north and west into the playpen where the Senators
are about to embark on their Terrible Twos.

There cannot have been a civic picnic, a family beach party
or municipal holiday anywhere in Quebec which was not
graced by a member of the team and the most nomadic
Stanley Cup in the history of the NHL.

Jacques Demers, the populist coach, is almost as ubiquitous. Everywhere you look there is the happiest man in Quebec who, barely a year ago, feared he had been blackballed
out of the league. This summer he bears the title of Stanley
Cup-winning coach with pride and just enough humility to
endear him even more with the Canadiens faithful, and even
some supporters of the dread Nordiques who are starting to
wonder about the icy demeanor of their mentor, Pierre Pagé.
And, although Demers's salary has just been tripled by a
grateful Serge Savard, and the length of his contract doubled
in the process, *l'homme le plus heureux au Québec* is starting to
show the wear-and-tear of a show-and-tell summer.

"I've had the best summer of my life, " he says, "but I'm
starting to look forward to the new season so I can have a
rest," he sighs. After the obligatory Stanley Cup parade and
several official post-Cup events in June, Jacques and Debbie
Demers treated themselves to two weeks in Paris, confident
that they could return and relax in preparation for the pressure-cooker of defending a Stanley Cup victory in 1993-94.

If they had known what awaited them upon their return,
they might have opted to rent a houseboat and slowly, very
slowly, cruise the canals of France for the entire off-season.
Golf tournaments appeared to ambush the roly-poly coach
at every turn, including his own and the Canadiens' official
summer gathering on the greens, as did every social service
organization in Quebec with a worthy cause in desperate
need of endorsement or support . . . and the laying on of
hands on Stanley.

And needless to say, that heady aroma of brewer's yeast and
hops never seemed to be too far away during the celebrations.

Jacques Demers is not complaining. On this morning in
August, he sits in his new second-floor office at the Forum,
next-door to the immortal Jean Beliveau's, patiently sifting
through hundreds of pieces of mail, almost all of which begin (in French or English): "Dear Mr. Demers, I represent . . ."
and then asks for his help or time to devote to a worthy
cause. A notorious self-described softie who leads with his
heart, Demers has trouble saying no. But he will have to;
there are only so many hours in a day, and the new season
beckons.

How sensitive is he to the plight of others? A week ago, a grateful Serge Savard gave Demers a contract extension of four years that will make him assistant general-manager at the end of the term, and that makes him close to a millionaire coach . . . a very recent phenomenon in the NHL.

Demers refuses to divulge his salary and benefits to the media. "There are a lot of people going through tough times, and I've been there," he said. "I don't want to sound like I'm rubbing people's faces in my success. It's hard times out there for a lot of people."

Demers is not only happy for the pecuniary aspects of the raise; the increased power profile in the Canadiens' dressing room is worth more than mere dollars. He also understands what comes with the job, and that is underscored by his latest move within the Canadiens' organization.

Demers is the first in a long line of Canadiens coaches to move upstairs; the rest have had to make do with a cubbyhole beside the trainer's room, across the corridor from the team's dressing room at ice level. That will remain Demers's "downstairs" or "game" office, for that half of his job which merely involves coaching the Montreal Canadiens during an eighty-four-game season and through, fortune willing, some twenty-plus playoff contests.

This new "upstairs" office is for answering mail, developing marketing opportunities and handling public relations: the other half of the coach's job, and in the 1990s, no less important than the downstairs task. Jacques Demers and the second-floor Canadiens have discovered that in the seven short years since the previous Stanley Cup victory, the world of the National Hockey League and professional sports had changed immeasurably. The game on the ice now is only marginally as strenuous as the Big Game off-ice — the game of selling the sizzle and delicious aroma of the steak while holding back on the prize sirloin itself. Today, everyone wants a sniff.

Part of that sizzle is the high salaries being paid to some of the top names in coaching — Mike Keenan of the New York Rangers, Scotty Bowman with the Detroit Red Wings, Al Arbour with the New York Islanders and (soon) Pat Burns with the Toronto Maple Leafs. In the 1980s, a New

Wisdom arose in the NHL, and even those who espoused it most fervently were hard-pressed to understand the reasoning behind it. The New Wisdom was, simply: "A coach should not stay with one team much more than four seasons because he, the team, or both would go stale." Examples of coaches who had succeeded in the early going, only to have the team turn on them, were legion. Or were these stories simply self-fulfilling prophesies? No one seemed willing to challenge the NW.

The NHL, like the rest of the world of pro sports, is built on a foundation of media hearsay, innuendo and front-office leaks. What one columnist muses in Calgary may become truth in Hartford a few weeks or months later. So it is easy for a theory or two to gain advocates, and spread quickly throughout the hockey world. The difficult part is tailing this disinformation back to its source, and debunking it. The four-year theory, it seems, kept Demers out of work for a couple of seasons.

He is happier this August than he has been for several Augusts for two reasons. The first is that he has fresh memories of what it was like to be on the outside looking in, as other coaches, many clearly inferior to him, prepared to take NHL teams through their training camp paces.

"At one point I asked my agent, Don Meehan, if I was blackballed," he says. "I couldn't understand why I wasn't behind the bench, and some of these guys were. Heck, I had two Coach-of-the-Year awards and I had left both St. Louis and Detroit without burning any bridges, and I left a lot of friends behind."

The second reason why Demers is happy is because he knows that his raise delivers a message to the dressing room, and is part of a movement in the NHL which will lay one nefarious myth — especially for coaches — to rest.

"I have no problem with Kirk Muller, Vincent Damphousse, Brian Bellows, Patrick Roy — the stars of the team — making a lot more money than me, because these are the guys who will win the big games for you. Where I have problems, and other coaches feel this way, is knowing that the twenty-third or twenty-fourth guy on the team is making more than the coach."

In other words, the super-salaries finally being paid to the super-coaches guarantees longevity and deliver a death blow to the "four-year itch" theory. "It is going to be easier in many cases to get rid of one, two or even three trouble-makers on a team, rather than have the coach pay for their mistakes," he adds. "It will be too expensive to automatically remove the coach when things aren't going well, and the guys in the room will get the message from the second floor when they hear that the coach is making that kind of money."

Demers is dead-on with his analysis. In today's professional sport, the astronomical salaries play with everyone's heads and an income hierarchy has developed. Simply put, millionaires need not deign to speak to peons. In the 1960s and '70s, the media and players enjoyed a symbiotic relationship, and there was a basic mutual respect, especially between veterans on both sides of the pen or microphone. By the late 1980s, especially in pro baseball, players making multimillion-dollar salaries felt that mere scribes who made less than six-figure salaries were beneath contempt. Needless to say, the ink-stained wretches and their blow-dried counterparts in the broadcast booth responded with the only weapons at hand, pen and mike, and relations soured further.

The greatest irony in all this is that the media, and the free marketing machine that they represent, are more responsible than the players for delivering the big bucks to sports. The biggest pies are media-generated, whether in newspaper columns, game reports, boxscores, pool results, event broadcasts, advertisements, televised commercials for a plethora of products, or simple appearances by athletes. The further removed some "superstars" became from depending on their talent, or their organization, for their money, the closer they got to biting the hand that feeds. And many journalists were not averse to seek retribution for slights, real and perceived.

A similar situation developed in many a clubhouse or dressing room. The team rarely got rid of the recalcitrant multimillionaire outfielder when the manager could be axed, with very few exceptions (right, José Canseco?). And if the superstar centre wasn't particularly receptive to his coach's occasional pleas to backcheck, he might do his level best to help hire a coach who just loved his goals and assists and was blind or indifferent to plus-minus figures.

Perhaps the most glaring example of money talking between the lines or in the dugout came in December 1992 in San Francisco, when Barry Bonds hired Dusty Baker, a close personal friend, to manage the Giants, after the team needed to bust the bank with a free-agent contract in the $45-million range. Those people who believe that Baker, a competent baseball skipper, was hired "upstairs" are incredibly naive.

More often than not, the manager or coach has to bite the bullet whenever "The Star" pouts or takes offense to the most microscopic perceived slight.

Is Demers sensitive to this fact? Every professional coach is, but Demers exceedingly so; even though he left Detroit with class and dignity, the story has it that several high-priced players had rebelled and run him out of town. "I don't have anything to say about leaving Detroit," says Demers, but you know the pain lingers. Like Sparky Anderson of the Tigers and Chuck Daly then of the Pistons, Demers was a players' coach who built relationships nurtured on loyalty, trust and respect. Detroit hurt deep inside.

"I am happy to be in Montreal, I am happy that we won the Stanley Cup, and I am really happy that Serge Savard has gone out of his way to show me and the players that he wants me here for a long time. It means a lot to me, believe me." What he didn't say was that Jacques Demers also would lobby in the world of marketing the sport, proving his mettle in all aspects of the game.

In 1993, the NHL still may have been poor cousins to the other major sports, but there was more money than even the most optimistic executive would have dared dream seven years previous. Consequently, the game changed so much that the men in suits began achieving the same high profiles, if not the exact results, of the players.

In 1986, one of the rising second-floor stars for the Canadiens was François-Xavier Seigneur, vice-president of marketing. You would not find his picture on a hockey card or poster anywhere, but he was a winner who would endure.

One of the first NHL executives to wholeheartedly espouse the cause of product marketing, Seigneur turned out to be so good at his job that he accelerated its headlong spin to redundancy. But that was okay; he had long ago set up his own company a block west in Westmount and, enjoying the best of both worlds in the 1990s, became a consultant to the team, with as much input as he had as an executive. (We told you he was good at his job.)

By 1993, a marketing vice-president for the Montreal Canadiens was about as necessary as a Federal Minister of Breathing in Ottawa. In half a decade the league had gone from the agony of endorsement defeat to the jaws (San Jose Sharks) of marketing millions. With Major League Baseball, the National Basketball Association and the National Hockey League, the NHL had become part of an $8.2-billion industry (August 1993) that had exploded around sports memorabilia and collectibles, and the mega-marketing of prominent players and teams.

When nonexistent teams like the San Jose Sharks, the Colorado Rockies and the Florida Marlins could sell multimillions worth of "logoed" collectibles, long before either franchise had played a first game or even drafted a first player, it became obvious that sports marketing was The Beast with No Name. With hundreds of prospective suitors lined up outside the front door, and halfway around the block like overnighting rock fans camped out for the first ticket, sports marketing had become, in its own 1990s vernacular, a no-brainer.

A conversation betwen the team's marketing guru and a prospective endorser/advertiser in 1986 went something like this: "Yeah, we have lots of room left in the official program and you can write your own ticket; it's not too expensive. We're thinking of experimenting with ads on the boards like they do in Europe; think you might be interested? We can even work out a poster deal for your stores, or you could distribute foldout schedules at your customer counters."

In 1993, the same people people would "take a phone meeting," the Canadiens' marketing guru probably on his Motorola hands-free, flip-up cellular while sitting in his golf cart at Royal Montreal or Elmridge on Ile Bizard and pondering his lie on his second shot.

"Talk to me, Sammy! Our official running shoe? That's long gone for top dollar. Oh, a cross-trainer? Well, that might be different, I'll have someone look into it. Even if it's clear, we'll have to see how you fit in our overall product marketing mix." Marketing the pro franchise in the mid-1990s now meant taking telephone calls, or "reluctantly" letting only the élite and best-screened supplicants into the Inner Sanctum for a consultation. In 1993, they queued for the chance to represent the "official" pyjamas, boardgame, Nintendo game, health socks, health drink, track suit, athletic shorts, polo shirts, colour film, bank, gasoline company . . . even a Montreal Canadiens credit card. Name a product, and see if we can't slap the old CH on it for mega-bucks. (Feel peckish after a robust NHL game at the Forum; maybe all those penalty box scenes with the Quaker Oats ads splashed above the heads of the belligerents have left you with a craving for good old stick-to-the-ribs porridge.)

Name an item and some enterprising soul would make a fortune slapping an official logo on it, and selling the bejeezus ouf of it. As this book went to press, the Walt Disney Co. which owns the Mighty Ducks of Anaheim, California, and which wrote the book on marketing before Snow White decided she was a sucker for height-challenged males, was preparing to sell the living heck (this is Disney) out of the Mighty Ducks — The Team. Major retailers from coast to coast in North America — not the least of whom was K-Mart — were awaiting their millions of dollars' worth of Mighty Duck inventory. Nobody wanted to bet, however, on whether Daffy Duck's beak would supplant the purple and black of the Colorado Rockies in the hearts of fickle sports fans.

When F-X Seigneur joined the Canadiens in 1984, he had set about establishing a long-term marketing policy for the club. The situation recalled "Tay Pay" Gorman's arrival in Montreal in 1934, when he had revived the "incidentals" — advertising, concessions and  sales of the game program, and put the Forum back on the road to financial respectability. Seigneur's job was to take a club that had become too staid and distant from its fans and return it to the people who paid the shot by upgrading and updating those same areas.

The Forum as High Church was out, came the official edict. "No more comparisons of the Forum with the Vatican," team president Ronald Corey told Seigneur when he joined the team. "This isn't a church. People are allowed to make noise and enjoy themselves."

The team president immediately went out and practised what he preached by unabashedly becoming the team's Superfan. During the 1986 playoffs, Corey startled many observers by reaching over and patting players on the back, yelling and gesticulating at stoic officials, and generally comporting himself with the decorum of a rabid fan fully dedicated to the parent company's two major properties, hockey and hops.

Seven years later, during the 1993 playoffs, Ronald's act was so familiar that there was a rumour of a new "over-under" bet on press row as the final game with Los Angeles wound down. The scuttlebutt was that either of the excitable Corey or the equally excitable Demers would mess up in their post-siren antics, kissing each other passionately and shaking hands with their wives before joining the players on the ice for a group grope.

Until Corey's arrival, the team president's position had been primarily ceremonial, and entailed sitting quietly behind the Canadiens' bench and maintaining decorum while all around were losing their heads. No more executive hand-sitting, Corey said.

One way to make the team more accessible to the fans was to bring the players to the people. The Canadiens had kept their faithful on starvation rations in the past, deigning only to distribute Molson Brewery calendars and mini-schedules, and to sign the occasional deal with a corn syrup manufacturer for coupon redemption of player pictures. The New Canadiens became marketing oriented, from Corey on down, and the *Club de Hockey Canadien* plunged into the burgeoning world of sports promotion. The small stand in closet-tight quarters in the southwest corner of the ground level of the Forum — that had made pennies with a few basic "souvenirs" — one or two models of hat, shirt, sweater and some pennants — now became a major emporium with all manners of merchandise available for sale, just in time for the Canadiens to win their '86 Stanley Cup.

Strategically situated mini-stands sprouted throughout the building to hawk pennants, banners, crests, mini-sticks in wood and plastic, and player cards. Within a year, there were Canadiens boutiques in shopping malls all over the metropolitan area, as well as at the airport, and deals were being negotiated with corporations such as Kraft Foods and Coca-Cola, and a major supermarket chain for special collector edition shirts, collector buttons and place mats.

The money changers invaded the Temple and the Temple was no more — except when it suited the purpose of the New Canadiens to evoke its exalted status, that is. Corey reasoned that if people from all over the world would travel far to to visit such famous Quebec shrines as St. Joseph's Oratory and St. Anne de Beaupré just outside Quebec City, then the Forum might prove the same draw for the religious hockey fan. So the Canadiens found themselves practising before 17,000 screaming kids (a joint promotion with a potato chip manufacturer) and the museum-cum-dressing room was opened to special tours, and the marketing race was on.

The Canadiens, thanks to Corey and Seigneur, got there just in time. By the time the Sharks, Lightning and Senators arrived on the collectibles scene, the Montreal Canadiens boutiques were in a position to benefit from sales of the new hockey sweaters and other paraphernalia.

Still, by 1993 Corey's vision of 1984 was as short of the mark as George Orwell's had been; neither man in his wildest dreams could have envisioned a marketing world gone berserk, with players signing autographs at card shows for a fee, with a developmentally challenged major league baseball player starting his own 1-900 telephone number, with super-hyper-mega-multi-stars like Michael Jordan and Shaquille O'Neil signing long-term representation and endorsement contracts for major corporations that would bring them in excess of $30 million a year, far and above their paltry salaries at $5 or $6 million per annum.

Between 1986 and 1993, the world discovered what "Bo Knows," saw Michael soar for Coca-Cola, only to go higher for Gatorade and play a Superman game of Horse with Larry Bird for a Big Mac, watched as O'Neil endured yet another Shaq Attack, and waited at home for Wayne Gretzky to deliver their Domino's Pizza (a quarter of a billion sold in 1992).

By 1993, teal and black and silver were the in-colours, worn religiously by upper-middle-class kids from Winnipeg to their less fortunate counterparts from Los Angeles' East-Side Barrio, and everywhere in-between on the continent, economically and geographically. North American teens, males and females, became walking billboards . . . a White Sox hat above a Rockies baseball shirt, over Raiders track pants, and $200 running shoes that either pumped you up, or prepared you to just to do it. And it was not unusual to see dad doing the groceries on Saturday morning in his Bulls jacket, or big sister heading out on a date that same evening in her satin Lakers outfit.

By 1993, the National Hockey League had gone from a league with two or three departments to a corporation with divisions like Communications Group (public relations) and NHL Enterprises Inc. (formerly the marketing department). And everybody involved in hockey paid for this change in orientation, from the stick manufacturers to the skate makers, and the guys who made the shirts, gloves, pants, socks and helmets. Those who balked were forced to black out their corporate logo, especially during televised games.

In 1986, F-X Seigneur could see only the tip of the iceberg, but he instinctively knew that the huge ice floe looming over his kayak was the tip, and that his job was to ensure that the Canadiens would obtain their fair share of what was going to become an economic pie of *Guinness Book* proportions.

A curious thing about passive consumers; the more you give them, the more aggressive they get. That meant providing more of a show at the Forum and taking the Cup to the people whenever possible which, of course, meant winning it. A new clock/scoreboard went up in the summer of 1985 and fans returning for the new season were greeted with a Snoopy-like dog leading cheers from his perch inside the inverted "CH," an animated "wave" that was synchronized with the Forum organist, and penalty-call cartoons.

And if the Forum got a little too quiet, the board and the organist would try to stir up the crowd with upbeat music and an exhortation of *"Bruit! Noise." Mon dieu,* is nothing sacred? Would they turn the Forum into a rink in Pittsburgh? The purists hated it, of course. One of the reasons the Forum had been so imposing in the past was that poor play by the home team would often be greeted with glacial silence, a big chill that was more intimidating than 10,000 boos.

These were new times. Late in one lacklustre 1985 game, the Canadiens were ahead by a goal when the scoreboard and organist conspired to start a wave. The mindless thousands stood up and waved their arms on cue (Pavlov; does that name ring a bell?) for a dozen or so passes around the stands; the noise reaching a crescendo totally inconsistent with the lack of action on the ice.

"Goddamn it!" swore one long-time regular and diehard in Section 32 of the whites. "I hope the other guys score just to stop this shit." He was more embarrassed by the *arriviste* attitude of his seatmates than worried for the outcome of the contest. The words were hardly out of his mouth when the puck was in the Canadiens' net. The goal had the desired effect; the fans turned their attention to the game at hand, almost guiltily.

"That's more like it," he snorted, all righteous indignation and pining for the cathedral presence of the past. During another game, the organist and scoreboard teamed up for another nauseating rendition of the "Hey, Hey Goodbye" song, played in every rink in the league when the home team has a lead late in the game. In this case, however, enthusiasm overcame judgment; eight minutes remained in a close contest and salutary song was squelched in mid-note by an opposition goal.

"He doesn't play that song any more," a visibly exercised Seigneur mentioned a few days later. New Age Marketing did not mean trying to rub the visitor's face in it. But F-X was not willing to listen to the complaints of the Old Guard, either. "We have given the team and the Forum back to the fans.

This was not done as a spur-of-the-moment thing. We work on a long-term basis and everything we have done so far has been researched carefully."

By 1993, there were no traces of the Old Guard. Curiously, there were no traces of the team organist either, the latter having been replaced by a disk jockey spinning tunes during every pause in play. It was not an improvement.

The Forum had become a thoroughly modern marketing emporium, with thousands of dollars worth of advertising on its boards and on the playing surface itself, and advertising and concession dollars squeezed into every nook and cranny.

And it was still not enough. In 1991, the word came down on the supreme marketing move by the Canadiens . . . the team would have to leave the most famous building in the sport.

The greatest irony of the sports marketing monster created by the major leagues was that it had begun to feed on itself. The Monster with No Name professional sports had created — a.k.a the mega-marketing sports franchise and communications entity — could not survive anymore in such a restrictive building as the venerable Forum. Crowds of 17,500 or 18,000 weren't good enough anymore; there would have to be 23,000 or 25,000. More importantly, sixty or seventy luxury boxes bringing in anywhere from $100,000 to $250,000 per year was not enough, either. There would have to be two or three banks of luxury boxes, in prime viewing areas, so marketing and salespeople could entertain their fellow marketing and salespeople from other companies in relative splendour, at huge and generally tax-deductible expense.

Word to this effect were parroted all over the major leagues as team owners in all sports sought incredible concessions from municipal authorities for expensive renovations to existing facilities, or heretofore unheard of ancillary benefits, such as control of concessions and parking revenues wherever possible. "Build me a rink, ball field, park, multi-purpose entertainment centre" became the great cry in cities all over North America. And if the city and its fans were unable to hold their noses long enough to say "Yes sir, yes sir, three bags full," the owner of the team or teams in question would threaten to leave for greener pastures. Immediately or sooner.

That the Canadiens won the Stanley Cup in 1993 was to the glory of the league and its most-storied franchise. That the league allowed Norm Green to move his franchise out of tradition-rich hockey territory in Minnesota and into the Texas humidity of Dallas, and then backed the insufferable Peter Pocklington as he threatened to move his Oilers out of Edmonton, was an indelible stain on its so-called commitment to hockey fans everywhere.

In 1993, the NHL and its new president Gary Bettman demonstrated clearly that the game on the ice will forever take second place in the future; marketing products and providing advertising space for Corporate America has become the primary bottom-line consideration of the NHL. No matter that a building that epitomized the sport and its development in the twentieth century was still functional, or that a city that was one of the richest cradles of U.S.-born talent still remained committed to the sport; the words on the pinstriped letterhead were unequivocal — there would have to be a new rink for Montreal, just like Boston, Hartford, Quebec City, Vancouver, Pittsburgh, Toronto, St. Louis, Chicago and almost all the rest. Just comparing the meticulously maintained Forum to slums like the Boston Garden, Maple Leaf Gardens and the St. Louis Arena smacked of sacrilege.

Conclusion: By the early 1990s, the suits had taken over the National Hockey League.

In the first edition of this book, we wrote about F-X Seigneur in his full splendour in 1986: *F.X. Seigneur is eating lunch and smiling a lot, the ever-congenial host. Occasionally we are interrupted as someone comes up to shake his hand.*

*The Forum and the Canadiens are different these days. They march to the tune of the 1980s and will continue the process of updating and modernization as long as Corey, Seigneur and company are around.*

*"We're into long-term plans and corporate objectives now," said Seigneur. "For sure, we will enjoy this summer, but we are already hard at work on next year and the year after."*

*They know that they are a corporation and operate not unlike others at the top of the heap. How corporate are they? The Montreal Canadiens are cited in a book titled* The 100 Best Corporations to Work for in Canada.

*The Lions in Winter Company Limited.*

*Because winter is never far away in Montreal.*

In 1993, we can update that a bit, as all of the Corey-Seigneur marketing plans have come to fruition, and more so.

It has become Lions in Winter Enterprises, Inc. — have team logo will travel. That is never more evident than on the night of March 21 when the Canadiens-Nordiques match-up before a full house of 17,959 fans unbelievably took second place to a beer commercial. Black Ice — Canadian Ice everywhere else in Canada because Quebec marketers are ashamed to use words like "Canadian" in their province — was launched literally in the middle of the NHL game. The boards in front of the Canadiens bench, the central camera position in any Forum hockey game, were done in the stark grey, black and white of the new product's logo. Television commercials were aired in black and white, and often the colours of the teams would stay on grey scale for many seconds after resumption of play.

In more than a quarter century of sponsoring hockey telecasts in Canada, Molson Breweries had never taken such an intrusive role in the broadcast of a game. This night, however, they went over the line, but the marketers were far from apologetic. In fact, they were crowing about their coup the following day and weeks when market surveys showed one of the highest product recall statistics ever for a Quebec launch. A survey of 352 families showed a recognition factor of 61 per cent, figuratively off the scale in market research terms. Extrapolate that over a television audience of 1.5 million and results jumped off the graph: one in seven Quebeckers would recall the product after a single promotion on a single hockey game. And Black Ice wasn't just being introduced on the Forum ice. Needless to say, the managers of other products stood up and saluted that flag.

It bodes well for marketing in the future. Less so, for the hockey purist.

## Part II — Downstairs

If the selling of the game changed substantially in the seven years between Cups in Montreal, the on-ice product and the game itself had found a wormhole that transported it light years away in the same interim.

For the Montreal Canadiens, the changes began happening on the flight home from Calgary, in the early morning hours of Sunday, May 25, 1986. As described elsewhere in this book, one of the most enduring images of the 1986 Cup-winning team was the "Alcatraz gang" celebrating at 30,000 feet. There were Claude Lemieux, Gaston Gingras and Serge Boisvert, all important contributors to Cup No. 23, showing no signs of tiring from celebrations in the wee hours. A few seats behind them, to the right, John Kordic, Craig Ludwig and Petr Svoboda wore their serious party faces while their usual howling partner and inspirational leader, Chris Chelios, uncharacteristically sat quietly beside his fiancée Tracey and behaved himself. Others like Shayne Corson, Stéphane Richer and Lucien Deblois, who saw little action in the final series, were restrained, as were veteran contributors Bob Gainey, Larry Robinson, Bobby Smith, Ryan Walter, Rick Green and Mats Naslund.

That Canadiens team — actually there were enough players to make two — was equal parts young and old and appeared ready to lay a longer-term claim on the Stanley Cup, even though many league observers claimed that the 1986 victory was a fluke. Up front, Jean Perron, the second rookie coach of the Canadiens to win a Stanley Cup, was accepting congratulations from all and sundry.

Few members of the organization could know that seven short years later, only Guy Carbonneau and Patrick Roy would be around to hoist No. 24 to their lips, and that the coach receiving the accolades would be twice removed from Jean Perron. Fewer could know that one of their number, John Kordic, would have died under suspicious circumstances, snuffing his life like a fiery roman candle in his last few years.

As well, few Canadiens, upstairs or down, could begin to believe that the league would be so different by 1993 — what with three expansions, the collapse of the Soviet Union and the influx of Russian players throughout the league, and the exploding marketing of hockey which would send their salaries soaring through the stratosphere.

The process of change, of course, started two minutes after the Stanley Cup parade. The Stanley Cup victory had served to obscure one fact: Jean Perron was not the man to coach this team. Serge Savard knew it, and had juggled that knowledge during the second half of 1985-86 with the fear that a team that changed its coach late in the season would not have much of a chance in post-season play.

"During that St. Louis meeting, I told the veterans that Perron was staying and that they would have to deliver," Savard reminisces. "We won the Cup, but the problem still wasn't resolved. The difference was, I was stuck — I couldn't change a coach who had won the Stanley Cup. It's not that Jean wasn't a nice guy, but he could not handle that group of players. They didn't have any respect for him."

Filling Jacques Lemaire's shoes had been a tall order. In less than two seasons at the helm, Lemaire had won the loyalty and respect of his veterans, and they took care of the rookies.

"Jacques Lemaire had come to me in July 1985 and recommended Jean Perron, but by late in the first season, I knew he had done this because Jacques was so desperate to get out from behind the bench that he would have said anything. As for the players, changing Jacques Lemaire for Jean Perron was like changing a Cadillac for a Volkswagen. It was very hard for them to accept. Too many veterans went around saying 'Jacques would do it this way' or 'Jacques wanted us to do this in a certain situation' and it was very, very hard for Jean."

Savard purposely kept his former coach and current general manager of the AHL team in Sherbrooke away from the big team. In fact, Lemaire would not get close to a Montreal coach again until the arrival of Demers in 1992. Then again, Demers did not feel threatened by Lemaire.

While the Canadiens veterans seethed quietly, the media was happy — Perron was popular with them, always good for a quick quote or interview. Larry Robinson and Bob Gainey were the two senior members of the team, and they went back to the Scotty Bowman era. They had seen a lot of changes in personality and substance behind the bench.

Robinson admitted his mystification when he originally had discovered that Perron was to be named head coach. "I truthfully could not understand the appointment of Perron. In my mind, he didn't have the credentials and he hadn't shown anything special the previous year as an assistant coach." The lanky Norris Trophy defenseman claimed no personality conflicts with his coach, because "I found him to be a very nice, if shy, man. He was fair and aboveboard with me in all of our dealings, but he came into this job with a strike against him. He had not gained the respect of some of the veterans on the team and after three years, that attitude had spread throughout the room. That's what hurt in the long run."

Perron tried to enlist the veterans in his cause, with mixed results and, at best, an armed truce. However, a major thorn in his side was Chris Nilan, the volatile team policeman who was oil to Perron's water, and who also felt threatened by Perron's reliance on Kordic in that role. The players felt that Perron was afraid of Knucks and would let him get away with murder, while riding roughshod over those rookies who committed the same transgressions. When those rookies became second- and third-year players, they took up more space in the dressing room and their displeasure over their perceived mistreatment doomed Perron.

Perron's ambiguous dispensation of justice caused all sorts of friction and this came to a head during a West Coast road trip in 1988. The Habs had stunk out the Forum against Hartford on a Saturday, lost to the Oilers in Edmonton on Monday, and flown into Vancouver on Tuesday for a Wednesday night game. During the Tuesday morning skate, Nilan and Stéphane Richer bumped on the ice, and then erupted into a full-fledged fight. Nilan was happily thumping away at the temperamental scorer when team-mates intervened.

There were other incidents: Claude Lemieux and Perron in a public shouting match, John Kordic loudly upset in another, and Robinson himself expressing his displeasure at watching young stars Sergio Momesso and Kjell Dahlin sitting in the press box night after night while other, less effective players, were automatically pencilled into the lineup.

The Canadiens finished second to Hartford in 1987, but appeared to hit their stride en route to a second straight Cup in the playoffs. They swept the Bruins 4-0 in the first round, while the Nordiques upset the Whalers, and then downed their provincial rivals in seven games to advance to the Prince of Wales conference finals. After splitting the first two games in Philadelphia, the Habs returned home and promptly lost the next two, 4-3 and 6-3. Facing elimination, they again travelled to the City of Brotherly Love and humbled the Flyers 5-2.

And then, one of the oddest incidents in playoff history. During the pregame warm-up, Claude Lemieux had developed a little superstitious routine at the Forum. He would linger on the ice, long after the siren had gone and after the ice-making crew had come out, and then fire a puck into the opposing team's net. It was a harmless gesture, since outlawed by the league, but the Flyers noticed it and schemed to stop the practice. That night, to prevent this, Flyers backup goalie Chico Resch turned the net around as he and the last few team-mates left the ice to go to their dressing room. Undaunted, Lemieux skated down the ice and scored into the empty net. As he looked up, probably in amazement, several Flyers were converging, among them a borderline no-talent named Ed Hospodar who in eight seasons with the Rangers, Whalers, Flyers and North Stars had managed to scored 17 goals and 50 assists, while compiling 1,216 minutes in penalties.

Hospodar and Resch attacked Lemieux. The word got back to the dressing rooms and players in various stages of undress streamed out on the ice to do battle. In the aftermath of this incident, the Canadiens lost Lemieux, the scoring hero of the previous season's playoffs and an important contributor in the 1988 post season, with 13 points in 17 games. The Flyers had Hospodar expelled, a player who wasn't even scheduled to play in the game. League officials, desperate to appear unbiased, totally blew the call and the Flyers' pre-game strategy bore fruit. The Canadiens eventually lost the game 4-3, and the series, 4-2, and there were a lot of veterans in the room who were angry at Perron for not raising a ruckus with league officials over the dubious decision.

"That was the time to get all over them," said Robinson. "We were suckered, and so were they, but our coach was more worried with appearances than results."

The following season saw the Canadiens rebound to win the Adams Division, with a powerful season-ending drive that saw the team go undefeated in 15 games. Ironically, the streak coincided with a major victory for Perron — the trade of Chris Nilan to New York Rangers on January 27. Nilan had scored a mere 7 goals and 5 assists in 50 games, but had racked up a whopping 209 penalty minutes as his frustration with his coach was taken out on opponents. Whereas a veteran agitator had often take his adversaries to the sinbin with him in the past, now he was going solo, serving misconducts and sportsmanship minors, or taking two minors to his opponent's one. The Canadiens were suffering for it, and they were struggling through a terrible powerplay when they had the advantage. When Knucks left, the relief was palpable.

Finishing strongly at the end of the season, 9 points ahead of Boston, the Canadiens inexplicably began to struggle during the playoffs. They downed Hartford in six games in the division semi-final, but the series was much closer than the final result showed, and too close for teams that had finished 26 points apart during the regular season. Meanwhile, the Bruins were also struggling with the Sabres, winning in six games as well, and no one knew what to expect when the Adams Division final began on Monday, April 18.

One thing they couldn't predict was a power failure that took out most of the downtown core of Montreal, and halted the television broadcast of Montreal's 5-2 win over the Bruins. To their everlasting chagrin, staunch Canadiens fans got to see the next four games, all Boston wins, as the Canadiens took their earliest playoff exit in three years.

Boston clinched the series on Tuesday, April 26, with a 4-1 victory at the Forum. Twenty days later, on Monday, May 16, Jean Perron was fired.

"I told Jean that day — we had a very good discussion over a couple of hours — that I thought he would be a very good assistant coach, but I didn't think he could be a head coach, the kind of person who demanded respect and was able to act with authority," said Savard. "I don't think he believed what I was saying at the time, but I had no choice. Jean originally was hired as an assistant coach in Montreal, and events conspired to have him become head coach."

Agree or disagree, Perron moved on to the Nordiques as assistant general-manager, and stepped in to replace Ron Lapointe behind the bench when the Verdun native was stricken with cancer. By season's end, he faced a rebellion in Quebec too, and the following season was a talk-show host in that city.

"The Montreal media were all over us when I let Jean go, but not one of these guys came back to say they were wrong when he was fired by the Nordiques," says Savard.

Savard, who had little choice in firing Perron because veterans Larry Robinson and Rick Green had threatened retirement if he returned, made no excuses for originally promoting Perron because every assistant who came to the team was told that he was hired with the hope that he could become a head coach one day. That was Savard's policy, and it stood in most cases, with a few exceptions such as Jacques Laperrière who steadfastly refused to be considered for the top position every time the opportunity arose.

When Perron was fired, the coach from Sherbrooke stepped in. The veterans on the team knew little of Pat Burns but what they had read in the papers; a former policeman with the Gatineau force, he had come up through the junior ranks with Wayne Gretzky's Hull Olympiques, and been an assistant coach to Bert Templeton with the Canadian Junior team that was disqualified from the 1986 World Championship after a brawl with the Soviets in Piestany, Czechoslovakia.

"Every year, I asked my people who was the top junior coach out there, and especially who was the best guy in Quebec," said Savard. "It was unanimous; everybody said Pat

Burns. I had also been considering Pierre Creamer for a full-time position and we went with Burns, and Creamer went to Pittsburgh. I didn't hire him as a policeman, but Pat came to Montreal with a reputation of a tough guy."

Burns had a strike against him, however. The French media was upset that their favorite had been fired and, although Burns had been raised in the St. Henri district a mere stone's throw from the Forum and was fluently bilingual, he became the whipping boy of several media commentators in his first year.

And it didn't take long for the flagellation festival to begin in earnest when the team got off to a 4-7-1 record in October, but Burns and the Canadiens turned it around with a 10-2-2 November and and 11-1-3 December to race out in front of the league standings with the Flames.

Savard's tinkering with the team contributed greatly to the turnaround, as did Burns's coaching, and two deals on the same day, November 7, would serve the club well in the future. In the first deal, Jean-Jacques Daigneault was acquired from Philadelphia for Scott Sandelin, a college-trained defenseman and Hobey Baker Award winner who never was going to make it in Montreal. The Habs were acquiring a reclamation project as well, an elegant skater who had had trouble breaking into the lineup in Vancouver and Philadelphia. Still, he had played for Jacques Lemaire in the Quebec Major Junior League and the former Canadiens coach vouched for him. Daigneault would spend the 1988-89 season in Sherbrooke before becoming a regular on Montreal's defense the following year.

The other trade was even more timely, and came compliments of Gord Stellick, John Brophy and Harold Ballard in Toronto. Going to the Leafs was a draft choice and a disgruntled John Kordic, a player who had increasingly alienated himself from his team-mates and the Canadiens' executive with his lifestyle and his vocal bitterness in the room. Coming to Montreal was a gazelle with a slapshot, Ross Courtnall.

Languishing on the bench because of a coach with a Jurassic Era mindset, Courtnall had scored only 1 goal and 1 assist in nine games, after seasons of 22, 29 and 23 with the

Leafs. So relieved was he to get out of Toronto, this perpetual-motion machine went all out for the Canadiens after his acquisition, contributing 22 goals and 17 assists in 64 games, and another 8 goals and 5 assists in 21 playoff contests. "The best part of acquiring Rusty was watching his speed scare the other teams half to death," laughed Larry Robinson. "You could see he loved being here, right from the beginning, and there was no question who won the trade." In 46 games with the Leafs, Kordic contributed 1 goal, 2 assists and 185 penalty minutes, and to the demise of both Brophy and Stellick.

Courtnall's addition gave the Canadiens the fifth-most potent offense in the league. While Calgary, Los Angeles and Edmonton in the Smythe, and Pittsburgh in the Patrick scored more goals, no team was as proficient on defense and Courtnall helped there too, joining the penalty-killing squad. The team had turned over a large number of players in the three years since the Stanley Cup win in Calgary. And a lot of the players moved were young ones, players who had been expected to play several years in Montreal, among them Tom Kurvers, Steve Penney, Lucien Deblois, Steve Rooney, David Maley, Serge Boisvert, Gaston Gingras, Nilan, Sergio Momesso, backup goalie Vincent Riendeau, Kordic and Mike Lalor. Newly arrived on the scene were Shayne Corson, Eric Desjardins, Donald Dufresne, Brent Gilchrist, Mike Keane and backup netminder Bryan Hayward.

"A lot of people don't realize that we turned over our team twice in the seven years between the two Stanley Cups," says Savard. "You can't let a team get old; you have to keep renewing it with good young players, and that's why we have a farm system. A lot of the young guys hate it when they have to play in the AHL, but two or three years later, after they've established themselves in the NHL, they thank you for it. They know that we'll be patient and let them develop, if they are going to develop, and that only helps them in the long run."

While the Canadiens had no one in the NHL's top twenty scorers, their offense came from many sources as eight players scored 20 or more goals, and eleven players had 40 or more points. They had size, speed, solid defense and goalkeeping, and with players like Skrudland, Lemieux, McPhee, Keane and Corson up front, enough toughness to play the physical game.

Leading the way in toughness was Burns, a man who the players felt was their man. He was tough, he rarely forgave egregious errors and certainly refused to accept anything but total effort. Even so, the players liked and respected him, and responded, and the Canadiens finished the season second overall in the league, three points behind Calgary, and 27 ahead of the Bruins atop the Adams Division (115-88).

That season also provided a rich harvest of league awards for the team, a rarity for Montreal, as Burns captured the Jack Adams Award as top coach; Roy and Hayward shared the Jennings; Roy also won the Vezina; Guy Carbonneau owned the Frank J. Selke Trophy as top defensive forward; and Chris Chelios won his first of two Norris trophies as the league's premier rearguard.

Thus, it was no surprise when the Canadiens blitzed Hartford 4-0 and Boston 4-1 to escape from the Adams Division, and then ousted the Philadelphia Flyers in six games, avenging the 1987 series. In the last game, a 4-2 Montreal win in Philly, goalie Ron Hextall lost it, attacking Chelios against the side boards and trying to pummel him with his blocker, his response to a vicious high stick Chelios had laid on the Flyers' Brian Propp the previous game. Hextall began the following season with a twelve-game suspension, a grievous punishment for his team considering the Flyers would miss a final playoff spot in the Patrick by two points. That incident, and others like it, would contribute to Hextall's premature exit from Philadelphia.

Like 1986, the Calgary matchup was an even one, but this time the Flames prevailed, four games to two. Like the previous Calgary final, the end result did not reflect the closeness of the series, but Savard, Burns et. al could rest easy that summer knowing that they had accomplished much that season.

But they didn't, or couldn't, rest.

We met Pat Burns in mid-June of 1989, in a downtown parking lot, ironically the former site of the Victoria Rink, the original hockey facility in Montreal whose 200-foot by 85-foot measurements dictated the dimensions of modern NHL ice surfaces. It was a humid, June Montreal afternoon, threatening thundershowers, and far, far away from the stresses of the NHL wars.

He was off to meet friends for a social drink but, as we discovered, there was no leaving the job at the office, even in the off-season. Everywhere Pat Burns went he carried the Canadiens' media monkey on his back. NHL Coach of the Year, a success with the fans and team executive (his contract would be extended prior to the new season), the former policeman was proving to be exceedingly thin skinned.

"Maybe we'll sit down and do my book one day," he offered, showing his teeth in a feral grin. "I've already got a title for it: 'Condemned to Win — The Life and Times of a Coach of the Montreal Canadiens.' Think it'll sell?"

This was the coach of a winning team? What might adversity bring? It wasn't too long before Pat Burns found out. He never returned to the Cup final again at the helm of the Canadiens, dropping three straight divisional finals to the Bruins between 1990 and 1992.

His remaining three seasons saw Serge Savard complete his retooling of the Canadiens. Gone in the fall of 1989 were veteran defencemen Robinson and Green, the former to Los Angeles after a salary dispute, the latter to premature retirement, and later to the Islanders, also over money issues. Within the next year, other veteran leaders departed, among them Bobby Smith, back to Minnesota, Ryan Walter, to his home province of British Columbia, and Mats Naslund to Europe.

Supposedly ready to step forward were the new leaders of the team, twin captains Chris Chelios and Guy Carbonneau, and young veterans like Shayne Corson, Stéphane Richer, Claude Lemieux and Petr Svoboda. It would never work out, and by the time that Jacques Demers joined the team in 1992, only Carbonneau would remain.

"Pat came to the Canadiens with the reputation of being a tough guy; he came and the right time and I think he did a helluva good job for us for a couple years," said Savard. "But the same thing happened to Pat at the end, as had happened with Jean Perron. He lost the respect of a lot of players, for a lot of different reasons. That's why coaches come and go. I think it is very hard to coach a team for more than three or four years."

What Burns discovered to his chagrin after the departure of Smith, Walter, Green and Robinson, was that the young veterans were not ready to assume the mantle of leadership. Chelios, Corson and Svoboda were notorious party animals, and the media were full of their escapades. And, like a famous veteran catcher with the Montreal Expos who had to be let go by team management because all of the rookie pitchers were showing up for games with hellacious hangovers, this trio had a way of taking young and impressionable team-mates with them down the proverbial garden path.

Lemieux and Richer were much more subdued in their extracurricular activities, but their problems stemmed from on-ice performance. It go so bad that Burns and the temperamental Lemieux could not share the same room, while Richer was as erratic a superstar you might find in the NHL, scoring 50, 25, 51 and 31 goals in consecutive seasons. A tough, physical forward with one of the hardest shots in hockey, great deceptive moves and excellent speed, Richer would generally leave one or two of his talents at home on most game nights, driving his coach to distraction. Both native western Quebeckers, Lemieux and Richer both wanted out of Montreal and away from the pressure cooker.

Chelios was traded to Chicago in a blockbuster deal for Denis Savard in June, 1990; Smith was dealt to Minnesota four weeks later and Lemieux got his wish in September, as Savard took a chance on another wounded bird, Sylvain Turgeon of the New Jersey Devils. Richer joined Lemieux in New Jersey, the following September in one of Savard's best-ever deals, straight up for Kirk Muller.

"I realized the problems Pat was having so I tried my best to make deals that would fix those situations, and bring some excellent talent to Montreal. In the Chelios case, we needed a high-scoring forward with good ability to put something back into our powerplay, and that's why we got Denis Savard. And to be fair to Denis, he did quite well for us that first year."

Perhaps he did, but the Denis Savard who came to Montreal after his share of difficulties with Mike Keenan in Chicago was no longer the whirling dervish or human highlight film he had been with the Hawks. He had lost a step, and also had difficulty in a system that asked him to visit his own defensive zone once in a while during hockey games. Savard remained in Montreal for three seasons, and by his third was a marginal player, alternating between winger on the fourth line and centre on the fifth. At season's end in 1993, and after fulfilling his primary career objective of winning the Stanley Cup, Denis was on his way to Tampa Bay. Chelios, the winner of his second Norris Trophy in the same year, remained in Chicago.

The Lemieux trade for Turgeon was a write-off as well, with the feisty former Canadien turning in seasons of 30, 41 and 30 goals for the Devils in three years, to Turgeon's 5 and 9 goals in a total of 75 games over two seasons with Montreal, and another 25 goals with the expansion Ottawa Senators in the third.

"We had no choice with Claude; he had to be traded to bring peace to the team, but nobody seemed to want him. His reputation had preceded him and clubs all over the league weren't interested, even though they knew he could still score a lot of goals and go into the corners."

All of these changes boded poorly, especially when Corson and Svoboda refused to lead the club.

"Petr was too selfish a player by then, and we had to trade him. And Shayne, it turns out, was more of a follower than a leader. Shayne was the kind of player who drives coaches crazy. He always did what he was asked, and was always agreeable to work with. But, there were many nights when he didn't show up, and we had the impression that we would be watching him wasting his ability for many years to come. Jacques Demers asked me to give Corson one more chance when I hired him, but I said, 'No, that's it. I'm not going to give him a chance to drive you crazy,' and I traded him to Edmonton a few days later."

These players let Burns down in different ways. Some he asked be moved, because of their attitude of lack of commitment and results on the ice. Others had to be moved for team unity; and still others he wanted kept. In the end, Burns joined them in the exodus out of Montreal.

Still, with all of the adversity of the last two years, many sports observers were surprised to hear that a coach who received a vote of confidence just weeks before had resigned and was moving to Toronto.

"I think the media closest to the team were more surprised when I appointed Pat again as head coach, a few days after we got beat by Boston," said Savard. "I didn't think that he deserved that treatment at the time, but I knew he had lost the respect of a lot of players on the club, and when that happens, it very, very hard for a guy to function. I don't know why the same techniques and methods will work for three or four years, and then suddenly not work anymore with the same players . . . maybe it gets boring."

When Savard replaced Burns with Demers, he again was sure that his team would respond to the new coach.

"Jacques always was my only real candidate for the job. He was a motivator, and we had a bunch of young players who could use that approach after our previous season. "

Some major alterations had to be made before the Canadiens embarked on their new season, and it took the managing director only 17 days to radically change his team, and launch it on the road to another Stanley Cup. On August 14, Mike McPhee was Minnesota-bound for a fifth-round draft choice, and defenseman Sylvain Lefebvre left six days later, en route to Toronto for yet another draft selection.

The two blockbusters came on August 27 and 31. On the 27th, Corson, Brent Gilchrist and WHL draft choice Vladimir Vujtek moved to Edmonton for Vincent Damphousse, a Montreal native who had been the top scorer with both the Maple Leafs and the Edmonton Oilers before his arrival in Montreal. Four days later, Savard announced the arrival of veteran sniper Brian Bellows from Minnesota for Russ Courtnall. Bellows had been Minnesota's first-round draft pick in 1982 and No. 2 overall, and responded with 342 goals and 380 assists in ten seasons with the North Stars. He was available because Bob Gainey felt he couldn't play the more defensive style demanded by him. Courtnall was available because, after falling in love with a Hollywood actress whom he later married, and suffering two injuries that kept him out of the lineup for all but 27 games in 1991-92, he tallied only 7 goals and 14 points. In the playoffs, he was even more brutal, with a single goal and 1 assist in ten games, though his overtime goal in the seventh game of the Adams Division semi-final eliminated Hartford and allowed the Canadiens to advance.

It all came together in the playoffs, with Damphousse leading the Canadiens with 23 points on 11 goals and 12 assists, just ahead of Muller's 10-7 — 17 and Bellows's 6-9 — 15, the same order of finish during the regular season with Damphousse, 97, Muller, 94, Bellows, 88 and Lebeau, 80, demonstrating an offensive capability that had long abandoned the Canadiens. Other kids with names like Dionne, DiPietro, Ronan, LeClair, Brunet, Brisebois and Bélanger also contributed under the new Demers system.

And, after a hiatus of seven years, Stanley came home. The "downstairs" bunch had been heard from once again.

*At 10 a.m., LeClair looked out in amazement at the hundreds of fans patiently waiting for their chance to touch the Cup, pose for a picture and garner an autograph. The event has been scheduled to begin at 11 o'clock and carry through until 4 o'clock in the afternoon, and as many as 2,000 Vermonters were expected, fully one-fifth the population of his hometown. Little did LeClair know that some of these fans he would meet that day had come from all over the North Country, from Syracuse, Tupper Lake, and Chateaugay in New York, to Georgia, Johnson, and Winooski, Vermont, and even from southern Quebec.*

*LeClair looked over the crowd and, his incredulity evident, sighed, "We'd better get started." Almost six hours of sauna-like conditions, and many, many glasses of soft drink later, an exhausted hockey player declares St. Alban's Feelgood Day to have been a success. Some 10,000 people have come by to say hi to their favourite hockey hero, and Canadiens hats and shirts were in evidence everywhere. This sports marketing was tough work, maybe even tougher than scoring a pair of overtime goals in La-La-Land. But the rewards were there, too, because Big John had managed to do something he usually can't do, even when delivering thundering bodychecks against Bruins in Boston Garden: he had single-*

*handedly pushed back the northern limits of New England to at least the southern Vermont border.*

*For now, Big John and the Habs rule in the North Country. On both sides of the border, both upstairs and down.*

# 18

# Patrick Roy
# The Lion at the Gate

*"L'audace, encore l'audace, toujours l'audace"*
*("Audacity, more audacity, always audacity")*

No other epigram more aptly describes the Gallic response to adversity than the immortal words uttered by Georges Jacques Danton during the height of the French Revolution, as he exhorted the lower classes to throw off the yoke of the nobility and storm the Bastille.

And the fact that its famous author would live that philosophy right up to his last moments at the guillotine is of no little consequence, either.

Ironically, a seemingly innocuous gesture by a great French-speaking athlete in the spring of 1993 gave that noble phrase new life; however, on this occasion, it was his Bastille that was under siege.

The scene was pure Hollywood — actually Inglewood — a freeway jaunt from Tinseltown, and much of the glitterati were in attendance at the Great Western Forum that hot evening in early June, including a former president of the United States, Ronald Reagan.

The Montreal Canadiens, having taken a 2-1 lead in the Stanley Cup final with a mathematics-defying ninth straight overtime win two nights previous, were back on their heels as the Los Angeles Kings attacked in waves. The game was tied 2-2 late in the third period, and the team in silver-and-white swirled relentlessly around the fortress defended by a tall, thin man in the signature scarlet of *Le Club de Hockey Canadien*, the most famous professional ice hockey team in the world.

The Kings played with controlled desperation: a loss meant returning to Montreal down 3-1 in the best-of-seven series, and an opportunity for the Canadiens to win the Cup before their rabid fans. This was a veteran team that so far had handled adversity well in post-season play, disposing of Calgary in six games, after losing two of the first three games; eliminating a much larger and more physical Vancouver Canucks which had owned them during the season; and then facing elimination twice against the Toronto Maple Leafs before pulling out a seventh-game win.

Most of the credit for the resurgence of the Kings could be laid at the feet of rookie coach Barry Melrose who proved to be a genius of motivation, and a rare coach who could earn the respect of his team. Anxious to take pressure off his players after the disappointing loss in the third game of the final, he held a family party at the Great Western Forum on Sunday, June 6. Instead of Wayne Gretzky and Tony Granato whirling about in those endless waves and descending on Kelly Hrudey in the team's one hundredth or so workout of the year, Ty Gretzky, age 3, shared the ice with Dominic Granato, age 2, the birthday boy, while their dads tried to recoup.

That tiny oasis of tranquility was ancient history late in the third period on Monday night. With an hysterical Hollywood crowd ballyhooing theirs on to victory — not so laid back as they would like us pale-skinned Easterners to think — and with millions more following the game on television, there was a sudden flurry at the edge of the Montreal goal crease. Two of the best snipers in the league, Luc Robitaille and Tomas Sandstrom, each apparently had the go-ahead goal on his stick only to be thwarted by a man whose name, ironically, means "King" in French.

As Patrick Roy froze the puck and the referee's whistle sounded a stop in play, the camera zoomed in for a close-up of adversaries Roy and Sandstrom, the latter bent over double, exhaustion and frustration etched on his face, gasping for air. And that face was scant inches away from the man who was the root cause of his most recent disappointment.

With millions watching, Roy looked up and did the unthinkable in a sport where talking trash is anathema: he gave Sandstrom a mischievous little smile . . . and a roundhouse wink.

Game over, Mr. Sandstrom.

A minuscule movement of Roy's facial muscles told Sandstrom and the world that the most storied team in professional sport was a dead, solid lock to win a twenty-fourth National Hockey League championship. The Canadiens on the bench and those others lining up for the crucial face-off already knew the Cup was theirs; during the previous intermission Roy had stood in a dressing room which was starting to exhibit signs of panic, and announced: "Just get one goal; they aren't going to score on me anymore."

The stuff of modern-day sports legend, he was true to his word.

Patrick Roy is one of those few people with the good fortune — or curse — depending on your point of view, who will go to their grave looking too young for their age. Tall and gangling when not swathed in his Koho Revolution goaltending kit . . . straw blond hair . . . twinkling blue eyes . . . a Stan Laurel smile without the sadness behind it, he will forever be The Shy Kid.

On this midsummer day, he shyly tries to dissect his greatest exploit, and while he is pleased to have been selected the Fourth Lion, his shyness keeps him back from a self admission that the accolade is well deserved.

"The Fourth Lion? I'm honoured." Actually Patrick, as he is known by millions of francophones, is embarrassed beyond belief. (One of life's little ironies is that while English North America makes such an effort to properly pronounce Roy [phonetically R-Wah], to French North America he is simply Patrick.)

To all of North America and the hockey world, what he should be, and should have been for several years by now, is recognized as the best goalie of this generation.

Many Canadian hockey analysts have had a problem with that in recent years, especially those in Ontario and points west. With Wayne Gretzky in gentle decline, brought about by the inexorable combination of a bad back, long career and the aging process, Mario Lemieux of Ville Emard, Quebec, stepped into his rightful place as the best forward in hockey in the 1990s. He dotted the i's and crossed the t's on that statement with two Stanley Cup wins and a pair of Conn Smythes as playoff MVP in 1990-91 and 1991-92. And then came the incredible 1992-93 season, the cancer diagnosis and treatment, and the scoring championship won on a half-season's play.

Eric Lindros notwithstanding, Mario Lemieux is the offensive player with the most impact in the first half of this decade.

And until Brian Leetch wrested the Norris Trophy away from him in 1991-92, a cruel joke to the knowledgeable hockey observer (try a mere +25 on 102 points and a +5 in the playoffs when the Rangers plummeted to the real world), Raymond Bourque of St. Laurent, Quebec, was universally acclaimed as the best defenseman in the NHL, winning the trophy four times between 1986 and 1991.

And as the 1990s dawned, the best goaltender in the league was Patrick Roy of St. Foy, Quebec.

What? The best forward, best defenseman and best goalie in this period were Quebeckers? There goes a lot of OHL and WHL mythology right down the drain.

As Sgt. Joe Friday would say, "Just the facts, ma'am."

Since 1969, and excluding the 1993 draft in Quebec City, National Hockey League teams had selected a total of 4,983 players, with the major single source being the Ontario Hockey League at 1,221 players. Next came the Western Hockey League at 967, and then the third member of the Canadian Hockey League, right? In the immortal words of the "other Wayne" — NOT!

Then came U.S. colleges with 741, international leagues with 568, U.S. high schools with 529 . . . and then the Quebec Major Junior Hockey League with 520. In its best year, 1977, the Quebec league had 40 of 185 players drafted for 21.6 percent of that class. However, since posting a 13.3 percent figure in the 1981 draft, the league never got into double figures again. The OHL's best year was 1970 with 44.3 per cent of the players selected, and while the league dropped into the teens through 1987-91, it had 21.6 per cent of the class in 1992, ironically tying Quebec's best-ever mark in a mediocre draft for Ontario. The WHL's best year proved to be 1979 with 29.4 per cent of the players selected and it, too, never drifted below double figures.

And the early totals flatter Quebec. Between 1980 and 1992, the OHL provided 596 draftees to the NHL, another 476 came from the WHL and only 238 from Quebec.

That begins to explain how hard it is for a Quebec-produced player to make it in the NHL, and especially gives a glimpse at why the hockey establishment, including the media, will give these players short shrift. North of the U.S.-Canadian border, there was a resistance to the notion, and still is, that Mario Lemieux had become the best player in the league, eclipsing Wayne Gretzky, about four seasons ago.

Bourque, consistently great, playing for a team with a history and millions of fans on both sides of the border, and perceived as English-speaking, received his due with little dispute.

Roy's treatment in the media, however, was closer to that afforded Lemieux — good — but that is patently ridiculous. Since his arrival in the NHL, Patrick Roy has won the Vezina Trophy three times (1989, '90, '92) and was runner-up once (1991). He has won or shared the William Jennings Trophy four times (1987, '88, '89, '92) and been runner-up twice (1990, '91). For those of you who claim confusion, you have a right to be. In its wisdom, the NHL introduced the Jennings award in 1982-83 and tried to differentiate between the best goaltender and the team with the best goals-against average (GAA). The reasoning was simple: a team with a mediocre goalie and a tremendous defense could win the Vezina year-in, year-out, while better goalies might be ignored.

That's right, simple reasoning, if simple is a synonym for stupid. The league was a tad upset because Montreal's Richard Sévigny and Denis Herron took the Vezina in 1981, so when the Canadiens once again had the best goals-against average in 1982, Herron and his new partner

Rick Wamsley received the brand-new Jennings, and Billy Smith of the Islanders garnered the Vezina. The following year, Smith and the Islanders allowed two fewer goals than the Boston Bruins and were awarded the Jennings, while Pete Peeters had his name inscribed on the Vezina. In this world, everyone has an opinion.

Ostensibly, the goalie judged to be the best at his position now wins the Vezina, while the team with the fewest goals scored against it claims the Jennings. From a pair of apples, the league has performed a marvel of recombinant DNA engineering and produced the proverbial apple and orange. Now we have a popularity contest for the Vezina. The league goofed, of course. The split trophy should have been the Norris which is awarded to "the defense player who demonstrates throughout the season the greatest all-round ability in the position." What this really means is that award goes to the highest-scoring defenseman, and too bad if his team's defensive zone is usually in another country. (For example, when Leetch won the Norris, Chelios was +24 on only 56 points, and a further +19 in the playoffs. Who would you rather have?)

Give Leetch a Jennings Trophy for highest-scoring defenseman — if he can take it away from Paul Coffey, Phil Housley et. al — and give the Norris to a defenseman, and not a fourth forward who hangs at both bluelines.

The Vezina-Jennings split has made it easy for the anti-Roy forces in the media to contest his title as the best goaltender in the game. The opposition will claim that he, like Herron and Sévigny before him, is the beneficiary of a great team of defensemen and a team that plays a hermetically sealed style that cuts down on the chances against him. They will also focus on a bad playoff year, or a bad goal scored from a distance. It is easy to make an anecdotal case against a player on the Canadiens because more than 90 percent of the team's games are televised.

It is not so easy, however, to make the same case when you read the numbers. Patrick Roy has taken his team to the Stanley Cup finals three times in the last seven years, winnning twice. In the same period, the following goaltenders made it that far: Mike Vernon, Calgary, twice;

Andy Moog, Boston, twice; Ron Hextall, Philadelphia, once; Tom Barrasso, Pittsburgh, twice; Grant Fuhr, Edmonton, twice; Bill Ranford, Edmonton, once; and Jon Casey, Minnesota, once.

None of the others has been able to do it more than twice, and none with a defense that was 100 per cent revamped. Calgary's defensive duo of Al MacInnis and Gary Suter played for both the 1986 finalist and 1989 champion; Ray Bourque and Glen Wesley led Boston's blueline corps in 1988 and 1990; Kevin Lowe, Charlie Huddy and Randy Gregg played on the Oilers' Cup champions in 1987, '88 and '90; and Pittsburgh's defensive leaders Larry Murphy and Ulf Samuelsson were given a precious boost when joined by Kjell Samuelsson in 1992.

Between Cup victories in 1986 and 1993, Patrick Roy's defense mutated 100 per cent. In 1986, a veteran defensive corps (total experience in years — 43) was led by future Hall-of-Famer Larry Robinson, who was ably supported by Rick Green, Craig Ludwig, Chris Chelios, Mike Lalor, Gaston Gingras and Petr Svoboda. This group was equal parts size — Robinson, Green, Lalor and Ludwig — and mobility — Chelios, Svoboda, Kurvers and Gingras.

In 1993, Robinson was in his first year of retirement, Green was an assistant coach for the Islanders, Chelios was winning the Norris Trophy in Chicago, Lalor was playing for Winnipeg, Gingras was playing in Europe and helping coach the defense on the Canadiens' farm team in Fredericton, and Svoboda was a Buffalo Sabre.

In their places were Eric Desjardins, Jean-Jacques Daigneault, Mathieu Schneider, Patrice Brisebois, Lyle Odelein and Kevin Haller, and occasionally Rob Ramage, Sean Hill and Donald Dufresne (total experience in years 42, but really closer to 27 when Ramage's 15 were subtracted). Right up to the NHL trading deadline in March, Montreal newspapers implored Serge Savard to beef up the blueline. Conventional wisdom described this group as mobile, but unable to move Mom out of the crease if she was on rollers. Big teams would stuff this defense and its goaltender into the net — along with the puck — during the Canadiens abbreviated foray into post-season play.

It is interesting to note that Roy was able to play above the entire revamping of the Canadiens' blueline corps. A single comparison should suffice to prove this point, as researched by Sylvain Robillard of Sportif weekly:

| Years | 86 | 87 | 88 | 89 | 90 | 91 | 92 | 93 |
|---|---|---|---|---|---|---|---|---|
| GAA Roy | 3.39 | 2.93 | 2.90 | 2.47 | 2.53 | 2.71 | 2.34 | 3.20 |
| GAA top 10 goalies | 3.30 | 3.25 | 3.24 | 3.06 | 3.04 | 2.88 | 2.92 | 3.07 |
| Difference (in %) | -3 | 10 | 10 | 19 | 17 | 6 | 20 | -4 |

Why the side trip? First, we establish that Roy is and has been the best goalie in the league for approximately six years. Having done that, we can then turn around and describe how truly bad he was during the 1992-93 season, and how he carried this psychological baggage into the playoffs.

How bad was Roy during the season? Patrick Roy was so bad that he was mediocre, a cardinal sin for a Canadiens goalie. And so bad that when a sports card company plastered teaser billboards all over Montreal exhorting the world to "Échange (trade) Roy" at mid-season, most hockey fans thought it was the work of one of their own, a well-heeled hockey fan who had been driven over the edge by yet another nonchalant performance between the pipes at the Forum. (In fact, the teaser encouraged hockey card collectors to trade Roy, the hockey card, and not Roy, the player. Needless to say, it was one of the most talked-about billboards in hockey card history.)

Patrick Roy is an inveterate hockey card collector, and you'll excuse him if he didn't get the play on words at first.

"Man, that was something," he reminisces. "I'm driving up the Décarie Expressway and there was this huge billboard right over my head with 'Échange Roy'. Talk about a message from above." And when Harry Sinden wanted to tweak his under-performing Andy Moog during the season, he compared him to Roy in the previous year's playoffs against the same Bruins.

As the playoffs beckoned, Roy was Horatio at the Bridge. Every playoff preview on the Canadiens started the same way: Montreal will go only as far as Roy can take them. Very little attention was paid to the Canadiens' improved offense and the fact that goals could come from many sources in a game, a most noteworthy change over the poast few seasons. The souped-up offense story had played well before Christmas, and although the Canadiens had scored 326 goals in 1993, compared with 267 the previous season, they had allowed 73 more (280-207). More offense wouldn't help the team escape the Adams Division if the puck wasn't stopped.

Compounding the problem, the Canadiens had fallen behind the Bruins and resurgent Nordiques in the last month of the season, relinquishing a supposedly insurmountable lead at the beginning of March and finishing third. Most of the season had these three teams jockeying to play the Sabres; that the Canadiens would have to start against the flashy Nordiques was perceived as failure.

As he sits in agent Pierre Lacroix's office, a participant in a high-stakes poker game with Serge Savard that will set him up for life, Patrick Roy is still just a shy kid from Ste-Foy, an affluent suburb of Quebec City. He looks like a modern-day Huck Finn: it wouldn't be a stretch to visualize a blade of grass or straw in his mouth, bare feet, a pole on his shoulder, patched jeans and a faded T-shirt, headin' for his favourite fishin' hole.

He has won his second Stanley Cup, and turned in what might be the all-time goaltending performance in post-season play in the history of the Cup, easily comparable with Terry Sawchuk in 1967, Ken Dryden in 1971, Bernie Parent in 1974 and '75, and himself in 1986.

And still the pain and puzzlement of Patrick's Paradox — a season and playoffs that were polar opposites — remains.

"One thing I realized going into the 1993 season was that this playoff was going to be the most important thing in my career. We had lost to Boston three years in a row, and it was extremely important that I play well in post-season. I think that this is part of the reason why I had an up-and-down season. My mind was on the playoffs and I tried to focus on how I was going to react when the playoffs came."

Was he bothered by the *Échange Roy*, or a poll in the *Journal de Montréal* in mid-season that suggested his value to the team might best be served as trade bait? And was that story true, about the Canadiens offering him and stars like Mathieu Schneider in a package to the Nordiques for Eric Lindros?

"I try not to be bothered by those kinds of things and stay focused. You can go crazy in Montreal if you take the sports talk shows or the newspaper columns seriously."

Focused or not, the playoffs started off better for the other Canadiens players than they did for their all-star goalie.

In the first game at Quebec, the Canadiens stifled the vaunted Nordiques' attack for 57 minutes and appeared to have a superbly sanitized 2-0 victory before a deathly silent Colisée crowd. Referee Paul Stewart was officiating his trademark game, letting the teams play, and had called only five minor infractions, four in the first and one in the second, when Gilbert Dionne threw an elbow at Alexei Gusarov behind the Quebec net. In the second period, Quebec's feisty Claude Lapointe had caught defenseman Mathieu Schneider behind the play with a crunching bodycheck, arguably from behind, and Schneider was out of the game and the series with a shoulder separation, his third injury in a season.

So both benches seemed surprised when Stewart's arm went up and he signalled the penalty to Dionne. At 18:31, Martin Rucinsky slipped the puck under Roy and the Nordiques were back in the game. Worse still, at 19:12 and with Ron Hextall sitting on the bench in favour of an extra attacker, Joe Sakic along the right boards mis-hit his shot, and the tantalizingly slow shot managed to elude Roy to tie the game. This was the explosive offense everyone had talked about all season long; you could shut them down for 58:30 and they still could could back in 41 seconds to lay waste a gallant checking effort.

Scott Young's overtime goal at 16:49 was almost an afterthought; there wasn't a person in the house who felt the Canadiens were going to win that night. The Nordiques, buoyed by that narrow escape, picked up where they left off two nights later, and were all over Montreal in the first period. Curtis Leschyshyn scored on a powerplay at 4:19, and then Young added a pair two minutes apart and the Nordiques were on their way.

To quote the inimitable Peggy Lee, "Is that all there is?" was the question making its way through the lineups for hot dogs and beer during the first intermission. Could it be that the Nordiques were that much better than the Canadiens, with all of their young studs and flashy scorers? Or could the Canadiens' balanced offense and defense, and superior goaltending, prevail?

When the Canadiens returned to the ice, they brought solace to the prognosticators who had forecast a six- or seven-game marathon. There was no scoring in the second period and Quebec enjoyed a 14-10 margin in shots, but suddenly Ron Hextall was forced to make the big plays. And, although the teams traded goals in the third period (Quebec's into an empty net) for a 4-1 final, the Habs returned home knowing they had outplayed their Quebec cousins in four of seven periods, with one drawn. But that was no consolation, down 2-0.

"After that second game, I felt I had to do something, anything to get myself and the team back to thinking about winning," Roy says. He and captain Guy Carbonneau sat together on the team bus back to the team's playoff hotel in Bromont, Quebec, 45 miles southeast of Montreal and, as they left the Quebec city limits, a despondent Roy turned to his team-mate and said, "That might have been our last playoff game in Quebec City together."

The next day, the Canadiens awoke to newspaper headlines that said "Nordiques Win Game, Battle of Goalies", and some pundits were even calling for backup goaltender André Racicot to start the third game of the series. At this point, Jacques Demers launched the Canadiens on the road to the Stanley Cup.

"Patrick Roy is my goalie. He got us here and we will win, or not, with him. I believe that he will win this for us. I will not get down on him and I would advise you not to either, or some of you might be eating your words before this is all over."

Roy was under siege by the media, and responded with a message to his teammates in fluent goaltenderese. "I think that we have given the Nordiques too much respect, like we believe their press clippings. We have to stop talking about how good they are, how nice they are, and say that we are as good as they are. Then we have to go out and prove it. And if we're going to do that, I'm going to have to do my job."

Roy recalls the stir his comments generated, but takes little credit for rallying his team.

"Jacques Demers was the big person because he was always working at building us up, even after we were two games down. He made us believe that the series was almost even, and convinced us that if we won the two games in Montreal, the pressure would be on them." What might have helped motivate the team preparing for the third game in beautiful bucolic Bromont was a broadcast of an Expos game from the Olympic Stadium. There in living colour taking in the game in a private box and casually brandishing some beers, were several Nordiques, Mike Ricci and Martin Rucinsky among them. These were young virile hockey players who were visibly enjoying their 2-0 lead over the Canadiens by partying at the Big O; they may almost have been players who were not mature enough to realize that their presence at the stadium, especially the "Hi Mom" routine before the cameras, would be the equivalent of a red flag in the face of the Canadiens.

Thus motivated, and braced by a prolonged ovation when they took to the Forum ice the following night, the Habs immediately fell behind the boys in powder blue at 1:17 of the first, on a goal by Mats Sundin. "Sometimes you can get too ready, too motivated," Roy says," and something like that is like a slap in the face. This time we all got together and turned up our game. They weren't going to embarrass us at the Forum."

What resulted was the pivotal game in the series, and a spectacular goaltending exhibition at both ends of the rink. Wave after wave of white shirts poured in on Hextall, only to be rebuffed by the lanky netminder who also had a history of stellar playoff netminding and his own Conn Smythe Trophy to prove it. Sundin, who had given his team the lead, helped pave the way for the Canadiens' comeback when he was sent off by referee Bill McCreary at 19:59 of the initial period for holding. When play resumed, Kirk Muller scored a powerplay goal to tie the game. But the issue would not be resolved until the fourth period.

When the siren sounded to end regulation play that night, no one on either team, or in the stands or anywhere where the sport is taken seriously, could have known that Patrick Roy and the Canadiens were about to launch the greatest string of overtime victories ever seen in their sport.

The 1993 playoffs will always be remembered for three things: goaltending, sudden-death overtime and The Streak. In 85 NHL playoff games, a record twenty-eight games went beyond the 60-minute mark. Only two series out of fifteen (Pittsburgh vs. New Jersey and Los Angeles vs. Calgary in the opening round) reached a conclusion within regulation time in all games played, five and six respectively.

When the 1993 playoffs began, Curtis Joseph and Félix Potvin had leaped into the headlines: Joseph because of his brilliance against a popgun Chicago offense, and Potvin because of his steady play and the omnipresence of the self-described "national media" in Toronto. By the time the 1993 playoffs had ended, Joseph and Potvin were asterisks and the oldtimers were mentioning Roy in the same breath as Sawchuk, Dryden and Parent.

What Patrick Roy and his teammates accomplished in Montreal's flabbergasting dash for the silverware defies mathematical probability:

- 96:39 minutes of playoff overtime hockey without allowing a goal (after Scott Young had beaten him at 16:49 of overtime in Game One of the Quebec series on April 18) on a total of 65 shots;
- A 16-4 playoff record, an .800 clip (previous best in the 16-wins era was Pittsburgh's 16-5 record the previous year);
- A league-record 11 straight playoff wins (Quebec 4/ Buffalo 4/Islanders 3) to tie the mark set in 1992 by the Penguins and Blackhawks;
- A team record of 12-0 in one-goal games once the streak began;
- Ten straight overtime wins, easily surpassing the six in 21 games registered by the New York Islanders in 1980;

- A 10-1 playoff record at home — a .909 clip;
- A 6-3 record on the road for a .667 average;
- A 2.13 GAA on 46 goals against in 20 games;
- A save percentage of .929, just behind Curtis Joseph's .938 achieved in only 11 games.

Going into the 1993 playoffs, Montreal held all playoff overtime records extant, including most games (103), most wins with 55 (55-46-2), most home wins with 31 (31-17-1) and most road wins with 24 (24-29-1).Toronto was next with 36 OT wins, and Boston with 35. In one playoff season, Montreal came close to doubling its two nearest rivals in this esoteric category, boosting its franchise record to 65-47-2, split in home (35-17-1) and road (30-30-1) contests.

"It is very interesting to know that you have contributed to the numbers that make this franchise the most successful one in the history of the NHL," Roy remarks, quite conscious of his role in Montreal hockey history.

"But the numbers would not have meant anything if Vincent Damphousse had not been able to win that first overtime game for us, and then we came right back and beat them in the fourth game to even the series."

And the numbers would have been meaningless two nights later when the teams returned to Quebec City for the fifth game in the series, had not team therapist Gaetan Lefebvre been able to work his magic on a stricken goalie. Both teams went to work with a vengeance that night, both sensing a six-game series with no seventh-game reprieve. Montreal opened the scoring on a Mike Keane goal at 4:24 of the first, but Quebec got the equalizer one minute into the middle frame when a slapshot caught Roy on the shoulder and he dropped like a stone. Andrei Kovalenko lifted the puck past Roy to tie the game and the celebration was muted as Roy lay in a heap for long moments after the play.

One of the quirks about playing at Le Colisée is the result of the idiotic rule that forces both teams to sit on the same side of the rink. In earlier times, when teams sat on opposite sides of the rink, they would simply walk out of their dressing rooms and sit at their bench, located on the same side of the building. With the advent of the same-side benches rule, weird things happened, like visiting players having to go to their room through Boston's bench door at the Garden, for example. Because the team benches take up so much space on one side of the rink in Quebec City, the visiting team's goaltender must sit in his own Coventry, all alone across the rink from his team-mates and beside the penalty boxes.

When Roy was helped from the ice, he and Lefebvre had to go past Racicot into the Canadiens' room and something in the starting goalie's demeanor seemed to rattle the substitute, like he knew that the playoffs now rested on his shoulders. Try as he might, Racicot wasn't mentally ready, and although the Canadiens stormed back with a pair of goals, the Nordiques got a pair on a netminder who seemed to be collapsing on every shot. It was 3-3 after two periods; the game and the series were in the balance, and a very long summer beckoned the team in the traditional red, white and blue. Could the Canadiens recover? Was Roy out of the series? Those questions raced up and down press row during the intermission.

When play resumed, both questions were answered. Roy was in the Montreal nets, and both teams had at each other hammer and tong. Sundin put the Nordiques ahead six minutes into the third, and Gilbert Dionne picked a corner at 13:23 to send the game into overtime.

"You talk about a lot of the games in overtime during our streak, but the 5-4 win in Quebec in Game Five was probably the biggest," said Kirk Muller, the man who would win it for the Canadiens, and start Ron Hextall on his way to Long Island. "Patrick kept us in the game in the third period and in overtime, and that gave us the series." The Nordiques tested Roy severely after his return, outshooting the Canadiens 15-7 in the third and 5-1 in overtime, 50-29 for the game. However, that lone shot in extra time went into the Quebec net, as Muller caught Hextall sliding across to his left to protect the short side, and then put it back against the grain to his right and through his legs. When the game ended, the Nordiques now tasted the bitterness the Canadiens had felt after the first game, coming out on the losing end of a game they owned.

Two nights later, Paul DiPietro guaranteed the Canadiens a restful summer with three goals and one assist as a visibly upset Pierre Pagé pulled Hextall from the game on two different occasions and lambasted some of his European stars in full view of the TV cameras.

*Échange Roy* was over; the new tune was *Échange Hextall* or Pagé. The kid from Ste-Foy was vindicated in his own backyard, and grandma Anna could rest peacefully.

"It is hard to describe what it means to be a goalie — no, THE goalie — for the Montreal Canadiens, especially the career I've had with this team. And it is even more special playing at home in front of the people I grew up with," Roy muses.

Roy always wanted to be a hockey player, from the earliest days in peewee with Québec-Sud and then the Citadelles at the famed Quebec Peewee Hockey Tournament, to his days in bantam when he moved to Cap Rouge and had to play for the Ste-Foy Gouverneurs. Like most of the kids growing up in Canada, he played ball hockey marathons between his busy practice and game schedule. Unlike many NHLers who came up through major junior hockey, he was the product of a very affluent family — his father, Michel Roy, is currently deputy minister of communications in the Quebec government, and his mother Barbara is a former nationally ranked swimmer who coached that sport in Quebec for years.

He and brother Stéphane, who would be selected by the Minnesota North Stars in the 1985 entry draft, were raised in one of Canada's more exclusive neighbourhoods, a cradle for top doctors, college professors, government administrators and corporate executives. The university track was no option here; quitting school to chance a career in professional sports was aberrant.

A little more than a decade after he left school in Secondary V (Grade 11), and during a summer when he ponders the eventuality of making more money in one year than many two-degree Laval University graduates will make in a lifetime, Patrick muses on how it might have been different.

"Like most kids, I never thought of playing in the NHL, it was more of a dream. When I began, I was Rogetien Vachon, and later when the Nordiques came, I pretended I was Daniel Bouchard. My parents were very supportive, and they gave Stéphane and I the choice to make up our own minds. We both decided on hockey and I decided on goaltending because I liked the look of goalie pads. I both lived and fantasized hockey."

Michel Roy is a demon tennis player who, his friends say, has a competitive charge in him that is a sight to behold. Barbara Peacock Roy was a competitive swimmer. The Roy brothers had the right genes; it became a question of whether they would have the right stuff for the pros.

"My mind was always on hockey and not on school and when Secondary V came along, I had an opportunity to move on to major junior hockey in Granby. I went to my father and he supported me. He recognized that I wanted to be a hockey player and the only concession was that I would return to school if and when I realized that I couldn't make in professional hockey. "

Part of his tenacity came from his maternal grandmother, Anna Peacock.

"Grandma Anna was a big Canadiens fan, while our house was all Nordiques, and her favourite player was Ken Dryden. My mom was coaching swimming most nights when I was young, so Anna would feed me my dinner and we would often listen to hockey games together on the radio. And she would speak French to me."

A lot of the mythology that has developed about Roy and his idiosyncrasies stems from his inability to speak English in his early pro career. The irony, of course, is that his mother Barbara and his grandmother Anna are English speaking. They improved their French in the unilingual provincial capital by constantly speaking French to their children and grandchildren. Anna and Patrick were very close, and her death in 1982 shook him. Her passing was a lesson in maturity for a young boy in high school.

"My grandmother had cancer, and at the beginning they thought it was Parkinson's disease. In my first year of high school, she would shake when she ate; by the second year, the shaking was so bad that by the time she got a soup spoon to her mouth, there was no soup left. The third year, she drank her soup through a straw and the fourth year was even worse. And then she died."

The last time Patrick saw Anna Peacock, in hospital, his grandmother was watching the 1982 Stanley Cup final between the New York Islanders and the Vancouver Canucks. Anna could never know that four years later "petit Patrick" would be standing in the Canadiens' crease at Madison Square Garden, stoning the surging Rangers, en route to Montreal's first Stanley Cup since Ken Dryden's retirement, while 17,000 New Yawkers adenoidally brayed "Roo-Wah, Roo-Wah" in a futile attempt at taking a rookie off his game.

"Anna was very important to me, and if I could have a wish, it would have been that she could have been there to see me play for the Canadiens. But, I think it might have overwhelmed her . . . she would have been very excited about such a thing."

Without realizing it, of course, Anna and Barbara Peacock's insistence on speaking French exclusively to Patrick led to several of his quirks. Like the famous story about his conversations with goalposts.

"In junior hockey at Granby, just about everyone on the team was French so I could communicate comfortably with my coaches and team-mates," Roy recalls.

"But when I came up to the Canadiens, I could hardly speak a word of English. When the team travelled, I always made sure I had some French player who could speak good English around me to help me, especially in interviews with the media. I wanted to make sure that I understood the question properly and I could answer. There were times when I would reply in French to my team-mate and he would translate for the reporter."

One day during the Rangers series in 1986, all of Patrick's Berlitz buddies were conspicuously absent while he fielded questions from a New York writer after practice. What Patrick generally does in the moment or two he turns to stare at his net prior to the start of a game is something that the sports psychologists call "visualization technique." Roy concentrates on the goal, and staring hard, wills it to become smaller. Baseball players "see" themselves hitting home runs, football quarterbacks "see" themselves throwing TD passes, and then go out and do it. It's the same mental process.

Patrick Roy could have explained the term "visualization technique" to a French-speaking reporter. To this New York scribe, however, he could only blurt out in broken English, "I talk to my goalposts," and science became superstition, all chicken entrails, black cats, and lucky charms. The Gotham media ate it up and a star was born.

"Yeah, they really loved that quote and started to have fun with it. I am superstitious and I do some things that people say are superstitious, like sit in a certain seat in a rink when I watch the other team practice, or follow the same rituals in pre-game preparation. I was turning around and looking at the net because a goaltender needs those things; the game is in your head and you need confidence before going out there, and I was using this to build my confidence. If they wanted to make a big deal out of it in the press, that was okay."

Visualization technique was one of many subjects broached with goaltender coach François Allaire in their budding year-old relationship at the time. After three years of vulcanization in Granby, with a team that was notoriously weak defensively and facing bombardment night after night, the Canadiens invited Roy to join the Sherbrooke Canadiens of the American Hockey League in April, 1985. In junior, Roy's goals-against average in three seasons was 6.26, 4.44 and 5.55, nothing to write home about or to inspire the team scouting staff, unless they could look past the numbers.

That spring, he played parts of two AHL regular-season games for Sherbrooke, beating New Haven 7-4 for his first pro victory. He fully expected to spend the playoffs in the stands, or on the bench backing up incumbent Greg Moffatt, until an equipment problem opened the door. "We were up 2-1 in the series against Fredericton Express [Nordiques' farm team] but losing 3-0 at home in Sherbrooke when Greg broke a pad and coach Pierre Creamer waved me into the game. I made a couple saves almost right away to keep the game close, and then we scored two quick goals before Moffatt returned from the dressing room. Creamer kept him on the bench and me in the game and we came back and won it." Moffatt, like the immortal Wally Pipp, never got back in.

By the time the playoffs were finished, Roy had 10 victories, three losses and a 2.89 GAA. And the Sherbrooke Canadiens, with Roy's former Granby team-mate Stéphane Richer, free agents Brian Skrudland and Mike Lalor, and Montreal draft choices Gaston Gingras and Ric Nattress, were the AHL champions. This performance did not go unnoticed by the brass on Lambert Closse; Steve Penney had skates of clay, as the Nordiques had demonstrated in their seventh-game victory over the Canadiens in the division final, and the parent club was actively seeking a skilled goalie. Roy's Calder Cup final series was played before a very discerning audience.

"The first difference I noticed was the big gap between junior and professional. It was a big step to take and the circumstance of playing in the AHL after our junior team failed to make the playoffs helped me a lot. Winning the Calder Cup made me confident that I could make the NHL the next season. The best part about Sherbrooke was meeting François."

Roy had his first full-time goalie coach and, best for his style of game, this coach was the kind who understood that any changes or improvements must happen within a style of play, and not by radical change to a player's game.

"He's a good coach and he understands; François is always looking forward, to correct small things, and to develop new ways to stop the puck or set yourself better." Roy and Allaire have been together since 1985, the kind of continuity and attention to detail that characterizes the Montreal approach to the game. Even today, many teams do not have a goalie coach, or even a goaltending consultant.

Today, Roy is not only the best goalie in the game, he is the most technically proficient. His team practices are not like most you will see in the NHL. Allaire and Roy always seem to be working on the mental or physical part of the game and have their own drills aimed at improving techniques for mind and body.

Roy is a butterfly goalie and, as such, tends to go down on shots too early, often leaving a short opening in the five hole (between the feet) or in the top corners. He and Allaire have worked on this aspect of his game for almost a decade, to the point that when he is down on his knees in the crease, with legs perpendicular to his torso to cover the corners at ice level, Roy's upper body is still erect and covers a great deal of the middle of the net. This came after years of work during practice sessions, and differentiates Roy's butterfly from all others except Félix Potvin's. Ed Belfour, for example, is considered by some to be the best goalie in the NHL, a claim will get a chuckle out of goalie coaches. On the ice, he is almost always out of control and has little or no technique with his upper body.

Ironically, one goalie who reminds many people of Roy is Kirk McLean, the Vancouver netminder who is a classic stand-up player. There are two reasons for this: the similarity in size and physique of the two players, and the fact that Roy in recent years has worked hard to improve his stand-up game: cutting down angles, letting pucks hit him, and deadening or swallowing rebounds with his pads. That, too, is the product of coaching and hours of workouts.

With the signing of Steve Shutt as offensive coach to work with Charles Thiffault, head assistant, and Jacques Laperrière, defensive coach, behind Demers, it is no wonder that 99 per cent of the most rabid Canadiens fans could walk right by Allaire in the street and not recognize him. There is no room for him behind the team bench during games, and he is so self-effacing it is even difficult to pick him out in practices.

Allaire is not a former NHL goaltender long on experience, short on technical grounding and career future. His background in academics and the serious study of all aspects of the position. Tall and lean like his prize student, Allaire in his horn-rimmed glasses looks more like the caricature of an author, accountant or computer programmer. If you guessed author, you would be partially correct — he has written an excellent technical manual on goaltending which, unfortunately for most netminders, is in French only.

"People ask me the difference between 1986 and 1993, and the answer is simple: I'm a much better goalie now than I was then," Roy testifies. "François and I have had seven more years to work together, refine things."

Comparisons between his two Conn Smythe playoffs have been legion since Roy raised his arms in triumph shortly atfer 10:40 p.m. Eastern Daylight Savings Time, on Wednesday, June 9, 1993.

"Many, many things had changed since then, on the ice and off. People are trying to compare the two defenses, but you can't. Both were two good groups of players, one older, the other younger. And it's hard to compare Robinson, Green, Ludwig and Chelios to the guys we have now. A lot of people forget that Petr Svoboda didn't play much in the '86 series, and that Gaston Gingras was a big man for us. In 1993, there was less talent than 1986, but still a lot of talent, and real hard workers in the star players like Mathieu Schneider, Eric Desjardins and Jean-Jacques Daigneault.

The major difference in the two teams was the man between the pipes. The Patrick Roy who started the playoffs against the Boston Bruins in April, 1986 was a red, raw rookie eight months removed from his first training camp. Sitting on the bench were veterans Penney and Doug Soetaert, and some veterans were outspoken in the club's treatment of the latter. During an injury-filled season, Soetaert had turned in a record of 11 wins, 6 losses, 2 ties and 3 shutouts in 23 games, for a goals-against average of 2.77. Penney was out of the picture, and didn't even travel with the team during most of the playoffs. Roy played in 47 games, winning 23 and losing 19, with three ties, one shutout and a 3.39 GAA. In twenty playoff games, he halved that latter stat, turning in a 1.92 GAA as the team won 15 of 20 games and the Cup.

"It's funny because I knew some of the veterans wanted Doug Soetaert to play more in the season, and even in the playoffs, but the veterans were the guys who played twice as hard to make my job easier. They didn't want any shots on me, and we had some periods in the four playoff series where I hardly had any. The whole team played amazing hockey."

Other differences came off the ice; the 1986 Patrick Roy was a kid who was being weaned off his fast-food habit by a nutritionist hired specially by the team, and a player who lived like a hermit in a basement apartment in Montreal, occasionally playing ball hockey with the neighbourhood kids. Seven years later, he lived in a mansion in suburban Rosemere with his wife Michèle and the proverbial 2.9 children, sons Jonathan, 4, and Frédérick, 2. The .9 child would arrive at the least, or most, opportune time in the 1993 playoffs, depending on your point of view.

After sweeping the Sabres in four consecutive 4-3 decisions, the last three in overtime, and then casting aside the giant-killers from Long Island in five games, another three in OT, the Canadiens sat back for their second eight-day layoff of the playoffs and awaited the winner of the battle of the pit bulls, Toronto and Los Angeles.

"I have to admit that I was surprised to see the Islanders beat the Penguins, but you play on the ice and anything can happen in a seventh game. We were a bit scared when the Islanders came to Montreal because they had beaten the best team in the league, but we played one of our best games of the playoffs and shut them down. The next game went into double overtime, and who knows what would have happened if Stéphan Lebeau didn't score to give us a 2-0 lead."

The most impressive scene in the series for Roy was a little talk Kirk Muller gave his team-mates before Game Five in Montreal. Muller delivered a very simple message: "Be ready. I'm ready."

"There is nothing more important for a team to have a leader like a Kirk Muller stand up in the room, say something like that, and then follow through on the ice," says Roy. The game wasn't a minute old when the Pride of Kingston (a prize shared with Doug Gilmour and Don Cherry), came out of the corner to Glen Healey's right and backhanded the puck through the goalie's legs. Later in the period, he combined with John LeClair on a nifty set-up of Mike Keane and the Canadiens were en route to the franchise's 35th Stanley Cup final.

The Kings finally prevailed in their seven-game marathon and swaggered into Montreal to thump the stale Canadiens 4-1 in the opening game of the final series. Wayne Gretzky, reborn after missing most of the season because of a major back injury, figured in all five goals scored in the contest, a goal and three assists for the Kings, and a puck deflected into his own net for the Canadiens.

Roy had barely time to duck the post-game media horde and speed out of the Forum to a midnight rendezvous; wife Michèle was scheduled to enter hospital at midnight and was going to be induced during the night.

"I didn't get out of the Forum until after 11 o'clock and we had to be at the hospital for 12, so even if Michèle was being induced, we had to hurry. We had decided on this because Michèle wanted me to assist at the birth and I was about to go to Los Angeles for four days where I wouldn't be much of a help to my wife, 4,000 miles away, if she went into labour on June 4th or 5th."

With help, Mrs. Roy went into labour at 4 a.m., had major contractions at 6:30, and Jana (for her two great-grandmothers, Jeanne and Anna) Roy arrived at 7:50 a.m. on June 2nd. Naturally, when the team got to Los Angeles, her proud and superstitious papa sat in seat J-2 while watching the Kings practice, instead of his traditional B-7.

Superstitions or not, you make your own luck; that was proved by the Canadiens when Jana Roy was only 39 hours old. Down 2-1 in the second game of the final and facing the longest plane trip in hockey, one-way to La-la-Land down a deuce, Jacques Demers called for the famous stick measurement on Marty McSorley, Eric Desjardins scored the tying goal with 1:13 remaining in the game, and completed his hat trick at the 51- second mark of overtime.

Five days later, on the Red Eye back to Montreal, the Canadiens were singing La-La, and the praises of their goalie. Everyone was talking about the Wink, even though the players hadn't seen it during the game. Like everyone else, they had to watch television replays to find out what all the fuss was about.

Roy had lauded Kirk Muller's leadership on and off the ice in the final against New York. Muller repaid the compliment two weeks later.

"When Patrick stood up and told us that all we had to do to win the fourth game was score one goal, because he wasn't giving up any more, there wasn't one guy in the room who didn't believe it. We didn't even doubt it a little. We knew that if we scored the one goal, we'd win."

The Wink and The Speech incidents prove one thing in modern sport: that despite the advances in technology (computers, freeze frame video, live Polaroid shots on formations in football, phones to spotters upstairs) that allow coaches to adapt strategies in mid-game, let alone mid-shift, the tried and true motivation of the "win one for the Gipper" spirit plays as important a role in determining outcomes of championships in the 1990s.

"When I first came to the Canadiens, I heard the criticisms that I was a motivator, but maybe not too advanced on the technical side of the game," Jacques Demers says. "Frankly, that is insulting. I remember one guy in Detroit once wrote that I said something to the effect that hockey wasn't all Xs and Os on a blackboard, and that diagramming plays wasn't important. What I meant to say is that all of it is important, from being able to find an opponent's weaknesses and shortcomings, to being able to get your team up in stressful situations.

"Patrick Roy stood up in the room at a time when some of the players were getting nervous and picked his team up with two short sentences. There will always be room for motivation in sports."

After worrying all year if he would be properly focused during the playoffs, Roy gave the world a lesson in the powers of concentration during the playoffs. And all of those doubts, memories, comments and experiences came to a head, if you'll pardon the expression, in a mere wink that spoke volumes. "Tomas Sandstrom is a very good hockey player, but he has a habit of coming late after a goalie," says Roy. "I wanted to show him that I was in control."

Two months later, Patrick Roy sits in Pierre Lacroix's office patiently awaiting his $16-million, four-year contract and dispassionately dissecting his playoff performance. The most recent sports poll in Canada has him as the most recognizable athlete in the country right now, bigger even that The Great One, The Greater One and The Next One. Gatorade has inundated Canadian convenience stores with a two-in-one poster of the goalie, separate poses on the front of a pair of 30-inch by 20-inch posters, which can be turned over and combined into a double-sized mural of the great save-master. IncROY-HAB-le (incredible) said one of the most imaginative banners displayed at the Forum during the playoffs.

Damn if he still doesn't evoke Huck Finn . . . those baby blues as faraway and as unfathomable as any Mark Twain creation . . . forever searching the horizon for the elusive perfect fishin' hole.

But, behind it all is stainless steel. Never mistake Patrick Roy's boyish charm for weakness.

He is a Lion. And Anna Peacock would be so proud.

# 19

# Les Fantômes

It is mid-afternoon on Tuesday, June 22, 1993. High up in the northwest corner of the Forum, a dark building today because most of the regular denizens are conspicuously absent, there is an phosphorescent glow. A moth to a flame, I must go.

I hear the voices before I see them . . . several men sitting around a card table, others lounging about on chairs away from the table, or standing and kibbitzing behind the card players. Off behind them in the haze, I sense movement, others sitting at tables, waiters swooping down like sea eagles.

I blink . . . and some of the images disappear into the haze. But at centre stage, the tableau I originally saw shimmers, and then crystallizes into sharply defined, solid forms.

"One no trump," says the bespectacled and portly gentleman with the crewcut. He looks across the table at his partner, a shortish, intense man with a high forehead, seemingly coiled to spring at the first loud noise. A small, young, man, he exudes vitality and nervous energy. Ironically, he wears a three-piece suit.

"Do you think they can figure out where I'm going with this, Howarth?"

"Don't know, Papa. Tommy would rather be playin' poker — bridge is a thinkin' man's game — and Tommy wants the action . . . a quick hand of five-card stud, the dice, the horses . . . a chance to bluff . . ."

"Ah shaddap Morenz," retorts the big-shouldered, handsome man, impeccably attired in a beautifully cut suit, a labour of love for fully a dozen or so of the best Italian tailors on The Main. He glances across the table at his partner, and snarls: "Come on-n-n-n, rookie. Say something. Anything. Bid your cards so I can take these guys to the cleaners. You don't talk, we go no place."

The fourth player is obscured by the wavering light, but his identity is given away by his mellifluous tones when he speaks: "Relax, Tay Pay. I'm just learning this game."

I've grown up with That Voice — "*Le but du Canadien . . .* Canadiens' goal . . . *compté par le numéro dix . . .* scored by number ten . . . Guy . . . . . La . . . . . . Fle-e-u-u-r!" — I look down at the big CH at centre ice and I swear I can see Lafleur acknowledging the cheers in his own inimitable way, skating in nervous little circles with his head down, stick resting across his knees and anxiously awaiting the referee's dropped puck at the feet of Jacques Lemaire, so that they can go to work on the next one. In my mind's eye, Claude Mouton turns off the mike and shares a joke with Cooper Smeaton, sitting next to him.

I think I can see it, anyway. My eyes focus, but the view is strange. . . . What is that huge fence-like screen just down below and in front of me . . . and where did the seats go? And where's the scoreboard and clock that hangs over centre ice? What in the world is going on? Where is this?

A movement to my right arrests that reverie. "It's been a few years since the good old days at the Press Club . . . yuh tomatacan, yuh." One of the kibbitzers has left the group behind the card players and is walking towards me. It's Harry Brown.

These are very strange doings.

"Harry, I hate to break it to you, but you're dead. Long dead. And while I'm on the subject of decomposition, why are you so much taller and whatever happened to your bow legs?"

"Up here, you don't have to be 85, ya dummy. I got my legs back. Hell, look at Claude over there . . . the weight's back on and he looks like a million dollars . . . awright, he *sounds* like a million dollars. And while we're on the subject, you haven't missed too many meals lately, have ya?" This is the real Harry, a shot a second. A real exercise in acid wit would be the two of us talking hockey with Al Strachan as referee . . . the Edward Scissorstongue Trio.

"Harry, where in hell's name are we? Or am I?"

"I wouldn't quite phrase it like that, young man," says the man in the crewcut who had opened the bidding, moments before.

"Although, having known Mr. Brown and Mr. Gorman on the other side, we were a wee bit surprised to have both of them join our little confab."

My eyes have to be playing tricks on me. This is Father Frank Selke, and the last time I saw him was Canada Day 1983, at Rolling Range Farm in Rigaud. Actually, that was the second-last time . . . the last time was downstairs in the Forum lobby, on another national holiday — July 4, 1985 — as he lay in state prior to his funeral. The dead give-away, no pun intended, is the Mr. Brown, Mr. Gorman. In the old days it was Mr. Richard, Mr. Beliveau, Mr. Harvey and Mr. Bouchard. Father Frank knew every person in the building, and was the epitome of courtesy and politeness. The feeling was mutual, a thousandfold.

"Sir, I'm not even going to ask what I'm looking at, or why I'm here . . . or even where is here," I reply. "But, if the entrance requirements to this gathering are what I think they are, I don't want to be a member. At least not just yet."

Off across the table, Tommy Gorman laughs, and it is a wonderful, rich sound.

"That ain't quite the way Groucho said it, kid, but it'll do."

I put one and one together . . . and get four. Standing right behind Gorman is the original Number Four, Aurele Joliat. "Ain't seen you in a few years, sonny. We sat in the dressing room together for a few minutes that night of the Dream Team, didn't we?"

"We sure did Aurele, and then you went out there and fell on your can in front of 18,000 people and a national TV audience."

"Yup. They loved the hat, didn't they kid? Heck, if I'd been a few years younger, I might have started a fad for one of those companies like Reebok and Nike and made a killing."

"There's that subject again," Selke chides gently.

"Let's get on with the game."

But, it is not to be . . . Tommy Gorman has lost even his most minuscule interest in bridge.

"Forget it Frank. You, Dick Irvin and H. Gordon Green can play this game in your dotage until you're blue in the face, or while you're talking chickens back home, but I need some pace. This is too slow. Anyway, enough of the smoke and mirrors. Howie's not interested, Mouton's scared to make a mistake and a bad impression, and Harry's driving me crazy with the whispering in my ear. By the way, the last time we played and you were partners with Irvin Senior, the chicken talk got a little suspicious. I began to notice that whenever you mentioned your favourite Rhode Island Reds, you ended up going for a contract in diamonds."

"Coming from you, Mr. Gorman, I might even consider that a compliment," Selke replies, an impish grin on his face.

To Gorman's right, Howie Morenz tosses in his cards.

"Tommy's right, Papa Frank. I think you should tell the kid why he's here."

Gathering up what courage I can muster, I volunteer, weakly: "Where's here?" A nagging suspicion has dawned but I don't want to offer an opinion just yet. Especially since I don't know if I'm a casual visitor, or about to become a permanent resident.

Harry jumps in, his legs are better, but you'd recognize that whine anywhere, on either side of the Great Divide.

"Come on kid. I played poker with ya, and ya wasn't half bad. Figure it out."

"Give me one clue. Or one answer, and I'll give you my opinion," I say.

Tommy Gorman looks over at Frank Selke, who nods to the shadows behind him. I move forward, squinting, and make out a tall, thin man with a thatch of white hair. Dick Irvin. Senior.

"1949," he says.

"1949?"

"1949."

"Got it yet, kid?" Gorman is relentless.

"Lemme try it. '49, a great year for the Yankees, so-so for the Habs. You finished third behind Detroit and Boston and ahead of Toronto, and damn if the Leafs didn't pop up and win the Cup." I look directly at Selke and continue.

"Yup, the first NHL team to win three Cups in a row. Connie Smythe must have been insufferable all summer."

Father Frank laughs, and retorts: "Nice show, young man. But it's not why you're here."

"This show's for me?"

"Only one question or clue," pipes in Irvin, Sr., "and you've had that already."

"Jeez, Mr. Irvin, what are you doing here. You spent as much time with the Hawks and the Leafs . . ."

"Stick to the matter at hand, young man."

"Okay, if this is my show, then '49 means something more personal. It's the year I was born; that's got to be it." I look down at the terrace below, and I feel the switch being thrown on the lightbulb in my mind: " . . . and that's the Millionaires' Section, the terraces you put in 1949 Mr. Selke, when you enlarged the Forum. My Dad stood and watched a lot of games up here that winter while my Mom was busy powdering my dirty derrière in an apartment on Delormier, right in front of Lafontaine Park. How am I doing?"

"Mr. Mouton, Mr. Brown . . . you were right. This young man is on the ball."

"You're doing my ego a world of good, Mr. Selke, but when I wake up and this dream is over — and I certainly hope I'm going to wake up — your opinion might be appreciated, but it won't mean a whole lot."

Gorman turns to me.

"Good going, kid. Frank isn't used to anybody figuring him out, especially the chicken references in the bridge games." He smiles across at Selke, and shrugs. "I'm a betting man, always have been, and I bet you've cottoned on to what this is all about."

"Let me figure this. You're the Ghosts of the Forum. Right? And you're telling me you exist. Right?"

"Correct."

"Why?"

"They liked the book, kid. Thought you did a thorough job, and Frank especially liked the shots you gave Connie Smythe," says Harry Brown.

"Tommy heard you were thinkin' of doin' an updated version, Claude confirmed it, and they convinced Frank to get our story in it. After all, that baby Sinden's been crying about us for years; we thought it might be a nice idea to drive Harry crazy by telling him he ain't."

This tableau smacks of Greek epic poetry; a minstrel or narrator recounting the stories of many past heroes, with the Greek Chorus chanting counterpoint in the background. As improbable as it seems, Harry Brown is the minstrel; Selke, Gorman, Irvin, Morenz, Joliat and Mouton are the heroes, and the voices off in the haze are the Greek Chorus. I'm feeling smug because I've got it all figured out. I even know something they don't — these guys are facing a potential Greek tragedy.

I turn to Harry.

"Know anything about dactylic hexameter, Harry?"

"Say what?

"It's Greek, Harry."

"Only Greek I ever knew was old Phed Vosniacos over at the Press Club. Damned sandbagger. I clunked him a cuppla good ones with my cane durin' poker games." I wince, remembering Harry and Phed flailing at each other drunkenly, cards flying everywhere. Where's Joe Servant when you need him?

"Never mind." I turn to Selke.

"At the risk of being repetitive, what *am* I doing here?"

"Mr. Gorman was right. We want you to tell them that there are real Ghosts of the Forum."

"Since Bill 101, that's *fantômes du Forum*," Gorman interjects, giving the French nasal Ns and rolled Rs a definite Hibernian intonation.

"The Forum Ghosts, excuse me. . . . *Les fantômes du Forum* are coming out of the closet?" Well, it's all the rage in the 1990s . . .

"Why?"

"It's time, kid," Gorman adds.

"We were all a little incensed two weeks ago when the New Kids won the Cup and all of the commentators and experts were saying we were a figment of somebody's imagination. Even Sinden admitted that the Ghosts didn't exist, the damned liar. It's real simple: we're here, we've been here for a long time, and we aren't going anywhere. Besides, I personally will not leave this place until those geniuses on the second floor put up the other two Cup banners that they've ignored for years."

"The Maroons?"

"Exactly. Two Cup banners are missing — 1926 and 1935. It's only right, this was their building first. A lot of people don't even know that Toe Blake's first Cup win came from playing with the Maroons in '35. The '35 team was mine, and the '26 team won the first Stanley Cup awarded in this building. And still no banners. I'm going to be up here until I see the two orange-and-maroon Ms up there."

"What about you, Mr. Selke?"

"I've always felt comfortable here, son, and I'm a frequent visitor, even though I spend most of my time at Rolling Range or H. Gordon's place in St. Thérèse. I'm still around because while I was proud of the job the boys did in 1986 and this year, although I also must say that I was disgusted by the poor behaviour of our so-called fans in the streets. Those aren't the Montrealers I remember, the seventh man that always made our teams so great."

"Reminded you a bit of St. Paddy's Day, 1955, did it?"

There is a gentle hint of annoyance in his reply.

"I don't think I have to point out to you the difference between righteous indignation and wanton vandalism, do I?"

"I apologize, Mr. Selke." I want to get back on his good side. "We all were embarrassed and disgusted by the idiots in the streets. They were our sons and daughters, and obvious proof that Benjamin Spock didn't have a clue. Some of those brats missed a few lessons growing up."

I look over at Claude Mouton, sitting quietly and unwillinging to venture too many opinions . . . very much The New Guy.

"I have a few messages for you, Claude. Denis, Kirk, Vincent, Brian, Patrick and Carbo all wanted to tell you that this Cup was dedicated to you, and that they were saddened because you almost made it, but weren't there at the end. They had a wee sip of champagne in your honour."

Do I catch a glint in the corner of an eye?

"I miss the kids," he sighs. "They showed me something during the year, and they reminded me a lot of the gang in '86. They were special. When you get back, tell them message received. And tell the guys at the 25th anniversary game at the Big O in August that I'll miss them too. Especially that catcher, what was his name . . . Bocca-bell-l-l-a?"

"Message received, Claude."

"The first two letters in champion and character are CH, Mr. Mouton," Frank Selke gently reminds him.

I address Howie Morenz.

"Jean Beliveau tells me your family has had a tough year too, what with Marlene's open heart surgery and the Boomer's prostate cancer."

He sighs, "That's certainly true. She was on the table for eight hours and they thought they had lost her a couple times. And Bernard has not been well, but her recovery has really picked him up."

I turn to the others, looking right at Gorman.

"If you guys are telling me that you are real, then I am led to believe that Harry Sinden wasn't just blowing wind when he started whining about you, was he? What happened so that he caught on? Did you do something to him?

Gorman's face lights up in a Cheshire grin, the kind that had most of Montreal's eligible belles, and some not quite so eligible, flocking to his side in the '30s.

"What's the best way of saying it — ah, we kind of let Harry know we were around a few times during the playoffs."

"You did? How?"

"Several ways. He might have been in the bathroom between periods, or walking in a quiet part of the Forum by himself, and he'd look up and see one of us. Afterward, something bad always seemed to happen to the Bruins."

This situation defies logic — what am I thinking — there could be no logic in a hallucination, obviously, and Faustian reveries are definitely not my style.

"Ah, now you think you've gone to the devil, is that it?" There is a magical but faint Irish lilt to the words. But a softer, more lyrical Maritime accent, not the harsh-edged Montreal working-class Irish of Gorman's.

I turn to yet another newcomer, and confront one of the gentlest, most popular men in hockey.

"Danny, how are you? You're missed, especially on the Hall of Fame selection committee. So how is it up here?"

Danny Gallivan replies, "I can't complain."

"You couldn't even complain when you were down here."

"It's good. Hewitt, Kelly and myself and been nicknamed the Heavenly Trio by these gentlemen and we're thinking of forming a barbershop quartet. . . . We're looking around for candidates."

"So I take it we're somewhere north of my first guess," I venture, "and if we're all here together under these circumstances, we must be receiving some sort of special dispensation from the Big Guy."

"Senateur Raymond?" Gorman smiles at his own joke.

"No, the Big Guy. The Lord. God. Whatever you want to call He, She or It."

"I think The Lord will do nicely," Father Frank interjects neatly.

"Okay, okay. Cut to the chase. If this is the good place, and you're all up here, how did you get permission to do what you did to the Bruins? Why would He pick on the Bruins? What have they done to annoy Him?"

"Never thought of it that way, young man," Gorman replied. "But, I can tell you one thing and it's, pardon the pun, God's honest truth."

"Truth with a capital T," came a whine from my right.

"Shaddup Harry. "

"So what's the Truth with a capital T? It sounds like there's Trouble here in River City. With a capital T."

"Like musicals, do you? The Truth with a capital T is that none of us has ever seen a Bruin up here. No Eddie Shore. No Dit Clapper. No Sugar Jim Henry. No Art Ross. No Bruins, with a capital B. Come to think of it, no Leafs, either."

"Well, we wouldn't expect Mr. Smythe to be anywhere near this place, would we," Selke smiles sweetly at Gorman.

"Maybe Heaven, or whatever they call this place, is divided by teams," I theorize. "Maybe Clapper, Shore, Henry and Ross are tipping a few brews in some celestial bar in Beatown right now, wondering why the guys in the red-white-and-blue never made it to the Big Game in the Sky. And maybe there's a Blue Room in Toronto with Smythe, Broda, Conacher, Horton, Punch and Ballard gnashing their teeth over the goings-on on Carleton Street. "

"Never thought of it like that, kid."

The interrogation machine is in high gear now.

"And if you did this to the Bruins for so long, why did you let them beat the Habs for three straight years in the playoffs?"

"We're not sadists, young man," Selke interjects, "and besides, I very much admire Mr. Bourque. He would have looked superb in the colours."

"So, how did you drive Harry Sinden nuts? What was your best coup?"

"The best one? That's easy. May 10, 1979 . . . at about 10:30 p.m., and then again at about 11:10."

"No kidding? The phantom extra player penalty in the semi-finals? The one that made Don Cherry's post-hockey career?"

"That's the one, kid," Gorman smiles.

"I'll never forget Harry's face because he was looking right at the bench when Tommy pushed the extra winger over the boards. Cherry still thinks the guy went out there on his own, but Tommy picked him up like a sack of potatoes and heaved him over the boards. And what was the guy going to do when he got back to the bench? 'Sorry coach, the Hand of God picked me up and threw me out there and there was nothing I could do.'?

"Harry was up there in the Bruins' box, and Tommy let Harry see him do it — we can do things like that. Sinden was fit to be tied because he turned to Tom Johnson and asked if he'd seen it, and Johnson looked at him like he'd lost his marbles," said Howie Morenz.

"When Lafleur scored the tying goal that sent it into overtime, Harry glanced away from the ice to the back of the lodge and there was Tommy Gorman sitting quietly, having a Molson. Tommy saluted him with the raised glass and when Harry started to say something like 'What're you doing here?', Tommy vaporized. By then the other Tommy, Johnson, knew Harry was crazy."

"I can vouch for the fact that Sinden went nuts that night," Mouton pipes in.

"I went up to the press lounge between periods and Harry was shredding a hot dog and muttering about ghosts to anyone who would listen. He was going nuts."

Gorman laughs richly. "And then there was my *pièce de resistance*," he adds.

"There's more?"

"When he came downstairs after the Lambert goal eliminated the Bruins in overtime, I shook his hand in front of the Bruins' dressing-room door, commisserated with him over his loss, and wished him the 'best of luck for next year.' And then I was gone, right before his eyes. I hear Harry wasn't the same at all that summer."

I'm in a daze. Looking back into the shadows, I am startled when all of the shadowy forms materialize into a sharp picture.

"Damn . . . that's Toe's . . . right down to the pucks, sticks, pictures and newspaper clippings on the wall and the two drafts for a quarter." A two-page *Montreal Herald* photospread of the 1957 training camp is crystal clear at eye-level, not more than four feet away from me. Below it, two regulars are enjoying the lunch steak special, the dark, rich gravy on their fries fairly bubbling.

The waiters at Toe Blake's Tavern, an All-Star aggregation of the art, are at high speed wending their way through the traffic, overloaded trays of glasses of foamy draft interspersed with quarts of Molson Export held high above their heads. Over there in a corner, Doug Harvey and Jacques Plante are playing shuffleboard. Across the room, a full house at one table, the Cleghorns — Ogilvie (Odie) and Sprague — are swapping lies with the Manthas — Sylvio and Georges. Joliat has moved to another table where he and Newsy Lalonde are playing a serious game of checkers for draft beers.

There seems to be a shortage of tables and chairs, however. At the real Toe's, neighbours were tossed together in intimate proximity, and liked it.

"Mr. Moore has several of the tables and chairs," Selke interjects, and I recall an emotional grey day when the furnishings of the tavern were auctioned off. The building has been replaced by a Cathedral to Yuppiedom called Le Faubourg Ste. Catherine. They call this progress?

"Mr. Moore will be returning the tables and chairs when the time comes," Father Frank assures me.

Fine, but hold on! Toe's didn't have a shuffleboard.

"Mr. Harvey brought that with him from the Press Club," Selke explains.

"He had some bad times near the end and we figured it would cheer him up."

I look over at Harvey, the bloom of youth on his features, very much again the man Bobby Orr would be compared to. The last time I had seen him, he sat aged and sad, quietly watching a Forum practice with his grandson. It was a poignant moment.

"Never mind the shuffleboard, explain Toe's," I continue, and as the words come out, a door off in the corner opens briefly and I hear the tell-tale rumble of the Leader bowling alley and pool room upstairs.

"Hector will be with us soon," Gallivan chips in.

"We've got a few things ready — his office is waiting for him." There is sadness, a contradiction in such a breathlessly boyish spirit. Danny Gallivan lived a life of perpetual curiosity and wonder and was genuinely loved and appreciated by all of us. He was forever young and this sadness is a surprise.

We share a quiet moment of reflection, looking inwardly at our personal visions of Toe Blake. Perhaps the Canadiens' most splendid warrior ever, on the ice and behind the bench, he has suffered the living death of Alzheimer's disease in recent years, and this knowledge affects us all. I glance quickly over to where the Cleghorns and Manthas are sitting . . . Alzheimer's was Georges Mantha's fate as well. He is youthful and animated, laughing up-roariously at one of Sprague's punchlines. I'm still looking at them when the image of Toe Blake's tavern fades, and only our original small gathering remains in sharp focus.

The afternoon must be waning, I guess. Or maybe this is one of those deals where time stands still in the real world and I'll come-to in an empty building, a few seconds after I supposedly fell asleep.

"Nah, it's about four o'clock, " Harry pipes in.

"You can read minds?"

"Like that guy Letterman on American TV . . . stupid party tricks," Mouton says.

"That's stupid pet tricks, Claude."

"Believe me, here it's the same thing."

I look around. Toe's has gone, and the 1949 Forum has returned to 1993. I turn back fully expecting the Million-aire's Club to have disappeared mysteriously as well. But they are still here, card table and all, looking at me expectantly.

Suddenly, a glacial chill envelopes us all. There is no breeze or hint of flowing air current . . . just an incredible cold that overwhelms the very marrow of the bone. An-other stupid pet trick, maybe? Am I the only one who can feel this?

"Jeez, what's that?" Gorman is shivering visibly.

"Like Peel and Dorchester on January 15th, with a thirty-mile-an-hour wind," volunteers Howie Morenz, the weath-erman. "I haven't felt anything like that in more than forty years."

I refrain from updating the Stratford Streak on Montreal street names and the metric system.

"Um, young man?"

"Yes, Mr. Selke?"

"We have not been entirely forthcoming with you."

"What do you mean?"

"You have asked us several times why you are here, and we have led you to believe that we summoned you so that you could tell our story to the world."

"Yes sir, that's how I figure it."

"To tell you the truth, we don't know why you are here. We didn't summon you. We can show ourselves to people, but we can't bring them here."

I feel the chill this time, but it doesn't seem to affect the men around me.

"Then . . . what am I doing here?"

The neon digital clock just opposite me reads: 16:00.00.

And realization dawns. I know why I'm here: I'm the messenger, not Harry Brown. I'm delivering a message to them, not a message from them.

Across town, six silver shovels have just made a half-dozen scalpel-like slits in the ground at the parking lot just west of Windsor Station. The biggest construction site in Montreal in recent years is about to open.

How do I broach the subject?

"Uh guys . . . ? Are you mobile?"